Contributors

Anthony Forder   Head of the Department of Social Work,
Liverpool Polytechnic.

Graham White   Lecturer in Sociology,
Department of Sociology,
University of Liverpool.

Ken Roberts   Lecturer in Sociology,
Department of Sociology,
University of Liverpool.

Kathleen Pickett   Senior Lecturer in Sociology,
Department of Sociology,
University of Liverpool.

Olive Keidan   Lecturer in Social Administration,
Department of Sociology,
University of Liverpool.

Eileen Holgate   Lecturer in Social Work,
Department of Sociology,
University of Liverpool.

Clive Davies   Lecturer in Sociology,
Department of Sociology,
University of Liverpool.

Contents

Charts

Tables

Foreword to the seventh edition
by Professor Lord Simey

I am very glad to take advantage of the opportunity my colleagues have given me to write the Foreword to this book, as Penelope Hall, whose memory it perpetuates, was both my colleague and my personal friend. I was, moreover, in at the birth, so to say, of this book, when we decided to collaborate together in writing an analysis of the development of the social services. This turned out to be impossible when my own preoccupations overwhelmed me, and she went on alone to a most successful conclusion. We are all only too glad that she was able to do so, and that the gift of the copyright to our Department has made it possible for us to make it plain how much we owe to her by producing a new edition of what has become a classic text. It is that alone which can justify or explain what might otherwise be the presumption of doing so.

The book that she wrote, and the editions of it that she produced, as time went by, are evidence of her scholarship as well as of her strength of purpose. Her industry was a constant reproach to one's own more questionable standards; her unflinching honesty, and willingness to speak the truth however much people might wish to brush uncomfortable things from sight, under the carpet, made her a constant threat to peace of mind, and an enemy of all who wanted to uphold the *status quo*, merely because to criticise it was to involve oneself in discomfort, or, still worse, to face the dangers that beset anyone who exposes injustice, oppression, or persecution. Her life was a long crusade for the common man's rights and against wrongs as she saw them. This made her a somewhat uncomfortable colleague, though it was a privilege to know her as a friend.

In the first instance, therefore, Penelope Hall was an author who displayed enviable standards of achievement which have illuminated the lives of a multitude of students. Not least, and of this I am sure they are fully conscious, these have been accepted by all who have collaborated together in producing this present book. Her meaning was always clear; she knew what she wanted to say, and she said it. There was, in fact, a certain deceptive simplicity about her writing. Her commitment to the values embodied in the services she discussed was complete, however unfashionable this might be; the technical quality of her writing was impeccable, in so far as she accepted an unqualified obligation to overcome the gigantic problem of keeping herself up to date about the multitude of events, theories, and strivings for which she made herself responsible. The ultimate objective of it all, the social welfare of her fellow-citizens, was one which lay very near her heart indeed.

Following the example of Penelope Hall, the authors of this book have been bold, or perhaps rash, enough to accept the same objectives. They are prepared to be judged by the same standards which she thought should be applied to her own work. They are intimidating, in so far as they extend to honesty of purpose and soundness of judgement as well as completeness of information and up-to-dateness of explanation. I am sure that the authors of what has now become so wide a collaboration would wish me to say that they will be more than satisfied if their work is generally regarded as displaying qualities of scholarship which are comparable with hers. That has been their aim, and it is in this way that they have paid a tribute to her memory.

Preface to the fourth edition

A writer rash enough to call her book *The Social Services of Modern England* is in the position of Alice in the grip of the Red Queen. Run as hard as this unfortunate child might, still the Queen cried 'Faster! Faster!' and when at last they paused, and she was able to look around, she found herself in exactly the same place as before. 'If you want to get anywhere else you must run twice as fast as that,' remarked the Red Queen acidly. Similarly at the end of each successive attempt to catch up with current legislation and research, I find myself, as always, a little behind the times, conscious that, like its predecessors, the newly revised edition contains statements of fact that were correct when the manuscript was written but which have become out of date during printing, and opinions which might have been modified had the findings of a government enquiry or piece of current research been available a little earlier. The way out of this dilemma is with the reader. If he wishes, as he should, to get 'anywhere else' he must himself consult the government publications and other original and specialist writings to which, as stated in the Preface to the First Edition, this book is intended as an introduction.

The present revision has been more thorough and extensive than previous ones and several chapters have been entirely re-written. I am grateful to those colleagues and friends who have helped me with it by their advice, criticism and encouragement. For the errors and inadequacies which still remain despite their generous help I must take full responsibility, and can but trust that they will be rectified by the student's further reading, observation and practical experience.

September 1958   M.P.H.

Editor's preface

It is an honour to be called upon to write this Preface to the new edition of *Penelope Hall's Social Services of England and Wales*, a book which has long been a classic of its kind and one which, over the course of its twenty-five years' history, has brought considerable prestige to Liverpool University's Department of Sociology or, as it was called until 1971, Department of Social Science.

By the terms of Pen Hall's will the copyright of her book was entrusted to the department, and it is in my present capacity as its titular head that I have acted as supervisory editor of this edition in succession to Mr Anthony Forder who, upon being appointed a lecturer at the Liverpool Polytechnic, relinquished a task which, as Pen Hall's successor, he had very efficiently carried out for several years. Fortunately, I was still able to call on him for help in preparing this new text, and to make use of his experience both as an editor and as an expert in the field of social administration. He has kept closely in touch with the design and contents of this new version and has, in addition, contributed three most important chapters. At the same time, I would like to pay an equally warm tribute to my colleague Mrs Olive Keidan, who, like Mr Forder, has acted throughout the long and detailed preparation of this text as a co-editor and an invaluable contributor. Indeed, my own task as editor-in-chief, as it were, has been made ridiculously easy by having two such capable and conscientious co-editors at my elbow, and I and the department are very much in their debt.

The regular publication of Pen Hall's book serves two very important purposes. In the first place, it keeps green the memory of a much-loved and widely respected colleague whose personal integrity and scholarship were, and still are, an example to us all. But she was more than the disinterested scholar. She was, above all, a committed individual who in her own life strove to live up to the ideals of social welfare and Christian responsibility, and it was this that gave the earlier editions of her book that stamp of moral enthusiasm which raised it high above the level of the usual academic textbook. It was typical, too, that under the terms of her will Pen set aside a substantial proportion of future royalties to provide a fund to help students of the department who are in any kind of financial distress.

In the second place, our departmental commitment to keep the text in being and abreast of changes in the ever-expanding sphere of the social services acts as a constant reminder of the department's past history and continuing interests. Although a few years ago we changed our title from Social Science to Sociology, it was not intended that this should to any great extent be seen as a change of focus either for our academic teaching or in our research policy. It is still true today that some half of our graduates ultimately proceed to a career in social work, or in some allied post in welfare or in social administration. The development of graduate and undergraduate courses in sociology has not, as in some other universities, led to a division into two opposed groups, the so-called applied and the solely theoretical. Although not all my colleagues might agree with me, I think the majority of us who teach here still hold with Durkheim that any neglect of the theoretical must be to the detriment of the practical and that one, at least, of the main purposes in studying society is in order to be in a better position ultimately to help to solve our social problems.

Such a view would, I know, wholly recommend itself to the original author of this book, and it is in such a spirit that we in the department now offer this ninth edition of her work to the public.

1975   JOHN BARRON MAYS

The authors have aimed to make this volume up to date at June 1974. Some legislation and reports after that date may be referred to in the text or in notes, but the reader should assume that events after June 1974 are not included.

TABLE 1 *Public expenditure on social services and housing in 1962 and 1972 expressed in £million and as a percentage of the gross national product*

	1962		1972	
	Total in £m	*% of GNP*	*Total in £m*	*% of GNP*
Education	1,173	4·6	3,508	6·5
National Health Service	971	3·8	2,644	4·9
Personal Social Services	75 ⎫		384 ⎫	
School meals, milk and welfare foods	98 ⎭	0·7	163 ⎭	1·0
Social security benefits	1,744	6·8	5,119	9·5
Total social services:	4,061	15·9	11,818	21·9
Housing	529	2·1	1,449	2·7
Total social services and housing	4,590	18·0	13,267	24·6

Source: Central Statistical Office.

Table 1 provides figures for public expenditure on individual social services in 1962 and 1972. The effect of increased costs, which is ignored in Table 1, is indicated in Table 2. This table is concerned only with current expenditure and so the figures do not agree with those in Table 1.

TABLE 2 *Current expenditure by public authorities and consumers in 1962 and 1972 in £million at 1970 prices showing percentage increase*

	£m 1962	£m 1972	% increase/ decrease
Public authorities current expenditure:			
Military defence	2,945	2,490	− 15
National Health Service	1,451	1,976	+ 36
Education	1,273	1,990	+ 56
Other	2,192	3,330	+ 52
Total	7,859	9,786	+ 25
Consumers' expenditure	26,269	34,115	30
Gross national product	—	—	31

Source: Central Statistical Office.

TABLE 3 *Post-war cycles in the British economy*

	I	II	III	IV	V
Period	1952–7	1958–61	1962–5	1966–70	1971–3
Duration	6 yrs	4 yrs	4 yrs	5 yrs	3 yrs
Real GNP rise (%)	16·4	12·1	13·4	11·2	10·9
Peak unemployment* (% average for year)	1·8 (1952)	2·0 (1959)	2·2 (1963)	2·3 (1968)	3·7 (1972)
Peak inflation† (% year-on-year)	5·3 (1955)	3·4 (1961)	4·7 (1965)	6·4 (1970)	9·2 (1973)
Peak payments‡ Deficit (% of GDP)	0·91 (1955)	1·12 (1960)	1·29 (1964)	§	2·07 (1973)

* Unemployed in GB excluding school-leavers and adult students.
† Change in average retail price level between calendar years.
‡ Current account in calendar years.
§ Masked by 1967 devaluation.
Source: Peter Jay in *The Times*, 1 July 1974.

Charts 1a and 1b show the trends in public expenditure in the UK over the period 1952–72, while Chart 2 compares earnings, wage rates and retail prices in the UK between 1961 and 1973. In the first, a rise in the proportion of expenditure on goods and services is evident during 1964–7, a period of Labour Government. The second shows how a reduction in expenditure on defence is associated with a higher proportion of public expenditure on social security benefits and education. Brian Abel-Smith discusses public expenditure on the social services in *Social Trends*, HMSO, 1970.

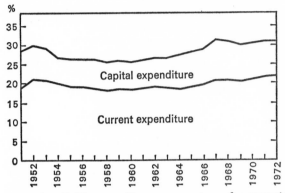

CHART 1a   *Public expenditure as percentage of gross national product (UK)*
Source: *Social Trends*, HMSO, 1973.

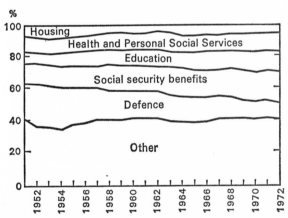

CHART 1b   *The pattern of public expenditure (UK)*
Source: *Social Trends*, HMSO, 1973.

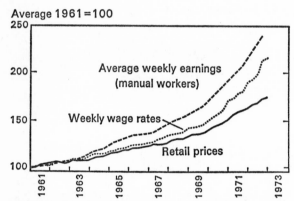

Average 1961 = 100

CHART 2 *Earnings, wage rates and retail prices (UK)*
Source: *Social Trends*, HMSO, 1973.

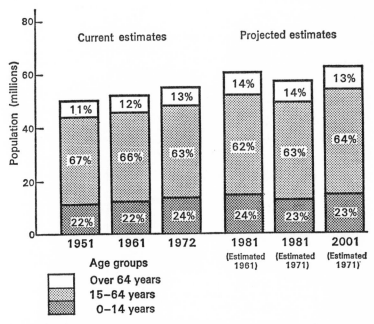

CHART 3 *Population of England and Wales: Registrar-General's estimates for 1951, 1961, 1972, 1981, 2001.*

This chart shows the growth in population from 1951 to 1972 and projections for later years, indicating where the pressure for increased social services is likely to come. The projections are more reliable for older age groups than for those not yet born. The most recent projections suggest that the total population will not reach such high numbers as was expected in the early 1960s – revised estimates take into account the continuously falling birth rate since 1965. Nevertheless, the number of elderly people in the population will increase until near the end of the century, though not to the extent predicted by the Phillips Committee (Cmd 9333) in 1954 which estimated that 18 per cent of the population would be of retirement age by 1979, so giving rise to much anxiety about the cost of pensions.

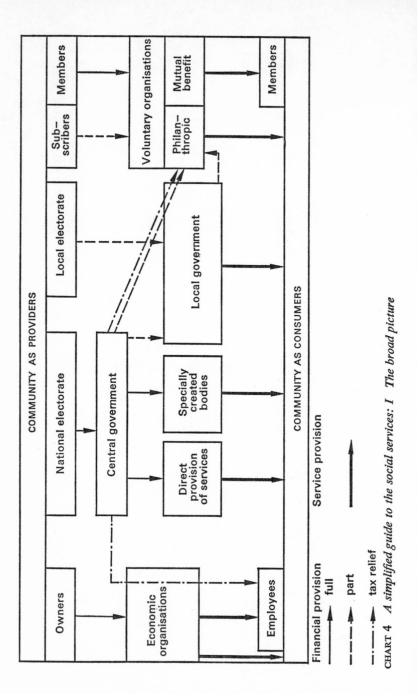

CHART 4 *A simplified guide to the social services: I   The broad picture*

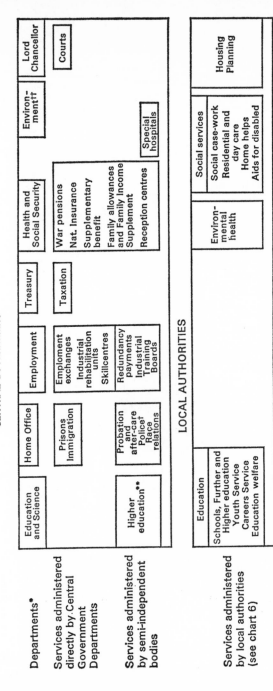

CENTRAL GOVERNMENT

Departments*	Education and Science	Home Office	Employment	Treasury	Health and Social Security	Environ- ment††	Lord Chancellor
Services administered directly by Central Government Departments		Prisons Immigration	Emploment exchanges Industrial rehabilitation units Skillcentres	Taxation	War pensions Nat. Insurance Supplementary benefit Family allowances and Family Income Supplement Reception centres		Courts
Services administered by semi-independent bodies	Higher education**	Probation and after-care Police† Race relations	Redundancy payments Industrial Training Boards		Special hospitals	Housing Planning

LOCAL AUTHORITIES

Services administered by local authorities (see chart 6)	Education	Environ- mental health	Social services
	Schools, Further and Higher education Youth Service Careers Service Education welfare		Social case-work Residential and day care Home helps Aids for disabled

CHART 5 *A simplified guide to the social services: II Government services*

* Administering or giving oversight to services below. The Welsh and Scottish Offices are omitted from the chart.
** Universities should be considered as voluntary bodies, but the University Grants Committee comes in this category.
† Responsibility shared with local authorities.
†† Has a general responsibility for the oversight of local authorities.

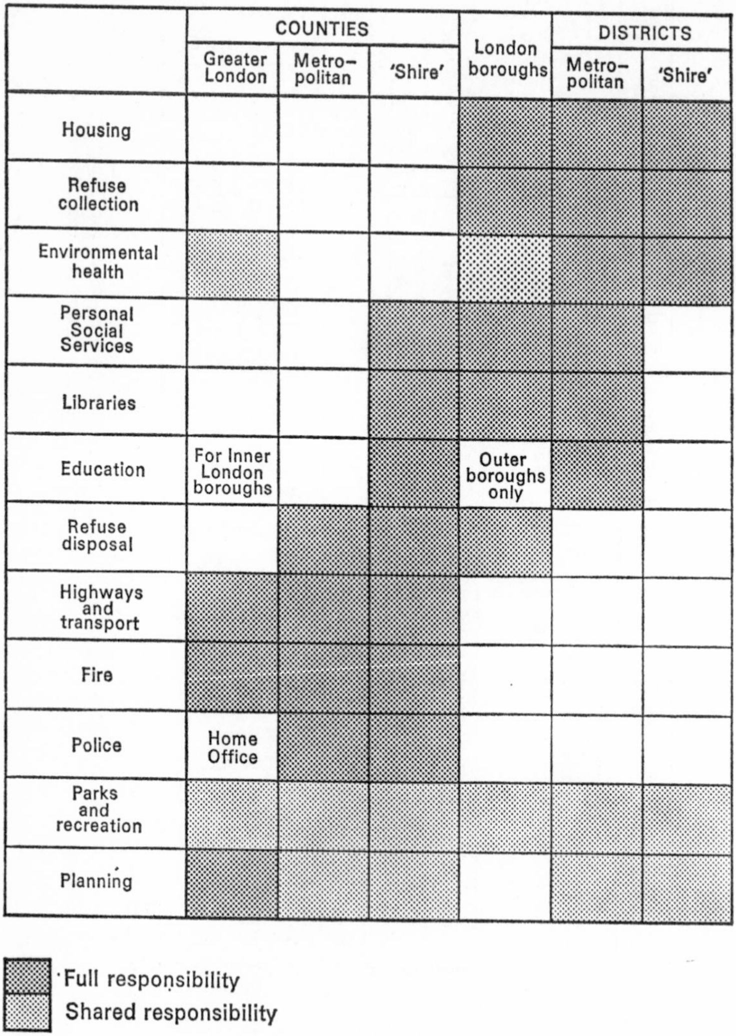

	COUNTIES			London boroughs	DISTRICTS	
	Greater London	Metro-politan	'Shire'		Metro-politan	'Shire'
Housing						
Refuse collection						
Environmental health						
Personal Social Services						
Libraries						
Education	For Inner London boroughs			Outer boroughs only		
Refuse disposal						
Highways and transport						
Fire						
Police	Home Office					
Parks and recreation						
Planning						

Full responsibility
Shared responsibility

CHART 6 *A simplified guide to the social services: III Distribution of local authority responsibilities*

1 Introduction
Anthony Forder

There is no general agreement on the definition of what is a social service.[1] There are, however, three implications of the word 'social' which help to set the boundaries. 'Social' in this context refers to the fact that the service is provided through collective action. Second the social services are designed to meet 'social' needs, that is those needs that are dependent for their fulfilment on the effective organisation of social relationships. Finally, it contrasts those services that are provided for a 'social' motive and those provided for an 'economic' motive, thus excluding many services provided for profit or primarily to meet the needs of trade and industry.

On this basis the definition of the social services is very wide and certainly much wider than the services covered by this book. Nevertheless the selection of these particular services for study is not without its rationale. They are services whose manner of operation directly affects the lives of individuals and is in turn affected by their reactions. Attitudes are at least as important as techniques in determining their effect. On this basis one can justify the omission of such services as sewage disposal, fire services and road construction. Somewhat less justifiable is the omission of discussion of such matters as library services, and the relationship between the public and the police, and the limited attention given to the penal system and the integration of minority groups into the community. These have all been omitted on grounds of space rather than reason.

However, in this introduction it is important to consider in more general terms the circumstances in which social services have grown up in this country and the factors that have affected the form they have taken.

Growth in the provision of social services is closely related to urban and industrial development. Even in ancient times municipal sewers were provided in Ur, and 'bread and circuses' in Rome. The association has been particularly marked with the rapid changes that have taken place as the industrial revolution has gathered speed. This is hardly surprising. Greater specialisation of function and greater physical proximity among large populations increases the dependence of individuals on each other for the satisfaction of their needs. Higher standards of behaviour and skill are demanded of people; higher expectations are raised by increased resources and new technologies. The individual in an urban industrial society faces hazards that fall to some extent at random, encouraging the sharing of risks. This is as necessary for the rich as for the poor, though there will be a difference in the risks they face and their attitudes to them. At the same time society as a whole needs literate, healthy citizens, able and willing to act responsibly in a variety of roles, as workers, voters, trade unionists, parents and so on. Thus 'enlightened self-interest' provides support for humanitarian impulses springing from the sense of identification of one human being with another or from the recognition that one has contributed, however indirectly, to another's misfortune. This support is necessary, because human capacity for sympathy is limited and unreliable, and also because even when sympathy is aroused there is too often a breakdown between humane impulse and humane action.

This is not of course to suggest that the interests of all members of the community are the same. While social services for all are to the benefit of the community as a whole, some groups can gain greater advantages according to the way the social services are provided. In particular, groups with greater income or low risks will benefit more if the risks are shared with people in a similar position. Healthy people with secure jobs can get better terms for insurance against sickness and unemployment if they join together and exclude the less fortunate. Wealthy people can gain better health and education services for themselves if they can separate their own service from that provided for others. Where there is disparity of income and influence it is only through state action that an equal disparity in the quality of service provided for all citizens can be avoided, though the state will not necessarily see this as its aim.

In some nations at certain periods of their history there is a strong prejudice against state action in domestic affairs. This prejudice may be justified if power has been misused to protect vested interests, or if adequate administrative machinery is lacking and cannot be created easily, as was the case in nineteenth-century England. Where this is true, social services may not be provided at all, or may be provided through other channels. These may include the economic market, charitable organisations, voluntary associations for mutual support, the local community network, or the family system. In many cases, even where state action is regarded as appropriate, the state may prefer to channel its efforts through these existing institutions rather than providing its own system.

The development of social services in England 1830–1939

In England in the mid-nineteenth century the rationalism of the Benthamite tradition favoured reforms,[2] but the main target of reform was the vested interests of the landed aristocracy which had for years supported legislative stagnation in the face of mounting social changes. The same rationalism, when allied with the individualistic philosophy, which was characteristic of protestant religious leaders and free-thinking philosophers alike, produced a strong opposition both to government control and to collective action. Additional support for this policy of *laissez-faire* came from a deterministic economic theory which stressed the inability of government action in the long term to change the position of the poor.

However, even at the height of the influence of Benthamite Liberalism there were other tendencies operating. Rationalist philosophers opposed unnecessary suffering. Evangelical Christians believed in a God of love. Both philosophies had an essential humanitarian element. Tories believed in the value of paternalism, while among 'the labouring classes' and some of their supporters faith in the effectiveness of collective action remained strong. Throughout the nineteenth century each of these elements struggled for expression in legislation. The most notable example was the agitation which produced the procession of Factory Acts from 1802 to 1898, giving increasing protection first to women and children and later to men in industry.

Gradually these humanitarian elements were reinforced by the pressure of events. The squalor of the poor areas of the growing towns was the breeding ground of crime, vice and disease that spread beyond their own boundaries to threaten the security of the prosperous. An amusing example is the persistent concern of Parliament up to 1857 for the effect of the stench of sewage from the Thames on its work.[3] Services to protect the public health and more effective crime prevention were among the first to receive government support, together with education which was necessitated by both the extension of the franchise and industrial development. From the second Reform Act, 1867, to the end of the century a whole series of laws was enacted by both political parties extending the role of government in the regulation of social conditions, and the protection of the weak, and sanctioning collective action by the working classes. At the same time more effective administrative institutions were being developed in central and local government to cope with the extension of activity in these politically sensitive areas.

3

However, even at the end of the nineteenth century the problems of poverty and of meeting the needs of individuals in distress had hardly begun to be tackled. From the point of view of today it is easy to be critical of the Victorians for their failure to face this problem – though not so easy now as it was a few years ago when even well-informed people were convinced that the problem of poverty had been solved in this country. There is little doubt that today poverty could be eliminated if the people of the country as a whole were determined enough. In the nineteenth century the size of the problem, the lack of understanding of its nature and causes, and the absence of the tools needed to tackle it all combined to place elimination beyond the capacity of the country. Faced with this situation the Victorians tended to assume that economic 'laws' made preventive action impossible. Alternatively, responsibility was laid on individual failure. Both attitudes were supported by the *laissez-faire* and individualistic philosophies of the time.

One instrument was available to the state, not for dealing with poverty as such, but with 'paupers', individuals who were 'destitute', i.e. lacking the means of subsistence, and who by virtue of the receipt of relief were given an inferior status as citizens. This was the Poor Law. It was inherited from the Elizabethans by whom it was created as an instrument for making the prevention of destitution the responsibility of the local community. Administered in a humane, paternalistic manner in the early years of the century, the Poor Law had manifestly failed to meet the conditions that were developing. The Poor Law Amendment Act, 1834, attempted to limit demand by an approach which, in the hands of people whose main concern was economy, became frankly deterrent. Those who accepted relief were stigmatised as paupers. Relief to the able-bodied was only to be given in institutions in which the regime had to be more unpleasant than the conditions which were generally endured outside these 'work-houses'. Contrary to the intentions of the Act the same conditions were applied to other destitute persons. The circumstances which made people destitute were very varied, including, as well as unemployment, physical and mental illness, old age, and the loss by children of parents. Because destitution was regarded as the primary problem, only gradually and to a limited extent were different methods and institutions developed to meet these varied needs. Even in 1944 the Curtis Committee was horrified to find some children in the care of local authorities in all-purpose workhouses of the type developed in the nineteenth century.[4]

Such a deterrent system could only be morally justified by the belief that the individual was responsible for his own condition. It was recognised that for some at least this was not true, but it was believed that the state could not provide separate treatment for these.

The needs of such people were left to private philanthropy, which could relate assistance to individual need in a way that the state could not. This philanthropy was the major outlet for the humanitarian impulses of the middle and upper classes. But philanthropists too had to limit demand, and did so by emphasising the distinction between the 'deserving' and the 'undeserving' poor which was the justification for so limited a state provision.

By the end of the century the thesis that the majority of the poor were responsible for their own condition was no longer tenable in face of the evidence against it. In particular the surveys of Booth and Rowntree had finally shown that the greatest causes of poverty were low wages in relation to the size of families and the risks of interrupted earnings through sickness, unemployment and old age. When these discoveries were supplemented by anxiety about the level of physical health and nutrition among recruits for the Boer War, the door was opened for a more energetic state campaign not only against poverty itself, but against those ills, such as squalor, disease, ignorance and crime, which were most closely connected with poverty. In 1904 a Royal Commission was set up to consider the operation of the Poor Law. This provided a sounding board for the various views on the causes and cure of poverty, and for information on the subject. The commission eventually produced a majority report, and a minority report reflecting mainly the views of Sidney and Beatrice Webb. The former recommended the retention of the Poor Law with modifications; the latter proposed the break-up of the Poor Law and the institution of a series of services to meet particular needs. Neither report was directly implemented, although the minority report was most accurate in its forecast of future developments, but the commission did clarify the need for change, and add to the impetus.[5]

The result of these various pressures was a remarkable programme of legislation particularly under the talented Liberal Government of 1906 onwards. It included measures for cheap meals and health inspections for school children; for health and unemployment insurance; for old age pensions; for the probation of offenders, the reform of juvenile courts, and the institution of borstal training; for the setting up of employment exchanges and the resettlement of the unemployed; and for the care of mental defectives.

Most of these reforms were based on the imaginative adaptation of methods developed by charitable organisations and voluntary associations in earlier years. Thus the system of health and unemployment insurance, while owing much to an examination of the German system created by Bismarck in the 1880s, made use of the voluntary Friendly Societies that had grown up for a similar purpose in England. The provision of school meals for necessitous children was an extension to the state of a service first pioneered in Liverpool

5

by the Liverpool Food Association. The development of probation involved the legal incorporation and extension of the work of the Police Court Missionaries. Voluntary organisations were seen as the pioneers of services, but they were also preferred as the channel for providing state services because they were felt to be able to provide an individualised, caring service that the state could not give. Thus it was regarded as an essential element of the probation system that the probation officers should not be directly employed by the state.

These measures enabled large numbers of people to receive assistance in time of need without enduring the stigma of the Poor Law. There were, however, many gaps, particularly as state intervention concentrated on the welfare of school children and employees, two groups for whom state help was most easily justified in terms of national need. Some of the gaps were stopped by further legislation on similar lines in the period between the two world wars. However, throughout this twenty-year period England suffered an almost continuous industrial depression in which unemployment sometimes reached 20 per cent of the working population and was rarely below 10 per cent. The effect of this on the social services was complex. On the one hand the shift in power in favour of the working classes, which might have been expected as a result of the growth of the Labour Party and the trade unions, was largely nullified by their weaker bargaining position in times of depression. The limited availability of resources tended to result in reduced growth or even cuts in the social services. The fear that demands for assistance would again outstrip the availability of resources helped to sustain the Poor Law attitude to the giving of relief. On the other hand the nature and extent of the unemployment, so clearly a product of the economic system, showed the inappropriateness of the Poor Law for dealing with the problem, while the large numbers that suffered meant a growing pressure against deterrent measures. The immediate result was that unemployment assistance was completely removed from the ambit of the Poor Law by the setting up of the Unemployment Assistance Board, though the old attitudes often remained in its administration. This was symbolised by the 'household means test' under which every earning member of a household was held fully responsible for the maintenance of other members. In the long run the depression meant that the rout of the Poor Law in 1948 was the more complete. It was no accident that the legislation of the 1940s took the form it did in the hands of the leaders of those who had suffered most in the inter-war period.

Post-war developments in social policy

In the Second World War a tremendous effort was required of the nation, combatants and civilians alike. The creation of national unity, which wars in any case tend to engender, was a conscious objective of government. Policies, such as rationing and price control, were developed to ensure a fair distribution of limited resources among civilians. The decision in 1941 to set up a Committee for Reconstruction to begin planning for after the war, was both an outcome of that sense of unity and a support for it. There was a determination that peace should bring the rewards of victory to all. Above all, mass unemployment and the indignities of poverty in the inter-war period were to be abolished.

The first fruits of this planning was the Beveridge Report on *Social Insurance and Allied Services*, which set the pattern for later thinking. 'The scheme proposed here,' said Beveridge, 'is in some ways a revolution, but in more important ways it is a natural development from the past. It is a British revolution.'[6] This description could justly be applied to all the legislation which set up the social services from 1944 to 1948, whether it was passed by the wartime Coalition, or the post-war Labour Government.

The revolution lay primarily in the acceptance by the state of a much fuller responsibility for the determination of social policy. Social development was no longer to be left as a by-product of economic development, with the state filling in the gaps left by private enterprise. There were two major prongs of this 'revolution'. First there was the management of the economy so as to maintain full employment. Second there was the abolition of the Poor Law and the development of a system of 'universal' social services, that is services available to all who needed them without regard to their income. The continuity with the past lay in the use made of methods already tried and accepted, like social insurance, and, wherever possible, of well-established institutions.

Management of the economy

The acceptance by government of responsibility for the maintenance of full employment was necessitated partly to avoid the damage to the welfare of the unemployed and their dependants resulting from the breakdown of the normal methods of income distribution in an industrial economy. But equally influential was the need of a highly capitalised industrial system for continuity of production to provide an adequate return on past investment and the confidence to invest in the future. Maintaining full employment meant managing the economy to an unprecedented extent, the full implications of which are only gradually beginning to emerge.

The maintenance of full employment has been achieved with remarkable success by all post-war British governments. Until 1967 the national average rate of unemployment was generally below 1·5 per cent, and rarely exceeded 2 per cent of the insured population despite much higher figures in some depressed areas. Indeed, the economy was rather hampered by the relatively slow growth of the labour force, which was only partially counteracted by immigration. Since 1967 unemployment has been rather higher but still well below the average level of $8\frac{1}{2}$ per cent for which Beveridge considered it was prudent to estimate.[7]

The price of this success seems to have been continuous and rising inflation coupled with an intractable problem in balancing our accounts with the rest of the world. The fundamental causes of the inflation are disputed by economists, but the expectation of inflation stimulates people to take defensive actions, which tend to increase the inflation further. Throughout the post-war period average incomes have more than kept pace with the increasing cost of living (Chart 2, p. xxiv), but this has not prevented a considerable sense of frustration developing. People are often more aware of the steady rise of prices than the intermittent rises of income to which they speedily adjust their standard of living. At the same time some groups whose bargaining power is relatively weak may suffer an absolute decline in their standard of living. To some extent we are learning to live with this and to mitigate its worst effects by, for example, building inflation proofing into wage agreements and pension contracts, and relating benefits to the cost of living index through regular reviews.[8] Attempts to control inflation have led successive governments reluctantly but inevitably to try to control wages and prices.[9] These controls, by operating at a specific point of time, have tended to fix relative incomes in an arbitrary manner and then to change them arbitrarily by operating more effectively on some incomes and prices than on others.

While inflation is a world-wide problem, so that the effect on any one country is mitigated, the balance of payments difficulties are particularly severe for Britain because of its reliance on trade for supplying its needs. Every significant rise in the rate of production has produced a corresponding crisis in the balance of payments. Governments have felt forced to respond by a severe curtailment of demand. As the balance of payments has improved they have then tried to stimulate demand to improve investment and production and the cycle has been repeated. This policy has become known as 'stop-go'. The recurrent cycles have tended to become successively shorter and more severe in their effects. This is shown in Table 3 (p. xxii).

The social services

In the new structure of universal social services, four services were central. The Education Act, 1944, was designed to provide equality of opportunity for children of all classes. It was based on the report of the Hadow Committee in 1926. The National Health Service was created by the Act of that name in 1946. Four Acts dealt with family allowances and social security.[10] The Town and Country Planning Act, 1947, was to enable the government to control the physical environment in which people lived. The problem of housing was not seen as requiring a universal social service in the same way. Instead reliance was placed on the continuance of wartime controls to ensure that resources went to the housing departments of local authorities.

The provision of universal social services received the support it did partly from the sense of national unity which persisted for a time after the war. This can be seen in the way in which the extension of wartime controls into peacetime was accepted by the community. Severe food rationing, for example, was continued until 1954, and then only abolished with misgivings on the part of many. At the same time political leaders were united temporarily in agreement about the necessity for new legislation, although individually they saw it as a stepping stone to different ultimate goals. Beveridge, for instance, saw the provision of a basic minimum income for all as the foundation for a policy that would leave the maximum opportunity for each individual to improve his own lot. On the other hand some Labour leaders saw the social services as a step towards greater equality among the people as a whole.

The sense of achievement in the country at the post-war developments in the social services was epitomised in the descriptive phrase 'the Welfare State'. However, behind the general use of this term were some important misconceptions. Most people thought, and many still do, that the generous provision of social services was a peculiarly British phenomenon. The fact that other European countries, including our greatest competitors, France and West Germany, had developed similar institutions was largely ignored. As a result many people regarded the provision of social services not as a necessity of industrial development, but as a luxury that could be reduced without damaging the social structure.

It was also generally believed that the new services represented a transfer of resources from the middle classes to the working classes. This was only partially true. Research has since shown that in the fields of education and health the greatest gains were made by the middle classes, who received services free which had previously only been free to those with lower incomes.[11] The advantages gained by the middle classes were a natural consequence of making the social services universal and free. The misconception about the nature of the transfer may have been strengthened by the relative decline of the incomes of professional and white-collar workers, which had taken

9

place at the beginning of the war independently of the development of the social services.[12] Large-scale publicity given to inadequate statistics also created the impression that taxation had had a very substantial effect on differences in income between different classes.[13]

The structure of the social services[14]

A broad and simplified picture of social services structure is given in Charts 4, 5, and 6 (pp. xxvi–xxviii). Chart 4 shows the interrelationship of the main types of institution involved in the provision of social services with special reference to the role of governments. Chart 5 gives more detail of the statutory services and can be seen as an enlargement of the central area of Chart 4. Chart 6 shows the distribution of responsibilities within the local authority system.

A quick glance at the charts shows that the structure is both complex and fragmented. One reason for this is the pragmatism which has preferred to make use of established institutions rather than develop new ones. But there are also issues of political principle involved. The increasing proportion of the gross national product channelled through government could have resulted in a dramatic increase in the power of central government as controller of the economy, provider of services and as employer. It could also have produced a stultifying rigidity that killed individual initiative. Fears of this encouraged a policy of delegation using existing institutions, setting up *ad hoc* bodies, and developing the work of the statutory local authorities. At the same time those who worked in the services, particularly professionals, have striven for a measure of autonomy through the vertical segmentation of the services on the basis of occupational skills.

Use of existing institutions

Before the widespread involvement of the state, the provision of services and the distribution of resources were undertaken by several different kinds of institution. These included the institutions of the economic market through trade and employment, families, local communities, philanthropic organisations and mutual-benefit or self-help associations. Religious bodies were at one time particularly important, combining the roles of mutual-benefit associations, local communities and philanthropic organisations.

The state has made use of all these types of institution, sometimes by encouragement, sometimes by compulsion and sometimes by providing financial support, with or without conditions attached. For example, the Poor Law placed responsibility for support of the destitute on local communities. The first Acts did so by exhortation,

10

later Acts by compulsion. The local authorities in turn enforced family obligations and only assisted where these could not be fulfilled.

In general the autonomy of these institutions has been valued and respected by central government. It has been reluctant to intervene in their internal affairs except to prevent exploitation and to curb damage to society. Examples are the protection of children, the regulation and inspection of homes and institutions, and the regulations of employer–employee and landlord–tenant relations. Even when financial assistance is channelled through these institutions, surprisingly few controls are applied. This is particularly true where the assistance is given through tax concessions, like the allowances on covenanted subscriptions to charities or on superannuation contributions. But as the issues involved become politically more important, central government is likely to tighten its control. So Griffith in his study of the relations between central government departments and local authorities found that the method and extent of central control tended to be influenced not by the efficiency or inefficiency of the services, but by their political importance.[15]

Each type of institution has its own pattern for the distribution of power and its own principles for the distribution of resources. For example employing bodies, which hire labour through the economic market, tend to allocate power on a hierarchical basis, and income and conditions of service tend to follow the same pattern. Thus the terms of employers' superannuation schemes tend to be more favourable to those with higher status in the organisation. In contrast, mutual-benefit associations, families and philanthropic organisations base their provision on the ideal of meeting need, although their power structures vary. Mutual-benefit associations are governed by committees accountable to members who are also the consumers of the services; philanthropic organisations are paternalistic with accountability to subscribers; and families are paternalistic with a very high measure of autonomy. When the state uses these institutions it has to accept these basic patterns, which it can modify only to a limited extent.

Local government

Local authorities differ from the institutions already discussed in their accountability to a local electorate composed of those who pay for the services and those who use them. This accountability is considered to justify giving the authorities a large measure of autonomy in the exercise of very considerable powers and the control of large resources raised through their own taxes or received as subventions from central government. They also undertake a very wide range of

11

tasks. Such delegation should make possible a flexible response to local needs and local opinion and the co-ordination of services at a local level. On the other hand it may make it more difficult for central government to ensure the maintenance of adequate standards in services over the country as a whole and may also interfere with national planning of the use of resources.

The pattern of local government that has recently been superseded was first instituted in 1888. It was based on the principle that the interests of town and country were separate, which was largely true at that time.[16] In the county areas, which were mainly rural and generally covered extensive areas with large but scattered populations, a two-tier system was introduced, county councils in the first tier, with urban districts, rural districts and non-county boroughs in the second tier. London was also made into a county with a second tier of London boroughs, with their own special powers. In other densely-populated urban areas, a single tier of all-purpose county boroughs was created. This system produced authorities of varied size in terms of both geographical extent and population at all levels.[17]

It has been long recognised that shifts in population, changes in mobility and the structure of communications, and extension of the responsibilities of local authorities, had made the principles underlying that structure inappropriate. As people with work and interests in the towns have chosen to live outside their boundaries, and country dwellers have made increasing use of the cultural and economic facilities of the towns, the interests of town and country have converged. At the same time, it was also generally agreed that extreme variation in the size of authorities has made it difficult to define their responsibilities appropriately.

For many services there are technical factors which set a minimum size for efficiency. In some cases there is a minimum population that must be served to make it economical to provide a sufficient variety of institutions and services. For example, with education a local authority could be relatively small if it had responsibility only for primary education (though special education for categories of the handicapped would be a problem). But secondary education, with a greater variety of subjects and standards, requires a larger catchment area, and higher education a larger one still.

Geographical factors may also be important. In areas with a low-density population, the minimum population size for economical provision may have to be sacrificed in the interests of accessibility and democratic influence. Transport, water and river control are also influenced by geographical factors.

The minimum size for efficient operation of different services will tend to vary, and so may the optimum size. But, if the boundaries for different services are allowed to vary to meet these criteria, co-

12

ordination becomes difficult, as in the different branches of the health service before 1974.[18] Any boundary will, therefore, represent a compromise, and within very broad limits there is no evidence that one compromise is better than another. On the other hand, if the authorities are larger rather than smaller, it may be possible to cope with the problem of remoteness by the creation of administrative districts of a smaller size but without the independence of a second-tier authority.

The size of authorities also affects relations with central government. A multiplicity of local authorities makes communication difficult. Griffith[19] found that communication with central departments was easier for those authorities near London and was carried on on a much more equal basis when larger authorities with chief officers and councillors of national standing were involved. Central departments had more confidence in larger authorities and some departments were more restrictive in their procedures generally in order to maintain effective standards in the weaker authorities.

If there was more confidence in the ability of all local authorities to act responsibly and efficiently, it would be much easier to remove what is at present the greatest limitation on the freedom of local authorities. This is the *ultra vires* rule, under which local authorities cannot provide any service, however desirable, unless they are specifically authorised to do so by legislation, except within very narrow financial limits.[20]

These problems were examined in the reports of three Royal Commissions for Greater London, England and Scotland, and in two White Papers on local government in Wales.[21]

Generally four levels of administration were recognised below the national level. These were regional or provincial, 'county', district, and 'local' or neighbourhood level.

The regional or provincial level was seen as involving some five to eight provinces in England together with the countries of Scotland and Wales. At the moment in England and Wales certain overall planning functions are undertaken by the Regional Economic Councils and Boards set up by the Labour Government in 1964.[22] The councils, following the general pattern of the National Economic Development Council, have voluntary representatives of local government, industry, trade unions and other local interests. They have been responsible for producing plans for regional development which are as important for social policy as for economic policy. The boards are composed of civil servants representing the regional interests of central departments with a general co-ordinating function. Both councils and boards have problems about defining their relationship with local authorities.[23] The pattern of regional administration is the subject of the Report of the Royal Commission on the

Constitution.[24] While having very great importance for planning and from a constitutional point of view, administration at this level is unlikely to have a direct influence on the social services in the immediate future.

Administrative bodies at the lowest level, the neighbourhood or parish, are generally regarded as representing communities too small to carry responsibility for essential services, but all the reports recognise the importance of this local level because it is here that people are most likely to feel a sense of belonging to a community,[25] so that citizen participation in local government can be more easily stimulated.

From the point of view of the administration of the social services it is the two central levels, county and district, which are of most immediate significance. In the various reports referred to, three approaches to county-district organisation were put forward. In areas with the highest population densities in England a two-tier structure was proposed, with major environmental planning functions in the upper tier and most of the personal social services in the lower tier. In areas of low population density in Wales and Scotland a two-tier structure was proposed with most of the social services in the upper tier, but with some functions such as housing management, environmental health and recreational facilities in the lower tier. Third, for areas of intermediate population density in England and Wales, unitary authorities were proposed with responsibility for all these functions.

In the event the Conservative Government of 1970–4 decided on two-tier authorities throughout the country based on the first approach for metropolitan areas, similar to that already created for London in 1963,[26] and based on the second approach for all other areas. A rough guide to the distribution of responsibilities between counties and districts in the Greater London Area, metropolitan counties and the 'shire' counties is shown in Chart 6.

Some of the advantages of delegation to local authorities have been lost through traditions that have developed in local government. The Maud Committee on management in local government[27] was set up because of concern about apathy in local government and the failure to attract able people for positions of responsibility as councillors and principal officers. It commissioned a series of most useful studies of councils, councillors and the attitudes of their constituents. Its broad conclusion was that despite much excellent work, the country was not getting full value for the time and money spent on local authority services. The most important reason for this was that councillors concerned themselves too much with the day-to-day details of administration. As a result, decisions tended to be pushed up to the highest levels, overloading councillors and their principal officers with detailed decisions, and leaving no time for the examination of policy. The heavy burden of routine decisions discouraged the recruitment of able people and left councillors with too little time to make contact with their constituents. At the same time, the work was fragmented between too many separate departments without effective co-ordination at any level.

To meet these problems the Maud Committee recommended a clearer division of functions and responsibilities between councillors and their officers and the adoption of 'the guiding principle that issues are dealt with at the lowest level consistent with the nature of the problem'.[28] It also recommended a much more centralised structure. A small management board, whose members might receive a part-time salary, would be appointed by the council from its own members. This management board, like the central government Cabinet, would be responsible for policy to the council. Its chief executive would be a clerk, not necessarily, as now, with legal qualifications, to whom the principal officers of departments would be responsible. There would be a smaller number of committees than at present, which would cease to be executive or administrative bodies. Their function would be deliberative, examining policy, calling for reports and making recommendations to the management board. These recommendations are an interesting attempt to combine efficient management with a balance of power that would prevent too much control falling into the hands of either committee members, management board or principal officers.

Subsequently further consideration was given to these issues by a study group on local authority management structures which prepared a series of recommendations to guide the councils of the new authorities.[29] These are known by the name of the chairman of its Working Group as the Bains Report. There is evidence that its recommendations have been very influential in determining the way many of the authorities have planned their structures.[30] In particular the new authorities are more likely than the old to have fewer committees and departments, a policy committee with sub-committees for personnel, land and finance, a chief executive with formal authority over other chief officers and no departmental responsibilities of his own, and a management team of chief officers holding regular and frequent meetings.

Ad hoc *bodies and direct provision*

It has already been pointed out that the most important reasons for using existing institutions to provide services are political. This is particularly true in the subsidising of voluntary organisations. The absence of direct accountability to a popular electorate is regarded as making it easier to pioneer new developments and to meet the needs of some of those who are in conflict with state institutions or the standards of society. Where a suitable voluntary body does not exist the state may set up semi-autonomous *ad hoc* bodies fully financed by central government. Examples are the Race Relations Board, the Community Relations Commission, and the Regional and Area Health Authorities of the National Health Service.[31]

It is really only as a last resort that social services are provided and administered directly by central government. Thus Beveridge justified central provision of social security benefits on the grounds (a) of the importance of uniformity of rates, conditions and procedures; (b) that social justice required that costs be met nationally, and this in turn required that expenditure should also be controlled nationally; and (c) on the grounds of economies of scale.[32] In addition he was probably influenced by the political importance of the issues involved requiring tight central control. Similar factors have tended to justify central administration of such services as the prisons, and the special hospitals for criminals who are mentally ill or subnormal.

This list of reasons justifying central provision serves as a reminder of the problems created by a policy of delegation to independent institutions. Broadly, while making possible greater flexibility, delegation also makes control more difficult to exercise. This in turn results in discrepancies in the provisions in different areas and problems of co-ordination between organisations with complementary functions.

Vertical segmentation of the social services

A policy of delegation results in horizontal discontinuities in the administration of services. But it is also evident that the British social services are divided vertically as well. This segmentation is based on the categorisation of needs in relation to the skills and knowledge required to meet them. The principle involved was clearly enunciated in connection with the division of responsibilities between Area Health Boards and local authorities, when the National Health Service was about to be reorganised:[33]

> After carefully considering the contrasting views expressed on these questions, the Government has decided that the services should be organised according to the main skills required to provide them rather than by any categorisation of primary user.

In other words, medical services should be provided through the National Health Service, social work services through the local authority social services departments, and these should be separated from other services such as education and environmental health provided by the local authorities.

In putting forward this principle the government was giving formal recognition to a long-term trend, which is particularly clearly seen in the departmentalism of local authorities. This phenomenon was discussed in the Maud Report. First the law requires local authorities to appoint certain officers and certain committees with specialist functions. But beyond this, with the growth of specialisation, there is a tendency[34]

> for specialists who do not head departments to seek principal officer status which, apart from considerations of pay, is often seen as providing:
> (a) an apex for a career structure for those specialists;
> (b) a degree of professional independence;
> (c) direct access to members in committee to whom professional advice can be proffered.

Thus departmentalism and vertical segmentation more generally are seen as proceeding in part at least from professional pressures for autonomy and influence. The department provides a territory within which professional knowledge and skills can be effectively employed and professional values given expression. Access to the committee gives opportunities for influence over policy and in the demand for additional resources. The career structure is seen as an added attraction for the able entrants that every profession needs. In this connection it is worth noting that the skills given recognition in separate organisations are the skills of those with relatively high status, who control in these organisations a large number of people with other skills with less prestige. In the health service doctors are outnumbered by other auxiliary workers; so are social workers in local authority social services departments.

Apart from the benefits to the staff of the services, segmentation on the basis of skills or processes does assist the development of services. A specialist service is able to define its values and goals – and therefore its priorities – relatively clearly, so that decisions can be made more quickly on the basis of consistent principles. It also ensures that the specific needs met by these specialist skills are not neglected. Unfortunately, the very advantages that such a structure creates also have their reverse effects. The focus provided by skills and processes is narrow in terms of the totality of human need, and provides the basis for conflict between departments both at policy level and in the services provided to individual consumers.[35]

At consumer level it leads to inadequate diagnosis and inadequate treatment. Specialists tend to diagnose a problem in relation to what they themselves can offer. If the kind of treatment they can offer seems to provide any hope of improvement they are likely to try it; if, before or after such a trial, they feel they cannot help, they are likely to turn the client away. They generally know too little about the skills and assistance available from other sources to be able to make effective referrals, or to compromise their own criteria for determining action in order to make a joint attack on a problem.[36] Many, perhaps even most, of the problems that face the clients of the social services require a combination of different kinds of assistance for their solution. To ensure that the right combination is in fact provided at the right time requires co-ordination, and this in turn seems to need the presence of a person with the authority to ensure that co-operation takes place. In a segmented structure like that of the British social services, there is unlikely to be anyone with formal authority at the right level to take such decisions. The emergence of someone with informal authority in any particular case is a matter of chance. In general the co-ordination role is left to the client, who usually lacks both the knowledge and the influence to perform it.

At policy level similar problems tend to arise. In particular externalities arise in the decision-making process, that is to say the decisions of one department fail to take into account the costs and benefits that their decisions create for other departments. Thus decisions in the hospital service to concentrate on patients who present the likelihood of improvement, and discharge chronic patients, may put additional costs and burdens on community services and on families which they may not be able to meet; while the failure of local authorities to provide adequate hostel accommodation may result in a more expensive form of care in hospitals. Similar problems occur between departments within a local authority, for example evictions by the housing department which throw costs on other services.[37] This is a useful reminder that putting separate functions in the same organisations will not result in co-ordinated activity unless appropriate administrative machinery is instituted. There is little indication that bringing together the separate Ministries of Health and Social Security has resulted in common policies. In contrast, in the same Department a real effort seems to be being made to relate health and personal social services through, for example, 'Policy Divisions', which attempt to identify the needs of particular groups such as the elderly and mentally handicapped persons, and to find ways of meeting their needs 'regardless of service boundaries'.

Two alternative approaches to these problems of co-ordination have been proposed and in some cases implemented. Where a single authority has diverse responsibilities a more centralised management structure has been considered appropriate with greater emphasis on management techniques in decision-making and the monitoring of results. This can be seen in the proposals of the Maud and Bains

Reports discussed earlier. It is also evident in the reorga
the National Health Service[38] and in the thinking of
Committee on the Civil Services[39] and the Seebohm Rep
authority personal social services.[40] The alternative app
retain separate organisations and to encourage co-ordination
joint committees, cross-representation on committees, and joint or
seconded appointments. This is the approach that has been necessarily adopted with regard to co-operation between the local authorities and the National Health Service,[41] and is recommended by the
Bains Report with regard to other issues.

It is not surprising that the problems of co-ordination revealed in
the statutory services are even more in evidence in relations between
the large number of independent voluntary organisations. The
National Corporation for the Care of Old People in its annual report
for 1973 noted 'the incredible patchwork of local bodies and branches
of national organisations . . . with varied accessibility and vast differences in expertise'. It pointed, too, to the difficulties created by the
persistence of voluntary organisations that lose touch with their
subject, and are ill-equipped to perform any function, having no
knowledge of the needs and conditions prevailing in their locality,
and no communication with other voluntary organisations. Lack of
communication can lead to competing activities with consequent
waste of resources, and the poaching of volunteers will lead to bad
relationships between agencies. The ideal situation as outlined in the
report is one where the statutory services are matched by voluntary
organisations that earn respect because of their expertise and involvement.

The National Corporation is one of a number of national bodies
which aim to co-ordinate and promote the work of voluntary agencies. Others include the National Association for Mental Health,
now called MIND, and Age Concern England, while the National
Council of Social Service has broad terms of reference, promoting
co-operation between agencies at local and national level.

At local level there are similar bodies, often affiliated to a national
body. In particular local councils of social service have been set up in
many areas. Considerable impetus was given to this movement
recently, when the changes in local authority boundaries were effected. Voluntary agencies that had formerly enjoyed local authority
or Council of Social Service 'support' were faced with the need to
establish new relationships in newly defined areas. Furthermore, the
requirement that voluntary organisations should be represented on
the Community Health Councils made it imperative that there should
be some organisational machinery through which the agencies could
arrange for representation. Councils of Social Service that were
already established were able to advise and assist the formation of

new councils in their own areas, while the national body outlined advisory and supportive roles.

Some of the important issues raised by these problems of structure and decision-making will be considered further in the final chapter.

Further reading

In attempting to cover more than a century and a quarter of history in a few thousand words, the truth is inevitably distorted by the absence of detail and by the personal elements in the selection of material. It is therefore particularly important that students should supplement this chapter by further reading on their own account.

The general history of the development of the social services can be covered by two complementary books:

M. BRUCE, *The Coming of the Welfare State*, Batsford, 1961 and 1966.

T. H. MARSHALL, *Social Policy*, 3rd ed., Hutchinson, 1970.

Bruce deals thoroughly with the earlier periods from the Elizabethan Poor Law to 1939, but is sketchy on the war and post-war period. Marshall is a small, very readable and valuable book giving an over-all view of problems from the end of the nineteenth century to the present day.

There is a very rich literature on the nineteenth century and the period up to 1913 and there is inevitably an arbitrary quality about any selection. In the list that follows, Dicey is a classic that still reads well, and is invaluable as a guide to nineteenth-century thought; the long introduction on 'Collectivism' in later editions can profitably be omitted. The Webbs' works are also classics. Government reports are often surprisingly interesting; only one or two can be mentioned here, but it is worth while following up references when they are found. Biography can be an entertaining and fruitful way of getting a picture of an age:

E. MOBERLEY BELL, *Octavia Hill, a Biography*, Constable, 1942.

G. D. H. COLE and RAYMOND POSTGATE, *The Common People, 1746–1946*, Methuen, 1949.

A. V. DICEY, *Law and Opinion in England in the Nineteenth Century*, 2nd ed., Macmillan, 1914.

S. E. FINER, *The Life and Times of Sir Edwin Chadwick*, Methuen, 1952.

J. L. and BARBARA HAMMOND, *Lord Shaftesbury*, Constable, 1923.

KATHLEEN HEASMAN, *Evangelicals in Action – An Appraisal of Their Social Work*, Bles, 1962.

DAVID C. MARSH, *The Changing Social Structure of England and Wales 1871–1951*, Routledge & Kegan Paul, 1958.

B. SEEBOHM ROWNTREE, *Poverty, A Study of Town Life*, Macmillan, 1901.

T. S. and M. B. SIMEY, *Charles Booth: Social Scientist*, Clarendon Press, 1960.

Poor Law Commissioners, *Report on the Sanitary Conditions of the Labouring Population of Great Britain*, HMSO, 1842.

Majority and Minority Reports of the Royal Commission on the Poor Laws and Relief of Distress, HMSO, 1909.

BEATRICE WEBB, *Our Partnership*, Longmans, 1948.

BEATRICE WEBB, *My Apprenticeship*, Longmans, 1950 (reprint of 1926 ed.).

SIDNEY and BEATRICE WEBB, *English Poor Law Policy*, Longmans, 1910.

SIDNEY and BEATRICE WEBB, *English Poor Law History, 2: The Last Hundred Years*, Cassell, 1963 (reprint of 1927–9 ed.).

For the period from 1914 to the present day the development of specialised social services means that one must increasingly go to books on individual services for further study. Details of these can be found at the end of the relevant chapters. Most of the books listed below provide useful background material. Mowat provides a very useful historical background to the inter-war period and gives the social services good coverage. Titmuss (1950) and Ferguson and Fitzgerald are essential reading for the period of the Second World War. Hackett gives a clear and readable account of the economic background in post-war Britain up to 1966 although events suggest that the authors may have been over-optimistic about the success of planning. Gregg is an economic and social history of Britain for the same period, and selected chapters fill in the social background missing from the previous book; there is an excellent collection of graphs and tables with sources. A knowledge of the general structure of British central and local government is important, but in view of recent changes it is difficult to recommend up-to-date books. Wilson is still reasonably sound on central government, but out of date on local government and the courts. Griffith is a valuable study of the relations between central and local government which is still relevant for understanding general issues even if some of the detail, particularly in the first chapter, is out of date. For local government, various reports mentioned in the text are obviously important in elucidating issues and alternative solutions and the first six chapters of Jones are particularly useful in describing subsequent developments. The latter also has some useful articles on important issues in the wider field of social policy such as sexual and racial discrimination and social class discrimination in relation to credit. Slack and Warham both provide introductions to the study of the social services, and both these two and Forder highlight in general terms issues which are discussed in relation to individual services in this book:

LORD BEVERIDGE, *Power and Influence*, Hodder & Stoughton, 1953.

A. M. CARR-SAUNDERS, D. CARADOG JONES and C. A. MOSER, *A Survey of Social Conditions in England and Wales*, Oxford University Press, 1958.

DAVID V. DONNISON, *The Development of Social Administration*, London School of Economics, 1962.

S. M. FERGUSON and H. FITZGERALD, *Studies in the Social Services*, History of the Second World War, UK Civil Service, HMSO and Longmans, 1954.

ANTHONY FORDER, *Concepts in Social Administration*, Routledge & Kegan Paul, 1974.

PAULINE GREGG, *The Welfare State*, Harrap, 1967.

J. A. G. GRIFFITH, *Central Departments and Local Authorities*, Allen & Unwin, 1967.

J. and A.-M. HACKETT, *The British Economy, Problems and Prospects*, Allen & Unwin, 1967.

KATHLEEN JONES (ed.), *The Year Book of Social Policy in Britain 1973*, Routledge & Kegan Paul, 1974.

C. L. MOWAT, *Britain between the Wars, 1918–1940*, Methuen, 1955.

B. SEEBOHM ROWNTREE and G. R. LAVERS, *Poverty and Progress, A Second Survey of York*, Longmans, 1941.

B. SEEBOHM ROWNTREE and G. R. LAVERS, *Poverty and the Welfare State, A Third Survey of York*, Longmans, 1951.

KATHLEEN M. SLACK, *Social Administration and the Citizen*, Michael Joseph, 1966.

RICHARD M. TITMUSS, *Problems of Social Policy*, History of the Second World War, UK Civil Service, HMSO and Longmans, 1950.

RICHARD M. TITMUSS, *Essays on 'The Welfare State'*, Allen & Unwin, 1958.

JOYCE WARHAM, *Social Administration: A Framework for Analysis*, Routledge & Kegan Paul, 1967.

NORMAN WILSON, *The British System of Government*, Blackwell, 1963.

For reference purposes details of social service provisions are often needed that cannot be included in a work of this kind. The National Council of Social Service's large work of reference is kept up to date constantly by loose-leaf insertions, and two pocket-sized works are produced by Penguin Books and the Family Welfare Association, the latter being revised annually:

National Council of Social Service, *Citizen's Advice Notes*, NCSS, 26 Bedford Square, London, WC1.

Family Welfare Association, *Guide to the Social Services*, FWA, Denison House, London, SW1.

PHYLLIS WILLMOTT, *Consumer's Guide to the British Social Services*, Penguin, 2nd ed., 1970.

Notes

1 For a discussion of different definitions see Kathleen M. Slack, *Social Administration and the Citizen*, pp. 11–13, Michael Joseph, 1966.
2 For a discussion of the role of Benthamism and Christian humanitarianism in social reform in nineteenth-century England see J. Hart, 'Nineteenth century social reform: a Tory interpretation of history', *Past and Present*, 31, 1965, pp. 38–61; reprinted in W. D. Birrell, P. A. R. Hillyard, A. S. Murie and D. J. D. Roche, eds, *Social Administration: Readings in Applied Social Science*, Penguin, 1973.
3 I am indebted to the Librarian of the House of Commons for this information, and for a copy of the report by Mr Goldsworth Gurney of 4 August 1857, giving details of the final solution of the problem.
4 Home Office, *Report of the Committee on the Care of Children*, Cmd 6922, HMSO, 1946, particularly paras 136–56.
5 For an interesting discussion of the majority and minority reports, see Una Cormack, 'The Royal Commission on the Poor Laws 1905–9 and the Welfare State', Lock Memorial Lecture, 1953; published in A. V. S. Lockhead, ed., *A Reader in Social Administration*, Constable, 1968.
6 *Social Insurance and Allied Services: Report by Sir W. Beveridge*, Cmd 6404, HMSO, 1942, para. 31.
7 *Op. cit.*, para. 41.
8 Reviews of social security benefits occurred irregularly in the 1950s and 1960s with intervals between reviews averaging about eighteen months. Under the Social Security Act, 1973, annual reviews became mandatory, but the Labour Government that first came to power in February 1974 has promised half-yearly reviews in its manifesto and appears to be putting this into effect.
9 Attempts to influence prices and incomes up to 1967 are discussed in J. and A.-M. Hackett, *The British Economy: Problems and Prospects*, chapter 7. In 1969 the Labour Government produced a modified policy in *Productivity, Prices and Incomes Policy after 1969*, Cmnd 4273. The Conservative Government of 1970–4, at first rejected all control over prices and incomes, but was later forced to take action. The second Labour Government of 1974, like its February 1974 Administration, is trying to achieve the same objectives by controlling prices and not incomes.
10 The National Assistance Act, 1948, the National Insurance Act, 1946, the National Insurance (Industrial Injuries) Act, 1946, the Family Allowances Act, 1945.
11 See R. M. Titmuss, *Essays on 'The Welfare State'*, pp. 208–9. See also Martin Rein, 'Social class and the health service', *New Society*, 20 November 1969.
12 See Guy Routh, *Occupation and Pay in Great Britain, 1906–60*, Cambridge University Press, 1965.
13 R. M. Titmuss, *Income Redistribution and Social Change*, Allen & Unwin, 1964. Studies by the Central Statistical Office on the incidence of taxation have shown that it is proportional over a wide income range.

Regressive indirect taxes and insurance contributions counteract the effects of a progressive income tax. The results of the studies were published in various issues of *Economic Trends* from 1962 onwards and are discussed in Adrian L. Webb and Jack E. B. Sieve, *Income Redistribution and the Welfare State*, Occasional Papers in Social Administration, no. 41, Bell, 1971.

14 For a fuller discussion on the issues discussed in this section see Anthony Forder, *Concepts in Social Administration*, Routledge & Kegan Paul, 1974, chapters 6, 7 and 8.

15 J. A. G. Griffith, *Central Departments and Local Authorities*, pp. 525–528. In addition Griffith found that each department had its own traditional attitude to its relationship with local authorities, which he classified as '*laissez-faire*', 'regulatory' and 'promotional' (p. 515 *et seq.*).

16 This issue is discussed and the evidence of the need for change presented in vol. III of the *Report of the Royal Commission on Local Government in England* (Redcliffe-Maud Report), Cmnd 4040, HMSO, 1960.

17 In 1965, of 172 counties, county boroughs and new London boroughs, 7 had populations of over 1,000,000, and 44 had less than 100,000. See J. A. G. Griffith, *op. cit.*, pp. 28–9, for a discussion of this.

18 See chapter 6, p. 193.

19 J. A. G. Griffith, *op. cit.*, pp. 528–9.

20 The absolute principle was modified by the Local Government (Financial Provisions) Act, 1963, Section 6, which empowered local authorities to incur expenditure up to the value of a penny rate for the benefit of the area or its inhabitants.

21 Recliffe-Maud Report, vol. 1, 'Report'; vol. 2, 'Memorandum of Dissent'; vol. 3, 'Research appendices'. Scottish Department, *Report of the Royal Commission on Local Government in Scotland* (Wheatley Report), Cmnd 4150, HMSO, 1969. Welsh Office, *The Reorganisation of Local Government in Wales*, Cmnd 3340, HMSO, 1967, and *Local Government Reorganisation in Glamorgan and Monmouthshire*, Cmnd 4310, HMSO, 1970.

22 'Regional economic planning machinery', *Board of Trade Journal*, 17 June 1966. See also J. and A.-M. Hackett, *op. cit.*, p. 191 *et seq.*, and Barbara N. Rodgers, *Comparative Social Administration*, Allen & Unwin, 1968, p. 271.

23 T. E. Chester and I. R. Gough, 'Regionalism in the balance', *District Bank Review*, March 1966.

24 *Report of the Royal Commission on the Constitution* (Kilbrandon Report), Cmnd 5460, HMSO, 1973, summarised and discussed in Edmund Ions, 'The prospects of regional government', in Kathleen Jones, ed., *The Year Book of Social Policy in Britain 1973*, Routledge & Kegan Paul, 1974.

25 Redcliffe-Maud Report, vol. 1, chapter 9; vol. 2, chapter 4; Wheatley Report, chapter 26.

26 Under the Local Government Act, 1963.

27 Ministry of Housing and Local Government, *Report of the Committee on the Management of Local Government* (Maud Report), HMSO, 1967.

28 *Ibid.*, p. xiii and paras 150–2.
29 Department of the Environment, *The New Local Authorities: Management and Structure*, HMSO, 1972.
30 Royston Greenwood, C. R. Hinings and Stewart Ranson, 'Inside the local authorities', in Kathleen Jones, ed., *op. cit.*
31 See p. 201.
32 Beveridge Report, *op. cit.*, paras 44–7, 161–5.
33 Department of Health and Social Security, *The Future of the National Health Service*, HMSO, 1970, para. 31.
34 Maud Report, vol. 1, paras 103–8.
35 Anthony Forder, *op. cit.*, pp. 53–4, 92–6; Olive Stevenson, 'Co-ordination reviewed', *Case Conference*, 9, 8, February 1963, reprinted in Eileen Younghusband, ed., *Social Work and Social Values*, Allen & Unwin, 1967.
36 Reference can be made to a study of professional education and identification by the Merseyside Interprofessional Working Party reported by A. Dufton, O. Keidan and G. White in 'Aspects of interprofessional training', *The New Era*, 6 June 1971. It was found that in general the participants had only a sketchy knowledge of one another's training courses and the scope of their work activities.
37 See pp. 137–8.
38 See p. 195.
39 *The Civil Service*, Cmnd 3638, HMSO, 1968.
40 See pp. 225–8.
41 See p. 199.

2 Education
Graham White

Historical introduction

Social histories of England and Wales illustrate the increasing role taken by central and local government in the management of people's lives. In taking over education the state assumed traditional socialisation functions of family and church, and from the struggles which ensued education has come to be seen unequivocally as a service, and increasingly as having a role to play in harness with the other social services. There is a continual reciprocal interaction between education and the other social institutions, such as the economy, the family, religion, politics and social class. An historical view highlights the complexity of that relationship and its effects upon education.

For most of the nineteenth century, education resembled moral training rather than the schooling of today, and was provided by voluntary bodies, mainly the churches,[1] who depended on subscriptions to finance building and running of schools.[2] Many such schools were small and ill-equipped. Attempts to assist them financially from the rates provoked bitter arguments based mainly on the nature of the catechism taught at the various schools.

The Elementary Education Act, 1870, was a compromise which kept the voluntary schools, but empowered the government to 'fill the gaps'. In districts where no voluntary school existed, or where provision was inadequate, local School Boards were elected with power to levy a rate in order to build and maintain elementary schools providing a basic education only. The churches were allowed one year's grace to fill the gaps themselves, after which time any schools they might build competed with state schools subsidised out of public funds. The religious traditions persisted into the twentieth century and were a feature of R. A. Butler's presentation of the Bill leading to the Education Act, 1944.

Previously major reform had come with the Education Act, 1902, which

(a) made available to voluntary schools money from local rates as well as taxes – which gave rise once again to bitter sectarian disputes;

(b) replaced the School Boards with general purpose county and county borough councils, together with some smaller authorities, with the statutory *duty* of ensuring adequate provision of facilities for elementary education; and

(c) gave permissive powers to the county and county borough councils to provide and grant-aid 'education other than elementary'. The fact that these powers were permissive meant that some authorities made generous provision whilst others made none at all. These disparities between districts have been inherited by our present educational system.

Towards the end of the nineteenth century 'higher grade' schools had grown up under the School Boards, providing a quasi-vocational technical training to complete the structure of elementary education for selected pupils.

Elementary education was compulsory up to the age of fourteen, and so it ran parallel with secondary education for several years without there being any fruitful contact between the two systems. In 1907 the Board of Education required all secondary schools maintained or aided by the local authority to reserve a percentage of places, usually one-quarter, for children from the elementary school who were awarded scholarships by their local authority. This was an attempt at creating equality of opportunity, but it was found in practice that it tended to benefit the children of artisans and small shopkeepers rather than the children of unskilled workers. Poverty and malnutrition formed a barrier to achievement even when opportunities were there. The Education (Provision of Meals) Act, 1906, empowered local authorities to provide meals and milk for children in elementary schools. This was the first time that benefits in cash or kind had been given outside the machinery of the Poor Law. It heralded the breakdown of that system and the coming of the 'Welfare State'. Although the meals and milk service was provided not as an end in itself, but only in order to ensure that state-subsidised education was not wasted, it helped to establish the principle that education did not merely involve the instruction of children but also extended to social care for them. Subsequent Acts soon compelled local authorities to provide medical inspection and treatment for the children in their care.

The Hadow Report of 1926, *The Education of the Adolescent*, recommended that at the age of eleven all children should enter a second stage of education which would be geared to their needs as adolescents. It suggested that the term 'grammar school' should be extended to include not only the older foundations, but also the county and municipal secondary schools which had been founded after the 1902 Act. These grammar schools would have a higher leaving age and a predominantly academic curriculum. Secondary education outside the grammar schools was to be provided in 'modern schools' with a less academic curriculum and with freedom of experiment. The report emphasised that these modern schools should be given parity of treatment with the grammar schools in terms of accommodation and equipment. Successive governments failed to raise the school-leaving age to fifteen, or to ensure suitable conditions for the development of secondary modern education. The Spens Report of 1938, *Secondary Education with Special Reference to Grammar Schools and Technical High Schools*, recommended a further diversification of the secondary system by including the junior, technical, commercial and trade schools which had been in existence for some time.[3]

This 'Tripartite System', although it was not specifically enforced by the Education Act, 1944, became the pattern on which most local authorities based their post-war planning of secondary education (see Chart 7). However, few technical schools were ever built and by the beginning of the 1960s this outline was further blurred as secondary modern schools were offering academic-type courses and were entering their pupils for the General Certificate of Education.

The 1944 Act tried to solve the religious question by ascribing aided or controlled status to voluntary schools, and by implementing a regulation for religious instruction according to an agreed syllabus.[4] On the whole the denominations came out of the 1944 Act needing only to show willingness to meet costs of building, maintenance and improvements to be able to retain control.[5]

For two decades after 1944 the unsettled co-existence and sporadic co-operation between local and national government continued, without any serious challenge to the general principles laid down by the Education Act, 1944. The Act left two Ministers responsible for educational policy and local authorities responsible for the administration of national policy, but the variety and scope of schools was left to local initiative. No effective coercive machinery was built in whereby central government could ensure control in crucial issues and the main decision-maker in educational policy was financial rather than legal. In spite of this imprecision there were only occasional organisation squabbles, until in 1964 the discontent about selection at eleven came fairly sharply to a head.

In recent years development of comprehensive schooling has been a feature of education in England and Wales. Such schools offer places to all children within an age group and they have been established in many local authority areas (see Table 4 on p. 32).

Another feature of education in England and Wales during the last decade at least has been the improvement in methods of teaching and facilities in primary schools. Willingness to experiment with new approaches leave many primary schools with classroom methods clearly in advance of those used elsewhere in the system. During roughly the same period there has been a growing insistence, albeit largely speculative, about the impact of so-called cultural deprivation on the school careers of children.

The Plowden Committee[6] recommended compensatory education

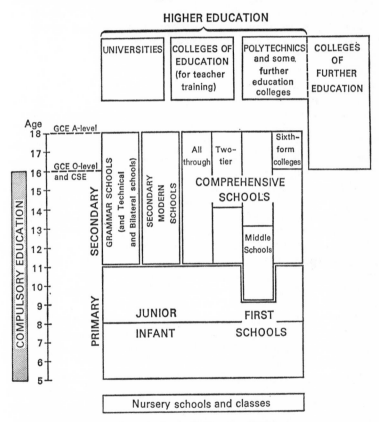

CHART 7   *Educational provisions in England and Wales*

This diagram shows the main elements in the provision of maintained schools and of higher education in England and Wales.

Source: *The Educational System of England and Wales*, HMSO, 1973, p. ii

29

to combat educational disadvantage caused by the physical, emotional and intellectual poverty of the environment. Upon the Plowden recommendations the government made £16 million available for Educational Priority Area Buildings over two years.

Plowden in a sense made public the findings of psychologists and sociologists[7] in the 1950s and 1960s that selection methods based on inaccurate tests placed great weight on a child's social background and this wastage of ability through selection inefficiency was enormous.

The Report made a number of recommendations aimed at not only the Department of Education and Science (DES), but at teachers, parents and indeed the community at large. The recommendations included allocation of resources to areas of cultural deprivation. As a forerunner of Seebohm, Plowden supported the idea of area teams of health and social service workers with specialists responsible for school problems.

Many suggestions were incorporated in relation to primary school organisation, looking for expansion in many school facilities and flexibility about ages of pupil entry and transfer. On school size the Report suggested 240 children on average for a first school, and 300–450 children in middle schools.

The committee was divided on religious education, and no changes were advised in that respect. Regular national surveys of attainment were supported, as was the total abolition of physical punishment in primary schools. Suggestions were made in detail about requirements for the training of nursery assistants, teacher aides and for fabric improvements. The committee also stated the need for clarification of the instruments of school management, and recommended the inclusion of teachers and parents on management bodies.

Other proposals echoed the desire for flexibility of organisation, including combinations of individual and group work in class, and variable school days, terms and years. Streaming was discouraged.

The committee felt there was a need for more generous staff–pupil ratios and considered part-time teachers and teacher aides as essential for expansion of the service, and also stressed the need for a full enquiry into teacher training.[8]

The James Committee was then asked to review and make recommendations about teacher education and especially to look into the content and organisation of teacher training courses. Its brief was also to consider whether intending teachers should be educated with Higher Education students who might be looking to other careers, and to assess the possible future relationships between the colleges of education, the universities, the polytechnics and the colleges of Further Education. The findings of that committee are included in the section on teachers and teacher education later in this chapter.[9]

The White Paper *Education: A Framework for Expansion*[10] presented to Parliament on 6 December 1972 contained a ten-year programme for the development of education in England and Wales.[11] The rates of development were acknowledged to be variable but the hope is that central government, the local authorities and the various voluntary groups will co-operate to implement the plans framed under five headings in the White Paper. As in the past, central government offers tentative guidelines only. These have been variously summarised,[12] but briefly the five areas for increased expenditure were:

1 a new programme for the development of nursery education;
2 expansion of school building programmes for primary and secondary schools as well as a plan for special schools;
3 expansion of the teaching force to improve pupil–teacher ratios in schools;
4 reorganisation and improvement of pre-service and in-service teacher training in pursuit of the James Report;
5 expansion of higher education opportunities, including the introduction of a two-year course leading to a new Diploma in Higher Education.

By June 1974 it was clear that some of these aims would be shelved, and recommendations as to the expansion of the training force, for example, positively rejected.

Structure of the present system

The law at present states that children must receive schooling from the age of five. Since 1 September 1972[13] the minimum age for leaving school is sixteen.[14] Parents may send their children to a publicly maintained school, free of charge, or pay for the children to receive another recognised form of tuition. Financial assistance is generally available to any student choosing to continue his education beyond school.[15] The number of children attending full-time education in the maintained sector is shown in Table 4.

Nursery schools

The under-fives may be catered for either in nursery schools or in nursery classes within the infant schools. Figures for 1972[16] show about 500 nursery schools in the public sector, accommodating about 40,000 children. In addition there is considerable provision in the private sector, where places are fee-paid. Well over half the children attending nursery education do so part-time. There are also more

31

than 310,000 under-fives in the infant departments of primary schools, approximately 166,000 of these being admitted in the term before their fifth birthday.

TABLE 4   *Schools: numbers attending full-time education in the maintained sector*

| | 1966 | | 1972 | |
	Schools	Pupils	Schools	Pupils
England				
Nursery	421	17,636	481	14,174
Primary	20,751	4,093,482	21,022	4,758,174
Middle	—	—	322	121,337
Secondary	5,412	2,638,603	4,728	2,980,584
Totals	26,584	6,749,721	26,553	7,874,269
Wales				
Nursery	41	1,781	46	1,269
Primary	2,071	272,890	1,977	308,169
Middle	—	—	1	172
Secondary	386	178,190	298	195,910
Totals	2,498	452,861	2,322	505,520

Source: *The Educational System of England and Wales*, HMSO, 1972, p. 23.

In the White Paper proposals of 1972 it was stressed that nursery education should become available to children of three or four, recognising Plowden's estimates of a 200,000 full-time by 1981. Expenditure on the under-fives was expected to rise from about £42 million in 1971–2 to £65 million in 1976–7.[17] No detailed proposal was laid down and directions were flexible in order to allow plans to reflect local needs and resources. Nevertheless it was hoped that priority would be given to areas of social deprivation and to children with special needs. Nursery provision was planned generally on a part-time basis, and the hope was that play-groups and other schemes should expand alongside maintained provision.

Primary schools

The first stage of compulsory education takes place at the primary school. The majority of primary schools accommodate children of both sexes from five upwards. Other schools are Infant only (5–7) or Junior only (7+ upwards). Generally primary schools cater for between 100 and 300 pupils each. Of the 2,000 Welsh primary schools those in Welsh-speaking areas instruct in the Welsh language and there are also bilingual schools in some English-speaking parts of Wales.

Middle schools

To enter secondary school pupils leave the primary phase at eleven, but in many areas middle schools are being developed. These vary in the age ranges catered for according to the preference of the local authority concerned, with an intake of 8–12-year-olds, 9–13-year-olds, or 10–13-year-olds. In January 1972 there were 323 such schools in England and Wales and more were planned. Although middle school units did exist in larger comprehensive schools, Wallasey was the first authority, in 1968–9, to begin changing to middle schools in the 9/10–13 age range, with upper schools for 13–18-year-olds. The DES paper *Launching Middle Schools* traces their development in one West Riding area. At Bradford the first purpose-built middle school opened in January 1969. As education reorganisation emerges it becomes clear that schools for the 9–13 and 13–18 age groups form an integral part of plans for the future. Cutting as they do across the old boundary at eleven between two educational 'stages', a great many new educational questions will be asked. As with all comprehensive schooling there is a great variety of middle schools though there is a clear general move towards unstreamed teaching.[18]

Secondary schools

Of the 5,300 or so secondary schools the majority take between 300–600 pupils each, the largest taking upward of 2,000 pupils. Selection and provision for secondary education exists in various ways. In some areas the tripartite pattern emerging after the Hadow Report of 1926 and the Spens Report of 1938, and which local education authorities generally adopted following the 1944 Act, still exists. Upon transfer to secondary education the child is allocated to a school according to a measurement of performance in a public examination, the eleven-plus. Ostensibly children are selected according to their level of academic attainment for education in different types of schools.[19]

In most areas the tripartite system is a misleading title since few technical schools were ever built. Where any form of selection does take place children enter either a grammar school, where a predominantly academic curriculum is provided for those in the 11–18 age range, or a secondary modern school, where a general curriculum is offered up to at least the minimum school-leaving age. In many secondary modern schools pupils have chosen in the past to stay on beyond fifteen. It remains to be seen if pupils will want to stay beyond the present school-leaving age. Many secondary modern schools offer an academic rather than a general course of study, others offer both, but increasingly their pupils enter for the GCE and, since 1965, the CSE examinations. The few technical schools offer specialist technical studies and purport to be the academic equals of the grammar schools.

Comprehensive schools

In July 1965, the Labour Government issued a circular[20] requesting local authorities to reorganise their secondary schooling on comprehensive lines, and including plans of six schemes already proposed or in operation, for local consideration. The schemes adopted reflect the resourcefulness and initiative, or lack thereof, of local education authorities, rather than any government direction. In consequence, without any legislative teeth, the responses of local authorities led to a total picture that was at best confused. Nevertheless, by 6 October 1967, the *Times Educational Supplement* could show that 159 of 194 local education authorities had submitted reorganisation schemes in response to Circular 10/65. The mixture of schemes so proposed went largely unchallenged by the DES even where plans which Circular 10/65 had advised against were included – especially proposals for middle schooling.

The lack of clarity about what was intended persisted so that no clear statement was made, for example, about the position of Direct Grant[21] schools, and the implication was that this should be left to local decision. The anomalies so presented were alarmingly exacerbated by the introduction in June 1970 of Circular 10/70 by the new Conservative Government without the customary consultation. Circular 10/70 made secondary reorganisation the responsibility of local authority enterprise. It had been recognised too late that only by law could comprehensive reform take place and the 1970 Education Bill was interrupted by the General Election and nothing reached the Statute Books. The cumulative effect of Circulars 10/65 and 10/70 was to pin the debates about comprehensives to the local level and fitfully the growth of comprehensive schools has gone on. Without central direction no comprehensive *system* emerged. In March 1974 the minority Labour Government issued a further circular in the saga. This repeated the election promises to end selection in education, though by the General Election in October 1974 legislation had still not been introduced. The bite in the circular came with the undertaking that only building programmes designed for comprehensive schooling would be supported.

The comprehensive schemes outlined in Circular 10/65 and existing today are as follows:

1 The 'all-through' school taking children from eleven to eighteen. This was the pattern favoured by the Wilson Government since it had already been a success in some local authority areas[22] and it came to be regarded at the time as the 'orthodox' scheme.

2 Tiered schools of broadly three kinds: first those where all pupils transfer at thirteen or fourteen from a lower school or tier to an upper one; second a parallel-tiered model where only some pupils, by choice or selection, go on to a higher tier; and third a type where at thirteen or fourteen pupils may opt, or be selected for, a long or short course.

3 The standard 11–18 format may be divided into a lower 11–16 school followed by either a sixth-form course or a junior college.

4 Middle schools, as described above,[23] leading on to one of the secondary comprehensive models.

Voluntary schools

Within the maintained sector there exist a number of voluntary schools. In January 1972 there were 8,780 such schools or departments. Of these some 3,672 were of Controlled status. Controlled schools are those where the facilities are the property of the voluntary body – these being in most cases affiliated either to the Church of England or Roman Catholic Church – but where recurrent and capital expenditure is met by the local education authority. Restrictions are imposed on the composition of managing or governing bodies of such schools.[24] In Aided schools playing fields are provided and internal repairs are undertaken at the expense of the local education authority but other repairs or alterations are the responsibility of the governing body and have to conform to set standards.

Non-maintained schools are fee-charging and the majority receive nothing from public funds. All such independent schools (about 2,650) are registered and open to inspection by the DES and about half reach the required standard, which is equivalent of the efficiency expected of a similar maintained school. Of the non-maintained schools receiving grant aid from the Department the main group is the 172 Direct Grant schools, which receive a *per capita* grant in return for an allocation of at least one-quarter of their places to pupils from maintained primary schools. The local education authority has then to pay the standard fee for such pupils. The remainder of the direct grant school intake is of children whose fees are paid, partly or wholly, by parents.

A number of independent schools, particularly those that are members of the Headmasters' Conference, the Governing Bodies Association or the Governing Bodies of Girls' Schools Association, are known as Public schools. The title *public school* is a misleading archaism as these schools are mostly independent, and are very exclusive in their intake. Originally the title appears to have referred to those better boarding grammar schools which attracted pupils from a wide area, and so were 'public' by comparison with others which were bound by the terms of their foundation to take only local children. Though many public schools are grant-aided in some way or another, the title still carries great prestige value, and received a certain official recognition when the President of the Board of Education set up the Fleming Committee[25] in 1942 to examine the relationship of the public schools to the rest of the education system. Many people feel that they are the strongest remaining bastion of privilege in the educational system, and wish to bring them into the maintained sector of education while at the same time preserving their educational excellence. About 7 per cent of secondary pupils attend non-maintained schools, three-fifths of these being at direct grant schools, and the rest in public schools.

Further and Higher Education

Further Education is a term used to embrace any form of education which takes place after the school career has ended, but may exclude universities and colleges of education, which are regarded as centres of Higher Education. It is the duty of local education authorities to ensure sufficient provision of facilities for full- and part-time education for people over compulsory school age. Each authority, having taken into account any local university or similar provision, adheres to a working plan for Further Education in its area which the Secretary of State must approve.

The field of Further Education is one of considerable scope, and courses in vocational as well as academic subjects are offered to craft or professional qualifications, to O- and A-levels, and to first and higher degree standard, the equivalent of Higher Education qualifications from the universities.

Diverse provision allows for considerable flexibility. There are no age restrictions and basic or advanced courses allow individuals to work up to whatever standard they can achieve. This is reflected not only in the wide range of courses but indeed in the variety of Further Education institutions. These include the new polytechnics which are now the main centres for Higher Education qualifications within the Further Education provision, and colleges of commerce and art, agricultural and technical colleges as well as the evening institutes. Attendance at these centres has increased steadily in recent years. By 1972 there were over 200,000 students on advanced courses. Almost half of these attended full-time or on an advanced sandwich course and about 42,000 and 20,000 were taking degree or higher diploma studies respectively. As well as full-time or sandwich courses, which have periods at college alternating with practical on-job training, study may be part-time, e.g. one day a week (day release) or for days or weeks at a time (block release) or on an evenings only basis.

In addition to the local authority-controlled colleges there are some colleges serving specialist interests. Many of them receive financial support from the DES, whilst others, like some secretarial or correspondence colleges, remain independent and largely rely on fees.

Liaison between local authorities and local industry and commerce in matters of further education is common. Since the Industrial Training Act, 1964, Industrial Training Boards have been established to embrace most areas of industry. The formation of these boards has had the effect of encouraging some industrial concerns to increase the number of their young people released for courses related to their employment. Firms favour a day or block release programme, often associated with formal in-work training. The qualifications for which such trainees study include the certificates of the City and Guilds of London Institute, and the regional training bodies. Occasionally specialist full-time short courses might be arranged to suit the needs of a particular group or industrial courses.

There has been fast development of the polytechnics in recent years. Local education authorities submitted plans for expansion in 1972 and indicated the potential for many regional polytechnics. There were 31 polytechnics in 1973, some formed by college amalgamation, offering full- and part-time higher education courses. They are wide ranging in both courses and intake, and provide teaching towards degree level or its equivalent as well as professional and higher national qualifications. Degree courses may lead to external University of London degrees but increasingly courses relate to the degrees for the Council for National Academic Awards.[26]

Colleges of education

The Secretary of State for Education ensures sufficient resources for teacher training. Where necessary a local authority may be directed to make provision for teacher training and other authorities may be required to assist in the expenses incurred.[27] It is necessary for teachers to be qualified in order to teach in maintained schools. Qualification may be obtained by completion of a course at one of the 159 colleges of education – formerly teacher training colleges – or at a university school of education or polytechnic department of education. The initial course of training in a college of education usually lasts for three years, but after any form of training course, teachers taking up first posts in maintained schools have to serve a probationary period of one year to demonstrate their practical classroom ability. Graduates used to be accorded qualified teacher status without undergoing a course of training, and this also applied to possessors of advanced specialist qualifications other than degrees. Such people qualifying in 1970, 1971–2 or 1973 could only teach in secondary schools, and since 31 December 1973 all such graduates are required to follow a one-year course of teacher training.

Exceptionally, students with appropriate experience or qualifications may train in two years or even one year. There are in addition four-year courses leading to B.Ed. degrees with professional qualification, and increasingly one-year postgraduate training courses are being offered by colleges of education. Twenty-eight university departments of education provide one-year postgraduate courses for teacher training, as do thirteen art training centres for students with advanced qualifications in art. Four colleges of education specialise in one-year training for those intending to teach in Further Education.

The James Committee Report concluded the desirability of a graduate teaching profession. This and its other main recommendations were accepted by the government in December 1972, and support was pledged for the development of colleges of education, polytechnics and of three-year courses leading to ordinary B.Ed. degrees, and thereafter to an Honours fourth year where suitable. Until these courses become available, or whilst the schools require them, certificate courses will continue.[28]

Universities

The British universities operate on a national basis so that suitably qualified people from any part of the UK may, if admitted, go to any of the universities in England, Wales, Scotland and Northern Ireland.[29]

Full-time university undergraduate courses to first degree level are generally of three years' duration.

Of all students in British universities about 25 per cent take science studies; the remainder are divided more or less equally between medicine, dentistry, the arts, social studies and engineering. About 20 per cent of full-time students are postgraduate, either working for higher degrees and diplomas or engaged in research. Compared with the education system in general a favourable staff–student ratio exists in the universities, at present averaging about 8:1. Within individual universities or departments there may be considerable variations in this figure, and as the economic cut-backs in 1973 and 1974 take effect the overall figure may become less favourable.

In addition to the conventional universities the Open University[30] offers part-time courses leading to degrees. Instruction is carried on by correspondence, short residential courses, tutorials and through the radio and TV media. The Open University differs in other respects in that there are no formal academic requirements of entrants, and qualifications are awarded on a credits system. Six credits are needed for the ordinary B.A. degree and eight credits for an Honours degree. Courses and credits may be combined in a variety of ways to cater for students' abilities, though for a degree with Honours a minimum of two credits must be at the higher grades 3 or 4 of academic content.

Adult education

The range of provisions of facilities for people over compulsory school age is extremely wide. Local education authority provision, extra-mural departments at universities and Workers' Education Association centres predominate, though HM Forces, the trade unions, the YMCA, the National Federation of Women's Institutes and other responsible bodies also make provision.

Courses range from full-time of one- or two-year duration, at residential centres like Ruskin College or Coleg Harlech, to short sessions provided by special organisations. Fees charged do not cover the cost of provision, in order to encourage all who wish to study to take part.

By 1973 there were about 1,600,000 students enrolled at the adult education centres and local education authority evening institutes, 500 or so students registering annually for the full-time courses at the residential centres. The DES grant aided such centres to about £2 million in 1972–3.

Special schools and education welfare provisions

Special schools

The Education Act, 1944,[31] laid down that special educational treatment should be provided either in special schools or provision made within ordinary schools elsewhere for pupils suffering from disability of mind or body. Some handicapped children may attend ordinary schools, or other maintained special schools, including hospital schools for in-patients, whereas others may go to non-maintained special, mostly boarding, schools of which there are some 110, where fees are paid in full by the local education authorities.

Special schools exist for certain categories of handicapped children, where the handicap is of such a nature and degree as to prevent the

39

child from benefiting from primary or secondary education alongside normal children.[32]

Special educational treatment is provided for pupils who are blind, partially sighted, deaf, partially deaf, educationally subnormal, epileptic, maladjusted, physically handicapped, delicate or suffering from speech defects not due to deafness.

The Education (Handicapped Children) Act of 1970 provides that certain severely mentally disabled children be regarded as needing special education. From 1 April 1971, the education service took responsibility for the 30,000 or so children concerned. Before that date these children were regarded as being unsuitable for education, and care and training arrangements were left to local health authorities.

The intention of special schooling is to provide a stimulating and diverse educational environment to endeavour to overcome the learning difficulties of the handicapped child, aiming at a degree of self-reliance and responsibility in adult life. Special schools are comparatively favourably staffed and in certain cases provide speech therapy, physiotherapy and other specialised treatment as well as special teaching facilities.

Of the maintained special schools about 75 per cent are day schools, although in some cases of severe handicap where day schooling is inappropriate or where long journeys to and from home may be necessary, boarding accommodation is provided free of charge. In circumstances where to remain at a special school beyond the age of sixteen is clearly an advantage this can sometimes be arranged.

In 1970, the Chronically Sick and Disabled Persons Act provided for consideration of special individual facilities for children suffering from blindness and deafness, autism and other childhood psychosis, and acute dyslexia, and in 1971[33] the DES stressed the need for skilled assessment of autistic children by experts from different fields.

The largest group in receipt of special schooling is that of the educationally subnormal. These are pupils who 'by reason of limited ability or some other condition resulting in educational retardation require some specialised form of education'.[34] They are children who are not necessarily intellectually backward, but who may suffer educational difficulties as a result of illness, environmental or emotional problems.

Identification of children in need of special education is the duty of the local authority. Any child of two or over may be called for medical examination; a legal notice may be served on parents if necessary, requiring them to submit the child for examination.

On the basis of the medical officer's report, with information from the educational psychologist and the teacher, the educational needs of the child are then determined. The parents' wishes are considered and should they disagree with the local education authority's decision they can appeal to the Secretary of State. Decisions regarding special schooling can only be made on an individual basis bearing in mind the social and psychological needs, as well as the educational and physical needs, of the child and the resources of the authority. The needs of the individual must be balanced against the needs of the group; a disruptive slightly handicapped pupil may be more in need of special school care than a stable but more severely handicapped child. The DES encourages provision in ordinary schools wherever possible in the belief that the more normal the environment in which the child develops the more easily will he find his place in the adult world.

In addition to traditional special education a few children are educated at home or in small groups. This work is undertaken by the local education authorities. Special provision may also be made for further education and pre-vocational training and guidance for young people who are blind or suffer from certain other physical handicaps. Vocational training may then be available through the Department of Employment.[35] In many cases today disabled persons are able to attend courses at ordinary centres of further or higher education. The White Paper *Education: A Framework for Expansion* recommended an increase in special schools building, particularly for the mentally handicapped. An increase from £11 million in 1972–3 to £19 million in 1976–7 was proposed to cover new building costs and the improvement of established premises.

Ancillary services

The Education Act, 1944, extended the powers of local education authorities to assist children whose education might suffer as a result of poverty or ill-health.

The School Health Service is discussed in chapter 6, and education welfare provisions, including meals, milk, clothing, grants and maintenance allowances, are included in the chapter on Income and need.

In addition to the provisions described elsewhere, local education authorities have a duty to provide free transport for fit children below the age of eight who have a distance of more than two miles to travel to school, and for older children with a journey of three miles or more between home and school; they are also empowered to provide it for shorter distances. Special services may be made available, but where public transport exists the local authorities may use it by paying the necessary fares.

Boarding education may be provided where the authority and the parents think it desirable. This may be free, or a charge may be made according to the means of the parents.

Children who are so unsuitably clothed that they cannot make use of their schooling may be supplied with clothing by the local authority. This provision exists for pupils of all maintained schools and all special schools, whether maintained or not. The authority is expected to recover clothing costs wholly or partly from parents who are not in financial hardship.

The Education Welfare Service

Education Welfare Officers – the one-time School Attendance Officers – deal broadly with problems of absence from school, as well as with assessments for educational benefits, transport attendance for children at special schools and other welfare-related tasks. Such work is closely associated with social work and the Seebohm Report recommended that the service be incorporated into local authority social service departments. In the main such amalgamation has not taken place. Education welfare officers, and indeed appropriately trained teachers, could greatly facilitate liaison between home, school and local authority social services. The welfare officers do not have a thorough social work training and such qualifications as are available to them do not confer professional status commensurate with the job they do. As a result the Education Welfare Service is more often regarded as an enforcement agency than one of understanding and help.[36]

The Youth Service

This service, always regarded as part of the education service, has never attracted the attention, glamour or finances of the other areas of education provision. Local authorities maintain their own youth centres, and assist voluntary agencies with youth work within their areas, so that the service is essentially one of co-operation between local authorities and voluntary organisations. In 1971 the report of the Youth Service Development Council[37] was not accepted by the government; the Secretary of State decided that the service should continue on its existing basis but that there should be 'certain changes of emphasis which should be reflected by corresponding changes in the financial support given by the Department'.[38]

A simplification of the grant-aiding system was felt to be needed, with more help being channelled into less prosperous areas and into experimental youth work. Since April 1972 new arrangements for capital grants have applied, local authorities becoming responsible for the finance and administration of projects to receive support and the DES then making grants proportional to the total cost and the local authority's contribution.[39]

The anxieties which this move created among the voluntary organisations proved unfounded. In April 1973 the Secretary of State was able to announce an increase of 50 per cent over the grant aid of the previous year under the old arrangement. In the decade 1961–1971 total government expenditure on the Youth Service increased from £3 million to £20 million, and the number of qualified youth workers increased from 700 to over 2,000.

Further recommendation by the Youth Service Development Council that the Youth Service should become a Youth and Community Service was rejected, and the council itself, after ten years' work following the Albemarle Report, was wound up.

A report was commissioned by the DES[40] in 1968 to describe the use made of the Youth Service and assess the facilities provided. It published its findings in June 1972, its only significant one being that the number of young people not attached to a club were fewer than previously believed. This finding might be partly explained by the definition of 'club' used by this report differing from that of the Albemarle Committee and other earlier reports.

The Young Volunteer Force Foundation, a development in youth work originating from outside the service, encouraged assistance to the community by young people, who were given short training courses before working for local authorities. For a time the future of the foundation was uncertain as it faltered in the face of financial difficulties; charitable money was coming to an end by 1972 and government grants could not be increased. Following a decision to appoint a Minister of State to co-ordinate government interest in voluntary social services, support for the Young Volunteer Force Foundation was transferred to the Home Office.

Education of immigrants and gypsy education

In maintained primary and secondary schools there are about 280,000 immigrant pupils. This represents about $3\frac{1}{2}$ per cent of all pupils. This rising figure is reflected in the DES's interest and concern for the needs of immigrant pupils in schools.[41]

In February 1972, Education Survey no. 14, *The Continuing Needs of Immigrants*, was published; the report of the National Foundation for Educational Research on educational arrangements for schools with immigrant pupils appeared at the same time.[42] The influx of refugees from Uganda in 1972 was provided for by local education authorities, either by special classes in resettlement camps, catering for both children and adults, or by the extension of existing school provision. Some costs for additional staff and building were met by the Uganda Resettlement Board.

Gypsy education is a topic which has commanded attention in

43

recent years. Since the Plowden Report commented that gypsies were 'probably the most severely deprived children in the country'[43] Lady Plowden has herself helped to form the National Gypsy Education Council. This and other interested pressure groups (such as the Gypsies and Travellers Education Council), studying the educational needs of the different gypsy groups, have witnessed the provision of the on-site Liverpool Travellers' School, an autonomous unit within the local education authority, with six specially appointed staff working flexible hours to suit the needs of the gypsy community. In addition there exists the West Midlands Travellers' School and two school-attached classes for gypsies at Blackburn and Sevenoaks. Action research in the West Midlands and in Liverpool may clarify the needs and demands of the various gypsy groups and so make way for provision which central government might feel should be supported.

Administration of the education service

Education in the public sector is administered through a combination of national and local government bodies.

The 1944 Act made it the responsibility of the Minister of Education to ensure the comprehensive provision and development of education in England and Wales. This involved the collaboration of local education authorities in implementing national policies for the education service. On 1 April 1964 the Secretary of State for Education and Science took over these duties and, in addition, responsibility for the universities of England, Wales and Scotland, which until then had been administered by the Treasury.

The Department of Education and Science has the Secretary of State for Education and Science as its political head. He is a senior Minister of the Crown who would usually have a seat in the Cabinet. He is assisted by two Ministers of State and two parliamentary under-secretaries. The department is staffed by civil servants whose appointments are non-political, their work being to deal with schools, further education and teachers in England and Wales, and with the universities throughout Great Britain. There are also specialist branches providing information and advice on particular topics, such as health, buildings and statistics. The Department's responsibilities in Wales are looked after by the Education Office for Wales, and after 5 November 1970 the Secretary of State for Wales took over responsibility for primary and secondary schools in Wales from the Secretary of State for Education and Science, who is now responsible for all education in England, for the universities in Scotland and for all post-school education in Wales.

Central Advisory Councils

Two Central Advisory Councils, one for England and one for Wales,[44] advise the Secretary of State, usually on matters referred to them regarding the theory and practice of education but also on those matters which in their opinion should have his attention.[45]

Not all forms of education come under Department of Education and Science control: education in the Armed Forces, or in community schools or borstals, falls outside its competence. It has only an indirect influence on university education through the University Grants Committee, and it does not yet have any powers to control the growing industry of private 'correspondence courses'. It does not run any schools or technical colleges, engage any teachers, or prescribe textbooks or curricula. The Department is primarily concerned with the formulation, interpretation and execution of national policy as laid down in Acts of Parliament and Regulations. Its functions also comprise the following:

(a) control of the rate, distribution, and nature and cost of educational building;

(b) control of teacher training and supply, and of the principles governing qualification for entry into the profession;

(c) the settlement of disputes, e.g. between a parent and a local education authority or the governors of a school;

(d) the payment of certain education grants from central government funds, e.g. in scholarships, for educational research, or through the Arts Council;

(e) the administration of a teacher superannuation scheme;

(f) with local authority consultation, predicting local authority expenditure to be considered when determining rate support grants;

(g) the administration of grants support to some special education institutions.

Since 1964 the Schools Council for the Curriculum and Examinations has advised and encouraged research programmes and development projects which schools may support if they choose. Composed mainly of teachers, it nevertheless represents the whole spectrum of the educational service, including the universities and the DES.

In addition the Secretary of State can create *ad hoc* committees to advise him on particular problems. He is represented on various autonomous bodies, such as, for instance, the National Foundation for Educational Research, which are often subsidised by the Department. Finally, the Department frequently consults, both formally and informally, the local education authorities, the churches, the teachers' organisations, and any other bodies which would be affected by a proposed course of action.

Although central government controls the overall nature of education, albeit in some measure through local education authorities, it does not control curricula in schools. A communication channel to schools is kept open by the 470 H.M. Inspectors of Schools whose job is to report to the Secretaries of State on work in maintained schools and colleges.[46] The inspectors are Crown officials and, although for administrative purposes this is merely a nominal distinction, it does symbolise a real tradition of independence in the inspectorate. Their principal function is the inspection of educational establishments other than universities, all schools being open to their inspection. They can only criticise, recommend, and advise; they cannot give orders to teachers, governors or local education authorities. They report direct to the Secretary of State, but must discuss their report with the school authorities before submitting it. Any teacher who is adversely criticised must be shown a copy of the report and be given a chance to reply to it. Once written, the report cannot be altered by anyone other than the writer – not even by the Secretary of State himself.

The inspectors are also responsible for approving independent schools for recognition as efficient. In addition the inspectorate gives professional educational advice to the Department and to local education authorities; provides a focus point for information on educational developments; conducts courses for serving teachers; and prepares advisory literature for teachers and the general public.

Local government

Following the Local Government Act, 1972, reorganised local authorities took over their new responsibilities on 1 April 1974. Of the forty-five new counties, all but six are responsible for education. In those six counties, thirty-six metropolitan districts have responsibility for education and with the eight new Welsh counties plus the existing local education authorities the total number of local education authorities in England and Wales is 105.[47]

Each such authority appoints an education committee, a majority of the committee members being by law members of the authority, but also including co-opted members who have 'experience in education and persons acquainted with the educational conditions prevailing in the area'. This illustrates the tradition in English government that legislative decisions should not be entrusted to specialists but should be made by ordinary citizens who have been elected to represent the community, and who can assess the opinions of specialists against broader issues.

The education committee in its turn appoints sub-committees to deal with special areas in the field of education, such as primary schools, secondary schools, and Further Education.

'A local education authority may authorise an education committee of an authority to exercise on their behalf any of their functions with respect to education, except the power to borrow money or to raise a rate.' However, Councils differ widely in the extent to which they delegate powers to their education committees. [48]

Education authorities have to provide schools, employ teaching staff, local inspectors of schools and education organisers. They must ensure sufficient equipment and provide education to meet all needs within the community. Costs for such provision are met from rates and the rate support grant, which is paid from Exchequer funds by the Secretary of State for the Environment. Except for housing and trading services all local authority services share in the grant although education is the largest of the services so financed.

All schools in the maintained sector have a managing body (primary) or a governing body (secondary). The general educational character of a maintained school is decided by the local education authority. The general direction of conduct and curriculum is the responsibility of the managers or governors in consultation with the head teacher who is usually given effective control over the day-to-day running of the school by the rules of management or articles of government. In practice the professional status of the class teacher means that he has considerable independence inside his own classroom.

The managers or governors of county schools are appointed by the local education authority (or by divisional executives to whom it may have delegated the necessary powers). A varying proportion of the managers or governors of voluntary schools are appointed by the voluntary body concerned according to the status of the school, the remainder by the local education authority.

In controlled schools two-thirds of the managing or governing body are nominated by the authority, which also meets all costs and appoints the teachers.

In an aided school two-thirds of the managers represent the voluntary body, who are responsible for repairs, improvements, enlargements or alterations to the school fabric. Central government grants are available for up to four-fifths of approved capital expenditure including the work of providing new schools or extensions to existing schools not previously eligible for grant. The local authority pays the teachers though their appointments are the responsibility of the governing body.

Special agreement schools, for whom local authorities pay between one-half and three-quarters of the cost of new building, also have two-thirds of their governors provided by the voluntary body.

Most Further Education colleges are local-authority maintained, and in some cases by more than one authority. Fees may be charged of students in Further Education but these do not cover actual course costs and are generally remitted. Students taking degree equivalent courses are in any case grant-aided. Further Education is co-ordinated by ten regional advisory councils which include representatives of colleges, universities, industry and commerce as well as from the local authority.

The governing bodies of polytechnics and Further Education colleges, which may include a student representative, are responsible for the general control of the institution, the principal overseeing internal organisation and discipline. The academic board plans, co-ordinates and develops the high grade academic courses.

Since the establishment by Royal Charter in 1964 of the Council for National Academic Awards, colleges may devise curricula and syllabuses of suitable standard leading to a CNAA degree or other qualifications and determine their own admission requirements and run their own examinations.[49]

Higher Education in Great Britain falls into two categories. There is an autonomous sector of universities with complete academic freedom to decide the number and quality of the students they will admit, the appointment of staff, the subjects taught, what degrees to award and on what conditions to award them. They have their own internal system of government, exercised in most universities by a court which is formally the supreme governing body, the council which administers finance, and the senate which is the chief academic authority. Faculties control day-to-day academic matters and are usually composed of departments representing different, though related, fields of study.

Oxford and Cambridge are self-governed, by senior members of the university, and self-financed by taxes and endowments. The ultimate authority at Oxford is Congregation and at Cambridge the Regent House.[50]

Candidates for first admission to a British university – other than the Open University – submit their preferences to the Universities Central Council on Admissions which sends the application to the universities concerned. Graduate applicants apply direct to the universities, who are quite free in all cases to admit students according to their standards and resources. Ninety per cent of students in the universities receive assistance from public monies. Undergraduates are normally financed by an income-related[51] local education authority grant. At postgraduate level government departments and research councils generally make grants, though since September 1967 DES bursaries are available for students in fields where other financial assistance is not forthcoming.

The government exercises its financial responsibilities in universities through the University Grants Committee. The committee's members are appointed by the Secretary of State from the academic and business worlds, though the universities are not directly represented. The main functions of the committee are to collect and diffuse information on university education in the UK, especially with regard to overall financial needs, and to advise the government on the use of Parliamentary grants, and to help in the preparation of plans for the development of university education. Grants made on the advice of the University Grants Committee represent about 18 per cent of the universities' recurrent expenditure, and about 90 per cent of their capital expenditure.

Recurrent grants, almost half of which go to pay academic salaries, are assessed quinquennially. Non-recurrent grants meet expenditure arising from government-approved annual building programmes.

The 1972 White Paper[52] announced the financial settlement for the quinquennium 1972–7 providing for 254,000 undergraduates by 1976–77, and 52,000 postgraduates, or 17 per cent of full-time student totals.

The public sector of Higher Education consists mainly of the polytechnics and the colleges of education. Rather more than two-thirds of the colleges of education are administered and financed by local education authorities, each authority contributing to a central fund in proportion to the average number of pupils attending maintained schools in their area. The DES meets the running costs of the remaining one-third – the voluntary colleges – and also contributes 80 per cent of the cost of approved capital expenditure. The academic oversight of the colleges is in the hands of twenty-three University Institutes of Education, which act as 'area training organisations'.

Since 1964 colleges have had greater freedom in running their own affairs, including students in aspects of college government in many cases.

The outcome of recently proposed changes means that some colleges may develop into, or merge with other colleges to form, new Higher Education centres, many of these taking a specialist function such as adult education, or in-service education for teachers.

Students may be grant-aided and are admitted by the colleges themselves, there being a clearing house[53] which circularises the applications of candidates not obtaining entry to any of the colleges of their choice. A similar scheme operates for graduate applicants for the colleges of education and university schools of education.

Parental and educational associations

These groups are taking an increased part in shaping the development of the education system. In schools teachers and parents are forming associations in increasing numbers in an effort to link the values and difficulties of home and school to the ultimate benefit of the child. The Plowden Report stressed the worth and the National Confederation of Parent–Teacher Associations encourages the development of such ventures. The Confederation of State Education, comprising over 100 local associations, seeks to co-operate with local education authorities in developing closer ties between school and community. A forum and information service is provided by the Advisory Centre for Education with its stimulating and well-informed periodical *Where?* and the Confederation for the Advancement of State Education has often expressed itself strongly on the serious gaps and deficiencies which still remain in our educational system.

Teachers and teacher education

The payment of full-time teachers in maintained schools and institutions of Further Education follows a national scale determined by machinery established under the Remuneration of Teachers Act, 1965. Salaries are negotiated in committees, known as Burnham Committees, composed of representatives of the DES, of the local education authorities, and of the teachers. In the event of disagreement there is provision for independent arbitration and the arbitrator's decision is binding on both sides unless set aside by Parliament. The remuneration of the teaching staff in colleges of education is decided at the national level by the Secretary of State for Education and Science on the basis of recommendations made by the Pelham Committee which represents both staff and their employers.

The 1972 White Paper[54] proposed an extension of the teaching force equal by 1981 to a 10 per cent rise over 1971 figures, in order to maintain standards. As a basis for planning the assumption might reasonably be that standards will decline if the figures are not met. In the face of an expanding school population including the large number of over fifteens, plus the nursery and in-service programmes, approximately half a million full-time equivalent teachers will be needed in maintained schools by 1980. Figures of this order would mean an overall projected pupil–teacher ratio of $18\frac{1}{2}$:1, compared with 22:1 in 1970. A breakdown of existing figures paints a slightly clearer picture, as is shown in Table 5.

The figures in the table contrast with the pupil–teacher ratios in non-maintained schools, which for 1971 showed 15·4:1 for direct grant schools and 12·8:1 in recognised independent schools, figures approximately fifteen years ahead of the maintained schools at the current projected rate of development.

Against this background teachers are often said to comprise a comparatively insecure, poorly respected and poorly paid profession.

This, whilst a debatable conclusion depending as it does in part at least upon definitions of professional and attendant questions on the viability of comparisons, contains some truth. As new professions grew up during the nineteenth century, a typical pattern emerged of small occupational groups which exercised strict control over admission, insisted on high standards of qualification and established codes of professional behaviour for the safeguarding of clients' interests. Membership carried prestige in society, and usually commanded a high salary. In view of the crucial role which our society attributes to education in terms of the personal development and future happiness of individuals, as well as its connection with economic expansion and technological progress, it might be thought strange that teachers have never, in the main, enjoyed commensurate status.

TABLE 5   *Number of teachers in maintained schools, England and Wales, 1972*[55]

	Full-time teachers	*Part-time teachers (FTE)*	*Pupils per teacher*
England			
Primary	171,273	10,921	26·2
Middle	4,991	339	22·8
Secondary	160,485	10,174	17·5
Special	10,983	438	9·6
Total	347,732	21,872	
Wales			
Primary	12,271	329	24·5
Middle	9	—	19·1
Secondary	10,640	272	18·0
Special	437	5	9·6
Total	23,357	606	

Source: *The Educational System of England and Wales*, Appendix tables A1, 1972.

Increasingly in industrialised societies teaching is becoming a profession for women and their predominance in primary schools has created problems. There is a high rate of 'wastage' among young women teachers, in that many of them marry soon after training and then give up teaching while they raise a family. The DES and local education authorities are offering various inducements in the form of flexible part-time posts to encourage married women teachers to re-enter the profession when their family responsibilities permit.

The National Association of Schoolmasters, which is exclusively male in membership, argues that its sister organisation, the National Union of Teachers, which has mixed membership, when involved in salary negotiations does not press for rates of pay which are related to the needs of a family man who has to maintain a professional standard of living, but tends to accept lower rates which are acceptable to the young unmarried women who form a large proportion of its membership.

The origins of the teaching profession, especially its religious context, have lent it a vocational quality, a job to be done for altruistic reasons rather than for reward. Such an ideal could hardly expect to command a wide following. Non-productive work could not deploy large finances, and so it could offer a social ladder only to members of the lower working class. This was most noticeable in boys' elementary schools, which constituted a self-perpetuating system, whereas teaching the poor was one of the few occupations deemed suitable for a middle-class woman of that period.

In addition the teacher associations have a reputation for being frequently concerned with salary and pension demands, as well as other aspects of public spending, to such a degree that any quest for status and professional standing may be damaged by their insistence upon the right to more money rather than insistence upon a quality of performance which will draw to public attention their merits. The more typical strategy of professional organisations has been to seek strong representation on all bodies which employ their members, or determine their pay and conditions of service.

As education is a service which must be provided continuously for the whole child population the teaching body will always be too large and varied to achieve the exclusiveness of a 'learned' profession. The teachers' organisations have successfully pressed for the extension of teacher training to a three-year course, parallel to the length of training in some established professions, and the creation of a four-year B.Ed. course in colleges of education.

Until now developments of this nature have been of little significance against the total background and output of higher education.

In December 1972 the government announced its acceptance of the main recommendations of the James Report[56] including the ultimate achievement of a totally graduate profession.[57]

The committee had been asked to consider the content and organisation of courses and the role of the colleges of education, the polytechnics, other Further Education institutions and the universities in the training of teachers. The report divided teacher education and training into three consecutive cycles – personal Higher Education, pre-service training and induction, and in-service education and training – and recommendations were made in respect of each cycle.

The first cycle would consist of not less than two-year courses leading to a diploma in higher education[58] appropriate for students who had not chosen their future careers, as well as for those wishing to become teachers.

The second cycle in the proposed teacher training scheme would last for a further two years, the first year of which would lead to recognition as 'licensed teacher' and be taken in a professional institution such as a college of education, or education department of a university or polytechnic. The second year would comprise a paid teaching assignment, with further regular training at a professional centre, leading to recognition as 'registered teacher' and to a new professional degree of B.A. (Education). In the third cycle all teachers would have the right to be released with pay for in-service education and training, at a rate equivalent to one term in every seven years and, as soon as possible, one term in every five years.

The Report proposed that administration of the scheme be in the hands of fifteen Regional Councils for Colleges and Departments of Education which should include representatives from universities, colleges of education, polytechnics, teacher organisations and local education authorities.

The initial reactions to the Dip. H.E. proposals were mixed, even among teachers themselves. Eventually, in the face of opposition from the National Union of Teachers and the Committee of Vice-Chancellors and Principals, among others, as well as the reality of the high costs of building and other development necessary, the government began to doubt the wisdom of the new teacher training proposals. Nevertheless, discussion of and reorganisation towards the goals encompassed in the James Report continue.

Selection and opportunity

The Education Act, 1944, was under discussion in a climate which suggested the strong intention to organise a new school system that would avoid early differentiation. In fact there emerged little that was new; selective schooling beyond eleven was retained and three kinds of secondary school were suggested: the former grammar school, unchanged, became the post-1944 grammar school; the secondary modern school was the senior elementary school renamed; and the technical schools were the junior technical schools upgraded. This reality was not obscured by the hope expressed in the Act that all forms of schooling would enjoy parity of status. The grammar schools were the avenues to university, and enjoyed commensurate esteem, though expansion in Higher Education soon meant that more people were involved. Against this background educational argument to justify the tripartite system used notions of secondary modern or grammar school 'types of mind' – mental characteristics conveniently corresponding to provisions aimed at the needs of these presumed categories of child.

The Act urged that secondary school provision should be made in accordance with pupils' different ages, abilities and aptitudes. In the face of challenge the view of types of mind corresponding to types of school was replaced by grades of ability matching the schools. Justification of selection by test at eleven became a priority.

After the Act the eleven-plus came under scrutiny and claims of objectivity on behalf of the test – that it was not so much competitive as allocative according to ability grade – necessitated close evaluation of the accuracy of 'intelligence'. As time went by and some secondary modern school pupils were clearly achieving academic levels not predicted for them the voices of sociologists, psychologists and educationists raised against the eleven-plus selection procedure came to be heard more clearly.

A growing understanding of the principles of psychological measurement revealed that IQ tests did not measure some absolute ability, but rather that 'intelligence' was, at least, partly an acquired quality which was profoundly influenced by such social factors as home conditions, size of family, educational experience and parental aspirations. Consequently, it was seen to be educationally wrong to decide the academic future of a child on the basis of such a criterion at the early age of eleven. Moreover, the critical point of the scale which determined selection for grammar school was dependent on such extraneous factors as the number of grammar school places available in a particular local education authority and the size of a particular year group in that area. Also it was known that the existing system resulted in a considerable number of wrong allocations, and once the children were segregated in different schools it became very difficult to detect and correct such an error. Thus, for a mixture of reasons both ideological and educational, administrators had been moving towards the idea of a unified system of secondary education where a wide range of subjects could be taught within one school, and where each individual would be educated in a range of subjects and to a level suited to his ability and aptitudes without anyone being labelled as a failure by virtue of a dubious system of selection.

In addition, for very much the same reasons, the systems of streaming in schools were criticised since any form of differentiation implemented might cause restrictive limits to be placed on a child's development potential.

Power was added to the zeal for reform by publication in the 1950s and early 1960s of sociological studies[59] relating selection processes in education to our society stratified by social class. Findings suggested that secondary modern school children, supposedly less intelligent, were predominantly from working-class families, and that the grammar schools, and more so the direct grant schools, were strongly middle class in intake. Thus the position in the pre-war fee-paying days still obtained in spite of 'objective' allocation. Statements were clearly made that all the intelligence test did was to reflect an academic view of what intelligence ought to be, i.e. the ability to perform the mental gymnastics necessary to absorb traditional learning presented on formal school lines. Once selection had thus been stripped of its pretensions the way became open for comprehensive reorganisation.

In July 1965 Circular 10/65 appeared, and by January 1967 only five local education authorities had refused to submit proposals; thirty-eight others had not yet submitted any, but were expected to do so. Inevitably, some felt that a doctrinaire programme was being rushed through without regard to parents' wishes or to the quality of education provided, particularly where the plans involved the merging of grammar schools which had enjoyed a long tradition of academic excellence.

Consequently the discussions came more and more into the political arena, and in time new sociological evidence suggested that not only was eleven-plus selection unsatisfactory, but also that the working-class child suffers cumulative disadvantages at every stage of his schooling, and that social barriers to educability are quite as important as the barriers to opportunity. Clearly, given the disadvantages under which large numbers of children labour, competition for educational advantage becomes meaningless. Moreover, since education provides the key to the individual's life-chances, fundamental questions of social justice are involved. However, these barriers cannot be removed simply by legislation and the need for social reform is clearly indicated.

Much of the more recent discussion about social class and educational opportunity has been centred on the 1967 Plowden Report, *Children and their Primary Schools*, which painted a clear picture of the vicious circle which existed in depressed areas, where education was inevitably seen as a brief prelude to work rather than as an avenue to further opportunity.

The proposals for education priority areas selected on the basis of eight criteria of need – the proportion of unskilled and semi-skilled workers in the area, size of families, proportion receiving state benefits, overcrowding and sharing of houses, truancy, handicapped pupils in ordinary schools, incomplete families and children unable to speak English – suggest that serious deprivation affects one child in ten and the Report urged that these areas should receive more financial aid.

The criteria listed are not primarily educational ones, but could be taken as evidence of the need for a wide range of social services. This helps to underline the present policy of viewing education in the wider social context of the community in which the school is set. So too does the complementary proposal from Plowden which consists of a complete programme for involving parents more intimately with schools so as to combat the lack of parental aspiration prevailing in these areas, often believed to be the most important of the external social factors influencing achievement.[60]

Modes of treatment were not precisely specified, though better teachers with extra allowances, links between teachers' colleges and education priority areas and development of nursery provision, extension of school and social work contact, and the implementation of the community school concept were all regarded as essential ingredients.

The organisation of the education priority areas scheme was envisaged in two stages. The initial stage, adding some £11 million to the expenditure on maintained primary schools, ran until 1971, introducing special measures aimed at combating the social evils described, and including an evaluative research project to judge the effects of different innovations. The second stage was intended as a long-term project designed to continue or extend schemes which were discovered to be successful during the experimental stage.

Dr Halsey's[61] action research programme into the education priority areas was completed in March 1972 at a cost to the DES of nearly £100,000 and to the Social Service Research Council of almost £75,000.

As action focused on the education priority areas, discussion and research in sociology, psychology and education moved on. Questions have been formulated and evidence sought about the way in which knowledge has been predefined by the society in which it is transmitted. More difficult, though more fundamental questions are being asked which may point the way ahead, and recently it has been argued frequently that until the whole management of knowledge is treated as a central concern, particularly in the Sociology of Education, such topics as 'the curriculum, the values of education and the relationship of education to wider social processes will never be given their proper consideration.'[62]

Further reading

In addition to published works referred to in the notes the following are suggested as further reading:

W. H. G. ARMYTAGE, *Four Hundred Years of English Education*, Cambridge University Press, 1964.

H. C. BARNARD, *A History of English Education from 1970*, University of London Press, 1963.

C. BENN and B. SIMON, *Half Way There*, McGraw-Hill, 1970.

M. BLAUG, ed., *Economics of Education*, I, Penguin, 1968, and *Economics of Education*, II, Penguin, 1969.

H. C. DENT, *The Educational System of England and Wales*, University of London Press, 1963, and F. H. PEDLEY, *The Educational System in England and Wales*, Pergamon, 1964.

K. RICHMOND, *The Literature of Education: A Critical Bibliography, 1945-70*, Methuen, 1972.

A series of government reports have examined different sectors of the educational system, and made recommendations, for example:

Day Release (Henniker–Heaton Report), HMSO, 1964. This deals with the development of day-release schemes in institutions of Further Education in England and Wales.

Early Leaving, Central Advisory Council of Education (England), 1954.

15 to 18 (Crowther Report), HMSO, 1959, vol. I, 'Report'; vol. II, 'Surveys'.

Half Our Future (Newsom Report), HMSO, 1963. This dealt with the education between the ages of thirteen and sixteen of pupils of average or less than average ability.

Higher Education (Robbins Report), with five separate appendices, Cmnd 2154, HMSO, 1963.

Public Schools Commission First Report (Newsom Report), with a one-volume appendix, HMSO, 1968, with independent boarding schools and how they might be integrated into the state system.

Public Schools Commission Second Report (Donnison Report), HMSO, 1970, with a one-volume appendix, and a further volume on Scotland, prepared by a separate committee under the chairmanship of T. Ewan Faulkner. This second report concerned itself with independent day schools and direct grant grammar schools. Direct grant grammar schools were not included in the Commission's terms of reference until October 1967.

The Demand for and Supply of Teachers 1963–1986, HMSO, 1965. The ninth report of the National Advisory Council on the Training and Supply of Teachers, this deals with the staffing of maintained schools.

The Youth Service in England and Wales (Albemarle Report), HMSO, 1960.

Women and Teaching, HMSO, 1963. This was a report by Professor R. K. Kelsall on a sample of women who entered teaching in England and Wales at various pre-war and post-war dates.

Youth and Community Work in the 70's, HMSO, 1969. Proposals for the future by the Youth Service Development Council.

Notes

1 Today the Churches no longer control the majority of schools in this country. Nevertheless the Education Act, 1944, made divine worship and religious instruction compulsory in maintained schools where no other subject is statutorily compulsory.

2 At the end of the nineteenth century the Church of England was responsible for almost 12,000 schools, and 2 million children. The Roman Catholic Church and other voluntary groups educated another ½ million. Local authority schools, though totalling far less, in fact themselves educated 2½ million children.

3 These had developed a liberal curriculum. They normally took boys and girls from elementary schools at twelve or thirteen, and were regarded as a form of post-school training.

4 Cambridgeshire, 1924. A committee of churchmen and teachers drew up a syllabus for religious instruction in schools. In 1942 over 800 local authorities used this syllabus and both the Minister of Education, R. A. Butler, and the Prime Minister, Winston Churchill, gave it their approval.

5 For an expansion of this point see R. A. Butler, *The Art of the Possible*, Hamish Hamilton, 1971.

6 *Children and their Primary Schools* (Plowden Report), vols 1 and 2, HMSO, 1967. One of a series of contemplative and exploratory reports by Central Advisory Councils.

7 For example, J. W. B. Douglas, *The Home and the School*, MacGibbon & Kee, 1964; B. Bernstein, 'Social class and linguistic development' in A. H. Halsey, J. Floud and C. A. Anderson, eds, *Education, Economy and Society*, Free Press, 1961; J. Floud, A. H. Halsey and F. M. Martin, *Social Class and Educational Opportunity*, Heinemann, 1956.

8 *Teacher Education and Training*, HMSO, 1972. Report of the James Committee, under the chairmanship of Lord James of Rusholme.

9 See p. 50 and n. 58.

10 Cmnd 5174, HMSO, 1972.

11 This includes in England and Wales, universities, primary and secondary schooling for which the DES is responsible, and education in Scotland except for the universities which are the responsibility of the Secretary of State for Scotland.

12 See especially DES, *Education and Science in 1972*, I, HMSO, 1973.

13 The Order in Council, raising the minimum leaving age to sixteen from fifteen, was made on 22 March 1972.

14 Pupils must remain at school until the end of the spring term of their sixteenth birthday, for those born between 1 September and 31 January, or until the end of the summer term for the remainder.

15 Voluntary post-school education may include universities, polytechnics, further education colleges, colleges of education, plus adult education and youth service. Financial aid applies to universities and college of education students and to many in Further Education establishments.

16 *The Education System of England and Wales*, HMSO, revised 1973, Appendix: Tables A1.

17 Cmnd 5174, HMSO, 1972. Plans included a 90 per cent provision of school places for four-year-olds and 50 per cent provision for three-year-olds, and they were expected to cater for all children whose parents wished for them to have nursery schooling.

18 See DES pamphlet *Towards the Middle School*, HMSO, 1970; also *ibid.*, *Launching Middle Schools*, HMSO, 1970.

19 *The Educational System of England and Wales*, p. 2.

20 Circular 10/65. This was a request document aimed at persuasion rather than legislation.

21 Schools not maintained by a local education authority, but in receipt of *per capita* grant from the DES, provided that 25 per cent of their entry was open to local authority pupils. By not taking up their quota of places, and thus diminishing financial support, local education authorities can put pressure on direct grant schools to accept maintained status.

22 For example, London, Anglesey, Bristol, Coventry.

23 See p. 33 and n. 18.

24 See p. 47.

25 *The Public Schools and the General Education System* (Fleming Report), HMSO, 1944.

26 See *Education and Science in 1972*, p. 19.

27 Provision made by the Education Act, 1944.

28 See p. 52 and n. 58.

29 Universities in England and Wales: Oxford and Cambridge, systems of related autonomous college units, over 10,500 students in each university; London federation of colleges, 33,000 students; Durham and Newcastle, before 1963 one University of Durham, 3,000 and 6,000 students respectively; Wales, federation of colleges, 15,000 students; Manchester, Birmingham, Liverpool, Leeds, Sheffield and Bristol, nineteenth-century civic universities, 6,000 to 9,000 students each; Reading, Nottingham, Southampton, Hull, Exeter and Leicester, younger civic universities – pre-1939 – 3,000 to 6,000 students; Keele (1949), Sussex, York, East Anglia, Essex, Lancaster, Kent and Warwick, the new universities, 2,000–4,000 students; Aston, Bath, Bradford, Brunel, City, Loughborough, Salford and Surrey, former colleges of advanced technology, universities since 1965, 1,500 to 3,500 students.

30 University standard work available also at the University of Manchester Institute of Science and Technology, the Manchester Business School, the Royal College of Art, the London Graduate School of Business Studies, the Cranfield Institute of Technology.

31 As amended by the Education (Miscellaneous Provisions) Act, 1953.

32 See *The School Health Service and Handicapped Pupils Regulations*, HMSO, 1953 and 1959.

33 Circular 6/71.

34 *The School Health Service and Handicapped Pupils Regulations*, 1953.

35 See chapter 3.

36 Report of the Working Party into *The Role and Training of Education Welfare Officers* (Ralph Report), HMSO, 1973. Membership appointed by invitation of the Local Government Training Board, to 'investigate

the functions of education welfare officers in order to identify common elements and to advise the Board on the most appropriate training for them (including a system of examinations)'. A new system of examinations for social work qualifications for education welfare officers comes into effect after the existing scheme is phased out in Spring 1975.

37 *Youth and Community Work in the 70's*, HMSO, 1969.

38 Secretary of State for Education in reply to a Commons question, 29 March 1971.

39 1972–3 grants: £1,672,177 for voluntary youth projects, £927,692 for voluntary village halls. For community centres the grant was £516,508 for projects previously dealt with directly by the DES.

40 *The Youth Service and Similar Provision for Young People*, HMSO, 1968. A report for the DES on behalf of the Youth Service Development Council, by the Social Survey Division of the Office of Population Census and Surveys.

41 Education Survey no. 13, *The Education of Immigrants*, HMSO, 1971; Education Survey no. 10, *Potential and Progress in a Second Culture*, HMSO, 1971.

42 *Organisation in Multi-Racial Schools*, National Foundation for Educational Research, 1972. A report sponsored by the DES.

43 Plowden Report, Special Groups S.155 and Appendix 12.

44 The Secretary of State must under Section 4 of the 1944 Act appoint these councils which replaced the Consultative Committees on Education. The Act specified that the councils would 'advise the Secretary of State upon such matters connected with educational theory and practice as they think fit and upon any questions referred to them by him' (Section 4[1]). Reports include Plowden, 1967, and her Welsh counterpart Gittins, 1967, Crowther, 1959, and Newsom, 1963. Council membership is for a period of three years in the first instance, and does not really exclude anyone, although responsibility ultimately lies with the Secretary of State: 'Each council shall include persons who have had experience of educational institutions not forming part of that system.'

45 Education Act, 1944, Section 4 (3).

46 In England there are 470 HM Inspectors, nearly 50 in Wales. See the DES pamphlet *Her Majesty's Inspectorate Today and Tomorrow*, HMSO revised 1974, for publication 1975. One aspect of the work of the inspectorate is to inspect independent schools for DES recognition.

47 Previously 146 in England and 17 in Wales. The present 105 local education authorities comprise 39 new counties, 36 metropolitan districts, 8 Welsh counties, 20 existing outer London boroughs, the Inner London Education Authority, and the Isles of Scilly.

48 Education Act, 1944, First Schedule, Part II.

49 Subject to the Council for National Academic Awards approval of compatibility with university standards.

50 The University of London colleges are self-governed, overall finances being controlled by a Court including outside members, and the supreme executive body, the Senate. The University of Wales colleges

are represented at Court, which is the chief governing and legislative body, Council being the executive body controlling finance; all academic matters are handled by the academic boards.

51 Determined by a means assessment of the student or his parents. Some of the Department's grants are available for first degree mature students.

52 *Education: A Framework for Expansion, loc. cit.*

53 Known as the Central Register and Clearing House.

54 *Op. cit.*

55 FTE (Full Time Equivalent) = numbers of part-time staff converted to a full-time equivalent figure for statistical purposes.

56 *Teacher Education and Training.*

57 Support was given to courses with an educational studies component leading to the B.Ed. degree and qualified teacher status. The B.Ed. award was introduced following the Robbins Report, 1963, and needed the sanction of the universities. After CNAA agreement to assist in validating such degrees, universities tended to follow suit.

58 From *Education and Science in 1972*, p. 5: '(1) The normal minimum . . . entry qualifications should be the same as for degrees or comparable courses; (2) courses should be offered by institutions in each of the main sectors of higher education; (3) the qualification offered after two years should be generally acceptable as a terminal qualification, and in particular as a qualification needed for entry to appropriate forms of employment; (4) courses should also be seen as providing a foundation for further study and be designed, where appropriate, in such a way as to earn credit towards other qualifications, including degrees; (5) courses should be validated by existing degree bodies; (6) it was the Government's intention that Dip.H.E. students should qualify for mandatory awards.'

59 See for example, J. W. B. Douglas, *The Home and the School*, Mac-Gibbon & Kee, 1964; A. Little and J. Westagaard, 'The trend of class differentials in educational opportunity in England and Wales', *British Journal of Sociology*, vol. 15, 1964, pp. 301–16; the excellent summaries and references in O. Banks, *The Sociology of Education*, Batsford, 1968.

60 Discussed in A. H. Halsey, ed., *Educational Priority*, vol. 1, HMSO.

61 Project directed by A. H. Halsey of the Department of Social and Administrative Studies, University of Oxford.

62 I. Davies, 'The management of knowledge: a critique of the use of typologies in the sociology of education', *Sociology*, 4, 1, 1970.

3 The employment services
Ken Roberts

Employment in modern Britain

The periods spent in office at the Department of Employment by
Barbara Castle, Robert Carr, Maurice Macmillan, William Whitelaw
and Michael Foot will undoubtedly be remembered for the contro-
versies that raged over strikes, pay controls and the law. It would be
unfortunate, however, if the fact was completely overlooked, that
these Ministers presided over an overhaul of the employment services
that will have implications for the lives of millions of workers. The
reasons why the government is anxious to provide satisfactory
employment services derive from the extremely important roles that
employment plays in the lives of the members of society. Employment is the main institution through which economic wealth is
created; it is also the major channel for income distribution and, in
addition, can perform various social and psychological functions
for the individual employee: for example, by providing an anchorage
point for his general social status and self-identity. In establishing
employment services, therefore, the state's interest is to ensure that
employment performs these functions in the ways most consistent
with the welfare of the public as a whole, and the work of these
services is to be judged in terms of the contributions that they make
towards this end.

There is a somewhat old-fashioned view that insists upon regarding
employment as an arrangement based upon a free contract between
employer and employee, and suggestions that this relationship should
be subjected to external constraints can still be relied upon to evoke
forecasts of economic collapse and social decay. The free contract
view of the employment relationship, however, has possessed little
resemblance to reality in Britain at any time during the twentieth
century. To begin with, a number of organised groups, the most

important of which are the trade unions and professional associations, intervene in the employment relationship and, given this situation, demands that the state should maintain a *laissez-faire* posture have become somewhat sterile.

The state has become involved in the regulation of employment partly in order to ensure that other organisations conduct their affairs in the public interest. Since the nineteenth century, the state has played a major role in setting up the system of collective bargaining by freeing trade unions from previous restrictive legislation, and encouraging industries and firms to establish negotiating procedures, whilst the Industrial Relations Act of 1971, amongst other things, attempted to superimpose a framework of legal controls upon bargaining relationships. In industries where trade unionism has been weak and wage levels low, the state has taken the initiative in setting up wages councils whose agreements, when endorsed by the Secretary of State, possess legal force. In 1973 there were fifty-three wages councils whose agreements covered approximately 3,500,000 workers. During the last decade, attempts have been made to regulate the growth of incomes by means of persuasion, compacts and more formally through the National Board for Prices and Incomes and its successor, the Pay Board. The state has also intervened in the development of professional associations mainly, in the past, by encouraging their formation with a view to promoting high standards of practice.

Apart from regulating the activities of other associations there is, of course, a long tradition of legislation in Britain in which the state had directly stipulated under what conditions employment may be practised. Since the nineteenth century, numerous Factory Acts have been accumulating on the Statute Book aimed at ensuring, amongst other things, that conditions of work should be neither unhealthy nor dangerous, and restricting the uses to which certain categories of labour can be put. The concern with health and safety at work continues to this day, and with the recognition that technological changes can introduce new dangers, the Employment and Medical Advisory Service Act of 1972 has led to the establishment within the Department of Employment of an advisory service staffed by specialist doctors which gives wide-ranging advice on all medical problems concerned with employment. The tradition of protective legislation has recently been broadened as a result of the Contracts of Employment Act of 1963, subsequently consolidated and replaced in 1972, which stipulates that every employee should receive a written copy of his terms and conditions of employment, and amongst its other important provisions, lays down minimum periods of notice that employees have to be given before they can be dismissed. The Redundancy Payments Act of 1965 secures financial compensation for employees made redundant, the amount of compensation being dependent upon length of service. The Industrial Relations Act of 1971, amongst its less controversial features, introduced further protective measures, most particularly against 'unfair dismissal'. Complaints under this section of the Act, currently totalling over 10,000 per year, are heard by the Industrial Tribunals which were initially created to settle disputes regarding redundancy payments. The aspects of employment with which the state concerns itself inevitably reflect more widespread changes in public attitudes, and in recent years the Department of Employment has been considering the problem of job satisfaction. It is difficult to envisage the form that legislation on this particular problem could take, but a steering group has been set up to study ways of enhancing satisfaction at work, and it is hoped that action will eventually follow.

There is, of course, a point of view that regards the employer–employee relationship as inherently incompatible with human dignity. Employment is considered to be an essentially exploitative relationship, with the weaker party – the property-less worker – invariably ending as loser. According to this view, employment services are wrestling with social ills the only fundamental cure for which lies in a recasting of the relations of production. Experience of various types of public ownership and control both in Britain and other countries, however, gives little cause for confidence that employment problems will disappear along with a simple transformation of property relations. Wherever economic power lies, there will always be a case for its deliberate regulation, and the evidence of British history suggests that the effectiveness of such regulation does not depend upon whether industry is privately or publicly owned. Conditions of employment have changed, and from the employee's point of view, improved considerably since the nineteenth century, and these changes have been due, at least in part, to the legislation described above. Furthermore, quite apart from legislative requirements, nowadays companies rarely treat their labour forces as mere economic details. Employers provide a variety of services for their employees including medical services, recreational centres, canteens, and even housing and other community services. The purity of the altruism behind some of these provisions is admittedly questionable, for it is now widely accepted in industry that good 'human relations' make sound business sense, and the more dependent a worker becomes upon his employer the greater is the weight of the sanctions that the latter is able to wield. Whether the provision of these services is altruistic or not, however, their existence should not be overlooked. Employers' provisions often act on substitutes for statutory social services and in recent years governments' social security policies have encouraged the spread of occupational pension schemes. This use of the employment relationship demands serious consideration from all who are concerned with the administration of the social services, and clearly accentuates the importance of employment itself.

The services that will be examined below have been established not so much to shape the institution of employment as to regulate its functioning in ways that meet the varied needs of the different members of society. Four main groups of services can be distinguished, most of which are administered from within the Department of Employment: there are services designed to ease the conduct of industrial relations; services intended to help individuals with various disadvantages to become integrated into the labour force; services concerned with vocational training; and finally those concerned with occupational advice, mobility and placement. In the case of each type of service, basic changes are either currently under consideration or have been recently introduced in response to developments in employment that have placed existing services under new pressures. For example, a number of interrelated changes in post-war industry have facilitated the emergence of a new type of grass-roots trade unionism, led to great involvement by the state in economic management, and thereby posed new questions for the industrial relations services. New disadvantaged groups have either appeared, as in the case of coloured immigrants, or become more visible and vocal, as with the resurgence of the women's rights movement. At the same time, technological developments have added to the handicaps of groups whose problems have long been recognised, such as the disabled and the ageing. The quickening pace of technological and economic change has also called into question established arrangements for dealing with redundancy, retraining, and job mobility. Hence, with the employment services, we are not dealing with a static situation. What have to be grasped are the nature and directions of the changes that are in process.

Industrial relations

In addition to laying the legal framework and encouraging industries to establish their own bargaining machineries, the state, primarily through the Conciliation and Advisory Service (formerly known as the Manpower and Productivity Service) which is operated by the Department of Employment, provides a range of industrial relations services designed to help the parties directly involved to reach agreement when negotiations through established procedures fail. The statutory foundations of these services are in the Conciliation Act of 1896, the Industrial Court Act of 1919, and the Industrial Relations Act of 1971.

Despite the public attention attracted by the Industrial Relations

Court, at all times during recent years informal conciliation has remained the most frequently used official industrial relations service. Apart from attempting to informally resolve all problems that reach the Industrial Tribunals, nationally and regionally based Conciliation Officers continuously keep in close contact with trade unions and employers and familiarise themselves with industry's problems. Consequently, when a dispute occurs that the parties involved are unable to settle amongst themselves, the Conciliation Officer should already possess sufficient background knowledge and suitable informal contacts to be able to act as a mediator. Conciliation is essentially an informal and voluntary procedure. The job involves meeting the parties involved in a dispute either separately or together, measuring the areas of disagreement that exist, making suggestions and, if possible, finding a basis upon which negotiations can be resumed. The informal atmosphere in which this service is provided makes it difficult to quantify its success. However, throughout the country conciliation officers make over 4,000 'contacts' per year; in 1973 they actually 'conciliated' in 866 disputes and in 78 per cent of these cases were successful in helping to arrange solutions. In addition to intervening in on-going disputes, the Conciliation and Advisory Service also offers more general advice and information to firms on all problems relating to personnel management, including how to make the most efficient use of manpower, and how to establish workable systems of industrial relations at factory level. This type of advice to industry is intended to help prevent disputes reaching the point of deadlock where conciliation would be required.

Arbitration is a further industrial relations service provided by the Department of Employment. If conciliation is unsuccessful and at the request of the parties involved, arbitration, usually by a single person nominated by the Department and acceptable to those concerned, can be offered as a means towards reaching a settlement. During 1973 there were sixty-three such arbitration hearings. Another means of intervention is the Court of Enquiry which can be appointed by the Secretary of State to investigate the circumstances surrounding a dispute, the object normally being to make all relevant facts and issues public, thereby prompting the parties to reach a settlement. The Court of Enquiry is probably the best known of the Department's industrial relations services, because such bodies are appointed to investigate disputes that are already attracting considerable public interest and concern. However, during the course of any single year there are rarely more than two or three Courts of Enquiry and the Department's normal involvement in industrial relations centres on its conciliation services, the effectiveness of which often depends essentially upon the absence of public attention.

At the moment in Britain there are no grounds for complacency as far as the state of industrial relations is concerned. It remains the case, however, that over 99 per cent of all working days are not interrupted by industrial unrest, and that most employees have never been on strike. Nevertheless, the number of working days recorded as lost due to industrial disputes has risen from less than 5 million in 1968 to a modern peak of over 23 million in 1972. From being a country where, in terms of international comparisons, strikes were relatively short and infrequent, Britain has acquired the reputation of a nation with a strike problem. The rise in the number of working days lost in recent years has been partly due to an increase in the number of stoppages, but mainly because disputes have taken longer to settle, and whilst the causes of these changes in the pattern of industrial unrest are complex and largely beyond the direct control of the Department of Employment, this must call into question whether the industrial relations services currently offered by the Department constitute the most appropriate response to the contemporary situation. Whether the present legal framework requires modification is itself a controversial issue, but quite apart from this, there are grounds for questioning whether the Department of Employment remains the right organisation through which to dispense industrial relations services. One problem is that during the last decade governments have become increasingly involved in regulating wage and salary levels, with the result that doubts as to the capacity of government conciliators and arbitrators to act 'independently' have been awakened in the minds of other parties to industrial disputes. Hence ideas have been floated envisaging a conciliation service operating independently of all government departments. The majority of disputes, needless to say, do not raise issues of national importance. Disputes where phases, codes and norms are at stake are the exceptions to the rule. Consequently, the Department of Employment's conciliation officers have continued to be active, often at the request of trade unions, even in periods when the unions have been resolutely opposed to the incomes policy of the government of the day. However, once the atmosphere surrounding the work becomes jaundiced, the general effectiveness of industrial relations services can suffer. Transferring social services from statutory to voluntary agencies might appear to be against the historical tide, but as central and local governments' administrative interests expand to affect widening areas of citizens' lives, it could be that pressures to 'hive off' social work type functions will develop in other spheres.

Until recently the Commission for Industrial Relations acted as a semi-independent body operating on the industrial relations scene. This commission was initially established and operated under Royal Warrant following the Donovan Report.[1] Its original function was to encourage what were believed to be good industrial relations practices by investigating and reporting upon matters referred by the Secretary of State, and its early enquiries, which were facilitated by the co-operation extended by trade unions and employers, covered industrial relations problems in particular firms and throughout entire industries. The 1971 Industrial Relations Act placed the commission on a statutory footing and subsequently its principal role involved investigating and reporting upon cases referred by the Industrial Relations Court. Since the majority of trade unions refused to co-operate in procedures surrounding the Industrial Relations Act and Court, the commission found itself working in a less receptive environment than it encountered in its early years, and consequently this body was allowed to disappear with the replacement of the Industrial Relations Act in 1974. The Department of Employment, however, is involved in discussions with the Trade Union Congress and the Confederation of British Industry, with a view to establishing an 'independent' conciliation and arbitration service, and if such a body is introduced it could well incorporate the type of work pioneered in the early days of the Commission for Industrial Relations.

Participation in the labour force

Several sections of the population suffer special disadvantages in the labour market and four such groups are singled out for discussion below: the physically and mentally disabled, ethnic minorities, women and the ageing. Being disadvantaged in the labour market is clearly a problem for the individuals directly involved. They suffer economically as a result of unemployment or confinement to the less desirable jobs that other workers try to avoid, and beyond this there are the wider social and psychological scars that can follow from the manner in which occupations influence the esteem in which individuals are held both by others and by themselves. Society at large, however, has reasons apart from a sense of justice for treating the status of the disadvantaged as a problem. If individuals remain unemployed or underemployed the value of their productive potential is lost and other means have to be arranged for their support. In addition, allowing sections of the population to remain and feel unfairly disadvantaged can generate further problems that may eventually be relied upon to thrust themselves to the attention of the wider community. Consequently, it is perhaps not surprising that a series of measures, admittedly varying in effectiveness, have been introduced to assist the otherwise disadvantaged to participate in employment.

The disabled

People suffering from physical or mental handicap of any description are clearly at a disadvantage in the competition for employment, and without special provision are likely to be denied the opportunity of supporting themselves and fitting in with the normal pattern of community life by participating in the labour force. Probably because their handicaps are so immediately apparent, the disabled are the disadvantaged group for whom special provision has the longest history. However, until as recently as the Second World War provision for the employment of the disabled was minimal. During the First World War rehabilitation departments were established in some military hospitals, and some government rehabilitation and resettlement centres were opened, but these facilities were not developed during the inter-war years. It was only during the Second World War that really serious consideration was officially given to the problems of the disabled. This consideration was related to the general attempts that were being made to create a Welfare State for post-war Britain, to the awareness that many returning servicemen would need rehabilitation, and to the expectation that large-scale unemployment would never return and that the economy would need all the available labour-power. The outcome was the Disabled Persons (Employment) Act of 1944, which remains the basis for provision today, having been subjected to minor modifications in 1958. The Act provides for a register of disabled persons to be administered by the Department of Employment. Anyone who is for some reason handicapped in the quest for employment and is likely to remain so for twelve months is entitled to register, provided that the person concerned is judged potentially employable, and approximately 600,000 individuals are currently registered.

Under the Act the Department makes special provision for the employment of these people, and it is partly as a result of these provisions that the vast majority of the registered disabled are in employment. In February 1974 65,469 were unemployed, only approximately 11 per cent of the total, though the fact that this unemployment figure (which has at times been as high as 15 per cent of the registered disabled) exceeds that for the labour force as a whole has recently been causing some concern. Disablement Resettlement Officers are available to give advice to their clients, assess the needs of individual cases and liaise with hospitals and employers. Furthermore, the law provides that any firm employing more than twenty workers must engage at least 3 per cent of its labour force from amongst the registered disabled. Less than 50 per cent of all firms actually meet this quota, primarily because there are not enough disabled persons to fulfil firms' legal requirements, which means that rigid enforcement of the law is impractical, but with unemployment amongst the disabled running at over 10 per cent there have been calls for stronger enforcement of the quota. Yet even when the law is less than rigidly enforced, as at the moment, the quota system ensures that some demand for labour is directed towards the disabled. Also it is claimed that the quota system has an educative value in so far as it accustoms both employers and other members of the labour force to accepting handicapped persons as ordinary members of the community once they have been given the opportunity to hold their own in employment.

The Department of Employment is also enabled by the 1944 Act to designate certain occupations as being reserved for disabled persons. So far only two occupations, electric lift operator and car park attendant, have been so designated. This is an effective way of ensuring that jobs are made available to the disabled, but the emphasis in the Department's policies has been upon integrating the disabled into 'ordinary' types of employment.

Industrial Rehabilitation Units are also operated under the 1944 Act. In 1973 twenty-five such units were functioning, offering places for approximately 14,000 persons per year. Courses are free, last up to twenty-six weeks, and maintenance allowances are paid to those taking part. The aim of the units is to enable disabled persons to tone up physically and so gradually adjust to normal working conditions. Some of the trainees are severely disabled, and at the moment only just over a half are being immediately resettled in outside employment. Little training in actual vocational skills is given, but such training can be made available when required at the Skillcentres that are run for the benefit of the general working population.

When reintegration into the general labour force is impossible, as with the more severely handicapped, sheltered employment can sometimes be offered. A non-profit-making company, Remploy, established by the Department of Employment, provides jobs for around 8,000 persons in all parts of Britain. In this sheltered employment disabled persons are able to earn a wage working in conditions and upon tasks especially suited to their limited capacities. Other sheltered employment, amounting in total to over 13,000 places, is provided in workshops run by voluntary organisations and local authorities. This type of provision recognises that even when in the case of a severely handicapped person employment may not be an economic proposition, occupational activity can, nevertheless, be of therapeutic value to the individual concerned. This principle has also been applied in the provision of occupational centres for retired workers (see below). As already implied, however, sheltered work is resorted to only when placement in outside employment appears impossible. During four weeks ending in February 1974, the Department placed 3,943 registered disabled persons in outside employment as against only 150 in sheltered employment. The main emphasis in the services is to enable disabled persons to become reintegrated into the normal labour force and there have been recent suggestions from within the Department of Employment that sheltered employment itself should be oriented towards rehabilitation rather than the maintenance of permanent enclaves.

It will already be apparent that the range of services offered to the disabled is certainly not above criticism, and the Department is currently considering possible improvements. The rise in the level of unemployment throughout the labour force as a whole that has occurred since the 1950s, coupled with mechanisation making more jobs less easily adapted to individuals' special needs, has left the disabled particularly vulnerable. The proportion of the registered disabled who are unemployed has been creeping upwards, and obtaining placements in outside as opposed to sheltered employment has become increasingly difficult. In addition to this, it is known that only a proportion of the disabled are actually on the register. Some are not accepted for registration whilst others (probably a half of all those who would be eligible) fail to register in order to avoid the stigmatisation involved. The employment made available for the registered disabled both in sheltered conditions and in outside industry is usually of low status, and the earnings of disabled workers fall well short of the general level of earnings in the working population. It is felt in some quarters that whilst in its early years the quota system may have possessed some educative value, it has now become ritualised as a means of channelling the disabled into the more routine and less desirable jobs that other workers try to avoid, and it is in order to avoid being labelled and channelled in this manner that some of those who would be accepted fail to register as disabled. Despite such weaknesses, however, it must be recognised that the employment services for the disabled do enable many to hold a job who would otherwise be idle. There is undoubtedly scope for improvement, but the strength of the situation resides in the fact that a comprehensive framework exists enabling both the needs of the disabled and the available services to be continuously reappraised.

Ethnic minorities

The presence of ethnic minorities within British society is no novel situation for immigrants have been entering the country continuously since the nineteenth century. However, the upsurge of 'coloured' immigration from the Commonwealth during the 1950s did make the presence of minority groups unusually visible, and by the early 1960s it had become evident that these newcomers were being clustered in

71

the less skilled and prestigeful types of jobs, this being but one aspect of the emergent 'race relations problem'. More recently, attention has been focused upon the similar difficulties facing the second generation, the 'coloured' school-leavers who have been educated and often born in Britain. Newcomers into any society do not normally possess the types of skill and qualifications required for entry into the more prestigious occupations in the host culture and, in addition to this, they rarely avoid some degree of prejudice and discrimination. Earlier waves of immigrants into Britain, including the Irish and the Jews, initially entered at the foot of the social scale before beginning the process of gradual assimilation, and the treatment of 'white' immigrant workers today in other Western European societies broadly parallels the reception of 'coloured' immigrants in this country.[2] In Britain, however, the predominant inclination has been to treat the problems of ethnic minorities as race relations issues, the solutions to which are seen as involving suppressing acts of 'racial' discrimination.

The Race Relations Act of 1968 comprises the main attempt to deal with the employment problems of ethnic minorities. Amongst other provisions the Act prohibits discrimination in employment on grounds of colour, race, ethnic or national origin (but not religion, sex, age or status), and is applicable to all types of occupations with the single exception of resident domestic work. The procedure prescribed by the Act is for individuals who believe that an instance of discrimination has occurred to complain directly to the Department of Employment, or to the Race Relations Board, or to one of its regional conciliation committees, who forward such complaints to the Department. In industries where representative bodies composed of employers and trade unionists have volunteered to investigate complaints made under the Act, the Department transmits complaints to the appropriate body. In other industries, the Race Relations Board is called upon to investigate. The intention of the Act is that, where possible, complaints should be dealt with by conciliation rather than by prosecution, and investigations are conducted accordingly.

In the year covered by the 1971–2 report of the Race Relations Board, 464 complaints were received, but in only approximately 5 per cent of these cases was discrimination found to have actually occurred, and all such cases are reported as having been successfully settled by conciliation. Since the working population contains approximately 750,000 'coloured' people, from the above figures it is apparent that either the problems leading to the passage of the 1968 Act must have been imaginary, or a dramatic change in behaviour must have occurred since the Act was placed on the Statute Book, or else the measure must be failing to tackle the situation.

Early comment from the Department of Employment claimed that the Act was working in a satisfactory manner, and hinted at widespread changes in personnel practices being provoked throughout the whole of industry. More recent assessments of the situation, however, particularly from the Race Relations Board, have manifested less complacency. Experience of administering the Act has shown how difficult it can be to prove that an act of discrimination on 'racial' grounds has occurred, and how unrealistic it is to expect generally disadvantaged victims to complain to an 'official' body. The Race Relations Board is now concerned that discrimination remains widespread, especially in promotion opportunities and in the white-collar sector. The Board has also learnt that the problem does not derive from a few prejudiced individuals, but from collective and tolerated discrimination. In the field of employment, this is a problem that we have hardly begun even to confront.

Women

In industrial Britain for working-class women employment outside the home has always been normal. Paid employment for women is no novelty in blue-collar households, nor is it recognised as a 'right' or 'privilege', but simply as a financial necessity. Nevertheless, the twentieth century has seen first the working woman, and more recently the working wife and mother gaining general social acceptance. Today over a half of all married women work, and this proportion does not vary greatly between the social classes. It remains the case, however, that women are still that greatest supply of human talent that the economy fails to utilise, and also that women suffer a number of disadvantages in the labour market.

First, even when doing similar work, women may be paid less than male employees. Second, several forms of covert discrimination combine to restrict women to the least skilled and lower paid types of jobs. Amongst school-leavers approximately 80 per cent of girls not continuing their full-time education enter jobs involving no systematic training, recruitment into skilled manual occupations is rare, and those professions in which women are now numerous tend to be associated with the domestic feminine role. There are few training schemes suited to the needs of the married woman contemplating a return to the labour force after her children have become independent. In some occupations such as teaching and social work, where the shortage of trained personnel has recently been acute, training programmes have been especially geared to the needs of older recruits, but these are the exceptions to the rule. Third, facilities to support the wife and mother in her domestic role, so as to make a prolonged interruption of her career unnecessary, are rarely adequate.

The short-fall in places at nursery schools and day nurseries is such that illegal child-minding businesses, often of an unsatisfactory character, have been able to flourish, and provision for the care of school children during holiday periods is rare. The net effect of these barriers is to largely relegate women to second-class jobs, and also to leave the female sex generally underemployed. Surveys conducted amongst married women have revealed a latent demand for employment which remains hidden because, not being eligible for social security benefits, married women available for work often do not register at an employment exchange and therefore do not swell the unemployment figures.[3]

Social policy towards the employment of married women has never been clearly defined. Whilst there have been periods when the economy has needed all the available manpower, the working wife has been accused (despite the weight of evidence to the contrary) of neglecting her family, precipitating delinquency, and a host of other social evils. In recent years, however, official ambivalence towards sex discrimination has been nudged by the advocates of 'Women's Lib'. There are plans to expand nursery education, and an even more concrete achievement has been the Equal Pay Act of 1970, destined to operate fully from 1975, which requires equal treatment between the sexes when they are engaged in 'the same or broadly similar work'. Complaints under this Act will be dealt with by the Industrial Tribunals, with the ultimate appeal being to the Arbitration Board (formerly the Industrial Court), the most formal type of arbitration offered by the Department of Employment, where business is conducted as in a court of law. In 1973 the government introduced a bill to remove unfair discrimination on grounds of sex in recruitment into occupations. Such a measure could potentially occasion more drastic changes in employment practices than insistence upon equal pay. It was proposed to establish an Equal Opportunities Commission to conduct enquiries and advise the government, and to enforce the law, as in the case of the Equal Pay Act, through the system of Industrial Tribunals. This particular bill failed to complete its passage through Parliament but since it enjoyed all-party support its early reintroduction is probable. Whether this type of legislation will prove more effective in dealing with sex discrimination than it has been in assisting ethnic minorities, needless to say, must remain a matter for conjecture.

The ageing

The employment problems of old people hinge upon the fact that ageing is an essentially gradual process. As people grow older their physical and mental abilities gradually deteriorate, and the problem of employment is to find a way of accommodating the organisation of work to the process of ageing. There is little dissent from the principle that the ageing should be able to continue in employment for as long as they wish to do so and are able to make a contribution to the economy. Upon retirement the incomes of old people are often severely reduced, which even if not involving a subsistence existence, may isolate the retired from the patterns of life to which they have been accustomed and are prevalent in their communities. Also men in particular often suffer psychologically from the loss of their roles as wage-earners, and society as a whole loses the value of the labour-power of people who retire, which is a serious problem at a time when the proportion of elderly people in the population is rising. All these are reasons why the ageing should be assisted to remain in employment for as long as possible, such assistance being no substitute but complementary to the provision of adequate services for those who must retire, for failure to help those capable of doing so to remain in employment can only aggravate the difficulties of providing for those who are obliged to give up work. Nevertheless, despite virtually unanimous agreement in principle, there are strong pressures rooted in the nature of contemporary industry that increasingly conspire to exclude ageing individuals from the labour force.

The proportion of the population that is economically inactive gradually increases with age, but rises sharply at the point when state retirement pensions become available, which is not the type of pattern that one would predict from our knowledge of ageing as a natural and gradual process. Surveys[4] have shown that deteriorating capacity is one factor that is involved in most decisions to retire, but in modern industry there are other forces at work which often precipitate retirement before the labour of ageing persons has ceased to be of any economic value, and before the individuals concerned would have ideally chosen to retire. Few firms enforce absolutely rigid retiring ages. A study conducted by the Acton Society Trust[5] found that only 19 out of 55 large companies studied demanded that their employees should retire at a stipulated age. There are, however, less formal pressures, built into the fabric of contemporary industry, which frequently result in premature retirement. As already stated, ageing is essentially a gradual process, and to accommodate the structure of industry to this process it would be necessary to arrange for employees to be transferred to less demanding jobs as their abilities became limited. In modern industry this tends to be difficult, for more jobs are now mechanised and the pace of work cannot be adjusted to match the capacities of the ageing employee. Also many formerly 'light' staff jobs, such as personnel work, are becoming professionalised and older workers can no longer be transferred into these positions, and when light work is available the claims of the ageing have to be balanced against those of other groups, particularly the disabled. The increasing pace of technological change has been transforming the mature skills and experience of the older worker from an asset into a handicap, and in an ageing society there is invariably pressure from younger people to have senior posts vacated in order to facilitate their own advancement. When these varied pressures are combined with the fact that state pensions, and often occupational pensions also, become available at a determined age, it is easy to see why many ageing persons should be either forced or allowed to drift into retirement before it is really necessary for them to give up work completely.

It also becomes easy to understand why the proportion of men aged over sixty-five who remain economically active should have been declining throughout recent decades (from 58·9 per cent in 1921 to 19·4 per cent in 1971). Similarly the difficulties faced by ageing individuals who become redundant in arranging reassimilation into the labour force become easy to comprehend. A survey of individuals registered as unemployed in June 1973 found that as many as 23·51 per cent were in the 60–4 age group, and such persons tended to remain unemployed for longer periods than younger workers. [6]

The ageing comprise the one clearly disadvantaged section of the labour force whose difficulties have not stimulated any major policy initiatives during the last decade. The Department of Employment has attempted to encourage firms to retain the services of older employees, but no one really believes that exhortation alone will override the pressures making for the underemployment of the ageing. Some local authorities and voluntary societies have instituted occupational centres which retired people can attend. Here the ageing can be allowed to work at their own pace under economically sheltered conditions, but are paid considerably less than what would be considered a normal wage in industry. These centres recognise the therapeutic value of occupational activity but are really no substitute for proper services to assist the ageing to remain in employment.

However, it is difficult to prescribe confidently forms of intervention to solve the employment problems of the ageing. Experience with other disadvantaged groups shows that we have yet to devise a totally benign formula. The history of race relations legislation indicates that outlawing individual acts of discrimination may fail to grapple with the crux of the problem. Requiring employers to engage a quota of disadvantaged persons, as has been the practice with the disabled, can have the side-effect of labelling and setting apart the group concerned from the remainder of the labour force in a manner that has unfortunate secondary consequences. It seems likely, therefore, that some sections of the labour force are destined to remain disadvantaged during the immediate future. Really effective solutions to the employment problems of disadvantaged groups may ultimately prove contingent upon broader changes in the attitudes and behaviour that initially impose disadvantages upon the groups in question. If the causes of disadvantage themselves cannot be tackled, employment policies may 'manage' but are unlikely to resolve the problems.

Vocational training

Vocational training is one of the two major groups of services supervised by the Manpower Services Commission that was established following the Employment and Training Act of 1973. The commission is appointed by and takes its general policy directives from the Secretary of State for Employment. It is hoped, however, that the creation of this 'buffer' commission will add to the vitality, flexibility and integration throughout a range of the employment services, the costs of which now exceed £100 million per annum. The Manpower Services Commission operates in a manner analogous to the board of directors of a holding company. Executive responsibility for vocational training lies in the hands of a Training Services Agency, which works within a budget and guidelines laid down by the commission and ultimately approved by the Secretary of State. Traditionally in Britain, vocational training has been left to individual industries and firms, with the state playing no more than a marginal role. During the last decade, however, the state's involvement has considerably increased both as a direct provider of training, and as a supervisor of training provided elsewhere, and the creation of the Training Services Agency is an administrative response to this growing involvement. It is now recognised that the effectiveness of the economy is affected by the quality of the labour that the working population is able to provide, that appropriate training opportunities can help mitigate problems otherwise associated with redundancy, and that young people's life-chances are heavily dependent upon the opportunities that are available to acquire occupational skills. Yet whilst its involvement in education has been long-standing, it is only since the 1950s that the state has even attempted to exert a major influence over 'on-the-job' training.

As a direct provider of training, the state's main interest has been through the Skillcentres (formerly called Government Training Centres). Like the Industrial Rehabilitation Units, the Skillcentres have their origins in the facilities initially provided to cater for the First World War disabled. After the war some of the centres were used to provide resettlement courses, and between the wars they were used both to retrain unemployed labour, and to provide some vocational training for young people who were unable to find jobs.

During the Second World War they were used to train civilian labour. After the hostilities they reverted to their role of resettling ex-servicemen, and later returned to what remains their contemporary function of offering training to civilian workers who wish to acquire occupational skills. As recently as 1962, however, there were only thirteen centres with a total of 2,500 places, and their contribution to vocational training was slight, but by 1971 fifty-two centres provided 10,650 places and there are plans to expand the system still further to eventually handle 100,000 trainees per year. Trainees are eligible for subsistence grants during the period of training which usually lasts for between six and twelve months. Training has so far been almost wholly in manual skills, but there are now plans to widen the range to cover some white-collar jobs. Approximately a half of all trainees are formerly non-skilled workers, whilst the majority of the remainder seek retraining following a contraction of demand for their existing skills. In earlier years the Skillcentres encountered some resistance to 'dilution' from craft unions, but trainees are now generally accepted throughout industry, and 90 per cent are placed in appropriate jobs immediately following their courses. The state, through its Skill-centres, is making an increasingly significant contribution to the country's pool of skilled manpower, and the Skillcentres themselves are playing an increasingly active role in identifying skills that are in short supply, arranging the required courses, and seeking the necessary trainees by methods which include television advertising.

In recent years a number of new developments have been pioneered, supplementing the standard Skillcentre courses, and designed to meet specific needs as they have arisen. Collectively the services offered are known as TOPS (Training Opportunities Scheme), and include courses for instructors who are subsequently equipped to train employees within industry, and special courses, for which a charge is made, to meet the needs of particular employers. In addition, grants have been offered to encourage firms to create training opportunities in development areas and for older workers, and college-based courses have been initiated in regions where industry-based training has been judged inadequate. The Community Industry Scheme, which was introduced in 1971 and which is run in co-operation with the National Association of Youth Clubs, is probably the best known amongst these recent initiatives. Under this scheme finance is provided to engage otherwise unemployed young people on work of social value. By 1973 a total of 565 individuals were engaged upon such projects, and it is planned to expand the scheme to 2,000 places.

Until 1964, government intervention in vocational training within industry amounted to no more than encouragement and exhortation. Employers, possibly subject to the approval of the relevant trade

78

unions and professional associations, trained however many workers by whatever methods they thought fit in whatever skills they believed to be appropriate. Numerous criticisms were made of this *laissez-faire* system. It was alleged that firms often found it cheaper to poach than train and that consequently not enough school-leavers were receiving training in occupational skills to satisfy the economy's need for skilled manpower, that the range and quality of training was often unsatisfactory, that there was no test of either the trainer's or the trainee's competence, and that the imposition of rigid age and time limits, such as five years to be served before the age of twenty-one for craft apprenticeships, was socially unjust and economically wasteful.

The response to these criticisms was the Industrial Training Act of 1964. Following this Act the Department of Employment established a Central Training Council, beneath which special Industrial Training Boards dealing with particular industries were created. Members of these bodies were appointed by the Secretary of State and usually included educators together with industrialists and trade unionists who were involved in the relevant industry. The job of each board was to ensure that sufficient training of a satisfactory standard was being provided to meet its industry's needs, and the main device used to achieve this objective was a system of levies and grants. The boards imposed levies upon the firms belonging to their industries, used the proceeds to cover their own administrative expenses, and distributed the remainder in the form of grants to finance training. Standards could be laid down that firms' training programmes were required to meet in order to qualify for grants; the engagement of training instructors, the provision of day-release, and an introduction to a stipulated range of skills could all be insisted upon. The boards were also able to set up their own training centres, appoint special training advisors, take the initiative in setting up joint courses provided by several firms, and to draw up syllabuses for use in training programmes. The major procedure used by the boards, however, was the levy–grant system, and by manipulating this it was intended to stimulate each industry to provide the right amount and quality of training. Following the passage of the 1964 Act, this new system was introduced enthusiastically and was heralded as a 'revolution in industrial training'.[7]

However, it proved to be a revolution that turned sour very quickly. The financial competence of the Industrial Training Boards became suspect, for some ran into debt as a result of paying out more in grants than they managed to recoup in levies and had to be supported by Department of Employment funds. From within industry there arose charges of 'red tape' as the boards declared criteria to be fulfilled in order to obtain grants and firms obligingly played the training game by appointing instructors, patronising conferences and courses, and arranging for as many of their recruits as possible to be designated as trainees. Sceptics began to query whether the 'training industry' that had arisen was really enhancing the quality of the vocational training actually received by learners, and the call was raised to let the people on the spot arrange training at their own properly informed discretion. Gaps, such as arrangements for redundant workers, that were left by having separate boards responsible for particular industries also began to appear. Consequently since 1972 the Department of Employment has been curtailing the system of grants and levies. The Industrial Training Boards are continuing in existence, but are concentrating upon the collection of information and advisory work, and the new Training Services Agency, with its broader responsibilities, is planning to dispense grants on a more selective basis, to act as the general co-ordinator, and to make arrangements to complement training in industry. Taken together with the development of the Skillcentres and allied training services, this change in the role of the training boards indicates that in the immediate future the state will be relying increasingly upon its own facilities in its efforts to influence the system of vocational training.

Whether this new revolution will remain more permanent than the last must be largely a matter for conjecture. However, the net result of all the developments that have taken place during the last decade is to leave the Department of Employment, through its Training Services Agency, with a varied set of procedures for appraising and influencing the system of vocational training. Training is a type of activity where the 'right' provision never remains appropriate for more than a short period. Redundancies affect different trades and regions at different times, technological trends create sudden shortfalls in particular skills, regional variations in the level of economic activity restrict opportunities in different places, and changes in the number of school-leavers entering the labour market can have a similar effect. Set against this context, the most hopeful feature of the current situation is that the Department, through the Training Services Agency, now possesses an administrative apparatus capable of appraising training arrangements as a whole, and has developed diverse ways of intervening which should enable it to respond flexibly to forever changing conditions.

Advice and placement

The final set of services to be considered are those that offer vocational advice to individuals and assist the placement of members of the labour force in their various occupations. These services can further several complementary objectives: they can promote the full use of manpower by bringing potential employers and employees into contact with each other; help to distribute labour throughout the occupational system in an efficient manner; and assist workers in finding jobs that are consistent with their abilities, capacities and interests. The provision of the relevant services, mainly through the national system of employment exchanges, has a fairly long history dating back to the Labour Exchanges Act of 1909. The exchanges were originally supervised by the Board of Trade, and subsequently by the other precursors of the contemporary Department of Employment – the Ministry of Labour and the Department of Employment and Productivity. This distinguished history has the advantage of making the availability of assistance at the exchanges well known throughout industry and to the public, but the complementary disadvantage is that the services tend to be burdened with an image based upon their past performances that bears little resemblance to current intentions.

The Employment Services Agency

Placement and advisory services for the adult population are now the responsibility of the Employment Services Agency, the second main division operating under the Manpower Services Commission following the Employment and Training Act of 1973. It is the declared intention of the agency to move away from the traditional labour exchange model and towards providing a range of services better attuned to contemporary needs.

The labour exchanges originated early in this century under what now appears to be a naïve belief that a method of bringing potential employees and employers into contact with one another would be a major step towards solving the problem of unemployment. Between the wars, however, handling mass unemployment was the main task with which the exchanges had to deal; during the Second World War they were used by the government to exercise compulsory controls over certain categories of civilian labour; whilst since 1945 their main purpose has been facilitating labour mobility, thus strengthening the economy by assisting the flow of labour out of declining and into expanding and efficient industries and firms, and promoting vocational adjustment by helping individuals to find suitable jobs. The exchanges' main problem in the post-war era has been that although their purposes have changed since their inception, their modes of operation have not changed in any significant way, and this constitutes the background against which the Employment Services Agency has recently been established.

The employment exchange service has been administered through approximately 900 local offices, each office attempting to meet requests for labour from employers and requests for employment from workers in its locality. When either an employer or a worker has applied for assistance his needs have been noted and filed. The attempt has then been made to match the needs of potential workers with the requirements of employers, applicants for work being directed to employers recorded as having a need for the type of labour that the worker can offer. If an applicant's needs have not been met locally, the case has been circulated regionally and, when necessary, nationally.

This method of operating made some sense when the main functions of the exchanges involved alleviating and keeping some check upon unemployment, but a growing body of evidence has indicated the failure of this type of service to meet contemporary needs. Employers have preferred to recruit labour, particularly into positions involving responsibility and skill, in other ways. Advertisements have offered access to a wider labour market, and either a firm's own personnel department or a private employment exchange has often been capable of providing a more highly skilled pre-selection service. A study of vacancies, undertaken at the request of the Department of Employment in 1973,[8] which included visits to thirty-four companies with registered vacancies, found that only 32 per cent of all these firms' vacancies had been notified to the employment exchanges. The prevailing view within the firms surveyed was that the Department's services were to be used only as a 'last resort'; they felt that 'good' candidates would probably not be registered at public employment exchanges. At the same time the investigators who conducted this survey concluded that the firms concerned were often aggravating their own labour problems by demanding unreasonable standards from recruits in terms of age, level of skill or appearance, and that the firms' approaches in publicising and 'selling' their vacancies were often unimaginative. Scope clearly existed for an employment service to make a contribution, but it was equally clear that the type of service being offered by the employment exchanges was not meeting the relevant needs. Studies of job-seekers have pointed towards a similar conclusion.[9] On the one hand, investigators have highlighted the frequent 'irrationality' of employees' labour market behaviour, meaning that it is often based upon either incorrect or very incomplete knowledge of available job opportunities, whilst on the other, such studies have revealed widespread dissatisfaction with the type of treatment received at the employment exchanges. Common complaints concern the jobs offered being poor in terms of levels of pay and skill, which is not surprising if firms recruit through the exchanges only as a 'last resort'.

It must be stressed, however, that many workers have found employment through the exchanges. It has been estimated that a fifth of all job changes are made in this way and if, in the absence of the exchanges, the search for work took an average of only a day longer, the value of the earnings and production consequently lost would exceed the cost of the employment exchange service. However, the creation of the Employment Services Agency marks the beginning of an attempt to develop an even closer alignment between the services provided and the contemporary community's needs.

Social security benefit payment is being separated from the employment services in an attempt to bury the dole queue image. New-style 'job centres' are being introduced which provide information about jobs on a self-service basis with access to advisers being available if required. Thirty self-service centres were in operation by 1973, the year when the first purpose-built new-style job centre was opened in Reading. An improved labour market intelligence service is also being developed in order to enable the Employment Services Agency to offer advice that industry will really value. Occupational guidance centres, staffed by specially trained officers and professional psychologists, are now available for the public in all parts of the country. At these centres no officer handles more than three cases per day, so that each client's vocational needs can receive detailed consideration. The type of special operation mounted in the past to deal with large-scale redundancies is being extended; for example, teams of officers from the employment exchanges are now able to visit construction sites where work is ending, having collected information about job opportunities on other sites. An Employment Transfer Scheme,which helped over 18,000 individuals in 1973, allows financial assistance to be provided for persons to travel and secure accommodation away from home in search of work. All these developments amount to a movement away from relying upon a standard type of employment exchange service throughout the whole country towards creating a range of services consistent with the needs of various employers and different sections of the labour force.

One of the longer-standing examples of these developments is the existence of special registers covering particular types of labour. 'Professional and Executive Recruitment' operates through a network of thirty-nine offices, and a computerised service provides almost instant national coverage of every vacancy and applicant. Refurbished offices are intended to convey an up-to-date executive image, 'consultants' provide advice for would-be employers, who since 1973 have paid a charge of between 5 and 8 per cent of the annual salary involved for the use of this service. The needs of employees, however, are given equal consideration, to the extent of organising 'self-presentation courses' to teach applicants the best approach when presenting themselves to a prospective employer. Other special registers deal with nursing and catering.

83

With the development of the Employment Services Agency's facilities, the scope for private employment agencies may well contract, particularly when the Employment Agencies Act of 1973 is brought into full operation. This Act forbids charging fees to job-seekers, and will require agencies to comply with standards laid down by the Secretary of State in order to obtain licences from local authorities.

It is necessary to point out that the employment exchange service in many parts of the country still remains close to its historical traditions. The new agency's plans will become reality only slowly, and a final assessment must await their implementation. However, with the Training Services and the Employment Services Agencies now jointly operating under the Manpower Services Commission, a structure has been created that should facilitate comprehensive provision for the problems of various groups. It should prove possible to assemble, for example, packages including guidance, information about job opportunities, retraining, and assistance with geographical mobility to meet the types of special needs that can arise in particular areas.[10]

The Careers Service

The Careers Service (formerly the Youth Employment Service) offers a parallel type of provision to the Employment Services Agency for young people in education (except at universities) and up to the point of entry into their first jobs. Careers Officers may advise and assist young people after their initial entry into employment if their clients choose to return for help, but once in employment individuals are able to use the Employment Services Agency facilities. The precursor of the modern Careers Service originated at the same time as the public labour exchange with the Education (Choice of Employment) Act of 1910. Special provision was made for young people since their needs were considered different from those of unemployed adults, and the relevant service has remained organisationally separate ever since. The service was renamed, its organisation and responsibilities modified, and it was placed on its present statutory footing by the Employment and Training Act of 1973.

The work of the Careers Service is concerned with education in the broadest meaning of the term as well as with employment itself, and the administrative structure of the Service is designed to facilitate contact with both the educational system and the remainder of the employment services. Overall responsibility for the administration of the service is vested in a sub-section within the Department of Employment, but whose staff is also recruited from those other government departments that are concerned with education. This central authority meets the greater part of the Service's costs, lays down general guidelines, and offers various types of support but does not directly operate the Service. The Careers Service is directly provided by local education authorities thus allowing some scope for local initiative. The intention is that the Service should respond to differing local conditions, benefit from its links with local school and college systems, and simultaneously from its association with the Department of Employment.

Whilst still at school and college, the Careers Service attempts to provide young people with whatever job information and vocational advice they require. Careers literature is issued through schools and public libraries, Careers officers give talks to audiences of young people, individual consultations are held, visits to places of work and even work-experience schemes may be arranged, and in some schools systematic courses of careers work extending over a number of years have been developed. In providing these services, the intention is that Careers officers should co-operate harmoniously with school and college staffs in general, and careers teachers and other counselling personnel in particular. The aim is to ensure that well before their point of entering employment and when facing educational decisions with possible vocational implications, young people are adequately informed about the types of jobs they will eventually find available, and beginning to consider the sorts of careers upon which they would like to embark. Few studies of school-leavers have complimented the Careers Service upon its effectiveness[11] but in recent years the amount of work done in secondary schools has greatly increased.

To help beginning workers find appropriate jobs, an employment exchange service is operated, and when it is necessary for a young person to leave home in order to enter suitable employment, the Careers Service is able to offer assistance in finding lodgings. Only approximately a third of all school-leavers who enter employment are recorded as 'placed' in jobs with the help of the Careers Service. To a large extent, this placement service appears to have suffered from the 'last resort' image that has plagued the employment exchanges catering for adults. However, in addition to formally 'placing' young people in jobs, Careers officers are able to offer a great deal of useful informal advice on where, when and how to apply for suitable opportunities.

Until 1974 the (then) Youth Employment Service dealt with all young people both in and out of school, up to the age of eighteen, and therefore followed up school-leavers and assisted young workers who required further advice or wished to change their jobs. As already mentioned, such young people are still able to seek assistance from the Careers Service if they wish but it is now primarily the responsibility of the Employment Services Agency to make the necessary

85

provision. This creates a situation that will clearly require monitoring in which responsibility for the welfare of young workers may be dangerously fragmented. A new situation has also been created in which employers wishing to recruit young people have two organisations with which to liaise. Another change is that previously the Youth Employment Service rarely concerned itself with young people in full-time Further and Higher Education since it was responsible only for the under-eighteens, whereas the Careers Service is intended to cater for all students outside the universities. However, like universities, most colleges have established their own advisory services and, in many cases, relationships with prospective employers. Exactly what role the Careers Service will play, therefore, is not entirely apparent. Similar uncertainties attend the Careers Service's future relationships with secondary schools, where trained careers teachers are becoming more numerous and careers education is becoming more widely provided by the schools themselves. Again, therefore, the type of role to be performed by an external Careers Service is far from self-evident. The type of 'supporting' role that Careers officers are likely to be called upon to play could probably be equally well performed by the Employment Services Agency. Whilst the needs of school-leavers may have differed from the problems of the unemployed to deal with whom the labour exchanges were first established, it is more difficult to argue the same case in relation to the range of facilities being developed by the contemporary Employment Services Agency.

Before it was renamed and its responsibilities modified, opinion within the Youth Employment Service favoured raising the age-limit of young people dealt with from eighteen to twenty-two in order to keep the Service viable. A more influential body of opinion within the Department of Employment, however, favoured making the Employment Services Agency responsible for the whole of the working population, thus increasing the comprehensiveness and attractiveness of its services. Whether the truncated Careers Service that has resulted will discover a role that it can play effectively will only become apparent as the new system of placement and advisory services as a whole becomes gradually established.

As has happened in many spheres of social administration, the British employment services originally developed in a haphazard way, different provisions being introduced at various times to meet needs as they became apparent. These services have rarely excited the imaginations of either politicians or the public at large, and consequently have never benefited from the stimulus of wide-ranging public controversy. The contribution that the employment services can make to the efficiency of the economy and to the well-being of individuals is nevertheless considerable, and for this reason the over-haul of many of the services that has occurred in recent years is welcome. It is an overhaul that has been largely conducted behind the scenes, mostly inspired by those directly concerned with the services' administration. Further gaps and weaknesses will doubtless become apparent, but the general movement is clearly in the right direction; namely, towards an integrated system of employment services capable of concerted attention to various specific problems and to the needs of particular groups.

Further reading

Comprehensive and up-to-date information about all the employment services is published monthly in the *Department of Employment Gazette*, HMSO.

For a full discussion of the system of industrial relations and government policy see, *Report of the Royal Commission on Trade Unions and Employers' Associations* (Donovan Report), Cmnd 3623, HMSO, 1968.

For background information about the problems of the various disadvantaged groups the following are useful studies:

S. CASTLES and G. KOSACK, *Immigrant Workers and the Class Structure in Western Europe*, Oxford University Press, 1973.

F. LE GROS CLARK, *Work, Age and Leisure*, Michael Joseph, 1966.

V. KLEIN, *Britain's Married Women Workers*, Routledge & Kegan Paul, 1965.

P. TOWNSEND, *The Disabled in Society*, Royal College of Surgeons, 1967.

On the system of vocational training see:

Changing Manpower Needs: A Study of Industrial Training Boards, Political and Economic Planning, 1970.

Training for the Future: A Plan for Discussion, Department of Employment, 1972.

LADY WILLIAMS, 'The revolution in industrial training', *Sociological Review Monographs*, 13, 1969, pp. 89–103.

On the problems of redundancy, mobility, and the role of the advisory and placement services see the following:

M. J. HILL *et al.*, *Men out of Work*, Cambridge University Press, 1973.

Into Action: A Plan for a Modern Employment Service, Department of Employment, 1972.

R. MARTIN and R. H. FRYER, *Redundancy and Paternalist Capitalism*, Allen & Unwin, 1973.

G. L. REID, 'The role of the employment service in redeployment', *British Journal of Industrial Relations*, IX, 1971, pp. 160–81.

'Vacancy study', *Department of Employment Gazette*, March 1974, pp. 222–3.

Information on the Careers Service can be found in K. ROBERTS, *From School to Work*, David & Charles, 1972.

Notes

1 *Report of the Royal Commission on Trade Unions and Employers' Associations*, Cmnd 3623, HMSO, 1968.
2 This point is argued in detail by S. Castles and G. Kosack, *Immigrant Workers and the Class Structure in Western Europe*, Oxford University Press, 1973.
3 See V. Klein, *Britain's Married Women Workers*, Routledge & Kegan Paul, 1965, and C. E. Arregger, ed., *Graduate Women at Work*, Oriel Press, 1966.
4 For example, *Retirement*, Acton Society Trust, 1960.
5 *Ibid.*
6 'Characteristics of the unemployed: sample survey June 1973', *Department of Employment Gazette*, March 1974, pp. 211–21.
7 Lady Williams, 'The revolution in industrial training', *Sociological Review Monographs*, 13, 1969, pp. 89–103.
8 'Vacancy study', *Department of Employment Gazette*, March 1974, pp. 222–3.
9 See G. L. Reid, 'The role of the employment service in redeployment', *British Journal of Industrial Relations*, IX, 1971, pp. 160–81; M. J. Hill *et al.*, *Men out of Work*, Cambridge University Press, 1973; and R. Martin and R. H. Fryer, *Redundancy and Paternalist Capitalism*, Allen & Unwin, 1973.
10 The former absence of this type of integration has been strongly criticised. See *Changing Manpower Needs: A Study of Industrial Training Boards*, Political and Economic Planning, 1970.
11 For a review of the relevant studies see K. Roberts, *From School to Work*, David & Charles, 1972.

4   Income and need[1]
Anthony Forder

Some theoretical considerations

In our society the primary sources of income are payments in return for labour and the use of wealth. For the majority of the population most of their income comes from employment either directly or indirectly through dependence on a wage earner. The size of the income is determined by status, skill, responsibility and bargaining power in the work situation. For a minority a high proportion of income derives from the ownership of land or capital goods or of cash deposits which can be lent at interest. There is therefore no reason at all to expect that income will bear any relationship to personal needs and responsibilities unless action is deliberately taken to ensure that it does so.

The first problem is posed by those who are temporarily unable to earn income in the normally acceptable manner because of sickness, accident or unemployment. A second problem is posed by the long-term dependencies of childhood, old age and permanent disability, and the dependency of the mother and housewife. A third problem is posed by those with high overheads, particularly the costs of housing and travel to work.

An important manifestation of long-term dependencies is the 'poverty cycle' or, to look at it from another point of view, 'prosperity cycle' that can be traced in the lives of individuals.[2] The single worker without dependants and the young married couple without children are comparatively well off. When children are born, the wife is likely to stop working, and the needs of the family increase as the children grow in age and numbers. In middle-class families the income of the husband generally increases annually over these first years, but probably not to the same extent as the demands on it. The manual worker reaches his maximum quickly, and there is little increase in income from employment as his family responsibilities grow. Later

89

as the children grow up and become more independent, the demands on the parents' income are reduced and the wife may go out to work again. This comparative affluence lasts for a few years, but is terminated by a sudden drop in income at retirement.

Types of income redistribution

Given a basic distribution of income related to earnings and the ownership of wealth, income can be redistributed in a number of different directions so as to take greater account of need.

First of all income can be redistributed over the life of the individual. To some extent this can be undertaken by individuals for themselves through personal savings. These can be reinforced by insurance through the economic market to meet contingencies like sickness, unemployment or a long life after retirement that are unpredictable for individuals but predictable for larger populations. Alternatively, provision can be made as part of the conditions of employment through sick leave and superannuation schemes. But some people have too low an income to cover all these eventualities without leaving themselves in continuous poverty. For others the cost of insurance may be particularly high because for them the risks of sickness, unemployment or death are very high. Some contingencies like having children or marital breakdown are uninsurable because the outcome is at least partly within the control of the people concerned. Such needs can only be met through state intervention.

Income can also be redistributed between individuals. Webb and Sieve[3] have distinguished two types of such redistribution, 'contingency' and 'income'. Contingency redistribution is designed to meet specific needs regardless of the relative incomes of those who lose or gain. This is the aim of 'universal' social services like the National Health Service as well as insurance schemes undertaken through the economic market. In contrast 'income' redistribution is more directly associated with income levels, and may be described as either 'horizontal' or 'vertical'. In horizontal redistribution the transfers of income take place between groups with the same income levels but different circumstances, as with earnings-related benefits and child tax allowances. Vertical redistribution takes place between different income groups and is positive if it takes place from richer to poorer, and negative if it is from poorer to richer. The latter is, of course, rarely a deliberate aim of policy. It is one effect of a free educational system whose selection procedures favour those with higher incomes. It was also the effect of a housing policy that controlled or subsidised rents and mortgages for a large proportion of the population but ignored the problems of those in furnished accommodation who were often particularly deprived.[4]

Another way of looking at vertical income transfers is to consider what proportion they represent of the incomes of the rich and poor. Taxes have traditionally been evaluated in this way. Progressive taxes represent a higher proportion of the income of the rich than of the poor; regressive taxes, like a poll tax or tax per head of the population, represent a higher proportion of the income of the poor than of the rich; proportionate taxes have an equal incidence throughout the income range. Benefits can be considered in a similar way. It is important to note, however, that a 'progressive' distribution of benefits, though favouring the poor proportionately, may still result in the rich gaining higher absolute benefits than the poor.

Redistribution over the life-span implies a redistribution of income over time. This is possible in monetary terms but rarely in terms of actual consumption goods. Services that are not used when they are on offer are completely lost. Most consumption goods deteriorate over time and in any case involve costs of storage, so the goods and services on which savings are spent after a long period of time mainly come out of current production. In real terms, redistribution over the life-span involves one of two systems. The goods and services that would be unused as a result of current savings may be used in such a way that future production is increased, that is to say they are invested. Alternatively, they may be used by other people today in return for an undertaking to supply goods of similar value when they are needed by the saver. In a simple society parents maintain their children and those too old to work in the expectation that their children will maintain them in their old age. In an industrial society more complex arrangements are required, and these are known as 'pay-as-you-go' systems.

The poverty line

In considering the adequacy of income, the concept of a 'poverty line' has proved a useful tool. The poverty line is a level of income per person or family below which they should not be allowed to fall. The original concept was developed by Rowntree[5] who devised an income scale that represented the minimum incomes on which families of different sizes could subsist while maintaining their physical health. Rowntree in his first survey was concerned to convince a sceptical country that poverty was a real problem, and chose a standard so exacting that no one could deny his conclusions. In a later survey[6] he used a rather more generous standard, which was used as the basis of Beveridge's calculations for an appropriate scale of benefits for the post-war social security scheme.[7] When Beveridge's scheme was first implemented, and even more in subsequent years, the scheme was modified to take account of political and other

91

considerations. Later scales, including the Supplementary Benefits Scale which succeeded National Assistance, have little or no relation to any objective assessment of need.[8] It is, however, generally used in research as a criterion of adequacy of income, on the grounds that it represents society's estimate of a minimum income.[9]

One of the criticisms of Rowntree's concept of a poverty line based on 'objective' criteria of need is that it takes no account of actual patterns of expenditure and the social pressures that influence these. Townsend,[10] for example, showed that families living on incomes equivalent to Beveridge's scale spent on average less on food than Beveridge considered that they needed. So the scale was in fact inadequate to ensure the maintenance of the physical standards at which it aimed. Many priorities in expenditure are determined by social conventions, the need for social interaction and the pressures exerted by state services for higher standards of child care. Such standards are strongly influenced by changes in the general level of earnings, so a poverty line should be related to average income in some way. This approach to defining standards has been called 'comparative need'.[11] It is one of the elements considered in determining current scales of benefit for social security.

Four methods of income maintenance

There are four broad approaches to income maintenance, each with its own limitations and advantages; income supplementation, compensation, earnings substitution, and proportionate compensation.

Income supplementation

Income supplementation means raising income as close as possible to a specific standard or poverty line. It involves an assessment of current income, or 'means test', and the payment of a sum that is approximately the difference between that income and the standard, or the remission of a charge which would reduce income below that standard. Typical examples are the supplementary benefits scheme discussed below, and the provision of free school meals to children of low-income families.

There are two major disadvantages to income supplementation schemes. The first is the effect on incentives to earn and to save. There may be little point in working if the result of this is a reduction in benefits which leaves income exactly the same. Similarly, there is little point in saving for old age or sickness if the extra comforts that the savings are intended to provide are lost through reduced benefits or pension. This is sometimes compared with the effect of 100 per cent rate of income tax, and referred to as an 'imputed marginal tax rate' of 100 per cent.[12] To counteract the disincentive effect some flexibility may be introduced into the system. Some income and some savings up to a specified maximum may be completely disregarded. Alternatively, or additionally, only a proportion of certain income may be deducted from the benefit. An example of this is the basic state retirement pension during the first five years after reaching pensionable age. Earnings up to a certain figure are disregarded, while above that figure deductions are made on a sliding scale. The Family Income Supplement achieves this effect by paying half the difference between the assessed income and the standard.

The second disadvantage of income supplementation is the reluctance of people to accept the feeling of humiliation that may be associated with an investigation of means.[13] This feeling of humiliation may be created by the manner of the investigation, which is sometimes deliberately designed to counteract the disincentive effect mentioned above.

Compensation

Compensation attempts to relate income more effectively to need by benefits designed to compensate specific conditions or handicaps, without considering the financial position of the recipient. Typical examples are the widow's pension and the industrial disability pension under the National Insurance scheme, and family allowances. The advantage of compensation systems is that they avoid means tests and have no disincentive effect (except perhaps to discourage private insurance). Their most serious disadvantage is that unless the condition is highly correlated with low income, they tend to be an expensive way of dealing with poverty, since the benefit tends to go to many who are not poor. There may also be problems in defining the precise criteria of eligibility, and particularly the criteria for ending eligibility. For example, a widow ceases to be eligible for a pension on remarriage. In order not to penalise marriage as such, the same condition is applied to co-habitation.[14] But co-habitation is difficult to define, and unlike a legal spouse, a co-habitee has no legal responsibility to maintain his partner.

Earnings substitution

This is designed to meet the financial needs of those who would normally expect to maintain themselves by their earnings but are unable to do so because of lack of employment, sickness, disability or retirement. It is frequently a special form of compensation for which the condition is lack of employment. Unearned income is not considered, but because of the nature of the condition of eligibility

93

incentives to work can be a major problem unlike other forms of compensation. Earnings substitution may also be in the form of income supplementation, as with supplementary benefits which cannot be paid to those in full-time work.

Proportionate compensation

Proportionate compensation is an earnings related compensation system in which the benefits increase the higher the income or the normal income of the recipient. Earnings related national insurance benefits, many occupational superannuation schemes, and many tax allowances come into this category. They are a form of horizontal income redistribution whose main purpose is to spread income more evenly over the life-cycle.

The major systems for income maintenance

It was in 1955 that Titmuss in an important paper drew attention to what he called 'the three divisions of welfare', the three parallel systems of relating income and need through the state social security provisions, fiscal allowances and occupational benefits.[15] These different systems developed initially independently of one another, sometimes on conflicting principles, although two were state systems and the third subject to state support. It has only been in recent years that serious efforts have been made to integrate the three.

Fiscal allowances

The most important fiscal allowances are those for income tax. The first allowances for dependants were introduced by the same Liberal Government that introduced so many other social reforms before the First World War. This was no coincidence. The reforms cost money; taxation had to be increased and it was easier politically to do this if allowance was made for particular responsibilities. It also fitted in with a general concern about the responsibility of the 'haves' for the 'have-nots'. The first such allowance permitted a stated amount of income to be free of tax for each child. Since then allowances have been introduced to cover wives and a wide variety of special needs and responsibilities. They include allowances for other dependent relatives; for the housekeeper of a widower; for a person looking after the children of a taxpayer with a single-handed responsibility for their care; for elderly taxpayers with low incomes, for blind persons, and for widows.[16]

Another reason for granting income tax relief has been that the same income should not be taken into account twice for tax purposes.

This seems logical when applied to pensions and pension contributions. If pension schemes are regarded as being a method of transferring income over the life-span of the individual, it is reasonable that the income should only be taxed at one point, and that the one where it is in fact used. It is also logical that if there is a direct transfer of income between two people without any service being performed as when an elderly parent is paid an allowance by her son, that this should only be treated as taxable income for one of them. If the income is transferred to a person or institution which pays no income tax or pays at a lower rate, there is an advantage to be gained. To limit the possibility of abuse, the income must be transferred under a 'covenant' of a minimum of seven years' duration. Since registered charitable institutions pay no tax on income, this has been a useful means of increasing the income of such bodies. The same means have sometimes been used or abused to reduce the taxation on a family's income. Much less logical is the decision that the same principles apply to income paid as interest in return for a loan. Under this arrangement interest paid on mortgage loans and bank loans has been excused income tax, because income tax is paid by the recipient.[17] Interest on hire purchase agreements has never been subject to a similar allowance.

Income tax allowances are a form of contingency redistribution on a horizontal basis with a regressive incidence. The higher a person's income, the higher the tax he pays both absolutely and as a proportion of his income, so the greater the relief he can receive for any specific contingency. Where taxes are not progressive, it is much easier to give reliefs that benefit those who have most need. In Britain the most important fiscal allowance outside the income tax system is the rebate of rates instituted by the Rating Act, 1966. Rates, which provide an important part of the finance for local authorities, are based not on income, but on the value of the housing occupied. It is a tax on householders and bears particularly hard on those with low incomes but better housing.[18] Rate rebates, by lessening the burden on low income households, are designed to enable local authorities to increase their revenue without penalising the poor.

Occupational benefits

The provision of assistance to employees in time of need, particularly in sickness and old age, has a long history.[19] Its origins often lay in a sense of obligation fostered by the acceptance of a paternalistic relationship between employer and employee. The arrangement was usually informal. With the development of a more formal relationship between employer and employee with increased industrialisation, this assistance has either been abandoned or put on a more formal footing through occupational benefit schemes. In the latter case the advantage for the employee is obvious, but the employer may also use these benefits as a means of attracting new workers and creating a stable work force. Naturally there has been a tendency for employers to develop schemes of this kind first for those employees whose services they most value. Salaried workers and skilled workers have been most favoured.[20]

Essentially occupational benefits are a method of redistributing income more evenly over the life-cycle with an insurance element for contingency redistribution. Because of the more favourable terms obtained by those with a better bargaining position, they are regressive in their incidence. Despite this they have been supplemented by fiscal allowances which have increased their regressive nature.

The state social security system

The state social security system has evolved from the original proposals made in the Beveridge Report published in November 1942.[21] Beveridge's aim was to provide a comprehensive plan to secure that all members of the community would be free at all times from want. To achieve this he recommended three schemes of benefit: social insurance payable on a contractual basis; social assistance payable on a test of need; and children's allowances payable to all without contract or test of need. These proposals were largely implemented by July 1948, but subsequent developments have given the system a quite different orientation from that envisaged by Beveridge.

Beveridge's central proposal was for a universal and comprehensive 'scheme of social insurance against interruption and destruction of earning power and for special expenditure arising at birth, marriage or death'.[22] This was instituted as 'national insurance' under the National Insurance and National Insurance (Industrial Injuries) Acts.

Initially contributions, subsidised by the state, were paid at a flat rate that varied in amount for the three classes of contributor: the employed (Class 1), the self-employed (Class 2), and the non-employed (Class 3). In return flat rate benefits were payable to those who satisfied certain minimum contribution requirements. The benefits varied for the different classes so that, for instance, only Class 1 contributors could claim unemployment benefit, and Classes 1 and 2 sickness benefit. Married women who worked had to pay a contribution to cover industrial injuries but could elect to pay the full contribution to entitle them to full benefits, including maternity allowance. Contributors who did not meet the minimum requirements were paid a proportionately lower benefit. Those in receipt of benefits were 'credited' with contributions so that future benefits were not prejudiced.

Essentially the Beveridge scheme was an earnings substitution scheme redistributing income over the life-span of individuals and families. Contributions were regressive and benefits progressive, but the net effect only involved vertical redistribution in so far as the contingencies the scheme was designed to meet, like sickness and unemployment, were more frequent among those with low incomes or costs were met from general taxation. As the costs of the scheme increased in the early years governments became reluctant to accept responsibility for the increasing share of the costs that Beveridge had recommended,[23] and in 1952 the state contribution was fixed at 18 per cent. The regressive effect of the flat rate contribution made it difficult to increase the income of the insurance fund without causing great hardship to low earners. So in 1959 the Government introduced an additional graduated contribution at the rate of 4·5 per cent of all income between certain limits.[24] In return contributors would receive an additional earnings related pension, but less than the economic value of the total contributions. This scheme was related to occupational pensions by allowing employers who provided adequate schemes with rights protected on change of employment to contract out of the scheme, but only on payment of a higher flat-rate contribution. In 1966 the Labour Government extended this principle by introducing earnings related contributions and benefits to cover the first six months of loss of earnings from other causes.[25] The aim of this measure, however, was not to balance the budget but to ease the problems of short-term loss of earnings, and to increase the mobility of labour.

The Social Security Act, 1973, aims to rationalise this system mainly through changes in contributions and in retirement pensions. Beveridge's three classes of contributor are replaced by four classes of contribution. Class 1 contributions, paid in respect of 'employed earners', will be a proportion of earnings between certain limits. Initially the employee's contribution was set at 5·25 per cent, and the employer's at 7·5 per cent of earnings between £8 and £48 per week. Married women may opt for a lower contribution of 0·6 per cent but their employer's contribution will not be reduced. Class 2 contributions will be at a flat rate, initially set at £1.68 per week, but supplemented by Class 4 contributions, a levy of 5 per cent on profits or earnings between £1,250 and £2,500 per year. Class 3 contributions, to keep a non-employed contributor in benefit, will again be at a flat rate, initially £1.33. These will be returnable to the contributor if no gain in benefit results. The new contributions begin in April 1975.*

* Further changes in National Insurance rates have been made since June 1974.

The benefits, which will be described later, will be for the most part on a similar basis to the present system, except for pensions. Certain non-contributory benefits for disabled people and those over eighty years of age, first instituted under the National Insurance (Old Persons and Widows' Pensions and Attendance Allowance) Act, 1970, are also consolidated into the Social Security Act.

Under Beveridge's proposals social insurance was to be supported by children's allowances payable at or very close to subsistence level irrespective of the income of the parents and whether they were in employment or not. This was essential to ensure that low-paid workers with families to support would not be living below subsistence level when employed, or, when not working, receive more in insurance benefits than their normal wage.[26] These allowances were instituted under the Family Allowances Acts, the new name indicating that they are intended for the benefit of the family as a whole and not to meet the specific needs of the individual children on whose behalf they are paid. They are a universal compensatory payment providing a progressive benefit. Their progressive nature is increased because they have always been subject to a progressive income tax. In addition, when family allowances were increased in 1968, the 'claw-back' principle was established. Under this a reduction in the child tax allowance nullified the effect of the increase for those who paid tax at the standard rate. This was one of the first attempts to integrate the fiscal and welfare systems.

Beveridge's proposals for social assistance were designed to provide a net for those whose needs were not met or not fully met through social insurance. Beveridge expected these to be a small minority, mainly of people who had failed to meet the contribution requirements for insurance benefits. The largest number, diminishing over the years, would be those not entitled to the full retirement pension because they had not contributed for a sufficient length of time.[27] This was instituted under the title of 'National Assistance',[28] changed to 'Supplementary Benefits' in 1966.[29] Payable on a test of means to those who are not in full-time employment, it brings income up to a scale calculated according to the number and age of child dependants plus a rent allowance which normally covers the whole rent paid by a family, or the interest on a mortgage for an owner-occupier. Supplementary benefits, like family allowances, are wholly financed by central government out of general taxation. The scheme is administered by the Supplementary Benefits Commission, a body with less independence than its predecessor, the National Assistance Board. Existing within the Department of Health and Social Security (DHSS), it has a full-time paid chairman, who is not a civil servant, and seven part-time members. It is serviced by officials of the Department and operates under regulations made by the responsible Minister.

It was the intention of the Ministry of Social Security Act, 1966, which introduced supplementary benefits, to make them an entitlement in a way that had not been true of National Assistance. These benefits, however, have two intrinsic characteristics which mean that they can never have the security of National Insurance benefits. First, they are subject to a means test. Second, there is a deliberate element of flexibility in their administration. For example, Section 13 of the Act gives an overriding discretion in cases of urgency; under Section 7 cash grants can be made to meet exceptional needs, such as replacement of bedding, clothing and household redecoration; and under the second schedule benefit may be varied up or down to meet exceptional circumstances. Such flexibility requires administrative discretion, which may be misused. In order to achieve consistency the Ministry has prepared a code of rules, the 'A' code, to govern the administration of supplementary benefits, but has refused to publish this as its critics have proposed.[30] Instead it has published a handbook giving in broad terms the general principles under which it operates.[31]

This difference between the two systems is also reflected in the different appeals procedures. For National Insurance benefits the procedures are basically those of the courts, with a legally qualified chairman. Decisions are based on precedents, and further levels of appeal lie to the National Insurance Commissioners, who are experienced barristers, and on points of law to the civil courts. Important decisions of these bodies are published.[32] In contrast the Supplementary Benefit tribunals have no legal chairman, hold their sittings in private (to protect the interests of appellants), and make each decision on its merits without reference to precedents – or to the 'A' code, which they do not see. There is no further right of appeal.[33]

These differences of principle between the National Insurance and supplementary benefits systems have also made another objective of the Ministry of Social Security Act difficult to achieve, namely the amalgamation of the two administrations so that enquiries and applications that related to both could be dealt with at a single point of contact. There have been some amalgamations of offices, but it has not proved possible to train staff of the calibre that the Ministry can recruit in the rudiments, let alone the complexities, of both systems.[34]

Beveridge's aim had been that National Insurance plus family allowances should normally be higher than the National Assistance scale, including the rent allowance. This has never been the case for the majority of those receiving insurance benefits. The difference between the basic insurance scales for single people and married couples and the National Assistance and supplementary benefit scales has never been sufficient to cover the rent of those who are householders. Family allowances were instituted at a level well below Beveridge's calculation of a subsistence minimum, and unlike other benefits were not increased with changes in the cost of living.[35] They were paid at a flat rate, as also were the additions to National Insurance benefits for dependent children, as compared with National Assistance scales for children, which were age-related. The result was that National Assistance was from the beginning mainly a method of supplementing inadequate National Insurance benefits, about three-quarters of weekly allowances serving this purpose.[36] The change to supplementary benefits, which was largely merely a change of name although there were some administrative improvements for pensioners, was designed to make this means-tested system more acceptable to recipients.

The failure to set and maintain family allowances at a subsistence level also had a serious effect on the position of low-wage earners. When in work their earnings kept their families at a standard of living below supplementary benefit level. When they were out of work they were paid benefits not on the normal scale, but at a level slightly below their potential earnings in work. This is the system known as 'the wage-stop'. Since the object of the wage-stop is to provide an incentive to work,[37] benefits are based not on actual earnings in the previous employment, but on an estimate of what they can reasonably expect to earn in the future. Since 1968 a minimum figure for a wage-stopped benefit has been set by the basic wage of unskilled manual workers employed by local authorities. The wage-stop principle also operates for earnings related insurance benefits which are restricted to 85 per cent of the average earnings on which the benefits are calculated. This is only likely to affect large families, and is a curious breach of the contractual principles of national insurance.

To make up for the failure of family allowances a pattern of benefits in kind and means-tested benefits, mainly for specific needs, has been developed. These benefits, which include educational benefits and the family income supplement described later, when combined with income tax, result in very high imputed marginal tax rates that sometimes exceed 100 per cent.

Meeting specific needs

Retirement pensioners

The provision of adequate financial support for those who have retired from work on the grounds of age has proved a particularly intractable problem in Britain. The numbers of retired people, though large, are not as large as the numbers of children,[38] and on average their period of dependency is shorter than that of children. But unlike children they are not regarded as the responsibility of particular members of the economically active population, while from the point of view of society as a whole the support of the retired population cannot be seen as an investment like the support and education of children. There is therefore a general expectation that people will provide for their own retirement by contributions made during their working life. Yet there are both practical and psychological obstacles to this. The practical difficulties relate to those with low earnings or without earnings, and to the effects of inflation on the value of contributions paid before retirement and the value of the pension after retirement. The psychological obstacles stem from the tendency of most people to discount the future, that is to say to give more weight to current needs and desires than to future deprivations. This tendency is likely to be more marked among the poor, whose current needs are particularly pressing, and those whose style of life discourages long-term planning, which is particularly frequent among manual workers. The problem is further complicated by the fact that women live longer than men. Yet women in our society generally spend a shorter period of their lives in employment, because of family responsibilities and an earlier retirement age, and also generally have far lower earnings than men.

The inadequacies of the state insurance scheme in meeting these needs effectively has been discussed earlier. The growth of occupational superannuation schemes might have been expected to compensate for these inadequacies. Surveys by the government Actuary showed a steady increase in the numbers of workers covered by these schemes from 8 million in 1956 to 11 million in 1963 and 12 million in 1967.[39] However, even at that date they covered only sightly over 50 per cent of the employed population, and provision was much wider for non-manual than for manual workers, for men than for women. By 1971 the fourth survey showed a decline of 1 million in the numbers covered, partly caused by a reduction in the work force but partly by a fall in the number of manual workers covered. Many of the schemes, and particularly those for manual workers, were also deficient in various respects. These deficiencies included lack of provision for preservation of rights on transfer of employment; a rate of pension well below 50 per cent of normal earnings; and no provision for augmentation of the pension after retirement to take account of inflation.

Both the main political parties have been committed to a reform of the state and occupational systems so that between them they provided a more comprehensive and effective scheme. The Labour Government of 1963–70 produced the 'Crossman Plan' which was incorporated into the National Superannuation and Social Insurance Bill, 1969.[40] This foundered with the change of government in 1970. It involved a massive extension of the state scheme on an earnings-related basis. It has a considerable vertical transfer element built into

101

it by the weighting given to the benefits of those with low earnings. Like the Beveridge scheme it was to be financed on a 'pay-as-you-go' basis in contrast to 'funded' occupational schemes. Inflation-proofing was to be built into it by regular biennial reviews which would ensure that all state benefits at least kept pace with inflation and if possible with increases in average earnings. The scheme would undoubtedly have made massive inroads into the private pensions sector. Only the most effective occupational schemes would have continued in being and then possibly in modified form. This could have affected the availability of finance for capital investment in industry. The terms under which employers could opt out of the state scheme were the subject of prolonged negotiations.

The Conservative Government of 1970–4, in accordance with its general philosophy, wished to strengthen the private occupational pensions system.[41] The Social Security Act, 1973, returned to Beveridge's concept of a flat-rate basic state pension, though financed by earnings-related contributions and reviewed annually to take into account the increased rate of inflation. Occupational pensions were to become compulsory, with minimum standards laid down under the Act for those employers who arranged their own schemes, and a funded state Reserve Scheme for others.

The provisions for the basic retirement pension under the Social Security Act, 1973, have been accepted by the new Labour Government,[42] but with half-yearly reviews. The Act provides for four categories of pension. Category A pensions are payable after the minimum age of 60 for women and 65 for men to those who have paid the requisite contributions during their working life. During the period of five years after reaching this age the insured person may elect not to retire, and provided this period of non-retirement exceeds eight weeks the pension when it is received will be increased by 0·125 per cent for each week during which this continues. If he does elect to retire he can still earn up to £9.50 without having his pension reduced, but after that figure it will be reduced on a sliding scale. Five years after the minimum age the insured person is regarded as having retired whether or not he ceases employment, and the pension is paid in full regardless of his earnings. Retirement earlier than the minimum age through ill-health is covered by invalidity benefit (see below) and through redundancy by unemployment benefit with its time limit of one year.

Category B pensions are payable to the wife or widow of an insured person after she has reached pensionable age. For a widow this is payable at the same rate as the Category A pension, but with additions at half the Category A rate for periods of non-retirement. For a wife the pension is at a lower rate. Under this Act the Category B pension is the wife's and is not a supplement to her husband's pension, so, for example, the husband cannot elect not to retire and so give up both pensions without his wife's consent, 'unless it is unreasonably withheld'.

Category C pensions are for people who were over pensionable age on 5 July 1948, or married to such people. Category D pensions are payable to people who are over 80 and not entitled to a Category A or B pension, or not at the full rate. These pensions are again payable at two rates, the lower being for a married woman. All retirement pensioners, of whatever category, who are over 80 also receive a small increase of pension known as an 'age addition'.

The improvement of funded occupational schemes was crucial to the Conservative programme. If a scheme was to be 'recognised' as an alternative to the reserve scheme it had to reach certain minimum standards. It had to provide a personal pension of at least 1 per cent of the total earnings on which national insurance contributions had been paid under the Act. This meant that the minimum pension after 40 years' service would be 40 per cent of a man's average annual earnings up to £48 per week over that period. Widow's benefit had to be equal to half the husband's minimum pension rate. The value of such a minimum scheme in relation to the income of the employee during the years that preceded retirement or death would of course be considerably affected by the rate of inflation and the increase in real earnings over the period of contribution. Once the pension had been awarded, a recognised scheme had to provide some cover against inflation either by relating the pension to the cost of living or by guaranteeing increases at least equivalent to 3 per cent per annum compound interest. All rights had to be preserved on change of employment. The schemes would continue to be supported by a tax allowance on all contributions.

If an employer did not provide a recognised occupational pension scheme, he had to join the state Reserve Scheme. Contributions would be at the rate of 4 per cent of PAYE earnings (1·5 per cent paid by the employee and 2·5 per cent paid by the employer). There would be no state subsidy or tax allowance on the employee's contributions. The scheme would have been fully funded. It would have provided a guaranteed pension of 34 per cent of average earnings for 40 years' service, but this would have been increased by bonuses dependent on the success of the Reserve Pension Board's investment policy, which would also provide funds for increasing pensions after retirement.

The Reserve Scheme is regarded by the Labour Government as completely unacceptable. They intend to produce their own proposals for a long-term plan in a White Paper. In the meantime the only part of the Act relating to occupational pensions which they intend to implement is that concerning the preservation of pension rights on change of employment.[43]

ment pension may be increased by a graduated pension
who have paid the appropriate graduated contributions
59 and 1974. Unlike the basic pension, which is regularly
and raised to meet changes in the cost of living and national
earnings, the graduated pension is fixed in cash terms, so
value will have been severely cut by inflation.

The retirement pension may also be increased by a supplementary
pension under a test of need if the total income of the retirement
pensioner and his family does not reach the supplementary benefit
scale. For pensioners this scale is increased by a 'long-term addition',
at present 50p. per week. In 1972 almost 2 million supplementary
pensions were paid, representing about one-quarter of all retirement
pensioners.[44]

Pensioners have also received an annual Christmas bonus of £10,
first instituted under the Pensions and Family Income Supplement
Payments Act, 1973 (discontinued in 1975).

Children

FAMILY ALLOWANCES These are a universal benefit payable
for all dependent children except the first child of the family. Eligibility is governed by responsibility rather than relationship. Legitimate
children, illegitimate children, stepchildren and even children un-
related to the claimant are all eligible, provided that the child is
maintained wholly or mainly by the person making the claim. Where
children are living away from their parents they can be included in
the family provided the absence is temporary or the parents are paying
at least 75p. per week towards the cost of the child's maintenance.
An exception to this is made where a child is removed from a family
by the order of a court or a local authority has assumed parental
rights under the Children Act, 1948. In these cases no family allowance is payable – or Insurance Benefit for the child – even if the
parents are paying the full cost of the child's maintenance. Family
allowances can be paid until a child leaves school or reaches the age
of nineteen, and for apprentices with low earnings up to the same age.
The present rates are 90p. per week for the second child and £1 for
the third and subsequent children.

Family allowances are the property of the mother of the family
and she normally signs the claim form, although either parent may
draw the allowance. They are payable at post offices on the Tuesday
of each week, and thus reinforce the housekeeping of hard-pressed
families at a midpoint between weekly pay days.

NATIONAL INSURANCE For all benefits, additions for dependent
children, including the first child of the family, make up the family

allowances to a standard figure. This is lower for short-term benefits than for long-term benefits. The Social Security Act proposes rates of £2.10 and £3.30 respectively. In addition a Maternity Grant is paid on the birth of each child (£25), a Guardian's Allowance for a parentless orphan (without regard to contributions), and a Child's Special Allowance for the children of a divorced woman whose former husband has died, both at the higher rate, for such additions.

SUPPLEMENTARY BENEFITS These include in their needs scale an allowance related to the age of the child, which is above the lower National Insurance addition for all children over five, and above the higher addition for all children over sixteen. This may, of course, be affected by the wage-stop.

FAMILY INCOME SUPPLEMENT[45] This is a non-contributory benefit payable to families, where the breadwinner is in full-time employment and there are dependent children, if the family income falls short of a prescribed scale. The scale was revised in April 1973 to £21.50 per week for a one-child family plus £2.50 for each additional child. It represents a simplified poverty standard that excludes an allowance for rent. Families are paid 50 per cent of the difference between their income from other sources and the scale up to a maximum of £5 for a one-child family and £6 for a larger family. Income is based on the average of the five weeks preceding the claim, and the supplement is granted for one year without further investigation of means.[46] Recipients are automatically entitled to certain other benefits such as free welfare milk and foods and relief of prescription, optical and dental charges. Although the supplement is only available to those in full-time work, it aids others on supplementary benefit since it is taken into account in calculating potential earnings for the determination of the wage-stop. The benefit also favours one-parent families since the scale is the same for them as for families with two parents.

EDUCATIONAL WELFARE PROVISION Since 1906 local education authorities have been able to assist children whose education was likely to suffer as a result of poverty. The Education Act, 1944, extended their powers and duties in this respect. It became a duty for local education authorities to provide school meals and these are subsidised by central government. In October 1972 about 5 million pupils (65 per cent) were taking school meals of which 16·5 per cent were provided free for those in families with a low income.[47] Milk was also provided for all school children and the whole cost met by government until this was abolished in 1971, except for children in infants' and nursery schools. Some local education authorities defied the government by continuing to provide free milk through the rates. It can still be given to junior children who are certified as needing it for the maintenance of their health. Under the same Act local education authorities can make grants to assist with the provision of school uniforms. They can provide clothing for children so poorly clothed that they cannot benefit from their education, recovering the cost in whole or part from the parents. They can also provide educational maintenance grants for children staying on at school beyond the age for compulsory attendance,[48] and, on a much more generous scale, for children going on to Further and Higher education.

In the case of school meals the income level at which meals should be provided free is determined by central government. For other school educational benefits local authorities determine for themselves the amount and frequency of the benefits and the income levels at which they are payable. As a result, different scales tend to operate for free school meals, school uniform grants and educational maintenance allowances; entitlement to one is no indication of entitlement to another, and separate applications may have to be made. Scales for maintenance allowances for students taking first degree courses are also laid down by the Department of Education and Science (DES). For other courses allowances are discretionary. The DES makes recommendations but local education authorities do not have to follow them.

WELFARE PROVISION FOR THE UNDER-FIVES Free milk and vitamin foods once provided on a universal basis are now only available to those receiving supplementary benefits, family income supplement or through a means test.

Unemployment

The main provision for the unemployed is through National Insurance (from January 1976 under the Social Security Act, 1973) and supplementary benefits. Provisions under the new Act are very similar in their effect to those they replace. Unemployment benefit is payable at the basic rate if in the previous contribution year (which is also the calendar year) Class 1 contributions have been paid or credited equivalent to 50 weeks at the minimum rate. No payment is made for the first three days of unemployment in any period. Unemployment benefit ceases after one year, but eligibility can be reviewed after paying 13 contributions. The earnings-related supplement is payable after two weeks' unemployment for twenty-six weeks. The unemployed person can be disqualified from benefit for a period of six weeks if the unemployment is 'voluntary' or due to misconduct. Where for any reason a man's National Insurance benefit is below the supplementary benefit scale, he is normally entitled to supplementary benefits (subject to the wage-stop where relevant), but a single unemployed man living in an area where employment is available may be refused benefit after four weeks.[49] Strikers may not receive unemployment benefit or supplementary benefit for themselves. They can, however, receive supplementary benefit for their dependants.

Redundancy payments are an additional benefit for some forced into a change of employment, whether or not they actually suffer a period of unemployment. Under the Redundancy Payments Act, 1965, payments must be made to employees dismissed after more than two years' service because of a change in the employer's circumstances or his requirements. The payments are made in a lump sum by employers and partially refunded from a Redundancy Payments Fund created by compulsory contributions on all insured employees. The payments are related to the age of the employee and to the length of his service with the employer. He receives half a week's pay for each year of service under the age of 22, a week's pay for each year between 22 and 40, and one and a half weeks' pay for each year of service over the age of 41. Appeals go first to a tribunal[50] and subsequently to the civil courts. The payments are treated as capital and not income for purposes of income tax and supplementary benefits. This system has many weaknesses, not least that the capital sums received are an inadequate substitute for a higher regular income in the absence of an effective retraining system.[51]

Sickness, invalidity and maternity

For practical reasons provisions for sickness and unemployment must approximate very closely together. It would be regarded as manifestly unfair to treat the sick less generously than the unemployed. If they are treated more generously then there is an incentive for unemployed people to get themselves certified as sick. This is likely to result in the wrong use of medical services. At the same time it may be more difficult to get a person back to work if he is registered as sick rather than unemployed.[52]

Despite this there is some discrimination in favour of the sick. Sickness benefit, unlike unemployment benefit, is available to the self-employed (Class 2 contributors). After 168 days of sickness, that is to say when earnings-related benefits run out, the sick person is entitled to invalidity benefit at a similar rate to the basic sickness benefit for which there is no time limit. In addition, a person who is more than five years from retirement age when the invalidity begins can receive an invalidity allowance of modest proportions which is higher for those who are invalided at younger ages. Those who are nearer retirement age than this will receive their retirement pension.

Benefits for loss of earnings due to sickness are heavily biased in favour of those who are in any case better off. Payment during sickness by the employer tends to be more likely and to continue longer the higher the individual's status. In some cases salary is paid without regard to entitlement to benefit, but even if sickness benefit is deducted from salary, the fact that it is tax-free means an increase in income for the sick person. A case could be put forward for compelling employers to accept responsibility for paying employees during short periods of sickness, although there is some danger that this might affect the employment opportunities for people with poor health records.[53]

Maternity benefit is a form of sickness benefit for employed women who pay the full rate of National Insurance contributions. Its purpose is to make it easier for them to discontinue work before the confinement and for some weeks afterwards. It is treated as sickness benefit for calculating invalidity. Maternity Grant is a cash grant payable on either the father's or the mother's insurance record, on the birth of a child.

Disability

For physically and mentally disabled people income is often primarily determined by the circumstances in which the handicap is received.

For those whose disablement occurs in the course of employment, even if it is due to the employee's own negligence, the Industrial Injuries scheme provides a comprehensive system of benefits. The degree of disablement is calculated according to certain principles by a medical board 'by comparison with a normal healthy person of the same age and sex' and is expressed as a percentage figure. The basic grant or pension is related to the extent of disability and can be supplemented by various allowances: the Special Hardship Allowance providing a supplement to compensate for loss of earnings, Constant Attendance Allowance, Exceptionally Severe Disablement Allowance, Unemployability Allowance for those permanently incapable of work, and Hospital Treatment Allowance for those receiving hospital in-patient treatment. Only the last two are subject to a limit on earnings, so the grants and pensions represent a genuine compensation for the disability and make it more likely that the disabled person will be able to obtain an income, including earnings, comparable to that received before the disability arose. War pensions are payable on a very similar but slightly more generous basis.

Another group to which the state has given special consideration is the victims of crimes of violence. The present scheme was set up in 1964 as a result of a campaign inspired by Margery Fry, an important figure in the field of penal reform. It is administered by the Criminal

Injuries Compensation Board, which was set up jointly by the Home Office and the Scottish Office. It provides compensation in cases where personal injury is directly attributable to a criminal offence or to attempting to arrest a suspected offender. The rate of compensation is based on awards made in the civil courts. [54]

If the disability occurs in other circumstances as a result of someone else's negligence compensation will be decided by the courts, but will depend on the wealth and income of the negligent person or his foresight in insuring against this eventuality. The driver of a vehicle is legally obliged to insure against third-party risks, but may disobey the law to the detriment of the victim. Legal proceedings are in any case often very prolonged and this causes much suffering to the disabled. A psychological condition known as 'compensation neurosis' in which physical symptoms are retained until the claim is settled often delays rehabilitation.[55]

Other handicapped persons, including those with a disability received at birth or in childhood, receive no assistance unless they are entitled to supplementary benefits on a test of need.[56] Even the blind, who receive more consideration than other handicapped persons, including a higher rate of supplementary allowance, receive no income for their blindness as such. For the employable, supplementary allowances are likely to be subject to the wage-stop, because their earning potential is low. The position of those with dependants is particularly difficult. Incapacitated housewives with husbands in full-time work are not entitled to supplementary allowances, and there is no compensation for the effect of their disability on family comfort and earnings.

A reform instituted in 1970[57] and incorporated in the Social Security Act is the provision of an attendance allowance for the severely disabled, physically or mentally, who require frequent 'attention in connection with his bodily functions', or 'continual supervision in order to avoid substantial danger to himself or others' either by day or by night. If such attendance is required by both day and night the allowance is at a higher rate. The allowance is only payable when the disabled person has already been subject to attendance for a period of six months. The allowances are administered by an Attendance Allowance Board, the majority of whom must be medical practitioners.

An interesting development in 1973 was the provision by the government of £3 million to set up a fund to meet the special needs of families caring for children under the age of sixteen with very severe congenital handicaps.[58] Known as the Family Fund, it is administered on behalf of the government by the Joseph Rowntree Memorial Trust, an approach which involves an interesting innovation. It provides grants to the parents of such children who, because

109

of their social and economic circumstances, are in need of help which the Trust considers should be provided. There is no means test, but the Trust is expected to form a judgement on the effect of the child on the circumstances of the family. The help is to relieve stress on the family while the child is at home and can be provided notwithstanding that it is within the power of other statutory services to provide it.

The need for consistency in the provision of income for the disabled is being increasingly recognised. A Royal Commission is at present examining the whole question of compensation in cases of civil liability. Its terms of reference are broad and include all cases of disability due to accident, whether or not negligence is involved and including disabilities due to injury before birth. Meanwhile the present Labour Government is committed in its manifesto to a compensatory income for all disabled people and it seems probable that such a measure if introduced would receive support from all Parties.

Widows

For widows the Social Security Act follows the National Insurance Acts. It takes into account the problems of adjustment in the period immediately after widowhood by the payment of the widow's allowance for a period of six months at a rate which is higher than the basic unemployment and sickness benefits, and like these can be increased by an earnings-related supplement. At the end of this period what happens depends on the age and responsibilities of the widow. A widow under forty without children receives no further benefit. A widow with a son or daughter under nineteen living with her receives a Widowed Mother's Allowance at the standard benefit rate. A flat-rate addition is payable for each child who is dependent on her. Since it is assumed that older women may have difficulty in finding employment, a widow receives a pension on a sliding scale according to her age when her husband dies or the last child reaches nineteen (see note 57 at the end of this chapter). If this occurs when she is under forty she receives no further pension. At fifty or over she gets the maximum rate. Since these benefits are now no longer subject to an earnings rule, they provide some compensation for the low level of a woman's wages for the support of a family.

The needs of widows and orphaned children have also been covered by some occupational pension schemes. The nature of the provisions has been very varied, like their provisions for superannuation.[59] They may involve a lump sum payment or a pension or a combination of the two. The cover may be additional to ordinary pension rights or a substitute for part of them. It may relate to the death of the employee before retirement or after. It may cover children or not.

110

The Inland Revenue Department again sets limits to these schemes. The maximum provision in a scheme for widows' pensions on the death of the employee before retirement would be approximately equivalent to a lump sum of two years' salary and a pension of a quarter of the salary annually. For widows' benefits after the retirement of the employee, the Inland Revenue makes a limit in approved schemes of 50 per cent of the husband's pension. In some cases protection for the widow may involve a reduced pension for the employee. These limits, coupled with the reluctance of employees and employers to face the costs of adequate schemes, mean that for most widows employment is essential to avoid having to live on an income at or little above the supplementary benefits level. Under the Social Security Act, 1973, a 'recognised' superannuation scheme would have to provide a widow's pension of at least half the minimum rate for the employee's pension.[60]

Almost all widows' benefits including those under occupational schemes cease if the widow remarries or during any period in which she co-habits with a man. The husband or co-habitee is expected to assume full responsibility for her and her children. Supplementary benefits depend on his application and eligibility. Co-habitation presents particular difficulties. It is hard to define and even when proved provides the woman with no legal claim on the man for herself or for the children (see note 14 at the end of this chapter).

Unsupported wives and mothers

For wives divorced or separated from their husbands, and women with illegitimate children, the first question is one of legal responsibility. A man is legally responsible for the maintenance of his children, legitimate and illegitimate; he is also responsible for the maintenance of his wife, unless when they are separated he can show that she is responsible for the situation. The Magistrates' Courts can make maintenance orders for a wife and her legitimate children payable by the husband, and affiliation orders for illegitimate children payable by the putative father. There is now no maximum to the amount which can be ordered for a wife and her legitimate children,[61] but the courts have always been influenced by the fact that it is easier to make an order than to enforce payment. An order for a small amount that is likely to be paid regularly may therefore be better than one for a large amount which will be resented and not paid. Other responsibilities of the husband, such as his co-habitation with another woman with children dependent on him, will also be taken into consideration. However, despite the relatively low payments required by some court orders many are not paid, or are paid irregularly, or only in part. The Maintenance Orders Act, 1958, attempted to deal with this by making it possible to 'attach' part of a man's wages for this purpose, i.e. making a court order stipulating that the employer should pay the amount of the order directly to the court. However, many orders are still not paid, since an attachment order lapses if the man changes his employment. Where the recipients of supplementary allowances have court orders or other agreements for the maintenance of themselves or their children, half the orders for divorced or separated wives, and one-third of the orders for mothers of illegitimate children, are paid irregularly or not at all.[62] The Commission have powers to bring proceedings to obtain maintenance and affiliation orders, and criminal proceedings for persistent neglect to maintain.

Where payment of a court order is not made regularly it is the practice of the DHSS to pay the woman supplementary benefits at a full rate and to obtain the woman's authority to collect from the court any money paid under the order. This ensures a regular income for the woman. The same problem of co-habitation applies here as for widows with the added difficulty that the whole allowance lacks the legal protection provided in the case of insurance benefits by the Commissioners and the courts.[63]

Single-parent families

Just as the income needs of disabled people are being considered as a whole, so it has come to be recognised that single-parent families have common problems, where the absence of one parent is due to death, divorce or separation before or after marriage, and whether the parent caring for the children is a man or a woman.[64] A minor recognition of this occurred in the administration of family income supplement. For the first time, in calculating needs, the requirements of a single parent were regarded as the same as those for two parents, and this was accepted for motherless as well as fatherless families. The most important recognition of this principle came in the appointment of the Finer Committee on One-Parent Families.[65]

The Finer Committee was concerned with all the needs of one-parent families (which represent about 10 per cent of families with children at any one time), but considered that their most urgent need was financial assistance. It has proposed a Guaranteed Maintenance Allowance sufficiently high to raise the income of 90 per cent of one-parent families above supplementary benefit level, and to give most such parents a genuine choice about undertaking full-time work. There would be a means-tested element in the allowance in that it would taper off to zero for those with incomes at about the level of average earnings. Until the allowance can be instituted, it proposes that more generous supplementary benefits should be paid to these families.

Housing

The cost of housing is one of the overheads of living which it i difficult for individuals, and even more for families, to control. result, given relatively fixed incomes, the cost of housing has a direct effect on the availability of income for other needs.[66] The importance of this is recognised in supplementary benefits by including an allowance that normally covers the whole of the rent, including rates, paid by a claimant. A reduced rent allowance may be paid if in the view of the Commission's officers the rent is unreasonably high. For house-owners only the rates and interest on a mortgage can be paid. It is not considered desirable that the Commission should make capital payments and thus contribute to the capital assets of claimants. This creates major problems for owner-occupiers with mortgages who are in receipt of supplementary benefits over a long period.

Other means of mitigating the problems associated with the cost of housing are discussed in the chapter on housing.[67] They include rent allowances under the Housing Finance Act, 1972, rent control, tax allowances on the interest on mortgages, and the mortgage option scheme. It is important to note that the transmutation of housing subsidies into rent rebates under the Housing Finance Act clarified that the major objective was then seen as income maintenance through supplementation rather than the encouragement of local authority housing.

Objectives and the future

If the various measures described in this chapter seem to lack consistency it is partly because a variety of objectives is being pursued without an evaluation of their total effect, and partly also because people are reluctant to face the changes in the basis of income distribution which the pursuit of these objectives requires.

One important objective has been to ensure that no person receives an income below a basic minimum or poverty line in relation to his responsibilities. This was Beveridge's main concern, and must be regarded as a minimum requirement for any system of social security. Britain is still a very long way from achieving this objective even if the minimum standard is taken as the supplementary benefits scale. Official estimates based on the *Family Expenditure Survey* of 1972 suggest that in that year there were 1,220,000 families with 1,780,000 members with incomes below that level (see Table 6). The Department of Health and Social Security believe that the figures are likely to exaggerate the numbers who appear to be below the supplementary benefit level but other estimates are considerably higher. The three main reasons for these high figures are low earnings,

113

the wage-stop, and failure to claim supplementary benefits when eligible.[68] This last appears to be directly due to the adoption of income supplementation under a means test as a primary element of policy. However, the supplementary benefits scale is itself an inadequate poverty line. It represents a very low proportion of average earnings, at least by the standards of the more prosperous Continental countries, and the numbers of people with incomes at, or only a little above supplementary benefit level are very high indeed.[69]

TABLE 6 *Estimated number of people with incomes below supplementary benefit level at December 1972, excluding recipients of supplementary benefit (in thousands)*

	Families	Persons
1 Over pensionable age (60 for woman, 65 for man)	760	980
2 Under pensionable age: With family head or single person:		
(a) normally in full-time work	80	250
(b) sick or disabled for more than 3 months	70	190
(c) unemployed for more than 3 months	120	190
(d) others	190	250
Total under pensionable age	460	880
of which in large families (3 children or more)	50	270
and of which single-parent families	(20)	(80)
Total in all categories	1,220	1,780

Note: Figures in brackets subject to very large sampling error; all figures rounded to nearest 10,000.

Source: Letter from the DHSS to Mr Brian Sedgemore, MP, quoted in F. Field, 'The poor people welfare benefits never reach', *The Times*, 8 July 1974. The figures are given as in the article, but there appears to be an error in the addition in the final column, which adds up to 1,860. This does not affect the argument significantly.

A second objective has been to maintain a greater stability in the relationship between income, needs and responsibilities over the lives of individuals, taking into account the standard of living to which they have been accustomed. Fiscal allowances and occupational benefits both contribute to this, but the latter have been so unequal in their incidence that the state has taken additional responsibility through the introduction of earnings-related benefits, and greater control of the private schemes through which such benefits are provided.

A third objective has been dictated by the acceptance of particular responsibility for certain groups such as those affected by war casualties, industrial injuries or crimes of violence. For these the aim has been to maintain an income more closely related to that received before the precipitating event, or at least significantly above the basic minimum considered acceptable for others. This has usually taken the form of a compensatory income, which is not affected by subsequent earnings. Pressure is mounting to extend the categories covered by such provisions, including all disabled people and one-parent families. The case for this is based largely on the grounds of social justice, which is the essence of compensation. But such allowances are also advocated because some of these groups are likely to include a high proportion of people with low earning power who are particularly likely to be below the poverty line.[70] Compensatory incomes are likely to enable them to avoid the need to apply for means-tested benefits.

These three main objectives have been complicated by a number of other aims of general or particular concern: making labour more mobile or trying to attach valued workers to a particular firm; maintaining wage differentials or creating greater equality of income; enabling children to benefit from their education and encouraging them to stay on at school longer; encouraging home ownership and relating rent to income. More recently butter at a subsidised rate has been made available to recipients of supplementary benefits and the family income supplement to reduce the stockpile created by the EEC agricultural policy. Similar proposals have been made for beef.

The confusion of objectives itself reflects a conflict of attitudes, which, while relevant to the social services as a whole, is particularly clear when monetary benefits are involved. Basically our society is committed ideologically to a system for the distribution of income in return for contributions to social well-being as evaluated through the economic market. There are two aspects to this commitment. On the one hand income obtained through the economic market, whether by investment or employment, is seen as an 'earned right', as part of a contract which, if it does not accurately reflect the value of the person's contribution, underestimates it rather than overestimates it.[71] Part of the contract is the right of people to make their own decisions about how the money is spent, which gives them their sense of autonomy. On the other hand the provision of income through the economic market is used as a means of social control, providing incentives for behaviour that is approved within the value system of the economic market. In general people accept the controls of the work situation in return for the freedom to spend time and money in their own way outside that situation.

In contrast to this, distribution through the social services is aimed

115

at meeting needs rather than providing rewards. The financial benefits of the social services provide for the needs of those who either
temporarily or permanently lack bargaining power in the economic
market, and give security to those who may lose bargaining power.
However, people are reluctant to accept the reduction in their monetary income that is required to provide effective services. They dis-
trust, or despise, those who receive income without submitting to the
controls of the work situation, hence the stigma attached to receiving
benefits and the emphasis on the prevention of fraud.[72] There are
widespread fears about the final results of loss of incentives.

Reluctance to accept the consequences of distributing a larger
proportion of income through the welfare system rather than through
the economic market has resulted in the adoption of a number of
measures that aim to meet need while reducing the effects of the
transfer. The increased use of selective means-tested benefits like
family income supplement and supplementary benefits involve a
lower rate of transfer as compared with family allowances and
National Insurance. At the same time they reduce work incentives for
the low paid so that resort is made to the wage-stop and other
deterrent measures. Discretionary benefits, like payment of supplementary benefit to the single unemployed under the four-week rule,
and financial assistance under the Children and Young Persons Act,
1963, also make possible some control over behaviour.[73] Benefits in
kind, like free school meals, control the use to which benefits are put.
An increased reliance on transfers over the life-span of the individual
through earnings-related and occupational benefits reinforces the
primary distribution through the economic market rather than
counteracting it.

This conflict between the respective roles of the economic market
and the welfare system in income distribution has only marginally
been reflected in the programmes of governments formed by different
political parties. It is true that the Conservative administration of
1970–4 introduced two major means-tested benefits, family income
supplement and rent rebates, but the former it intended to replace
with the tax credit system discussed below and the latter was to
replace a complex system that was manifestly unfair and for which
the Labour Party had no solution. It is also true that the Labour
Party has based its pensions policy on an extension of the state
scheme for social insurance while the Conservatives have relied on
controlling and extending occupational pension schemes. Yet both
schemes are earnings related, and the major differences are not in the
amount of the compulsory transfer of personal income but over
funding, which affects investment, control and the extent of guaranteed inflation proofing. In other respects their policies have been
remarkably similar

Jordan has made out a strong case for the view that the whole tendency over the last thirty years has been a reintroduction of the principles of the Poor Law and for the very reasons that those principles were first established.[74] Before accepting this view it is worth noticing the contrary tendencies. One of these has been the increased use of compensatory payments for groups of people such as widows and certain disabled people, and the pressure to extend these to all the disabled and to all one-parent families. Another has been the Conservative proposals for a tax credit scheme.[75] This is essentially a compromise between two alternative systems that have been put forward to meet the problem of poverty, negative income tax and social dividend schemes.[76]

Under a negative income tax system all income tax payers whose income falls short of their total tax allowances receive a proportion, 50 per cent in some proposals, of the difference between the two. These schemes would operate like the family income supplement, but since they would be operated through the tax system, no special claim would be required and under PAYE it would be paid through the employer.

Under social dividend schemes a standard tax-free allowance would be paid to every man, woman and child at a minimum poverty level, thus replacing all the main elements of the social security system. All other income would be taxed at a standard rate. Atkinson calculated in 1969 that to provide standard allowances at the current supplementary benefit rates would require a tax rate of about 50 per cent.[77] The tax credit proposals of the Liberal Party are in essence a social dividend scheme. They are outlined in the Party's February 1974 Manifesto, 'Why Britain Needs Liberal Government', on pages 11-12.

Under the proposed tax credit scheme every person earning over a minimum figure (£8 was suggested in 1972) would be credited with a sum for himself, his spouse and his dependent children, from which would be deducted tax at a standard rate on all earnings. At a later point it was agreed that the tax credit for dependent children should be paid to the mother like the present family allowance. As the proposed rate was £2 for all children including the first this would have been a very significant improvement of the family allowance scheme. Essentially, however, the tax credit is a social dividend applied only to earners and with the scale well below any conceivable poverty line. Its advantages would be threefold. It would dispense with the need for family income supplement machinery while ensuring that all, or almost all, those eligible would receive the benefits. It would reduce high imputed marginal tax rates. It would simplify the tax system with consequent administrative savings for employers and government. Its disadvantages would lie chiefly in making the

117

tax system much more inflexible. It would also result in the abolition of only one means-tested benefit and exclude many of those most in poverty including non-employed and all self-employed people, since it would apply only to employees. Its effect on poverty would depend on the level of credits and the rates of taxation implemented. The scheme has been criticised because the increased taxation (estimated in the Green Paper on the rates proposed at £13,000 million) could be used more efficiently to combat poverty. Nevertheless it could represent an important shift in the balance of resources distributed through the welfare system rather than the economic market, particularly if the whole of the tax credit was eventually paid to the housewife or mother.

However, the tax credit scheme even if implemented, would be far from providing a minimum income, and implementation is unlikely in the near future. Effective compensation schemes are slow in coming and are also generally far from generous. The question must therefore be raised whether, if redistribution results in so much resistance, the basic system of distribution of income can itself be influenced. If there was greater equality in the original distribution of income then redistribution over the life-span, which is relatively acceptable, could better meet the need for social security.

Some attempts have been made or proposed to effect that initial distribution. In the prices and incomes policies of successive governments to deal with inflation and balance of payments problems, emphasis has been placed on ensuring that the low-paid gain relatively larger increases. Over many years the TUC has been advocating legislation for a minimum wage related to national average earnings. The same proposal is also included in the Liberal Party Manifesto of February 1974. This could only be effective if differentials were reduced. Neither of these goals has been successfully pursued, because the pressure to maintain differentials has been too strong. An alternative approach through the control of prices of essentials, specially food, has been equally ineffective. The reintroduction of subsidies by the Labour Government in 1974 still relies on redistribution through taxation.

One can only conclude that in a period of rapid inflation and slow growth in the gross national product a more effective attempt to relate income to need will depend on people giving a much higher priority to social justice than they seem willing to give at present.

Further reading

For the history of these services before 1939, Gilbert and de Schweinitz are useful supplements to the more general works listed at the end of chapter 1. George (1968) covers general development from

118

Beveridge to 1968 very thoroughly, King a more specific area. Stevenson is a very good account of the work of the Supplementary Benefits Commission, avoiding the issues raised by the more radical critiques of the social security system in George (1973) and Jordan. Of these two George's work is the more scholarly, but Jordan's is full of interesting insights. Atkinson is still the clearest exposition and analysis of the various ways used and put forward for tackling the abolition of poverty defined in terms of supplementary benefit rates. Burns, Richardson and Rodgers provide useful analyses of the principles involved in different forms of provision, with international comparisons which are to varying degrees dated. Wynn provides the basis on which a rational system of family support might be constructed, with many fascinating tables and charts. Lynes is a useful reference book:

A. B. ATKINSON, *Poverty in Britain and the Reform of Social Security*, Cambridge University Press, 1969.

E. M. BURNS, *Social Security and Public Policy*, McGraw-Hill, 1956.

VICTOR GEORGE, *Social Security: Beveridge and After*, Routledge & Kegan Paul, 1968.

VICTOR GEORGE, *Social Security and Society*, Routledge & Kegan Paul, 1973.

B. B. GILBERT, *The Evolution of National Insurance in Great Britain*, Michael Joseph, 1967.

BILL JORDAN, *Poor Parents: Social Policy and the Cycle of Deprivation*, Routledge & Kegan Paul, 1974.

SIR GEOFFREY S. KING, *The Ministry of Pensions and National Insurance*, Allen & Unwin, 1958.

TONY LYNES, *The Penguin Guide to Supplementary Benefits*, Penguin, 1973.

J. H. RICHARDSON, *Economic and Financial Aspects of Social Security: An International Survey*, Allen & Unwin, 1960.

BARBARA N. RODGERS *et al.*, *Comparative Social Administration*, Allen & Unwin, 1968.

KARL DE SCHWEINITZ, *England's Road to Social Security*, University of Pennsylvania Press, 1943.

OLIVE STEVENSON, *Claimant or Client?*, Allen & Unwin, 1973.

MARGARET WYNN, *Family Policy*, Michael Joseph, 1970.

Notes

1 In the two previous editions a historical approach was taken to this subject starting from the Beveridge Report. In the interests of economy of space this approach has been abandoned in favour of a greater concentration on analytical description of the present situation. A

number of theoretical issues, some of which were interspersed through-out the earlier text – and often consequently ignored by students – have been brought together in an initial section. Those who prefer a historical approach may still find value in referring to the earlier editions.

2 First described by B. Seebohm Rowntree in *Poverty, A Study of Town Life*, Macmillan, 1901.

3 Adrian L. Webb and Jack E. B. Sieve, *Income Redistribution and the Welfare State*, Occasional Papers in Social Administration no. 41, Bell, 1971.

4 See Adela Nevitt, *Housing, Taxation and Subsidies: A Study of Housing in the UK*, Nelson, 1966.

5 *Op. cit.*, chapter 4.

6 B. Seebohm Rowntree, *Poverty and Progress, A Second Survey of York*, Longmans, 1941.

7 *Op. cit.*, paras 217–32.

8 For a discussion of the evidence on which such a scale might be based see Margaret Wynn, *Family Policy*, Michael Joseph, 1970.

9 An approach first used in the study of Brian Abel-Smith and Peter Townsend, *The Poor and the Poorest*, Occasional Papers in Social Administration no. 17, Codicote Press, 1965.

10 Peter Townsend, 'Measuring poverty', *British Journal of Sociology*, June 1954.

11 J. Bradshaw, 'The concept of social need', *New Society*, 496, 30 March 1972, pp. 640–3.

12 This approach is particularly associated with P. Kaim-Caudle. See his articles in *Social Services for All?*, Fabian Society, 1968, and *Lloyd's Bank Review*, April 1969. See also A. R. Prest, *Social Benefits and Tax Rates*, Research Monograph no. 22, Institute of Economic Affairs, 1970. There is very little evidence of the actual effects on incentives of any tax rates. See C. V. Brown and D. A. Dawson, *Personal Taxation, Incentives and Tax Reform*, PEP Broadsheet 506, 1969, for a discussion of the evidence.

13 See Sheila Kay, 'Problems of accepting means-tested benefits' in David Bull, ed., *Family Poverty*, Duckworth, 1971.

14 DHSS, *Co-habitation: Report by the Supplementary Benefits Commission to the Secretary of State for Social Services*, HMSO, 1971. See also 'The co-habitation rule: a guide for single, separated, divorced or widowed women claiming supplementary benefit or national insurance', Poverty Leaflet no. 4, Child Poverty Action Group, January 1972.

15 R. M. Titmuss, *The Social Division of Welfare*, Rathbone Lecture delivered in 1955 and published in *Essays on The Welfare State*, Allen & Unwin, 1958. Titmuss was not the first person to draw the analogy between the systems but stimulated a more general interest in it.

16 Allowances are amended annually by the Finance Acts and details can be obtained from Inland Revenue departments.

17 In general there has been a tendency for Labour Chancellors to remove these concessions for family trusts and interest on loans other than mortgages. Conservative Chancellors have tended to reinstate them.

18 For a discussion of the disadvantages of rates and the difficulties of replacing them see *The Future Shape of Local Government Finance*, Cmnd 4741, HMSO, 1972.

19 A brief historical account is given in G. D. Gilling Smith, *The Complete Guide to Pensions and Superannuation*, Penguin, 1967.

20 *Occupational Pension Schemes 1971 – Fourth Survey by the Government Actuary*, HMSO, 1972, and earlier surveys.

21 Beveridge Report, *op. cit.*

22 *Ibid.*, para. 17.

23 *Ibid.*, paras 292–5.

24 Under the National Insurance Act, 1959.

25 The National Insurance Act, 1966.

26 Beveridge Report, *op. cit.*, para. 308.

27 *Ibid.* paras 369 *et seq.*

28 National Assistance Act, 1948.

29 Ministry of Social Security Act, 1955. An excellent if somewhat bland account of the administration of supplementary benefits is provided by Olive Stevenson, *Claimant or Client? A Social Worker's View of the Supplementary Benefits Commission*, Allen & Unwin, 1973.

30 Tony Lynes, 'The secret rules', *Poverty* no. 4, autumn, 1967.

31 DHSS, Supplementary Benefits Commission, *Supplementary Benefits Handbook*, HMSO, 1970 with later revisions.

32 But for evidence of the extent of variation in tribunal decisions see Kathleen Bell *et al.*, 'National insurance local tribunals', *Journal of Social Policy*, vol. 3.4, vol. 4.1, October 1974 and January 1975.

33 Kathleen Bell, 'Supplementary benefit appeals tribunals', *Case Conference*, November 1968. Also *Guide to Supplementary Benefit Appeals*, Child Poverty Action Group, undated. Obtainable for 5p., from CPAG, 1 Macklin Street, London, WC2.

34 The DHSS Annual Reports no longer give information on progress in this respect. For a discussion of early difficulties that almost certainly still continue see Anne Lapping, 'Social security: how new a Ministry', *New Society*, no. 245, 8 June 1967.

35 In 1942 Beveridge recommended a rate of 8s. per week (40p). Rates have been raised as follows: 1946, 25p.; 1952, 40p.; 1956, 2nd child, 40p., subsequent children 50p.; 1967, 90p.; and 100p.

36 DHSS, *Annual Report for 1971*, Cmnd 5352, HMSO, 1972, table 108, p. 335.

37 The DHSS, however, denies that this is the objective but sees it as protecting the position of wage-earners, as the co-habitation rule is seen as preventing unfairness to married people. See Ministry of Social Security, *Administration of the Wage Stop*, HMSO, 1968, paras 4–7. The graphic picture of the life of the families presented is well worth reading.

38 See Chart 3.

39 Summarised, except 1956 figures, in the 4th survey, *op. cit.*, para. 3.1.

40 DHSS, *National Superannuation and Social Insurance*, Cmnd 3883, HMSO, 1969. The Bill was based on proposals formulated in Opposition, see *National Superannuation*, Labour Party Publications, 1957. See also Brian Abel-Smith and Peter Townsend, *New Pensions for Old*,

Fabian Society, 1955; *National Superannuation: A Critical Review of the Labour Party Proposals*, Association of British Chambers of Commerce, 1958.

41 DHSS, *Strategy for Pensions: The Future Development of State and Occupational Provision*, Cmnd 4755, HMSO, 1971.

42 *The Times* Parliamentary Report, 20 May 1974.

43 *Ibid*.

44 DHSS, *Annual Report 1971*, HMSO, 1972, table 125, p. 353.

45 Introduced under the Family Income Supplement Act, 1970, and the Family Income Supplement (Computation) Regulations.

46 Originally the supplement was payable without reclaiming for six months. This period was extended by the Pensions and Family Income Supplement Payments Act, 1973.

47 DES, *Education and Science in 1971*, HMSO, 1972, para. 34.

48 The issues have recently been re-examined in a Report of a Select Committee of the House of Commons published on 3 September 1974 by HMSO.

49 Tony Lynes, 'Four weeks misrule', *New Society*, 20 January 1972.

50 The tribunals are those set up by the Industrial Training Act to hear appeals from employers against training levies imposed by the Industrial Training Board.

51 S. Mukherjee, *Through No Fault of Their Own*, Macdonald (for PEP), 1972.

52 These points are vividly made in R. M. Titmuss and B. Abel-Smith, *Social Policies and Population Growth in Mauritius: A Report to the Governor of Mauritius*, Methuen, 1961.

53 See Ministry of Labour, *Sick Pay Schemes*, HMSO, 1964, for information about existing arrangements and discussion of the questions raised.

54 Home Office, *Report of the Working Party on Compensation for Victims of Crimes of Violence*, Cmnd 1406, HMSO, 1961; *ibid.*, *Compensation for Victims of Crimes of Violence*, Cmnd 2323, HMSO, 1964. The work of the Criminal Injuries Compensation Board is reviewed in its annual reports published under the auspices of the Home Office from 1965 onwards.

55 Henderson and Gillespies's *Textbook of Psychiatry*, 9th ed., revised by Sir David Henderson and Ivor R. C. Batchelor, Oxford University Press, 1962, pp. 170–2. For a full discussion of the weaknesses of the legal system for settling compensation including its expense see Terence A. Ison, *The Forensic Lottery*, Staples Press, 1968.

56 An exception to the rule that supplementary benefits cannot be paid to a person in full-time employment is made in favour of self-employed disabled persons, earning substantially less than other workers similarly employed.

57 Under the National Insurance (Old Persons' and Widows' Pensions and Attendance Allowance) Act, 1970. The same Act introduced the sliding scale for pensions for widows between 40 and 50 years of age, and a pension of £3 per week for old persons and their widows who were too old in 1948 to be insured under the National Insurance Act.

58 For an account of the setting up and administering of the fund by the

director of the Joseph Rowntree Memorial Trust see Lewis E. Waddilove, 'The Family Fund', in Kathleen Jones, ed., *The Year Book of Social Policy in Britain, 1973*, Routledge & Kegan Paul, 1974, chapter 12.

59 G. D. Gilling Smith, *op. cit.*, chapters 14 and 15; *Occupational Pensions Schemes 1971 – Fourth Survey by the Government Actuary*, HMSO, 1972, chapter 12.

60 This, like other sections of the Act concerning occupational pensions, is awaiting a decision of the Labour Government.

61 The maximum rates for an order for the maintenance of a wife or child were abolished by the Maintenance Orders Act, 1968, on the recommendation of the report of the Committee on Statutory Maintenance Limits, Cmnd 3587, HMSO, 1968.

62 Ministry of Social Security, *Annual Report, 1967*, HMSO, 1968.

63 For a study of the situation of women without male support and living on supplementary benefits, see Dennis Marsden, *Mothers Alone: Poverty and the Fatherless Family*, Allen Lane, 1969; see also Margaret Wynn, *Fatherless Families*, Michael Joseph, 1964.

64 Victor George and Paul Wilding, *Motherless Families*, Routledge & Kegan Paul, 1972.

65 DHSS, *Report of the Committee on One Parent Families* (Finer Report), Cmnd 5629, HMSO, 1974.

66 Beveridge, following Rowntree, discusses this problem in his report, *op. cit.*, paras 197–206.

67 See pp. 146–7.

68 A. B. Atkinson, *Poverty in Britain and the Reform of Social Security*, Cambridge University Press, 1969, p. 43.

69 *The Times*, 8 July 1974, p. 11.

70 R. M. Titmuss, *Commitment to Welfare*, Allen & Unwin, 1968.

71 Ironically there is some evidence that lower paid people are less liable than those not in poverty to believe they are exploited. Ken Coates and Richard Silburn, *St Ann's: Poverty and Morale*, Nottingham University Press, 1967, pp. 75–80.

72 Pressure to take action on fraud resulted in the appointment of the Fisher Committee to examine this: see DHSS, *Report of the Committee on the Abuse of Social Security Benefits*, Cmnd 5228, HMSO, 1973. No committee on tax abuse has yet been set up.

73 See Bill Jordan, *Poor Parents: Social Policy and the Cycle of Deprivation*, Routledge & Kegan Paul, 1974, chapter 6, 'The making of a public welfare agency'.

74 *Ibid.*

75 Treasury and DHSS, *Proposals for a Tax Credit System*, Cmnd 5116 (Green Paper), HMSO, 1972. The proposals are discussed in Michael H. Cooper, 'Tax Credits: problems and proposals', *Social and Economic Administration*, vol. 7, no. 2, May 1973. This article has a full list of references.

76 A. B. Atkinson, *op. cit.*, chapter 9 discusses the various proposals put forward.

77 *Ibid.*, pp. 173–4.

5 Housing
Kathleen Pickett

Among those commodities which may be considered basic to normal
civilised life – food, clothing, fuel and housing – housing poses
peculiar economic problems. The cost of buying a house is very high
relative to annual earnings and so the great majority of people need
to obtain a loan if they wish to possess a house of their own, or
alternatively must be content to obtain one by paying rent to its
owner. In either case, the cost is reduced to one which can be paid
out of earnings. Nevertheless, such payments are affected by rising
interest rates which could increase them to an unacceptable extent.
To meet this threat, a number of devices are possible. At the building
stage, the standard of housing may be reduced or a greater number of
dwellings may be built on the same area – that is the density of housing is increased. After this stage, maintenance may be neglected or
the density of population increased by overcrowding. All are a means
of reducing the cost of housing per person as well as of increasing
profits.

In addition, the long life which houses normally sustain means that
only a small proportion of the existing stock are of recent construction. Old dwellings, of however high a standard when built, may well
deteriorate into slums and so give rise to conditions which will lead
to intervention by some form of authority. Yet housing is a comparative newcomer to the field of social services. The needs of the old,
the sick and those in extreme poverty have been recognised by the
charitable for many hundreds of years. It was only after the upheaval
of the Industrial Revolution with its mass movement to the new
factories, and the resulting overcrowded, insanitary and disease-
ridden communities in the central urban areas that society generally
was forced into recognising that some control over housing conditions
in those areas was essential. It was in this context, with the fear of
epidemics spreading from such concentrations of squalor, that the

first housing legislation was introduced in the second half of the nineteenth century.

Gradually, after the First World War, when the promise of 'homes fit for heroes' became a discredited and derisive catchphrase, good housing was recognised as a need for which society must accept some responsibility. This social approach to housing with its implication that economic considerations must, if necessary, take second place where need accompanies an inability to pay, at least in full, is now largely accepted. However, the extent and the form of aid is still very much a matter of controversy.

Where the public pays the price through tax or rates the cost of meeting such a need must inevitably be a matter for close scrutiny, especially when there are so many competing demands to be met and the cost is so high. No doubt this is why housing under the public sector has never yet achieved an adequate level and has been and is still supplemented to a significant extent by bodies largely independent of the government. Early examples of the private provision of housing may be seen in the tied cottages and, in a few cases, the model villages of the landed gentry. Similarly, many manufacturers made prosperous by the industrial development of the nineteenth-century built tied houses for their workers close to the factory or mine, not a few of which are still occupied today. During this period also charitable trusts endowed by wealthy patrons began to provide dwellings for the working class at low rents. These trusts led to the formation of non-profit-making housing associations which play an important part in the provision of low-cost housing today.

As good housing became recognised as a right, it was also seen as one of a complex of amenities necessary to a satisfying environment. These include access to shops, schools and open space, and facilities for recreation and association conducive to the development of good relationships between fellow residents. Until the advent of comprehensive planning powers, such amenities were largely supplied, if at all, on an *ad hoc* basis and subject to the whims of individual developers. The failure of this system to meet growing expectations became more apparent during the inter-war years as urban sprawl encroached upon the surrounding countryside. Ribbon development, coastal shanty towns and a general lack of care for natural amenities led to the introduction of an increasing number of controls. Rudimentary powers of planning and conservation in urban areas had been available to local authorities, though not generally used, since the early inter-war years. These were later extended to rural areas, but the establishment of a Ministry of Town and Country Planning at the end of the Second World War marked the beginning of the system of controls over all forms of environmental development which we have today. Only the ownership of land remains largely a private preserve and even here freedom is far from total and is likely to become more restricted in the future.]

Closely associated with such changes has been a change in values and expectations. For the majority of people in this country economic improvements have provided opportunities available only to a favoured minority before the last war. The increasing proportion of home owners, although currently prejudiced by unprecedentedly high rises in the cost of houses and mortgages, reflects this change. Nevertheless, the improvement has not been universal and for a few it appears that the difficulty of establishing an adequate home environment may have increased, or perhaps their needs are more easily overlooked in the general preoccupation with new and enlarging experiences. Around those with few resources, particularly the old, large families and those with single parents, or the mentally or physically ill-equipped, the vicious circle of multiple deprivation appears to have become more firmly closed.

In examining housing as a social service, four separate strands must be followed: first, the construction of new houses at a cost or for a rent which can be afforded by those on low incomes; second, slum clearance and renewal; third, the improvement and updating of structurally sound houses which have fallen below current standards; and fourth, the care of the general environment which is implicit in the term 'planning'. At different periods, different strands have been in the ascendant, but ideally a strong housing policy requires equal weight to be given to each. In the first half of this chapter, a historical account of housing legislation under successive governments since the mid-nineteenth century indicates how the emphasis has changed between these aspects; in the second half a more general discussion of special problems illustrates the need for adequate support in each area.

Early housing policies and control

The Victorian period

The massive overcrowding of the nineteenth century has disappeared, but one legacy remains in the recognition of the need for controls in the housing field. During the first half of that century, as new factories proliferated in the developing industrial towns and cities, migrants from declining agricultural areas streamed in to find work and a more prosperous life in urban centres. To answer their need cheap houses for rent were rapidly constructed, and became a popular and rewarding form of investment, while in many older houses each room contained at least one family, perhaps of eight or nine people. Lawton[1] describes conditions in Liverpool at this time where, as in other cities, back-to-back houses were commonly built round courts which were entered from the street by narrow, badly lit alleys. Octavia Hill[2] vividly describes the state of such houses in London where hardened mud caked the kitchen stairs over which hung the 'foul smells which the heavy foggy air would not allow to rise'. In Liverpool, 20,000 residents lived in cellar dwellings often below water-level, in 1841.

In all urban areas mortality rates rose astronomically; there was a high incidence of tuberculosis and a constant risk of epidemics of typhoid, cholera and other contagious diseases. Concern at these conditions and dangers grew and culminated in a study sponsored by the 1832 Poor Law Commission under its secretary Edwin Chadwick. This *Report of the Sanitary Conditions of the Labouring Population of Great Britain* was published in 1842 and was followed by a Royal Commission[3] which reported in 1844 and 1845.

The ensuing legislation in 1848[4] was largely an attempt to raise the standards of public health by establishing local Boards of Health to secure the supply of clean water and to improve sanitation. In 1868, however, the Artisans' and Labourers' Dwellings Act was passed, which although still primarily concerned with the health aspect was the first measure to enable intervention in the housing situation. Under this Act, houses could be declared unfit for human habitation by the medical officer of health for the authority and their owners required to make improvements or to demolish at their own expense. Later nineteenth-century legislation increased the power of the local authority to clear areas of unfit housing and to rebuild under an improvement scheme. However, little use was made of these powers for they were expensive and largely impractical because of a requirement to rehouse a number of people equivalent to those displaced. Nevertheless, the principle of slum clearance was established.

From 1851 local authorities were empowered[5] to build new dwellings for rent, but again few took advantage of this opportunity and the scale varied. Liverpool Corporation was one of the earliest, constructing a block of tenements, St Martin's Cottages (part still standing, modernised and occupied). But against the background of massive private enterprise absorbed in the creation of suburban areas, and the redevelopment of central areas for the new railway complex as well as for commercial undertakings, the efforts of the public sector at this time are insignificant in spite of the exacerbation of an already serious problem by wholesale demolition.

In the face of this neglect by authority, charity – a major force in the Victorian period – stepped in. In London, Octavia Hill persuaded Mr Ruskin to put forward £3,000 to buy cottage property, which she renovated with the help of occupants needing employment. Her use of the housing situation to put into motion a whole series of improvements, including employment, leisure activities and education, although on a local scale, was an example of social service at its most effective. Her example was followed by others and led in time to the development of housing management as a professional service.

During the same period a number of charitable trusts of differing sizes were set up to provide low rent housing for the 'working classes'. These were the forerunners of today's housing associations and some, such as the Bournville Village Trust and the Sutton Dwellings Trust, have remained active. Set up initially by private funds, the rents were used to provide more houses. In 1909 support was given by Parliament to these organisations by their recognition in the Housing, Town Planning, etc., Act as Public Utility Societies, which enabled them to obtain loans on special terms.

The same Act was the first to facilitate a move beyond the small scale 'improvement scheme', which had so little success, by giving borough, urban and rural district councils powers to formulate planning schemes for new building. These would take into account amenities and layout as well as ensuring proper sanitary conditions – a continuing government preoccupation. Attempts to make these schemes compulsory failed; nevertheless, the effect was generally to raise the standard of housing design and layout. The end of the nineteenth century and the beginning of the twentieth century had seen a growing interest, fostered by a few outstanding individuals, in the improvement of the urban environment. Often marked by strongly anti-urban views, hardly surprising in the context of the times, men such as Ebenezer Howard dreamed of the creation of residential areas which would combine the best qualities of urban and rural life. The realisation of these dreams can be seen in the two Garden Cities of Letchworth and Welwyn, and Garden Villages such as Port Sunlight and Bournville. This idea of a total environment which would provide for outdoor recreation in areas of open space and for the intellectual life in access to libraries, art galleries and other cultural facilities has been firmly established in accepted planning practice since that time.

The inter-war years

During the First World War, house building and house repairs were at a standstill. At this point in time, the great majority of houses were rented from private landlords and only the very wealthy could afford to buy their own. Few municipal dwellings were available: the public utility societies were the main providers of low-rent housing. A high proportion of houses were multi-occupied and sharing between parents and their married children was usual.

At the end of the war the Coalition Government realised that changes must be made and more houses become rapidly available.

Although the association between housing and public health remained, in that both were the responsibility of the Ministry of Health and would remain so until after the Second World War, housing was established as a need in its own right for which the government must take responsibility. During the inter-war years, the periodic increase and decrease in house construction reflect the ability and will of successive governments to provide some form of support to builders in the public or private sector. The days of low-cost materials and labour, which allowed a good return to the property investor, had passed apart from a short period leading up to the Second World War.

Certainly in 1919, costs had risen too far for any large-scale development to be expected from the private sector or the unaided local authorities. To meet this difficulty, the Housing, Town Planning, etc., Act of 1919 empowered local authorities to use the product of a penny rate for new council housing of a standard fixed by the government, any difference in cost to be met by an Exchequer subsidy. A subsidy could also be claimed for slum clearance schemes, but in the event few such schemes were submitted – the shortage of housing was too acute to allow any loss of housing of however poor a standard. The scheme for a virtually open-ended Exchequer subsidy was soon abandoned when it was found to entail an average cost of £60 a house each year – a quite unacceptable amount by the standards of that time – and once more the number of house constructions fell sharply. As an alternative the decision was made to subsidise building for sale,[6] in the hope that private builders might be more ready to keep costs low, and that the movement to these houses would release older ones for rent and so relieve overcrowding. At the same time, rent control, introduced during the war, was removed from lettings when vacant possession was obtained in the expectation that this would lead to an increase in privately rented accommodation. None of these hopes was realised before the Labour Government came into office in 1924.

Under the new government the 1924 Wheatley Act[7] introduced a programme for the construction of $2\frac{1}{2}$ million houses during the next fifteen years. All building agencies were to co-operate – private, local authority and housing associations – with a fixed Exchequer subsidy of £9 a house to be paid annually for 40 years while the local authorities contributed £4 10s. towards each of their own. Rents were again fixed at approximately pre-war level, though decontrol on vacant possession remained for private lettings. By the end of the 1920s nearly half a million council houses had been built with a small amount of slum clearance. Nevertheless, problems all too familiar today remained: the improvement had barely affected those in greatest need, for whom council house rents were too high, and the slums grew rather than diminished. Of the two aspects of government

129

concern at this time – construction for 'normal housing requirements' and slum clearance – the first had received the most support while the second had been largely inhibited by the cost of compensation and rehousing. Fresh measures were required if there was to be any serious attempt to shift the balance of advantage towards those at the lower end of the income scale, and in the 1930 Housing Act a new government introduced new procedures and new subsidies which provided a basis for a more effective approach to slum clearance and the provision of low-cost housing.

Under this Act, the balance between council housing and slum clearance changed, and for the first time clearance took priority. Criticisms had been made that council house rents were too high for all but the skilled worker. Studies of Becontree[8] and Watling[9] confirmed that there was a high turnover rate in these estates. Many new residents found that they were unable to meet the added expense, in particular the cost of the journey to work, and so returned to the city centre. After 1930, and even more when economies under the Housing (Financial Provisions) Act, 1933, led to the abolition of subsidies for 'general need' housing, the first aim was slum clearance and rehousing. Until the outbreak of war in 1939, this proceeded at a rate never reached before or since. Nevertheless, 'general need' subsidies returned in 1935 for the balance had swung too far.

The 1930 Act also replaced the old definition of 'unfit' – closely associated with protection from disease – by a new definition which took into account 'lack of air space or of ventilation, darkness, dampness, absence of adequate and readily accessible water supply or sanitary accommodation or of other conveniences and inadequate paving or drainage of courts, yards or passages'. Five years later[10] overcrowding became an offence.

Another change in the housing situation occurred after 1932 when, with a degree of economic recovery, the speculative builder was able to take advantage of a good market for cheap houses for sale and for the first time owner-occupation spread to lower income groups. Although the workmanship was often poor, these houses served a useful purpose at a time when council housing had become more difficult to obtain. At the same time there was renewed interest in property investment and smaller houses were bought for letting. The 1933 Rent Act also decontrolled houses of high rateable value entirely, allowed decontrol on vacant possession for those of moderate value but controlled rents on those of low value. Under these conditions, housing societies were also widening their scope and though still seeing their function as the provision of houses for the 'working class', they did not confine their attention to the poorest section. In 1935 the National Federation of Housing Societies was formed and given official recognition in the 1936 Housing Act.

The spate of building during the 1930s inevitably led to problems of control and preservation. Government and public were still not ready for any stringent measures and this was a time when freedom for the builder was almost complete. The 1932 Town and Country Planning Act reflects the rather grudging admission that while the urge to build and to renew must be given encouragement, some restraints were required and some attempt should be made to maintain minimum aesthetic standards. On the one hand, the Act drew attention to the need to preserve certain amenities such as areas of natural beauty and historic buildings, while on the other it insisted upon the availability of essential services such as roads and water supply before development commenced. A rather weak piece of legislation – it was essentially local in its application and inhibited by the acceptance of large claims for compensation – it nevertheless prepared the ground for the post-war period. Then, with the experience of five years of controls in all areas of life, associated perhaps with the successful termination of the conflict, the British people were ready for some curtailment of freedom in order to achieve an improvement in their environment.

By the time the Second World War commenced, when, as in 1914, all housing developments were quickly brought to an end, each of the four aspects of housing need were established in some degree. The 1930s had given an impetus to the construction of new houses and to slum clearance and replacement, greater than at any previous period. Improvement and updating, however, was hardly considered in the public sector and little outside since the days of Octavia Hill and her associates. Planning, although in its infancy, had arrived and had many influential supporters. These would emerge after the war and take part in its development into a discipline in which architects and geographers would associate to found a profession whose power would extend at an unprecedented speed. Even before the end of the war, in 1943, a Ministry of Town and Country Planning was created and the Town and Country Planning (Interim Development) Act of that year imposed development control over all land not already subject to a local authority scheme. Three reports published at the beginning of the war had exposed a number of problems which required far-reaching powers for their solution: the Barlow Report, *Distribution of the Industrial Population,* the Uthwatt *Report of the Expert Committee on Compensation and Betterment,* and the Scott Report on *Land Utilisation.*[11]

In addition the inter-war years had seen the use of two instruments of policy, whose varied application provides evidence – not always to be taken into account – of their effectiveness in making housing available at a cost which can be met by households on low incomes. One of these was rent control, in force at the start of the period, relaxed in 1923, preserved only for 'working class' houses after the 1933 Rent Act and, after relaxation in 1938, saved from a final abandonment by the outbreak of war.

The second was the use of subsidies to stimulate house construction. At first available for both municipal and private dwellings and, like rent control, seen as a temporary measure, they have survived in some form to the present day. Between 1933 and 1935 they were given only for local authority houses provided as replacements for demolished unfit dwellings but this restriction may well have prevented other council house construction. Both rent control and subsidies have played an important role in government housing policy in the post-Second World War years – some might say with at least as much effect on political events as on the supply of dwellings.

Post-war developments

The end of the Second World War, like the end of the First, saw problems of housing need compounded by years in which no domestic building had taken place. By 1945 this had been aggravated by the loss of many houses through enemy action. Once more, slum clearance was a luxury which must be postponed while all efforts were given to providing additional accommodation. During the immediate post-war years, a considerable amount of legislation affected all aspects of housing provision and environmental control and the foundations were laid for many new developments in the ensuing years. Each of the four main areas concerned in meeting housing needs will be considered in turn although none can, in effect, be isolated from the influence of the others, or from those two instruments of policy, rent control and subsidies, with their continuing cycles of imposition and relaxation. The current situation here will also be discussed at the end of this section.

New housing

During the immediate post-war years, priority was given to council housing while a strict system of licensing restricted all other developments. From 1948 to 1952, 80 per cent of post-war houses were built by local authorities with the help of an increased government subsidy, yet even so every authority had long waiting lists and systems of allocation were introduced which took into account family size, present accommodation, war service and often most important of all, length of residence within the authority. Various types of selection schemes have remained, which will be considered in more detail below under 'Council housing'.

After the advent of a Conservative Government in 1951, restrictions in private building were relaxed and since that time the proportion of houses built for owner-occupation has increased remarkably, so that today half the dwellings in England and Wales are owner-occupied compared with a little over a quarter in 1947, and nearly one-third are rented by local authorities compared with 12 per cent in 1947 (see Table 7).

TABLE 7   *The tenure of dwellings in England and Wales, 1947, 1961 and 1972 (in percentages)*

Tenure	1947	1961	1972
Owner-occupied	27	44	51
Public authority	12	25	31
Privately rented, etc.	61	31	18

The figures in the table are taken from *Annual Abstract of Statistics*, HMSO.

The increase in the proportion of these tenures has accompanied and is a consequence of the fall in privately rented accommodation, which has become progressively less worthwhile financially. It may be said that today owner-occupation is the goal of the great majority of households and home ownership now extends over a considerably wider portion of the population than in pre-war days. Building society figures show that currently approximately 40 per cent of home-owners with mortgages are manual workers and this is associated with the economic improvement of this group, particularly those in skilled trades. Nevertheless, there still remain many unable to raise sufficient capital for the deposit as well as those unwilling to take on the responsibility of ownership, and for these council houses or other types of rented accommodation are still required. Income clearly acts as a constraint to those looking for a house, but the proportion of income which a household is prepared to spend on its purchase or rent varies considerably and is a choice available to all except the poorest.

Private building

Little control has been exercised over the standard of private building since subsidies were withdrawn from this sector. A minimum standard of construction is laid down through building bye-laws but frequent inspection is required to ensure its maintenance and this is not always feasible. In 1946 the National House Building Registration Council was set up, representing a variety of interests which include the Royal Institute of British Architects, the Building Society Association, the Town Planning Institute, building operatives and local authorities. It operates as an independent certifying body which can be used by any builder.

Few people are able to buy a house outright, especially since the inflation of house prices which brought about massive increases between 1970 and 1973. The majority obtain a mortgage loan through a building society, which will advance a proportion of the value which is placed by the society on the house; this will often be rather less than the price paid by the purchaser. Loans, for which the house acts as security, vary according to the age and condition of the property and may be as high as 90 per cent for a newly built house. Repayment is made over a number of years which is usually twenty-five but can extend to thirty-five at the time the mortgage is taken out. The interest is related to bank rate, and as a result has risen from 8 per cent to 11 per cent over the last four years. The increase in monthly repayments which this has caused added to heavy initial down-payments as house prices soared, has led to difficulties for many young house-owners buying their first home. It has recently been proposed that there should be a redistribution of interest payments on mortgages for first buyers, so that total repayments will be lower initially, when income is often less and commitments greater than in later years. The price of new houses has more than doubled over the whole country since 1963, but increases were relatively steady until 1970 (see Table 8).

TABLE 8 *Purchase price of new houses in Great Britain, 1963–72 (1963 = 100)*

1963	1966	1968	1970	1971	1972
100	126	141	161	181	232

Source: *Social Trends*, HMSO, 1973.

In the South of England, price rises have been even greater, and in Greater London were half as much again between 1970 and 1971 as those in the Midlands and North. Schemes to reduce interest rates over the initial years for first buyers have been proposed but so far have not been operated. Some help is given to those already holding mortgages by providing the option, when interest rates rise, of extending the repayment time rather than increasing the monthly account. This has led to repayment periods of fifty years or more – often beyond the likely life-span of the buyer.

Building societies originated in the late eighteenth century when their members raised money to buy land on which to build their own houses; once done, the society was dissolved. During the nineteenth century the two functions of investing and house purchasing became distinct and since then the societies have raised money from the public which is lent at a higher rate of interest to the house purchaser. The rate of interest allowed to the private investor must compete with other forms of investment and to a great extent decides the rate paid on the mortgage loan. In 1973, while the price of houses was a major political issue, building societies found that their loans were outstripping their investment funds, and so applied to the government for the necessary permission to raise their interest rates. In the face of public concern, a bridging grant was provided to the societies by the government on the understanding that the rise was to be delayed: this was extended to six months and has since been twice renewed. A further attempt to conserve funds was the government's withdrawal of tax relief on mortgages for second houses, brought in with the 1974 budget proposals.

Most local authorities also operate mortgage schemes[12] and are allowed to lend up to 100 per cent of their valuation repayable over thirty years with interest. Money available for this purpose is limited and authorities tend to operate selection procedures so as to provide such loans to applicants who do not qualify for a building society mortgage – perhaps because the house they wish to buy is considered by the society to be too old or on too short a lease. Loans may be obtained through insurance companies combined with endowment assurance or through a bank, but the latter usually expect higher repayments over a shorter period than do building societies.

Tax allowances may be claimed for mortgage repayments, the amount of tax relief being related to the tax liability and, therefore, highest for those who have big loans for expensive houses – generally those in the higher income brackets. Until the government's option mortgage scheme was introduced in 1968, those with low tax liability because on small incomes were not able to obtain any tax relief. Under this scheme,[13] purchasers may opt for a subsidy rather than income tax relief, which effectively reduces the interest on their loan by 2 per cent unless the interest rate falls below 6 per cent – virtually this occurs only where an annuity mortgage at a fixed rate of interest has been taken out, an arrangement discontinued some years ago.

The recent high cost of housing is closely associated with the rising cost of materials, labour and building land, the latter now in especially short supply in the larger towns and cities. In order to release more land for building and so reduce the price a number of measures were proposed by the government in 1973.[14] These included the release of some Green Belt land and a charge to be levied on land for which planning permission is granted if it is not developed within four years of outline permission or three years after full permission has been granted: measures designed to counter 'land hoarding' by developers who wait for prices to rise on their land. However,

135

these proposals were overtaken by the dissolution of Parliament in early 1974, while at the same time the price of houses passed its peak as shortage of money forced building societies to restrict the number of mortgages made available. The situation remains to date that if land is not developed within five years of outline planning permission and three years of full permission, a new application must be made. Changes will doubtless be associated with the proposed nationalisation of all development land which the Labour Government hopes to see in force during 1975.

Council housing

The great majority of houses built by local authorities are for rent, although a few may be built directly for sale. All such housing qualifies for subsidies, whose operation will be examined in a later section.

In the light of changing standards, in particular concerning the allocation of space, a report by the housing management sub-committee of the Central Housing Advisory Committee in 1968[15] suggested that one of the most difficult problems now is to 'match' the size-distribution of dwellings and households. In some areas of pre-war council housing there may be considerable under-occupation[16] where families have grown up and the children have left. In many post-war estates the same problem will arise in the not too far distant future, especially in the case of houses built in the 1950s, when the urgent need for housing led to fast construction and occupation by families whose age and composition fell within a narrow scope.[17] Often in such estates there is a demand for houses from second and third generation households who have found that they must move back to the city in order to qualify for a house in their home area. Here there may well be a long waiting list for vacancies, in spite of under-occupation.

Many overspill estates have been constructed outside city boundaries since the war, as city land has become more scarce and expensive. In such estates housing has been administered by one authority, perhaps some miles away, and other services by a second, leading to confusion and a belief by many residents that they have been 'dumped over the border out of the way'. This situation may be improved by the 1974 local government reorganisation. Responsibility for housing rests with lower tier authorities, but these usually extend over a larger area than was administered previously by a single authority.

Those who obtain council houses fall into four main categories: from the housing list, through demolition and slum clearance, by exchange or transfer, or for medical reasons. A smaller category includes key workers who may be needed for local industry or by the

136

authority, for example as social workers. The housing list contains the names of people who have themselves applied for a council house and in areas where houses are in short supply may well be inflated by those who have found alternative accommodation, those who have moved away and those who have put their names down for more than one authority. On the other hand, some who are eligible for a tenancy may not be aware of this and may not apply – for example, rehousing one coloured family may lead to an upsurge of applications from other coloured families who did not appreciate that council housing was available to them.[18] As the normal situation is that there are more housing list applicants than tenancies available, selection procedures of some kind must be applied by the local authorities.

There is a statutory duty under the 1957 Housing Act to give reasonable preference to persons occupying insanitary or over-crowded houses, who have large families or are living in unsatisfactory conditions of some kind. Following a recommendation of the housing management sub-committee, the Seebohm Report[19] urged a broader interpretation of their housing responsibilities on the part of local authorities and also suggested that more attention should be paid to those in greatest need, especially those at greatest risk of becoming homeless or grossly ill-housed. The particular difficulties faced by such people in obtaining a council house are that they tend to be mobile, and so may not fulfil the residential requirements, and often migrate to areas with a serious housing problem, such as the inner areas of cities, to find work. Their low income means that they may have difficulty in paying rent regularly. The housing management sub-committee, reinforced by Seebohm, asked local authorities to relax their residential qualifications for such people and to consider means of helping them financially through rent rebate schemes.

Selection procedures vary considerably between local authorities. In most cases there is a points system, in others a personal decision by the local authority housing manager, or in the few cases where there is a surplus of council housing, a simple date order based on application time. It has been pointed out[20] that subjective factors, such as the strain of living with in-laws, are not measurable and so tend to be ignored, and that it is physical rather than social needs which are assessed. Housing managers usually visit the home of applicants before allocating houses, and on this basis they are 'graded' as being likely to take good care of their new house or as potential risks. This may lead to neighbourhoods or whole estates winning a reputation for 'roughness'[21] and the newest council housing goes to those seen as the 'best' tenants. Some authorities take up a moralistic attitude believing that council tenancies should be given only to those who 'deserve' them – thus unmarried mothers, dirty families, and 'transients' tend to be grouped together as 'undesirable'.[22] Nevertheless, the housing management sub-committee recognised the problem of the social deviant and suggested that in these cases the social services should be involved.

Where people have been displaced from houses compulsorily acquired by the local authority, in most cases because they have been living in a slum clearance or redevelopment area, local authorities, where such houses were unfit, have a statutory obligation to rehouse owner-occupiers, tenants, sub-tenants or married children, though not individual lodgers. Where they have been moved out of technically fit property, even though sub-standard, some authorities will consider that owner-occupiers who have been paid the market value for their houses should find accommodation for themselves, although tenants will usually be rehoused. There appear to be substantial differences in policy here between authorities and there are certainly difficulties in areas of housing pressure where it frequently occurs that houses, in however poor condition, will be bought or rented if clearance is likely, in order to qualify for a council house when this takes place. Many authorities will refuse to accommodate recent arrivals although such action is the consequence of desperate housing need.

The ease with which exchanges and transfers – the former to tenanted, the latter to vacant housing – can be made either within or between estates can vary a good deal from one area to another. Some authorities co-operate more readily than others although few yet operate local bureaux through which such changes can readily be made. Housing management sub-committees in successive years have seen the process as one way of redistributing tenants so as to minimise under-occupation though the policy at present is more to facilitate such exchanges than to positively encourage them through financial inducements. Transfers to other members of the family on the death of the tenant responsible for payment is also a process where no general procedure is followed. An adult son or daughter who has lived for many years with parents in a council house will have a strong case, but separated or deserted wives will often find themselves in difficulties.

Under the Housing Finance Act, 1972, local authorities were required to fix 'fair rents' for their tenants and rent rebates could be claimed by low-income households. Rebates were previously available only where local authorities chose to provide them, subject to a means test of variable stringency: the 1972 Act standardised the procedure. Rent rebates will be discussed below under 'Rent control and security of tenure'.

There has been much controversy in recent years over the sale of council houses, a policy generally encouraged by Conservative governments and strongly opposed by Labour. In 1973[23] authorities were urged by the government to sell council houses to those tenants wishing to buy, and a 20–30 per cent discount on the market value was suggested, restrictions on resale to be applicable for at least five years. Again a change of government reversed this policy, although the decision remained in the hands of local authorities.

Housing associations

Housing associations[24] were defined in the 1957 Housing Act as non-profit-making societies whose object is to construct, improve or manage houses. Before 1919 they were the chief providers of low-rent housing for the 'working classes', but as this role was taken over more and more by local authorities the associations diversified their interests. Today many cater for special needs, in particular for the elderly, but also for other groups such as the disabled, ex-prisoners, un-married mothers and students. Others provide rented accommodation at economic rents for those with higher incomes. Others again are formed by groups who wish to build their own homes and dissolve when these are completed. There has been rapid growth of the 'new style' associations since the Housing Corporation was set up in 1964 with powers to assist in the development of societies, make loans and acquire land. Houses must meet Parker Morris[25] standard – the standard required for local authority building – and where dwellings are built for letting, they must remain so.

Housing associations are generally able to operate a more flexible letting policy than local authorities, for they are not bound by the same obligations. On the other hand, loans for construction are often provided by local authorities, who may then in return nominate tenants from their own lists. Such nominees have in the past been able to obtain rent rebates where available, though not other housing association tenants except where their association had charitable funds for this purpose. However, the 1972 Housing Finance Act placed the financial position of tenants as regards rebates on a similar basis to those in other types of rented accommodation (see under 'Rent control and security of tenure' below).

Privately rented accommodation

The fast decline of privately-owned rented accommodation in post-war years has been a major factor in the growing scarcity of low-cost accommodation. Worthwhile profits may still be gained by building and letting high-quality flats at economic rents, in London or in retirement towns, but low-cost rented accommodation owned privately is almost always old and very often in poor structural condition, lacking basic amenities or providing them only on a shared basis. Rent control, imposed or removed, has been used alternately to protect the tenant and to encourage the landlord, but has had little apparent influence on the supply position.

Slum clearance

Slum clearance[26] was resumed in the 1950s, associated with redevelopment plans for many urban inner areas. The 1951 Census had revealed a high proportion of houses without basic amenities and further information was supplied by local authorities in 1954 providing an estimate of 845,000 slum dwellings out of a total of 13 million permanent houses. Unfortunately, standards of assessment based on a new definition of unfitness varied between authorities and it is generally believed that this figure was much too low. This definition took into account the state of repair, stability, freedom from damp, natural lighting, ventilation, water supply, drainage and facilities for food storage and cooking and is considered to be too narrow by current standards. The addition of internal layout to the criteria in the 1969 Housing Act was a small improvement.

A later survey[27] in 1964 estimated 1·8 million unfit dwellings and a further 6 million sub-standard. Shelter[28] has suggested that at present rates it could take at least twenty years simply to clear all unfit houses and it has also been estimated[29] that there is a need for a 1 per cent annual replacement rate (141,000 houses) if account is to be taken of the fact that slum clearance is not a finite problem and that as standards rise there will be an increased need for improvement. Optimistic predictions in the 1960s that the disappearance of slums was in sight were made without allowing for this factor as well as the continuing process of obsolescence.

Overcrowding is frequently an exacerbating factor in sub-standard property although it is not by any means confined to such dwellings. Statutory overcrowding is based on a standard which takes into account the number of persons by sex and the number of 'habitable rooms'; this is again recognised as too narrow today. Housing authorities have a duty to relieve overcrowding, although it has been not infrequent for them to let houses to young families which require only a single increase to become statutorily overcrowded. Nevertheless, where tenants are selected for council houses on the basis of overcrowding, the standards used are generally higher.

Overcrowding is most often associated with multi-occupation, especially common in the inner areas of the larger cities. Where houses are occupied by more than two families or four lodgers, they must be registered with the local authority. In order to encourage the improvements which are often required in such houses, registration has been conditional since 1969 on those necessary being carried out, although as a concession grants may be given for the installation of basic amenities, even when these are not for exclusive use.

Improvement

The continuing existence of slum areas and their slow clearance has led to an increased interest in improvement. Until the Dennington Report in 1968,[30] the cost of improvements required to bring older houses up to acceptable standards so as to guarantee a minimum life of fifteen years was considered to be too high for this work to be worth undertaking on any large scale. The 1969 Housing Act, however, gave local authorities the power to declare General Improvement Areas in which an effort would be made to upgrade the total environment, an innovation supported by the success of the Deeplish study.[31] Deeplish, a deteriorating but socially stable area of nineteenth-century terraced houses in Rochdale, was chosen for an investigation into the practicability of rehabilitation by the Ministry of Housing and Local Government in 1964. The findings were encouraging, suggesting that improvements were feasible on a limited scale to houses and environment and could appeal to the majority of residents.

Within General Improvement Areas, local authorities were able to acquire land and buildings and to buy houses for improvement and conversion or demolition if this was necessary to the plan for the area as a whole. In addition, house-owners were to be encouraged to improve their houses by an increase in the grant available, and in the case of landlords, by allowing rents to be increased over a period after the tenancies had been certified as reaching the required state, this to include basic amenities (indoor WC, fixed bath, wash basin, hot and cold water, sink) installed and in good repair. In the process improved 'controlled' tenancies became 'regulated' tenancies and so qualified for 'fair' rents.[32]

Grants for improvement have been available since 1949, and now fall into two basic categories: 'discretionary' grants, paid by local authorities to owners improving their homes to a certain standard, and 'standard' grants, which could be claimed by right by owners who installed basic amenities. In General Improvement Areas, the 'discretionary' grant was to be used, and amounted to £1,000 for house improvement and £1,200 per flat where buildings of three or more storeys were converted.

After a rather slow start, grants were taken up in increasing volume and in particular by landlords seeking to qualify for 'fair rents' and property owners converting old houses into flats. Unfortunately the results was often not to the benefit of those in most need, especially in London, where pressure for housing has become so great that high profits can be derived from the modernisation of old dwellings; in the process low-income residents have frequently been forced to move out and have been replaced by others more able to pay the substantial rents which may be charged after such conversion. In addition, grants were used to improve property which was then sold for a grossly inflated figure – again this was most common in the London area. The scheme produced some notorious cases and it was generally believed to have afforded more benefit to the speculator than to those in need of adequate housing.

Town planning

The comprehensive system of planning controls introduced after the war basically remain, modified only to a limited extent by more recent legislation. Since that time planning permission has been required generally for the development and use of land and buildings even though a variety of minor developments are free of this control. In considering applications for planning permission, the local planning authorities often – and increasingly – seek to inform themselves about local opinion before reaching decisions. If permission is refused or granted subject to conditions, the applicant has a right of appeal to the Secretary of State at the Department of the Environment. Development without planning permission may lead to a court order to demolish, and if this is ignored, to a fine or imprisonment. In certain special circumstances compensation may be given where permission is refused, where a discontinuance order is made to cease existing use or where permission is revoked because of a change in circumstances. Also in special circumstances, an authority may be required to purchase property in respect of which permission is refused and for which there is no other 'beneficial' use.

Until 1968, planning authorities were required to produce development plans for their areas in which existing and permitted land uses were shown. For example, undeveloped land might be shown as agricultural land, land on which only residential development would be permitted or land on which industrial development was possible. After approval by the Minister this became a legal document, and any substantial departures from it had to be referred back to the Minister. Revisions to the plan were required at at least five-year intervals.

An inherent lack of flexibility, however, led to criticism and in the Town and Country Planning Act, 1968, development plans were replaced by a new plan system comprising structure plans and local plans. The structure plan is largely a statement of policy and takes into account a wide range of social and economic factors relevant to an area's future together with the resources required and available for implementation. More detail is provided by the local plan, which is usually the responsibility of the local planning authority alone, while the structure plan must be approved by the Secretary of State. These changes were accompanied by a move towards greater public participation in the planning process. The increasing impact of planning proposals upon the public, for example, in the siting of motorways, the expansion of airports or the construction of oil terminals, has highlighted a corresponding interest and concern on their part.

The Skeffington Report *People and Planning*,[33] published in 1969, considered ways in which public participation in the planning process might be facilitated and encouraged. It suggested that there should be early involvement with the public – at the time when plans were were being formulated – and that, later, alternative proposals should be provided for comment and discussion, together with information which would enable a reasoned assessment of their benefits and disadvantages to be made. The problem of how to involve those who, though concerned, lack confidence in their power to influence authority and the danger that vocal and articulate minority pressure groups will gain the greatest attention, worried the committee. They suggested that Community Development Officers should be appointed by local authorities, whose responsibility would be to work with those people whose voices are rarely heard at public meetings and stimulate discussion among them. Community forums could be set up in which discussions would take place and information be provided. There has been more difficulty in convincing both planners and public of the benefits of participation than was appreciated by the Committee, and the delay in completing and implementing plans when advantage is fully taken of the opportunities for participation can be considerable and so lead to increased costs. Even so the principle of participation has been accepted and a required minimum effort is now part of the plan-making procedure – even though this is more superficial than the report suggested ought to be the case.

Over the last few years increasing attention has been paid to regional planning policy and the need for long-term strategies which will take into account all aspects affecting the growth and prosperity of the area and will provide a framework for structure plans. A series of regional studies began in the South-east and continued in the West Midlands, East Anglia, the North-west and the North.[34] The later strategic plans in particular have examined and assessed economic and social prospects and resources as well as those matters more traditionally associated with 'planning'. Arising from these studies and given additional impetus by the Kilbrandon Report[35] is a growing belief that regions should be given a more direct responsibility

143

for budgeting decisions at present taken by central government and often appearing to emphasise national at the expense of local requirements and sectional rather than interdepartmental interests. The *Strategic Plan for the North-west* called for an independent regional fund to be administered by some form of regional authority which would also be concerned with up-dating strategies and implementing regional policies, a recommendation in line with that of the Kilbrandon Commission for greater devolution of government.

Superimposed on these trends is the reorganisation of local government in England and Wales in 1974. Reorganisation has split the planning function between districts and counties as well as creating two kinds of county area – metropolitan and shire. Equally significantly reorganisation has been accompanied by considerable heart-searching about the way local authorities operate and has led to the widespread introduction of a diversity of methods of 'corporate planning' and 'corporate management' – the aim being to integrate the individual services offered by an authority in pursuit of common objectives.

The planner's task has thus steadily broadened in scope since the early post-war years; his role has become diversified and a whole range of new basic disciplines have been drawn into the practice of planning.[36] Town Planning, which grew out of a concern for health, housing and sanitation in the late nineteenth century and became a land-use regulating device in the mid-twentieth century, now appears to be increasingly concerned with the total spread of community action. Yet wherever it is practised meaningfully it is still primarily concerned with people and how to discern and meet their needs.

Rent control and security of tenure

Security of tenure is closely associated with rent regulation, particularly at times of decontrol or permitted increases, and the two are therefore considered here together. Some form of security has been given to tenants since the war, though with greater effect for those in unfurnished than in furnished accommodation; much furnished accommodation consists of a single room in a house occupied by the owner who, it may be argued, should have the right to decide whether he should share his home or not.

In post-war years, the cycle of rent control and decontrol continued as governments changed although some form of regulation, at least for the lowest rented houses, has always remained. 1957 brought decontrol for all houses above a very low rateable value, though even here small increases were allowed where repairs had been carried out. It was hoped that decontrol would encourage more people to let their property and also induce a redistribution of tenants, in particular persuading those in under-occupied property to move into smaller accommodation – in the event, neither aim was achieved to any significant extent.[37]

The 1965 Rent Act gave security of tenure to all but those in the most expensive accommodation; such 'protected' tenancies could be those controlled under previous legislation or 'regulated' tenancies. 'Regulated' tenancies are generally private lettings of unfurnished dwellings whose rateable value currently falls below £1,500 in Greater London and £750 elsewhere. Landlords may apply to a Rent Officer to determine a fair rent for their tenancy and can then obtain a 'certificate of fair rent'. Tenants may make a similar application if no agreement can be reached with the landlord. Appeals against the rent officer's decision can be taken to a Rent Assessment Committee and further appeal to the High Court is possible. The fair rent is then registered and may not be reviewed in less than three years unless changes in the tenancy occur, for example, in the services provided or in the state of repair.

'Controlled' tenancies are those controlled under legislation prior to 1965 – mainly small dwellings with very low rents. They may become 'regulated' if the local authority certifies that the dwelling reaches a certain standard of repair, with all basic amenities. The 1972 Housing Finance Act provided for the transfer of groups of controlled tenancies every six months, according to their rateable value, or if the tenancy passed to a member of the family who is a 'second successor' – that is following a previous member who has obtained the tenancy on the death of the original tenant.

In both 'regulated' and 'controlled' tenancies, protection is given to the tenant and a court order is required in order to evict, which may be allowed only for special reasons such as that the tenant refuses to leave at the end of a letting or after being given notice for non-payment of rent, or that the landlord wishes to re-occupy the dwelling.

Furnished accommodation provided by a private landlord is not subject to rent control. However, in those properties where the rateable value falls below the same amount as that of 'regulated' tenancies, the landlord or tenant may request the local Rent Tribunal to determine a fair rent. Security of tenure is then awarded for a renewable period of six months in order to protect the tenant whose application for an assessed rent has succeeded. An application for increased rent after the determination has been made will only be allowed when conditions of the tenancy have changed. The Rent Act of 1974 brought many residential furnished tenancies into the full protection of the 1965 Rent Act. Where the landlord does not live on the premises, these become 'protected tenancies' under the same terms as unfurnished accommodation.

Under the 1972 Housing Finance Act, the concept of 'fair rents' was extended to local authority dwellings. Rents were assessed on the basis of age, size, condition and area as the amount which would be paid on the open market or, alternatively, the amount needed to pay off the cost of building and maintenance. In the majority of cases this resulted in a considerably higher rent, for the policy of most authorities was to subsidise, in effect, newer houses through the rents obtained on the older housing stock. Although higher rents were normally asked for newer dwellings, these were rarely 'economic rents', the difference being made up in part by rate support and in part through the rents of older houses which had already had their cost covered. Both means of reducing council rents were to be removed by the 1972 Act. Many authorities protested at having to impose the increases while a few, among which the best known was Clay Cross Urban District Council, refused to do so. The refusal by this council resulted in the appointment of a housing commissioner to operate the scheme, and a surcharge imposed by the district auditor on the recalcitrant members of the difference (£7,000) between the rent paid and the rent which should have been paid.

A right to appeal against the 'fair rent' was available to the council tenant through a new body, the Rent Scrutiny Board – whose word was final. The increases were to be spread over a number of years, the first increase of £1 a week being made in two steps between 1972 and 1973, the second of 50p. a week between 1973 and 1974. Further increases of 50p. a week were to be made in the following years until the 'fair rent' level was reached. In the event, only the first increase was put into effect, for a new government in 1974 prevented any further rise by freezing all rents, and made preparations to repeal the 1972 Act.

The 1972 Housing Finance Act aimed to support those in greatest need through new rebates, while ensuring that those able to afford an economic rent should pay. Such a policy can only be effective, however, where rebates are taken up by all entitled to them and extend over a wide enough range of tenant incomes – such evidence as is available suggests that neither condition has been satisfied, in the past at least. The 1972 rent rebates for council tenants were standardised rather than left to the discretion of the local authority, and assessed by a formula which took into account the gross income of the tenant and the number of dependants. An entirely new departure was that an equivalent rent allowance could be claimed by private tenants paying a 'fair rent'. A substantial part of both rebates and allowances was contributed by the government, the rest from rates. Further support to the low-income householder, whether owner-occupier or tenant, was given in the Act by an extended rate rebate scheme.[38] Inflation and the costs involved in local government reorganisation led to greatly increased rates in 1974, in some areas by more than twice the 1973 figure, and a rebate to all those paying more than 20 per cent above the 1973 rate was provided that year.

One further aspect of security of tenure is the prevention of harassment by landlords attempting to obtain vacant possession. In 1965 the Milner Holland Committee[39] commented on this and as a result stronger penalties were imposed. Nevertheless, the practice continued and in some areas such as London appeared to increase. Substantially greater penalties for harassment and unlawful eviction were to be introduced in a new Bill, but this was lost in the dissolution of Parliament in February 1974.

Housing subsidies

No direct subsidies for private building have been given since the war, although the option mortgage scheme is a form of subsidy to the owner-occupier, and plays a particularly important part in co-ownership schemes developed by housing associations.[40]

Subsidies for council houses have followed a similar course to rent control: curtailment following increase, and followed by restoration. One aim of the 1972 Housing Finance Act was to place the financing of council houses on a more stable footing. It was expected that 'fair rents' would provide increased revenue to the authorities and the Act therefore allowed for a withdrawal of subsidies over the following four or five years. Instead the government was to pay 75 per cent of any deficit incurred by the local authorities on house building and slum clearance up to a certain cost, while at the same time, if rent income provided a surplus, this would pass to the government. During the year following the Act, many local authorities had great difficulty in keeping within the cost limit for subsidies, because of the rise in the price of materials and labour. With a change of government it seems probable that the withdrawal of subsidies will not occur.

Housing associations which build dwellings in co-operation with local authorities may be given the appropriate subsidies if the authority is willing but there is no obligation to do so. The withdrawal of subsidies under the 1972 Act therefore placed the associations who had relied on them in a difficult position, particularly in conjunction with the rent freeze introduced by the new government in 1974.

Social trends

While on the wholly physical side the aim of adequate accommodation for all is in principle a relatively simple objective which may even be ultimately achieved, associated social needs are often more complex and certainly less constant. A new house, whether moved

147

into from choice or from necessity, requires a readjustment to a new social situation by its occupants. Where choice has been exercised, there is likely to be a greater readinesss to accept new standards – some would say to conform – than where the decision has come from some anonymous authority. Where there has been a move, for example, from the inner city slum to a peripheral housing estate, the new environment will be strange in many ways and the adjustment may be painful – a familiar street full of variety is lost to a suburban landscape peopled with strangers.

Since the Second World War, many thousands have undergone this experience as new housing estates and New Towns have been constructed. Planners and housing authorities, although aware of the problems entailed, have tended in the past either to see them as beyond their responsibility or as requiring facilities which were not available. However, a gradual move towards acceptance of the need for social planning to accompany physical planning does appear to be taking place and may be observed in the history of the post-war estates and New Towns which follows.

Housing estates

Land shortage resulting in high prices for building plots has ensured that the bulk of new residential development whether private or public, takes the form of estates. During the 1950s and most of the 1960s, when pressure was at its greatest, massive council estates were rapidly constructed, many on the periphery of the cities from which the 'overspill' was to come. The motto often appeared to be 'any housing is better than no housing' and with depressing frequency the all too well documented errors of pre-war days were repeated: a lack of facilities, especially shops, long journeys to work by poorly serviced public transport and no entertainment to keep the children occupied. These and other complaints, including higher rents than had previously been paid, reflected especially the increased cost of a move to the new areas which largely nullified the benefits obtained. The series of community studies by sociologists, especially those of the Institute of Community Studies in Bethnal Green,[41] built up a stereotype of the council estate as a dreary, lonely place where people 'kept themselves to themselves' and where there was a general nostalgia for the warmth and life of the city. Perhaps it was unfortunate that, among many problems, these studies ensured that the loss of close community life, however important, made most impact, so that the search for a formula which might recreate a situation basically arising as a protective device against poverty and deprivation, obsessed the planners to the exclusion of those other factors which might have been more readily corrected.

148

A general characteristic of council estates is the homogeneity of their age and household structure. Especially where an estate population is largely drawn from the housing list, intake families tend to be young, larger than average and with children of school age or less. Such households tend to be most vulnerable in the housing situation, especially where the father is unskilled and in casual labour, and receive priority under the points system of allocation (see p. 137). When rapid development has taken place, the population tends to fall within narrow age limits, the birth rate is initially high and a third or more will be less than fifteen years old. Such a structure brings both short- and long-term problems. In the short-term, many places are required in schools, as well as clinics for infants and ante-natal care. Later the schools may well have places to spare, while there is a great need for youth employment and training facilities for school-leavers. As time goes on, houses become under-occupied as children leave home.

Estates on which some residents have obtained houses through redevelopment or exchange tend to have a broader age spread including a far higher proportion of elderly, as do those which have grown more steadily. The New Towns Committee, with such problems in mind, recommended that there should be gradual development after the initial stage so as to minimise population imbalance.

In 1967, a sub-committee of the Central Housing Advisory Committee[42] suggested that there should be increased government control over housing development, commenting that to build houses without ancillary facilities would 'result in the unnecessary creation of social problems'. It suggested that where families have been moved away from areas in which they have been established for many years, welfare services should give more support, and that more accommodation should be found for the elderly so that families might be reunited and a more balanced population develop. When large-scale development took place a social development plan should be prepared to co-ordinate the provision of facilities and officers appointed to give information and help to new arrivals. Although not universally put into practice, a growing number of authorities have now adopted many of these recommendations.

A problem also mentioned by the sub-committee which has caused and continues to cause discussion is the housing of young families in high-rise flats. Introduced in the 1950s in the belief that industrialised building would be economical and speedy, little advantage has been gained by their construction in the long run. Neither economical nor speedy, for work was often delayed in a wait for components, they were from the start highly unpopular with their occupants.[43] Clearly inappropriate for young children and for the elderly also except where special arrangements are made, badly insulated against noise and isolating their residents from life at street level, they often appeared to symbolise the inability of architects, planners and housing authorities to recognise the needs of ordinary families. Controversy on all sides culminated in official discouragement in the 1967 Housing Act, when the extra subsidy for buildings more than six storeys high introduced in 1956[44] was withdrawn. Perhaps the final blow was the partial collapse of systems-built flats at Ronan Point in 1968. Few authorities will now place young families in high blocks and the majority have now ceased to build this type of flat.

New Towns

Post-war New Towns were seen by politicians and planners to provide an opportunity to put into concrete terms aims and ideals which had developed over many years. Their early prototypes were the Garden Cities of Letchworth and Welwyn, established at the start of the century: these were a product of deeply felt anti-urbanism which originated at the time of massive industrialisation and the rapid expansion of towns with the accompanying dirt, squalor and disease. Largely the inspiration of Ebenezer Howard, and incorporating the idea of Robert Owen's industrial villages, the Garden Cities aimed to combine the advantages of urban and rural living, the first in their provision for industry and other sources of employment and the second in their generous allotment of open space: the objective, 'a Town designed for healthy living'. Their success, which was financial as well as social, encouraged those who, forty years later, believed that New Towns would help to contain expanding urban areas so that access to the countryside would remain within reach of their residents and at the same time provide enough accommodation to reduce the pressure on the cities. This was the practical aspect, but other aims spelled out by the Reith Committee[45] in its guidelines for New Towns reflect the spirit of the time – the widespread desire to maintain the co-operation and comradeship of wartime years. The towns were to be 'self-contained and balanced communities for work and living' and 'of diverse and balanced social composition', 'locating skilfully the sites for houses of all classes in the various neighbourhoods'. Although 'balance' was not defined it has been generally taken to mean that the age and occupational structure should reflect that of the country as a whole and it was considered of the utmost importance that there should be no resemblance to the one-class towns which had grown out of large-scale council estates before the war.[46]

To achieve self-containment, industries which can provide a wide range of occupations must be encouraged to move to the New Towns. The Development Corporations which manage New Towns[47] at least

150

until they are established, allocate most of their houses to those who have obtained local employment. In doing so, the achievement of 'balance' is prejudiced, for New Town industries rely largely on skilled workers and provide relatively few openings for the unskilled. For this reason New Towns do little to alleviate the urgent housing problems of the big cities – rather perhaps increasing the pressures which result in the concentration of low-income and immigrant families in the inner areas.

Again, within the New Towns 'social mix' was an elusive target. The early 'Mark I' towns such as Crawley and Harlow used neighbourhood units to encourage the development of a community spirit. Each contained a population of 5,000 to 12,000, its own primary schools and local shops and a variety of housing which would hopefully produce a cross-section of income and social groups equivalent to that of the town as a whole. This imposed interaction, though well-meaning, achieved little success and neighbourhood units were criticised as prejudicing the development of the town as a unit. Mark II New Towns such as Cumbernauld and Skelmersdale were built at higher densities and concentrated facilities in central areas but were unpopular with residents and suffered from traffic congestion. More recent New Towns are built on a linear principle while densities have once more been reduced. The majority also take the form of 'expanded towns', where an already established area provides a base on to which New Town development is grafted: an arrangement which can pose problems of integration,[48] but overcomes some of the initial difficulties resulting from a lack of facilities.

An increasing proportion of New Town houses, rising to 50 per cent, are for sale; often such houses are situated on the periphery and invariably they are segregated. Professional workers, though mainly employees rather than self-employed, have been attracted to the New Towns especially in the South-east, but there is an increasing tendency for higher-income households to move outside and commute. 'Self-containment' is breaking down, as once a house has been let or sold it cannot be forfeited if the householder goes to work elsewhere. Current thinking favours a more regional approach to new development with controlled expansion of existing areas.[49] Nevertheless, the achievements of New Towns should not be underestimated, not least the opportunity they have given for architectural innovation and the development of new ideas in transportation systems.

The homeless, coloured immigrants and gypsies

From the standpoint of certain sections of the population, estate and New Town residents must be seen as greatly advantaged, for whatever their difficulties they are no longer in need of adequate housing.

151

While recognising that an unshared and structurally sound house or flat is not necessarily sufficient in itself to satisfy every requirement for an adequate environment, the aim must be to secure at least this minimum for the many whose housing needs are basic. Three such groups whose problems appear to grow rather than diminish are the homeless, coloured immigrants and gypsies or travellers.

The homeless

'Homeless' tends to be defined according to the interests of those making the definition. Central and local government explain their preference for restricting this term to those who are literally without a roof over their head, as a need to concentrate on the most pressing cases. Some voluntary organisations, on the other hand, include all those living in unsatisfactory conditions, so producing massive figures whose impact may set in motion some new form of alleviation. For example, official figures for 1971 were 26,900 while Shelter, two years previously, estimated over 1 million.[50]

Official counts of the homeless include only parents and children in local authority temporary accommodation, but even in this limited sense, numbers have been rising steadily. Between 1960 and 1968 they almost doubled, while between 1968 and 1972 they increased by more than one half. Variation in the size of the problem over the country is considerable, but London stands out as being in by far the worst position: applications for temporary accommodation there forming 43 per cent of the national total in 1972,[51] a product largely of the increasing number of people moving into this area. The dwindling amount of low-priced rented accommodation in the face of this pressure particularly affects large young families on uncertain incomes and such is the problem of housing in London that middle-class households are now competing for the same accommodation.

Two recent studies of homelessness, the first in London and the second in South Wales and South-west England,[52] show that although the pressure is greatest in the London area, the type of household affected and the basic factors that lead to homelessness are much the same in both areas, as are the gaps in provision and support for those affected. As a response to these and other reports the government recommended a number of new measures in early 1974.[53] The most important of these was the implementation of a recommendation made in the Seebohm Report that housing authorities should have the practical responsibility for providing accommodation for the homeless rather than the social services, who should be concerned with preventive measures and support to those with problems which contribute to homelessness. Co-operation between the two departments was urged and also with those voluntary organisations which have a special interest in the homeless. Local authorities were asked to take into account in their building programmes the special needs of small households and single people, considering the use of self-contained flats or bed-sitting rooms as well as hostels.

Until the 1960s most of the homeless families applying to the local authority for help were placed in hostels where they lived communally. There is no legal obligation for local authorities to provide housing for the homeless – only temporary accommodation for 'persons who are in urgent need thereof'. Dismal conditions, which often included the separation of wives from husbands and children from mothers, were expected to encourage those accommodated to move on quickly, and a time limit operated. Publicity in the mid-1960s from a number of directions, including the television play *Cathy Come Home*, led to some improvement and to an increasing extent hostels are being replaced by 'family units' in which the whole family is kept together. These are sometimes in sub-standard council housing due for eventual improvement or demolition or sometimes in converted larger old property.

During the early and mid-1960s the increasing need for help to the homeless resulted in the formation of a number of voluntary organisations as well as intensified efforts on the part of already established housing associations. Among the new organisations was the Simon Community, the Notting Hill Housing Trust and the fund-raising body Shelter.[54] Voluntary associations tend to specialise in the needs of particular groups and have become increasingly involved in the improvement and conversion of old houses as a relatively low cost and speedy method of providing accommodation. Some also provide an advisory service and the recently formed S H A C (Shelter Housing Aid Centre) also helps those wishing to buy their own houses. The ability of these organisations to deal with problems unhampered by the restraints experienced by local authorities is their strength. For example, local authorities have difficulty in giving direct help to battered wives, who may not be considered 'homeless' in any rigorous sense, but who now have a few houses provided by Women's Aid, grant-aided by the Greater London Council. The 1974 circular 'Homelessness', urged local authorities to work closely with the voluntary housing movement and to be ready to make loans or grants to help them.

One further activity which gained impetus during the mid- and late-1960s was squatting.[55] Begun as a protest movement against the restrictive rules in local authority hostels, it developed into an action group placing homeless families in empty houses and using the law against forcible entry to prevent re-occupation. It has had some success in gaining the co-operation of a few London authorities who allow squatting families to stay until demolition. The Family

153

Squatting Advisory Service is now allocated short-life empty houses for homeless families by the Greater London Council, and a number of other councils.

Coloured immigrants

Where pressures are severe, groups which pose particular difficulties or who may appear to increase already critical problems will inevitably arouse hostility and sometimes conflict. The housing situation is one of shortage and high prices and many see the coloured immigrant as at least an exacerbating factor, even a cause. Immigrants certainly compete for low-cost rented accommodation, for many arrive with little money and unlikely to find any but the lowest-paid jobs available. Without residential qualifications they are not eligible for council housing and they tend to move to areas where shortages are greatest because these are the places where there are most opportunities for work.

The coloured immigrant, whose misfortune is that he is recognisable, in addition faces positive discrimination in the search. Given the money to consider buying a house, building societies are generally unwilling to advance mortgages and estate agents will ensure that the houses made available to them are in 'suitable' areas. Houses bought by immigrants tend, therefore, to be those in areas of decay and twilight zones, where poor structural conditions combined with short leases reduce the price, usually met by a short-term loan with a high interest rate. Many large old houses in 'zones of transition'[56] pass to immigrants in this way, their rooms let out to cover the cost and provide an income. In London, such houses tend to be in the inner 'stress' areas, centres of multiple deprivation which have a particularly adverse effect on any children.[57] Inevitably ethnic groups concentrate in such areas in all the big cities, coming together in part for mutual support but also because of the combination of pressures through which all but a privileged few are barred from the normal dispersion process which is a stage in the assimilation of the immigrant.

The housing management sub-committee in 1969[58] commented on the low proportion of council tenants who are coloured immigrants, although authorities strongly deny discrimination. Nevertheless, certain of the rules used to decide eligibility for a council house operate against the coloured immigrant, especially residential qualifications, while cultural factors which produce unconventional family patterns and fear or ignorance in approaching authority also operate against them. Dismissing positive discrimination and compulsory dispersal, the sub-committee urged that reliable records of their residential coloured population should be kept by local authorities so that where they have not received treatment on a par with white residents remedial action can be taken. Their limited recommendations reflect the difficulties of a situation which has little if at all improved.

In 1971, Fair Housing Groups were set up in Manchester, Nottingham and Sheffield to identify the needs of minorities such as coloured immigrants and to see how they could be met.[59] In each of the areas, records of immigrants housed and on the waiting list were not available in spite of the importance, as they also saw it, of such information. Their recommendation was that local councils for community relations should interest themselves more closely with the housing situation of coloured immigrants which remains an area in which a great deal of additional help is required.

Travellers and gypsies

Almost alone in being unaffected by the shortage and cost of housing, accommodation problems have increased for this group as for others. Although the Caravan Sites Act of 1968 appeared to be to their advantage, for it required local authorities to provide 'adequate accommodation for gypsies residing in or resorting to their area', provision was made for exemption from this obligation for a variety of reasons and full advantage of this has been taken by many authorities. Exemption can be granted in cases of land shortage, and no more than fifteen caravans need be accommodated. Since 1972 loans have been available for the purpose of providing sites but even so, only 94 local authority sites were available at the end of 1973 in England and 6 in Wales, of which 19 were temporary. It appears likely that in spite of official discouragement the travelling population in this country will increase, in part because of continuing immigration from Ireland and in part because they will inevitably receive new recruits from the homeless population.

Current developments

Against the background of legislation problems of many kinds remain to be solved. Rising environmental standards are expected, if not always obtained, by the majority of the population and there is continuing pressure on planners, builders and architects to make improvements, while as they do so their efforts are increasingly subject to examination. Today when changes are to be made which will affect people's environment they will expect to have some say in the final decisions. The Skeffington Report reflected this growing demand for participation and suggested ways in which it could be met. Perhaps most advantage has been taken in areas where improvement can be a substitute for redevelopment and residents have been able to make their views known on the changes they wish to see. One example of this was in an inner Liverpool area where Shelter, with the co-operation of Liverpool Corporation, helped residents to design an improvement scheme.[60] A more recent similar exercise was in the Kensington area of London, conducted by the Greater London Council with the help of a housing association.[61] These projects suggest that while full participation by the public on large-scale decisions is problematic, on a small scale it is feasible and advantageous to planners as well as residents.

Nevertheless, circumstances arise in which a proposal may be highly unpopular with the great majority of residents in an area but must still be imposed for the benefit of a greater number of others. This is, of course, the argument used to support those large environment-destroying undertakings such as motorways and in this context may legitimately be contested where alternatives are available. More problematic are difficulties such as those faced by Inner London councils who wish to build estates in the outer areas to rehouse some of their population in desperate need of accommodation, but are blocked by residents fearing for their amenities. In such cases, who participates in the final decision?[62]

London's housing problems certainly appear of a different order from those in the rest of the country. Differential house prices have previously been mentioned and the loss of a great deal of cheaper rented accommodation through replacement by luxury flats and offices. Since the protection of furnished accommodation under the 1974 Act, this also has become in shorter supply. 'Stress' areas have been defined by the Greater London Council where overcrowding, high rents, high density, harassment and illegal evictions are at their worst. Recommendations have been made that Greater London Council powers should be strengthened, an overall approach should be made to include population redistribution, renewal and planned overspill and the council itself considers that a strategic housing authority might be the most effective agency to implement such changes.[63]

The problems experienced by London occur in all other cities though on a less gigantic scale. The urban situation gains attention, for this is the environment in which more than 85 per cent of the population lives today. Nevertheless, parallel situations arise in rural areas, perhaps with even less chance of remedy because less publicised and so unlikely to arouse interest in reform. Here, as in the cities, the stock of rented accommodation is well below the requirement and much is in the form of tied cottages, generally accepted as an inappropriate and inadequate form of accommodation today, providing as they do so little protection to the tenant. The price for which country cottages can be sold to the urban emigrant is proportionately even higher than for town properties, taking into account size and structural standards, but life in the countryside is the goal for many city dwellers and they are ready to pay for their dreams. Some move out and commute, others wait until retirement. A growing number buy a second home for weekends and holidays. Villages expand as new development is increasingly permitted while older properties are transformed into homes with urban amenities.

Too often urban migrants form segregated communities which contribute little to the area in which they live. The town remains the provider of employment, entertainment and shopping facilities – even the local school will often be rejected.[64] Weekenders will bring all they need for their short visits and their empty houses during the week cause added resentment: many appear to have little understanding of the countryside and its ways. The younger villagers must often move into the towns to find accommodation they can afford, while a minimum of local employment, except to builders, is provided by the newcomers.

So far little has been done to redress the balance which is so much to the advantage of the urbanite, but in a report from Denbighshire[65] it is suggested that the stock of agricultural cottages is so low that pressure is bound to grow. A possible answer is the expansion of schemes such as that on the Lleyn Peninsula where a housing association has bought houses to let at low rents to locals. Another possibility is that holiday villages should be built on poor agricultural land. The removal of tax allowances on mortgages for second houses in the 1974 budget may have some impact, while local government reorganisation will bring many rural areas with a high proportion of commuters under the same authority as near-by towns and cities. A greater contribution to the rates required from rural residents, while causing much resentment from those – mostly urban migrants – in high-rated property, should be to the advantage of both communities, for the town provides roads for the commuters while the village needs money if it is to give help to its locals.

One important aim of local government reorganisation is to encourage increased co-ordination and co-operation both internally between departments and externally where conflicting requirements arise. Too little time has passed for any judgement to be possible, but it will be on the success of reconciling such areas of disagreement as those between ex-urbs and locals that the final judgement will be made.

Further reading

The chapter on housing (chapter 15) in W. E. Baugh, *Introduction to the Social Services*, Macmillan, 1973, gives a general account of housing legislation up to the 1972 Housing Finance Act. More detail is given in H. Ashworth, *Housing in Great Britain*, Skinner, 1957, as well as information on housing finance and town and country planning.

Planning in its widest sense is examined in J. B. Cullingworth, *Problems of an Urban Society*, Allen & Unwin, 1972, in which volume 2, 'The social content of planning', is most useful for the housing aspect. Other accounts which discuss housing policy are provided in J. B. Cullingworth, *Housing and Local Government*, Allen & Unwin, 1966, and D. V. Donnison, *Housing Policy since the War*, Occasional Papers in Social Administration, no. 1, Codicote Press, 1960. A popular style commentary on housing problems is S. Alderson, *Housing*, Penguin, 1962.

On the financial aspect, useful books are L. Needleman, *The Economics of Housing*, Staples Press, 1965, and Adela A. Nevitt, *Housing Taxation and Subsidies*, Nelson, 1966. On the development of town and country planning in this country, the most recent is G. E. Cherry, *The Evolution of British Town Planning*, Hill, 1974, while W. Ashworth, *The Genesis of Modern British Town Planning*, Routledge & Kegan Paul, 1951, remains worthwhile reading.

Many community studies of the transition from inner city to suburban council housing estates were written in the 1950s and early 1960s. The best known, M. Young and P. Wilmott, *Family and Kinship in East London*, Routledge & Kegan Paul, 1957, should still be read, though not uncritically; and from a different standpoint, H. Jennings, *Societies in the Making*, Routledge & Kegan Paul, 1962. Two books which trace the movement of residents from inner Liverpool to a housing estate outside the city boundary are C. Vereker *et al.*, *Urban Re-development and Social Change*, Liverpool University Press, 1961, and K. Pickett and D. Boulton, *Migration and Social Adjustment*, Liverpool University Press, 1974. The latter includes an account of a privately owned suburban estate.

On the problems of commuter villages: R. E. Pahl, *Whose City?*, Longmans, 1970.

On London's housing problems: D. Donnison and D. Eversley, eds, *London: Urban Patterns, Problems and Policies*, Heinemann, 1973.

On New Towns: F. Schaffer, *The New Town Story*, Macgibbon & Kee, 1970.

On living in high flats: P. Jephcott, *Homes in High Flats*, Oliver & Boyd, 1971, and E. Gittus, *Flats, Families and the Under-5s*, Routledge & Kegan Paul, forthcoming.

On homelessness: J. Grieve, D. Page and S. Grove, *Homelessness in London*, Scottish Academic Press, 1971, and B. Glastonbury, *Homeless near a Thousand Homes*, Allen & Unwin, 1971.

Statistics of house construction, slum clearance, housing loans and associated information are provided for England and Wales by the Department of the Environment in *Housing Statistics*, and for local authorities in *Local Housing Statistics*, both quarterly. A guide to housing data will be available in the Social Science Research Council publication S. Farthing, *Housing in Great Britain*, vol. VIII of W. F. Maunder, ed., *Reviews of United Kingdom Statistical Sources*, Heinemann.

Statistics of housing from a number of government sources, with a commentary, are published annually by the Central Statistical Office in *Social Trends*.

Notes

1 R. Lawton, 'An age of great cities', *Town Planning Review*, 43, 1972, pp. 199–224.
2 O. Hill, *Homes of the London Poor*, Macmillan, 1875.
3 *Royal Commission on the State of Large Towns and Populous Districts: First Report*, HMSO, 1844; *Second Report*, HMSO, 1845.
4 The Public Health Act, 1848.
5 By the Labouring Classes Lodging Houses Act, 1851.
6 In the Housing, etc., Act, 1923 (Chamberlain Act).
7 Housing (Financial Provisions) Act, 1924.
8 T. Young, *Becontree and Dagenham*, Becontree Social Survey Committee, 1934.
9 R. Durant, *Watling: A Study of Social Life on a New Housing Estate*, London, King, 1939.
10 In the Housing Act, 1935.
11 *Report of the Royal Commission on the Distribution of the Industrial Population* (Barlow Report), Cmd 6153, HMSO, 1940.
   Report of the Commission on Land Utilisation in Rural Areas (Scott Report), Cmd 6378. HMSO, 1942.
   Report of the Expert Committee on Compensation and Betterment (Uthwatt Report, Cmd 6383, HMSO, 1942.
12 Under the Housing (Financial Provisions) Act, 1958.
13 A simple guide to the scheme is *Your Guide to the Option Mortgage Scheme*, HMSO, 1967.
14 *Widening the Choice: The Next Step in Housing*, Cmnd 5280, HMSO, 1973.
15 Ministry of Housing and Local Government, *Council Housing Purposes, Procedures and Priorities*, Ninth Report of the Housing Management Sub-Committee of the Central Housing Advisory Committee, HMSO, 1969.
16 See, for example, Department of Social Science, 'A Norris Green study', *Journal of the British Association of Social Workers*, July 1971.
17 For example, Kirkby, near Liverpool; see K. G. Pickett and D. Boulton, *Migration and Social Adjustment*, Liverpool University Press, 1974.
18 See *Council Housing Purposes, Procedures and Priorities, op. cit.*, p. 15.

19 *Report of the Committee on Local Authority and Allied Personal Services* (Seebohm Report), Cmnd 3703, HMSO, 1968.
20 R. N. Morris and J. Mogey, *The Sociology of Housing*, Routledge & Kegan Paul, 1965.
21 See O. Gill, 'Housing policy and neighbourhood decline', *Social Work Today*, vol. 5, no. 18, 12 December 1974.
22 See *Council Housing Purposes, Procedures and Priorities*, *op. cit.*
23 *Widening the Choice: the Next Step in Housing*, *op. cit.*
24 A useful account is given in Department of the Environment, *Housing Associations*, HMSO, 1971. A working paper of the Central Housing Advisory Committee.
25 The Parker Morris recommendations are published in a report of the Central Housing Advisory Committee, *Homes for Today and Tomorrow*, HMSO, 1961.
26 A comprehensive account of slum clearance legislation is provided in J. English and P. Norman, *One Hundred Years of Slum Clearance in England and Wales – Policies and Programmes 1868 to 1970*, University of Glasgow Press, 1974.
27 M. Woolf, *The Housing Survey in England and Wales, 1964*, Government Social Survey, HMSO, 1967.
28 *Face the Facts*, A Shelter Report, 1969.
29 Gillian R. Vale, *Is the Housing Problem Solved?*, Housing Centre Trust, 1971.
30 Ministry of Housing and Local Government, *Our Older Homes: A Call for Action* (Dennington Report) and *Old Houses into New Homes*, Cmnd 3602, HMSO, 1968.
31 Ministry of Housing and Local Government, *The Deeplish Study*, HMSO, 1966.
32 The definition of these terms is given under the section entitled 'Rent control and security of tenure'.
33 Ministry of Housing and Local Government, *People and Planning, Report of the Committee on Public Participation in Planning* (Skeffington Report), HMSO, 1969.
34 South-east Joint Planning Team, *Strategic Plan for the South-east*, HMSO, 1971; SPNW Joint Planning Team, *Strategic Plan for the North-west*, HMSO, 1974.
35 *Royal Commission on the Constitution, 1969–73*, Cmnd 5460, HMSO, 1973.
36 D. Eversley, *The Planner in Society: the Changing Role of a Profession*, Faber, 1973.
37 A. Nevitt, *Housing, Taxation and Subsidies*, Nelson, 1966, argues that in fact decontrol of rents leads to a lower supply of rented accommodation because a better return can be obtained from the commercial sector.
38 Rate rebates had been available outside the National Assistance scheme since 1966.
39 *Report of the Committee on Housing in Greater London*, Cmnd 2605, HMSO, 1965.
40 See *Housing Associations*, *op. cit.*, pp. 63–4.

41 The best known is M. Young and P. Willmott, *Family and Kinship in East London*, Routledge & Kegan Paul, 1957.
42 Ministry of Housing and Local Government, *The Needs of New Communities*, HMSO, 1967.
43 See a comprehensive account of the difficulties imposed by such flats in E. Gittus, *Flats, Families and the Under-5s*, Routledge & Kegan Paul, forthcoming.
44 The Housing Subsidies Act, 1956.
45 *Interim Report of the New Towns Committee*, Cmd 6759; *Second Interim Report*, Cmd 6794; *Final Report*, Cmd 6876, all HMSO, 1946.
46 No doubt the committee had been influenced by *Becontree and Dagenham, op. cit.*
47 See *The Ownership and Management of Housing in the New Towns*, Report submitted to the Minister of Housing and Local Government by J. B. Cullingworth and V. A. Karn, HMSO, 1968.
48 See R. Berthoud and R. Jowell, *Creating a Community*, Social and Community Planning Research, 1973.
49 See W. Bor, *The Making of Cities*, Hill, 1972.
50 *Face the Facts, op. cit.*
51 *Homelessness*, Joint Circular from the Department of the Environment, the DHSS and the Welsh Office, HMSO, 1974.
52 J. Grieve, D. Page and S. Grove, *Homelessness in London*, Scottish Academic Press, 1971; B. Glastonbury, *Homeless Near a Thousand Homes*, Allen & Unwin, 1971.
53 *Homelessness, op. cit.*
54 An account of the formation of Shelter and its campaign is given in D. Wilson, *I know it was the Place's Fault*, Oliphants, 1970.
55 A history of this movement is given in R. Bailey, *The Squatters*, Penguin, 1973.
56 An account of a Birmingham zone of transition is given in J. Rex and R. Moore, *Race, Community and Conflict*, Oxford University Press, 1967.
57 See N. Deakin and C. Ungerson, 'Beyond the ghetto: the illusion of choice', in D. Donnison and D. Eversley, eds, *London: Urban Patterns, Problems and Policies*, Heinemann, 1973.
58 *Council Housing and Purposes, Procedures and Priorities, op. cit.*
59 J. Perry, *The Fair Housing Experiment*, PEP, 1973.
60 *Another Chance for Cities, Snap 69/72*, Liverpool Shelter Neighbourhood Action Project, 1972.
61 *The Swinbrook Case: Report of the Housing Committee to a Meeting of the Greater London Council on 6.3.73*, Greater London Council, 1973.
62 An interesting recent development is the sale of houses in private estates in outer London to inner authorities, because private buyers are not available.
63 Aspects of London's housing problems are discussed in *London: Urban Patterns, Problems and Policies, op. cit.*
64 See R. E. Pahl, *Whose City?*, Longmans, 1970.
65 *Second Homes in Denbighshire*, Tourism and Recreation Research Report 3, County Planning Office, Denbigh, 1972.

6 The health services
Olive Keidan

This chapter was revised during the period when the National Health Service Reorganisation Act was being implemented, and was completed within a few weeks of the appointed day. Since the changes in the service were concerned with the management and organisation of the service not the basic principles and institutions, and were evolutionary in nature, the structure of the chapter has been left largely as it was in the last edition, with descriptions of and comment on the changes based on the 1948–74 provisions. Any assessment of the new organisation at the time of writing is speculative and tentative. The student can follow informed criticism of the new organisation through journals.

The most widely known legislation relating to health is the National Health Service Act, 1946, recently revised by the National Health Service Reorganisation Act, 1973,[1] which laid a duty on the Minister of Health not only to provide medical, nursing and ancillary services care for everyone needing it, but to aim for improvement in the physical and mental health of the people.[2] The Act did not, however, attempt to define 'health'. The World Health Organisation suggested it is 'a state of complete physical, mental and social well-being and not merely the absence of disease or infirmity'. In such an ideal state chronic boredom would possibly be the greatest menace. This brief statement, however, links together the three major factors that are involved and interdependent in any consideration of what we mean by 'health' and the lines along which efforts must be made to promote improvement.

It has long been recognised that ill-health makes for inefficient social functioning and it is therefore costly to the community in general. The more complex and urbanised the society, the more necessary it becomes to take account of the effects of illness and to try to mitigate these effects by preventive measures and treatment.

Apart from the economic and social aspects of the health of the community, we have, as a nation, long expressed humanitarian concern for the sick and disabled; they have been respectable objects of charity for centuries. The early legislation relating to begging makes exception of the 'impotent' beggar,[3] and the boom in hospital building and endowment by philanthropists in the eighteenth and nineteenth centuries was an expression of this concern in the face of increasing and uncontrolled urban development.

When we consider what kind of personal health service provisions should be made we find many complicating factors. The acceptable standards of physical and mental fitness vary between one individual and another, and between one community and another. Individual expectations of health are affected by differences in the age group, the sub-culture, educational level and social class, and people tend to seek advice and help when their health is not conforming to their own expectations. The decision when and where to seek help is affected by factors other than disease, including emotional and social attitudes to sickness, doctors and hospitals.[4] The responsibility for the first step in diagnosis and treatment is left to the individual, and his action may depend more on his personality and social circumstances than on a rational decision. The value of health education has been acknowledged fitfully and some areas of practice such as health visiting have long had some responsibility in this. Its importance was given recognition in 1968 when the Health Education Council was established by the government.

The value of preventive services relating to personal health, such as child welfare provisions, and pre-symptomatic examinations, depends not only on the quality and comprehensiveness of the service provided but also on the active participation of the people for whom they are provided, and on a sensible use by them of these services. To provide a service may not be enough, it may also be necessary to provide instruction on the use of the service and in some instances to take the service to the people most in need, but who may through apathy or ignorance not avail themselves of its benefits.

It has been increasingly recognised that the benefit derived from medical treatment can be lost because of adverse social and economic conditions, such as poor housing, unsuitable employment, poor standards of nutrition and personal care, and apathy.[5] For the patients affected by sub-standard conditions some of the expenditure on medical care is wasted, unless there is improvement in their life situation. This depends to a large extent on services outside the health service.

The community's attitude to the health and sickness of the individual has undergone considerable changes over the centuries. Crisis situations such as the cholera outbreaks in the nineteenth century,[6]

163

and the alarm at the poor physique of so many of the volunteers for the Boer War, made the nation aware of the increasing interdependence of the people. The developments in social services in general, in preventive measures relating to health and in the way provision of medical treatment is made for the individual reflect the assumption of greater responsibility by the state.

Rising standards of living and demographic changes cause changes in the patterns of disease and demand for health care. The health services have to adjust to these, but as the social services tend to lag behind the community's needs they inevitably exhibit tensions. To understand the anomalies and uneven provisions of the services today we need to look to the past to see the needs they were provided to meet and the subsequent adjustments to later demands. A proper historical perspective is necessary; for example it is a mistake to think of the hospitals of the nineteenth century as treating the 'sick', they were for the care of the 'poor-sick'. There was an intimate relationship between poverty and sickness, a two-way cause and effect,[7] a relationship that has been rediscovered in the modern hospital.[8] Improvements in the care of the sick and in preventive measures are the result not only of technical and scientific developments, but also of the organisation of other social services, of changes in standards of living, in expectations of health and service, and the extension of professional training in many fields.

The main concern of this chapter is with the personal health services. However, these services have been dependent on the prior development of the environmental health services, which are discussed in the next section. New developments in environmental health, following the reorganisation of both local authorities and the health service, are also briefly mentioned.

Environmental services and public health

Reform of insanitary living and working conditions began mainly in the nineteenth century. The 1832 Poor Law Commission did not fail to notice the close connection between poverty and sickness. One of the problems facing sanitary reformers such as Edwin Chadwick[9] in those early days was in establishing actively interested local health authorities and effective central control. The General Board of Health set up in 1848 to try to effect these reforms lasted only ten years but the zeal of the reformers continued until the Local Government Board was established in 1871, having control over health and Poor Law provisions and creating stronger central and local administration. Occupational health was not within its province and is still outside the scope of the National Health Service.

The medical officer of health which each local authority had to employ, full- or part-time, after 1872 was a sanitarian concerned largely with environmental conditions, and it was not until the twentieth century that personal health provisions began to be included in his province.

The Ministry of Health, established in 1919, took over the work of the Local Government Board which included all aspects of public health provision, except for school health services and occupational health, and responsibilities relating to housing and the Poor Law. In 1929 the Local Government Act put the management of all public hospitals and environmental health services under one local authority health department, which also had duties under Factory Acts, relating to the hygiene and sanitary provisions within work premises; under the Food and Drugs Act, relating to sampling and inspection; under the Housing Acts, and under the Port sanitary regulations, involving such work as de-ratting ships. By the beginning of the Second World War the public health duties of the local authorities were very wide, although there was a 'pronounced tendency for Medical Officers of Health to concentrate their attention on the personal health services, and to lose interest in the older subject of sanitation'.[10]

The achievements of the environmental health services have been taken for granted by the public – perhaps that is their greatest achievement – but new problems are having to be met.

In the discussions and plans for reorganisation of the National Health Service in 1974 (referred to later in the chapter) allocation of responsibility for community health had to be made between the local authorities and the Service. Clearly the local authorities would be responsible for control of environmental sources of disease, while the National Health Service would be responsible for the protection of the individual by immunisation and treatment, but prevention of food poisoning and the spread of notifiable diseases would involve action and the use of skills from both. In discussing this overlap area the Working Party on Collaboration between the National Health Service and Local Government[11] felt that prime responsibilities could not rest with the National Health Service as the public might find the exercise of control necessary to contain an outbreak of disease more acceptable from the elected body. On the other hand as the social services have been 'organised according to the main skills required to provide them'[12] it would be out of line with this policy if the local authorities appointed their own medical staff. Instead a duty to collaborate in areas of mutual concern has been imposed on both authorities by the National Health Service Reorganisation Act, 1974,[13] and arrangements have been made for specialists in community medicine, called community physicians, to be seconded to the local authority as 'proper officers',[14] in which role they will be directly accountable to the local authority.[15]

A satisfactory physical environment is acknowledged as the basis for good personal health, consequently the increase in pollution of land, sea and air is regarded as a serious international problem. Control over the environment in this country is exercised by several different central and local government departments, but a Standing Royal Commission on Environmental Pollution was appointed in 1970 to overview the whole situation.[16] Health hazards to local communities from noxious and dangerous industries are also a matter of concern, but again responsibility for planning and control is divided between different departments. The public health problems of the technological era may yet be regarded as being as formidable as those of the industrial era.[17]

Health care before the National Health Service

Developments in personal health care before the advent of the National Health Service can conveniently be grouped into three main areas: hospital and institutional care, domiciliary services, and the care of school children.

Hospital and institutional care

Hospitals were founded partly for the destitute sick and the poor, and partly to protect the community from the spread of infection. They were rather dangerous places to be in until towards the end of the nineteenth century when developments in medical science and staffing changed their functioning and direction. Institutional care grew up along different lines, catering for different needs with no form of central or even local planning.[18]

Under the Poor Law the destitute sick were treated, or at least housed, in infirmary wards or separate infirmaries under the Boards of Guardians. Medical care was minimal and 'nursing' was done by the pauper inmates of the workhouse, although conditions improved with the gradual introduction of trained nurses. These institutions, for want of other provisions, also came to offer care to sick people who were not destitute[19] and many were ultimately taken over by the local authority health departments after the Local Government Act, 1929, and turned into municipal general hospitals. By this time qualified medical and nursing personnel were available to man them and the standard of many became very good.

The local health authorities had already established fever hospitals and sanitoria under public health provisions and could have established general hospitals had they wished, although few did. By the end of the 1930s there were about 1,750 local authority hospitals of all types.[20]

The special needs of the mentally disordered were recognised by legislation which in 1808 allowed for the provision of county asylums, and by new developments in their care. Physical restraints gave way to more humane methods but apart from sedatives little treatment was available. Increasingly the poor who became mentally ill were placed in asylums rather than workhouses, but as with prolonged physical conditions the consequence of being ill was destitution. The Lunacy Act of 1890 reflects the anxiety about responsibility for maintenance of patients, on admission and on discharge, and the ever-present fear of overburdening the rates.

The concern of this Act with the legal status of the lunatic was expressed in the complicated procedures governing admission, detention and discharge. It also imposed duties on local officers to protect lunatics at large from ill-treatment and neglect, and on the local authorities to build asylums for persons of unsound mind, which included the mentally subnormal. However, because of shortage of staff and the numbers needing admission, the kind of personal care and attention that would have been of value in treatment was not available; and because of the slow development of psychiatry there was little else to offer patients. It was only towards the end of the nineteenth century that systematic psychiatry began with Kraepelin making the first satisfactory classification of mental illness. Psycho-analysis was also making progress in the treatment of very limited numbers of patients. Clinical psychiatric teaching did not begin in this country until the beginning of the twentieth century. The most famous teaching hospital in the country, the Maudsley, was endowed for this purpose in 1907, but for a variety of reasons did not start as a teaching unit until 1923. A few other voluntary hospitals, such as St Thomas's, started psychiatric out-patient clinics at the end of the nineteenth century.

A new era began with the Mental Treatment Act of 1930 which encouraged people to seek early treatment by allowing for voluntary admissions to mental hospitals, and for public hospitals to have out-patient clinics. Psychiatry having started to develop more effective treatments was thus given further encouragement.

In the 1944 White Paper the number of public hospitals for the mentally ill was put at 101, with 130,000 patients; but there were also about 12,500 persons of unsound mind in other local authority hospitals and public assistance institutions.[21] The mentally subnormal numbered 37,000 in the 61 certified institutions and 9,500 in public assistance institutions.

The voluntary general hospitals, of which there were more than 1,000 in 1944, varied enormously in size, age and function. Some were endowed in medieval times, many were founded in the last 200 years. Some became great medical teaching centres, with splendid

167

specialist and consultant services, others were tiny cottage hospitals using the services of the local general practitioners. Some were provided by trades unions for their members. They were financed by voluntary contributions from charities, endowments and later from patients' payments. The voluntary hospitals tended to treat acute conditions, sending the chronic sick to the Public Health hospitals or Poor Law infirmaries. The teaching hospitals, which were a small proportion of the voluntary hospitals, needed the patients as teaching material, and therefore admitted the interesting cases. The distribution of voluntary hospitals was very uneven, and, as the major hospitals attracted the services of the more outstanding doctors, distribution of the latter was uneven too.

From the beginning of the twentieth century there were growing problems relating to finance and co-ordination in the various hospital services. Some neighbouring voluntary hospitals united together under one administration, in an effort to make more effective use of their funds and to cope with the rapid developments in medical science and the consequent need for investment in new buildings and equipment. Some help came from Hospital Contributory and Provident Schemes which developed rapidly after the First World War. By small weekly payments people could cover part or all of the cost of any hospital service that they or their dependants might need.

Illness amongst the well-to-do was treated at home, at spas, or in the doctor's house until hospitals became safer.[22] Private paying patients were admitted to teaching hospitals or to private clinics and nursing homes which were run for profit. These paying patients were the main source of income for the voluntary hospital consultant or 'honorary'. The reputation of the doctor in the paying sector of the community was often related to his work in the voluntary hospitals, and his standing as a consultant there. Many doctors thus had a curious role, being on one hand the paid medical attendant to an independent and sometimes 'fashion'-conscious group of people and on the other hand being the benefactor of a large number of poor, dependent patients. The doctor's appointment to a voluntary hospital and the patronage of eminent specialists would certainly improve his career prospects while satisfactory attendance on influential private patients would enhance his income. For the young hospital doctor starting a career the early days would be fraught with anxiety, but the prospects were very enticing.

Domiciliary care

The development of public, voluntary and private care in the home was haphazard, dealing with areas of need as they were identified.

This led to complicated systems that were not sorted out in 1946 and still present problems.

Personal medical care in the community was given by doctors of a wide range of training and ability. In 1858 the Medical Act established the General Council of Medical Education and Registration which laid down minimum requirements for qualification and kept a register of practitioners. The qualified doctor was thus identified, but while the standards of training were supervised the standards of care given were often limited by the financial situation of his patients.

Under the Poor Law the destitute sick could be seen at home by the medical officers of the Board of Guardians, but the adherence to principles of deterrence and economy meant that the service often came too late or was inadequate.[23]

Out-patient advice and treatment was available to the needy who could present themselves at hospitals, charity clinics and public dispensaries without referral from family doctors. Again the adequacy of the care was limited, not only by the state of medical science, but by the need for economy and the ignorance of the consumers.[24] The essential prerequisite of the patient's responsibility to obtain treatment for his condition – which Beveridge saw as the 'duty' of the sick person – was health education, and some local authorities began to use health visitors to offer health advice to households where infectious disease had been notified.[25]

The majority were cared for by general practitioners for a fee. Patients could choose the doctor and doctors were free to charge what they wished, but were obviously limited in the size of fee by the capacity of the people to pay. Many doctors in poor areas had difficulty in extracting even small payments. Some commissioned collectors who settled bills by weekly payments. Others used a flat rate – perhaps sixpence – for all consultations. The problem of payment, often at a time when income was reduced by sickness, put an unenviable burden of decision about priorities, diagnosis and prognosis of families. The wage earner and children were often first in line for care, the housewife and aged took second place. The doctor's position was difficult in that it would be uneconomic for him to give more care or medicine than that for which the patient could pay. Some workers' Friendly Societies and Provident Clubs were formed to ensure that money would be available for members to cover medical costs when necessary.

If an employed person is unable to work because of illness, it is obviously economically desirable that he should be helped to return to work and self-sufficiency as quickly as possible. The evidence given to the Poor Law Commission, 1909, showed some of the dangers to the community and the individual of lack of early medical advice, often leading to prolonged sickness and destitution. A radical change, creating a precedent in state action, occurred when Lloyd George's National Health Insurance Act was placed on the Statute book in 1911. This Act entitled insured persons not only to weekly payments to help maintain a minimum income level during sickness, but also to free doctoring from the doctor of their choice, provided he had agreed to participate in the scheme. The general practitioners who did participate, known as 'panel doctors', were paid on a *per capita* basis. This method of remuneration had been the doctors' own choice; they rejected the idea of a salary.

At its inception the scheme covered about one-third of the population, but by the time the National Health Service Act came into force more than a half were covered. The scheme did not provide hospital or specialist care, and made no medical provision for dependants. Nevertheless this spread of contact between the public and general practitioners encouraged the idea of the family doctor. It also ensured better and regular pay for many doctors. Although this was a compulsory national scheme the financial side was administered by 'Approved Societies'. These were either co-operative undertakings, organised by trades unions and Friendly Societies, or were private companies. The Societies varied in their resources and some were able to give extra benefits such as help with dental care and spectacles. This method of administering health insurance proved to be cumbersome and costly.[26]

As there was no way by which the Insurance Committees could oversee the individual GP's work a system was instituted whereby a patient could complain to the local committee if the doctor failed to carry out the work he was contracted to do. This system was taken over by the Executive Councils after 1948, and the Family Practitioner Committees after 1973.[27]

At the other end of the economic scale the rich used the services of eminent or fashionable doctors. Although medical and surgical specialisms were growing in the teaching hospitals, these doctors were frequently used by their patients as general practitioners. Because their income came largely from private practice, the hospital specialists had to keep a careful eye on the paying patient. 'Keeping in' with the patient could be time-consuming and frustrating.

Dental care, except for extractions, was almost unknown among the working population. Routine school medical inspections, starting in 1907, revealed something of the extent of dental disease. Little was done to improve matters except in the school health service and the maternity and child welfare services, although popular indifference, shortage of trained staff and their uneven distribution combined to keep these services minimal. The debilitating effects of dental caries were not widely known and people with little money to spare would be moved to seek care only by toothache, and then would take the

170

cheapest and easiest cure – extraction. There was little charitable provision for dental care apart from the teaching hospitals. Popular dental education and a positive attitude to dental care was sadly lacking even in 1946. By the time the National Health Service Act came into operation the number of people who needed dentures was much greater than had been imagined.[28]

A home nursing service for the sick poor of Liverpool was started by William Rathbone in 1859. The value of this work led to the founding of Queen Victoria's Jubilee Institute for Nursing in 1887, financed by the money collected by the women of the nation to celebrate the Queen's jubilee. The name was shortened to the Queen's Institute of District Nursing in 1925. Although many local health authorities took over the functions of district nurses there were still some in 1948 who left the task to voluntary nursing committees.[29]

The development of maternity nursing and care was one of the striking achievements of local authorities. In spite of great advances in epidemiology during the nineteenth century maternal and infant mortality remained high. The first legislation in the personal health field was the Midwives Act of 1902, which laid down standards for training, maintained a register, and prohibited untrained women from practising. The qualified midwives remained private practitioners, or worked for voluntary nursing associations.[30] With the passing of the Midwives Act, 1936, local authorities had to ensure that an adequate number of midwives was available in their area, which gradually brought domiciliary midwifery under local authority control as a public service.

Legislation relating to infant welfare lagged behind maternity care, in spite of concern about the declining birth-rate at the end of the nineteenth century.[31] Little was done to save the infants who died because of their insanitary surroundings and the ignorance and poor health of their mothers. Attempts to improve this situation were first made in 1862 when the Manchester and Salford Sanitary Association employed women visitors, the forerunners of the health visitors, to advise mothers on the care of infants. The results so impressed the local authority that it gave financial support to the work. Other local authorities started different schemes with similar aims, which were considerably advanced by the compulsory notification of all births to the local health authority after 1915. In 1918 the Maternity and Child Welfare Act established the local authority services for expectant and nursing mothers and children under school age. At this time there were already 3,000 health visitors employed in local health authorities.

The provisions of this Act meant that the care of large numbers of mothers and infants was undertaken by local authority midwives, doctors and health visitors, working from infant welfare clinics, and

171

not by general practitioners. For the family able to pay, ante-natal and post-natal care and infant care were given by the general practitioners, helped by the private midwife and the nursery nurse. Thus there grew up two different systems of care for mothers and babies; and when hospitals began to offer the kind of specialised care that some people required, yet a third system was added, with pre-natal, post-natal and infant clinics attached to the maternity hospitals and wards.

Health care of school children

The school health service developed as part of a two-sided attack on the poor physique of school children. The complementary service was the provision of school meals to undernourished children. These were accepted as functions of the educational service.

This wider conception of education was born with difficulty and grew slowly. The pioneers of school feeding and school medical inspection and treatment, often the teachers and inspectors who knew from first-hand experience how great was the need, had a hard struggle to convince both legislators and the public generally that, in accepting responsibility for the education of its children, the nation had, whether wittingly or not, accepted responsibility for their health and general well-being, since the effective discharge of one responsibility was impossible without undertaking the other. Further, these pioneers had not only to contend with the passive resistance of the indifferent, but also with the active opposition of those who regarded any material help given by the state, unless safeguarded by a deterrent Poor Law, as a threat to family solidarity and responsibility.

The London School Board appointed its first school medical officer in 1890. The Inter-departmental Committee on Physical Deterioration, reporting in 1904, strongly recommended the systematic medical inspection of school children. By 1905 eighty-five local education authorities had appointed school medical officers. The Education (Administrative Provisions) Act, 1907, compelled local education authorities to have the children in elementary school medically examined at least three times during the school career. Unfortunately, the bogey of undermining parental responsibility, and the fear of intruding into the sphere of the private doctor, prevented an equally strong line being taken with regard to the provision of facilities for treatment and this remained optional until 1918.[32] The duties placed on local authorities by the Education Act, 1907, necessitated the creation of a Medical Branch at the Board of Education, and the first Chief Medical Officer was appointed in the same year. When the Ministry of Health was created in 1919 the Ministry of Health Act transferred all the powers and duties of the Board of Education concerned with medical inspection and treatment of children to the new Ministry. An arrangement was made by which these powers and duties were exercised by the Board of Education on behalf of the Ministry of Health and as part of this the Chief Medical Officer of the Board became also the Chief Medical Officer of the Ministry.[33] This arrangement was reflected in the local authorities, where the medical officer of health was also the principal school medical officer, as had been recommended in the 1904 Report.

Children's psychological needs were only slowly dealt with. Between the wars developments in psychiatry and psychology offered greater understanding of and interest in maladjusted children. The Child Guidance movement started in the USA and with American help the Child Guidance Council was founded in this country in 1927 as a training and propaganda organisation, although its influence spread slowly. Some voluntary hospitals started out-patient clinics and some private bodies started day clinics.

The first local education authority child guidance clinic was opened in Birmingham in 1932. By 1939 there were 48 clinics in all, 17 of them wholly maintained and five partly maintained by local education authorities.[34] The war indirectly stimulated further acceptance of the need for such clinics. By 1945 the total number of clinics was 79 and of these 63 were wholly or partly maintained by local education authorities.

From their early days a characteristic feature of child guidance clinics has been their teamwork. The team is usually made up of a psychiatrist, a psychologist and a social worker.[35] The 'team' activity led to some difficulties in the 1974 reorganisation as the allocation of the three main workers on the basis of their skills would be to three different authorities.

The Chief Medical Officer of the Ministry of Education in his report for 1939–45 discussed the provisions relating to the school health service contained in the Education Act, 1944. He made a strong case for the school health service to continue under the Ministry of Education as before. One of the most cogent reasons for having a health service administered by the education authority was that 'The presence of children in schools made it possible to arrange effectively for their inspection in school.'

The Education Act, 1944, anticipated the National Health Service Act by ending the charges to parents for treatment given to school children. The duty of the local education authority under the new Act was to ensure that comprehensive facilities for free medical treatment were available, either at clinics, or hospital out-patients departments or as in-patients. Domiciliary care was not included, but orthopaedic appliances and spectacles were. The local education authorities were to pay for hospital treatment, and to make arrangements where necessary with general practitioners and private dentists for care of children.

The Department of Education and Science has continued to look after the health needs of school children providing school clinics through the local authorities, but supervision of the health of children in the care of local authorities was undertaken by the Children's Department of the Home Office, until the work of this department was transferred to the Department of Health and Social Security (DHSS). This unsatisfactory splitting of child health between three central government departments was brought toward integration in 1972 when a Child Health Division was set up in the DHSS combining the work formerly carried out by the Home Office and the child health work of the Maternal and Child Health Division of the DHSS.

The need to maintain a preventive service for children was stressed in the Sheldon Report of 1967 and the view taken that the work could be done by the family doctor in an integrated health service.[36]

The National Health Service

Planning and advent

Between the wars the personal health services were subject to scrutiny and planning from two different points of view. First, from 1920 onwards several reports and studies considered the inadequacies of medical care for the general population and the need for a more orderly service.[37] Medical resources were unevenly distributed both geographically and by social class. The medical and hospital provisions were not integrated nor were they planned on an efficient scale. The various studies suggested that as sickness was costly to the community people should be encouraged to seek treatment early and that it should be available regardless of ability to pay.[38]

Second, the growing threat of war focused attention on the need to plan for civilian and military casualties.[39] Titmuss, in describing this says, 'the pattern of the hospital services at the end of the war is due as much – if not more – to the kind of war that was expected as to the kind of war that happened'.[40] The Emergency Medical Service was established under the Civil Defence Act, 1939, and put under the control of the Minister of Health, who had power to direct voluntary and local authority hospitals, assumed responsibility for the civilian and military victims of the war, and organised a 'nationally planned and financed service based on regional groups of hospitals',[41] which was administered alongside and in the same hospitals as the services for other patients. Inevitably, it became increasingly difficult as the war went on to keep the two services apart. From this experience of planning on a nationwide basis there was no question of a permanent return to the pre-war inadequacies.

The broad principles of the post-war policy for health were contained in Beveridge's *Report on Social Insurance and Allied Services* published in 1942 in which the proposals for national insurance rested on the assumption that there would be a comprehensive health and rehabilitation services for the prevention and cure of disease: 'Restoration of the sick person to health is a duty of the State and the sick person, prior to any other consideration.'[42] Beveridge agreed with the Medical Planning Committee[43] that medical administration should be separated from income maintenance and that access to medical care should not depend on insurance contributions.

The 1944 White Paper, *A National Health Service*, was generally acceptable in outline but problems arose regarding administration and finance. The three main parties involved with the government in the discussions – the local authorities, the voluntary hospitals and the medical profession – were divided over these issues. The doctors, many of whom had been employed by local authorities, or Poor Law Boards,[44] and had experienced the disadvantages of lay control over medical practice without appreciating the advantages, rejected the proposal that the local authorities grouped into Joint Boards, should administer the health services. The medical profession played a large part in determining the new structure of the health service, which left the local authorities with considerably reduced responsibilities for health.[45]

The question of pay split the medical profession. The hospital-based doctors accepted a salaried service, but it was rejected by the family doctors,[46] and in the clashes between them and the Minister of Health, Aneurin Bevan, they threatened to boycott the service. The financial scheme they settled for was much like the panel system set up in 1911, whereby the GPs received a capitation fee for each patient on their list,[47] which has the disadvantage that it rewards good and bad practice alike and offers little incentive for improvement. The assessment of income appropriate for hospital doctors, GPs and dentists was undertaken by three separate committees, all chaired by Sir William Spens.

The National Health Service Act, 1946, provided a broad plan for extending a comprehensive and free service of medical and ancillary care, advice and treatment to all; thereby encouraging the maintenance of good health, rather than the treatment of ill-health. The intention of the Act was to uproot as little as possible. No one was to be compelled to participate either as consumer or practitioner. Private fee-paying practice was to be available.

The day appointed for the Act to come into operation was 5 July

1948, which gave less than two years to prepare detailed plans at the local level. In view of the number and variety of agencies involved – local authorities, central government departments, voluntary agencies and individual practitioners – and of buildings, from nineteenth-century workhouses to up-to-date clinics, as well as the complex financial problems, it is surprising that the structure that evolved was as orderly as it was. Not only was there a great diversity in services, staff and buildings but also in the people who were to use the new services, ranging from the co-operative and intelligent to the apathetic 'uncomplaining poor',[48] from the belligerent to the thoughtless.

The tripartite system

The structure set up under the National Health Service Act, 1946, was the now famous tripartite system, which organised the health service in three separately and differently managed parts, joined administratively only at central government level. There have been many changes in its twenty-five years of life from July 1948 to April 1974, not the least of these being in the structuring of the government departments. In 1968 the Department of Health and Social Security was created. It united the Ministries of Health and Social Security and was also called upon in 1971 to oversee the new Social Services Departments, making it responsible for three major interdependent areas of social provision. In 1969 the responsibility for the Welsh Health Service was transferred to the Secretary of State for Wales.

There have been changes too in the way advice is made available to the Secretary of State on the performance of his duties. Ever since the Ministry of Health was set up in 1919 there has been a Chief Medical Officer who gives professional advice and reports annually on the nation's health.[49] Over the years he has been joined by chief officers from other professions. In addition under the 1946 Act the Central Health Services Council was set up which also advises the Department, working through standing committees, and setting up *ad hoc* bodies on its own initiative, or at the request of the Department to report on any matters of concern;[50] and in 1969 a Hospital Advisory Service was set up following the publication of the report on the treatment of patients at Ely Hospital.[51] Concentrating initially on hospitals where patients are most vulnerable to abuse such as those for geriatric patients and the mentally subnormal, the service has visited and advised hospitals on patient care, and has informed the Secretaries of State (DHSS and Wales) of the conditions in hospitals. It is an independent body in that it has its own offices and staff, and its director reports directly to the Secretary of State. By guidance, advice and a ready flow of information to and from the centre it is hoped to raise standards where this is necessary and increase the allocation of resources.[52]

The three operational parts of the National Health Service were the Hospital and Specialist Service administered mainly by 14 Regional Hospital Boards in England directly responsible to the Ministry of Health; the General Medical, Dental, Pharmaceutical and Ophthalmic Services administered by the 134 Executive Councils to which the individual practitioners were contracted, and finally the community services provided by the county and county borough councils. The hospitals and Executive Council Services were financed directly by central government through taxation, and that part of National Insurance contributions specifically earmarked for the National Health Service,[53] while the local authority services were financed from the rates, which also include a rate support grant from the Exchequer.

The hospital and specialist service

This was the greatest innovation of the National Health Service. The nationalisation of the hospitals secured a better distribution of staff and other resources, and the enlargement of the administrative areas beyond local authority boundaries made for a more efficient operational size. The fourteen Regional Hospital Boards (RHBs) based on the wartime Civil Defence regions, were responsible for hospital in-patient and out-patient provision, for domiciliary consultations and for the appointment of senior medical staff.

They had the task of planning the hospital service in their areas, deciding priorities and controlling finances. By employing the senior medical staff directly, they controlled the distribution of specialist services over the whole region. They allocated money to the hospital management committees in their area. The hospitals, grouped or separate, were administered by these committees, who were responsible to the RHBs.

The members of the boards and committees were unpaid laymen appointed, in the case of the RHBs, by the Secretary of State and in the case of the hospital management committees by the boards. The members were selected not elected, which led to some disquiet at a situation in which large sums of public money (in 1972 over £1,000 million) were at the disposal of non-representative bodies.

The special needs of the hospitals associated with universities in medical teaching, and the anxieties of the staff about standards of education in this new untried structure, were acknowledged by having them administered by Boards of Governors directly responsible to the Secretary of State. Since 1948 the fears of the universities that their voice would not be heard have generally been allayed and

177

increasingly clinical instruction has been provided in RHB hospitals as well as teaching hospitals. The Todd Report on Medical Education,[54] reporting in 1968, suggested that the teaching hospitals should come under the RHBs. The fears that caused separate arrangements to be made have receded into the past, and apart from the London teaching hospitals which provide pre-clinical education, the teaching and RHB hospitals have become less and less distinguishable.

Finance and control are closely connected. The Minister in 1947 wanted the RHBs, on venturing into the unknown, to feel 'a lively sense of independent responsibility'.[55] However, the financial difficulties of the early years of the health service, when the original estimates proved to be too low, suggesting overspending and extravagance, led to a tightening of control by the Ministry, with consequent confusion in the RHBs about their role. The Guillebaud Committee, set up in 1953 to review the cost of the National Health Service,[56] reported that the charge of excessive spending could not be substantiated. On the contrary it appeared that the portion of the total national resources allocated to the National Health Service had fallen and that the increasing cost was due to rising prices and the post-war increase in the population. Nevertheless, the sobering lesson was that health service expenditure, high as it seemed, was as yet inadequate, and the hospital service, already making the greatest demand for resources of the three parts of the service, was far from ideal.[57]

The Chief Medical Officer of the Ministry in his annual report for 1966 looked back to the 1950s as an era of reorganisation of the 1948 inheritance, and to the 1960s as an era of planning. The money available to the hospital service for the first five or six years was spent on patching and improving existing hospitals, but after 1955 it was possible to start thinking about major schemes of development. This presented a need for planning on a scale unknown before. In 1962 the Hospital Plan for England and Wales was published, to be reviewed and carried forward annually. It presented the idea of the District General Hospital covering a population of 100,000 to 150,000 people including all types of hospital and specialist services, that did not require a substantially larger catchment area,[58] an idea that was basic in the reorganisation plans.

It became apparent in the 1960s that certain groups of patients had fallen behind in the scramble for finances, and indeed had never had equal access. These included the young chronic sick, the mentally handicapped and the elderly. In 1969 the RHBs were asked to review their services for long-stay patients and make a more generous allocation of money, while the Secretary of State earmarked £3 million for improving services for the mentally handicapped. In 1970 the new government took this protection further and allocated a further £93 million over 4 years for all groups of chronic sick and handicapped who appeared to suffer the added handicap of being less eligible to their own RHBs than other patients.[59]

The Guillebaud Report also drew attention to the muddled and irritating situation regarding responsibility and consultation between the hospital boards and committees and the Ministry, recommending a clearer definition of powers and functions at all levels.[60] Problems of management in the hospitals, and indeed in the whole health service, not clearly identified in 1948 were examined in this and other reports in the 1950s and 1960s.[61] Several concerned the involvement of hospital staff in management. The report of the Salmon Committee[62] on senior nursing staff structure proposed new patterns of administration with preparation for management at all levels and clear lines of accountability. These proposals have largely been implemented. The doctor's managerial function was considered initially by the Advisory Committee for Management Efficiency in the National Health Service,[63] and subsequently by a joint working party of consultants and Ministry staff.[64] The difficulties discussed in the working party (called 'Cogwheel') arose from the continuation in the 1948 structure of a long-standing system whereby most hospital consultants had equal clinical and administrative status. The control exercised by the RHBs, by whom the consultants were appointed after 1948, was indirect and limited largely to the allocation of resources. Apart from a few departments such as radiology there were no hierarchical structures as there were in nursing. It became increasingly clear that while the medical staff, because of their clinical autonomy, had control over, and responsibility for, the allocation of resources to their patients, there was little overall co-ordination of their individual activities. If the resulting inefficiency and waste were to be remedied and at the same time clinical autonomy protected, the doctors must be involved much more closely in administrative and management affairs.[65]

In the Cogwheel system specialists in the same area of practice, such as surgery, together discuss their clinical arrangements, while the chairmen of the specialist groups form a committee to plan the administration of clinical matters as distinct from the administration of the hospital. In this way the medical staff can be involved in assessing priorities.

Lay administration of the hospitals rested with the voluntary members of the hospital management committees advised and aided by permanent officials. Training for the professional administration has been provided by the DHSS at the Hospital Administrative Staff College and by university courses.

Private beds have always been available in RHB hospitals.[66] Consultants who worked part-time for the RHB could admit their private patients, who paid for treatment and maintenance. The number of private beds has declined since 1949 and the take-up has been far from complete, being little over 50 per cent. Private insurance schemes, through which most of the private care is financed, have, however, increased both their membership, from about 50,000 in 1949 to about 1 million in 1972,[67] and the provision of private nursing homes. Group membership, arranged for example through employing bodies, has shown a particular increase. Membership of a private scheme has no significance at all in the treatment of acute or emergency situations, while privacy has always been available at a very low cost in the form of amenity beds, and the opportunity to choose a consultant oneself has become less relevant as medicine has become more technical, where several specialists might be involved in one episode and where the consumer often has no adequate criteria for choice. As the subscriber is not benefiting markedly in these matters, the value of private care must be sought elsewhere and it has become apparent that what he and his employer are often buying is the opportunity to choose when to be admitted to hospital for treatment of non-acute conditions, and freedom from the restraints of ward routines so that they may continue to pursue their own employment. However, it can be argued that private patients in RHB hospitals use public resources 'out of turn'.[68]

The advantages and disadvantages of a private sector in the National Health Service have been debated almost continuously since the service was in embryo and refer particularly to the hospital service. On one side there is a belief that the consumer should be allowed choice. D. S. Lees suggests that 'medical care is a personal consumption good, not markedly different from the generality of goods bought by consumers'.[69] It is also argued that a private sector brings in much-needed resources, to the ultimate benefit of all users. Certainly consultants can supplement their incomes at no extra expense to the taxpayers. On the other side Titmuss and other contributors to the Fabian literature believe that a two-class service would operate. The redistributive effect might be horizontal rather than vertical and there might even be a loss of resources from the free sector to the paying sector. In a comprehensive service, used by almost all the population, the standards of care would be of concern to all.

The 1974 Labour Government was committed to a phasing-out of the private sector in the National Health Service. A Working Party was set up by the Secretary of State, including representatives of the profession, to discuss the whole question of private care. It began its work in an atmosphere of growing militancy not only among the hospital doctors, but also among the para-medical workers.

Although the aim of the 1948 legislation was the provision of a comprehensive and universal service this has not been achieved. The

Guillebaud Report of 1956 recognised that the concept of a health service which would reduce demand for care by improving health was an illusion – 'at least for the present', the report adds[70] – and that shortages would continue. In the hospital service the distribution of resources remains uneven although, as the 1970 Green Paper points out, there has been a great improvement and specialist services are within reach of all. Some of the uneven distribution in hospital provision reflects a maldistribution of other resources, and illustrates the interdependence of many factors in any area. For example the figures for 1966 of facilities in psychiatric hospitals show that of all the regions Liverpool had nearly the lowest number of trained nurses, but nearly the highest number of untrained nurses, ward orderlies and domestics, which might be more of a comment on educational rather than hospital facilities.[71] In many areas hospital beds are still used to meet social as well as medical needs.[72] The reasons for differences in demand are numerous and complex, but make for resistance to any attempt to have a nationally uniform provision of hospital beds proportional to the population, as proposed in 1962 in the Hospital Plan, particularly in areas where community resources are inadequate.

The mental hospitals have been particularly liable to use for social rather than medical needs. In 1948 the RHBs had the unenviable inheritance of lunatic asylums and mental deficiency institutions many of whose patients were no more in need of medical care than the rest of the population. The National Health Service Act integrated these hospitals with all others in one administrative framework, while the 1962 Hospital Plan included services for the mentally ill in the District General Hospital.

The Plan also proposed a reduction in the number of beds for the mentally ill and subnormal.[73] In his report for 1968 the Chief Medical Officer said that the District General Hospitals would totally replace the old mental hospitals, assuming that community services and geriatric services provided full support. The RHBs in December 1971[74] were advised to plan for psychiatric units to replace the old hospitals, but the plans did not refer to the elderly who constituted nearly half of the inmates of the condemned hospitals. They were dealt with in a circular to the RHBs in 1972[75] which analysed and advised on the varying needs of old people. The enthusiasm for change in the care of the mentally disordered which urged the closing of the large institutions has been tempered by the realisation that these hospitals represent a valuable source of sheltered accommodation,[76] and that community care is not yet at the standard required.

There have been dramatic changes in admissions to mental hospitals since 1948. The number of residents reached its peak in 1945 at 3·5 per thousand of the population. A century-long upward trend was reversed and by 1971 the hospital population had fallen to 2·25 per thousand.[77] The major change has been in the short stay and younger section of the population. On the other hand the number of admissions and readmissions has been steadily rising. The admission rate nearly trebled between 1949 and 1971, and it has been estimated that the lifetime chances of admission to mental hospital now are one in six for women and one in nine for men.[78]

The pattern of mental illness and psychiatric provision has approached more nearly the pattern for physical illness. Out-patient facilities and day hospitals have expanded, partly a reaction to, and partly a cause of, changes in treatment and legislation. The Mental Health Act of 1959[79] replaced all previous legislation. It was made possible by new drugs by which disturbed behaviour could be controlled, and by the separation in 1948 of income need from health need – an important factor in long-term illness.

The term 'mental disorder' is used to describe all conditions of mental illness and deficiency, psychopathic and 'any other disorder or disability of the mind'. As far as possible mental disorder is treated on an informal basis. Compulsory admission to hospital is used only where necessary to protect the patient or others. Over 90 per cent of the admissions to hospital are on an informal basis – a dramatic reversal of the situation following the 1890 Lunacy Act.

A patient can be detained in hospital for observation for up to twenty-eight days under Section 25 of the Mental Health Act on the recommendation of two doctors, where application has been made by the nearest relative or a social worker. Detention for treatment up to one year can be ordered under Section 26. The treatment procedure can be used for a patient of any age who is suffering from mental illness or severe subnormality. However, a subnormal or psychopathic patient may only have a treatment application made for him before the age of twenty-one and this lapses at twenty-five unless he is a danger to himself or others.[80] These age limits are not applicable to hospital orders made by the courts.[81] Section 29 allows for compulsory admission for seventy-two hours in cases of urgent necessity, with only one medical recommendation supporting the application.

Appeal against detention can be made to the hospital managers, who until reorganisation were the hospital management committee, and beyond them to the local Mental Health Tribunal which has legal, psychiatric and lay members, and can order discharge. In 1972 tribunals considered 753 applications and directed that 101 should be discharged.

Trends in treatment since the Mental Health Act have been away from admission to a mental hospital to an increasing use of out-patient and day-care facilities, and psychiatric units in District

General Hospitals. The annual report of the DHSS for 1972 noted changes since 1966 in the diagnostic conditions admitted to hospital. Alcoholic psychoses have trebled and personality and behaviour disorders have doubled, conditions that may not be suited to treatment in a busy acute hospital.

Another group posing problems is that of the mentally abnormal offenders. Henry Rollin[82] has pointed out that mental illness and deviant behaviour are not mutually exclusive. The care of the mentally abnormal offender, he suggests, has been complicated by the provisions of the 1959 Act. Although psychiatric units have been established at some prisons (coming under the control of the Home Office, not the National Health Service), he reports a 'flood' of mentally abnormal offenders into his hospital, a high proportion of them also having no fixed abode. Others report a similar rise.[83] The needs of such people, or rather, of the community, are particularly at variance with the new concept of the mental hospital as a therapeutic community in close contact with its environment. These abnormal offenders may abscond easily from the open hospitals. The Act in Rollin's view has 'cast mental hospitals in an unenviable and difficult role in relation to the care of the mentally abnormal offender'.

The least satisfactory part of the mental health hospital provision seems to have been for the mentally handicapped and the psychogeriatric patients. As noted the Hospital Advisory Service was set up following disclosures of ill-treatment at some of the large institutions.[84] Patients detained for their own protection have been left unprotected from the rigours of life in understaffed, badly managed institutions. Positive attitudes towards patients in long-stay hospitals are encouraged by the provision of community facilities to which these patients can be sent. In 1969 a drive to improve facilities was launched, with the determination not to let patients who were out of sight be out of mind.[85]

The physically disabled have needs that go across service boundaries. The hospital and specialist service has been concerned with rehabilitation of the disabled, in particular with artificial limbs and vehicles. Artificial limb and appliance centres deal with assessment, fitting and training. The intention is to have them all sited by District General, or special rehabilitation hospitals. The vehicle service for the disabled has been under discussion (see the chapter on personal social services). Lady Sharp in her report on the Mobility of Physically Disabled People, 1974, was emphatic that the social as well as physical needs should be taken into account when considering eligibility for a vehicle, or help with running a car. Eligibility for a vehicle has already been extended from loss of limbs, to other conditions which impede mobility, such as chronic lung or heart conditions.

Community care

This was the concern of the local health authorities and the Executive Councils.[86] The latter were responsible for the financial administration of general practitioners, dentists, pharmacists and opticians,[87] who were independent contractors with the Councils, which could exercise only limited control over their work.

The general practitioners

General practitioners were very unevenly distributed over the country in 1948. The Medical Practices Committee, set up to remedy this, identified areas that were under-doctored and for these 'designated' areas there were positive financial inducements to practise. In the over-doctored areas permission to practise would normally be refused. The ratio of doctors to patients has varied, partly because the number of doctors going into general practice has not been constant. As hospital work and opportunities overseas expanded in the late 1950s so the number of GPs declined. Projections about need in the Willinck Report of 1957, based on incorrect assessments of the future size and shape of the population, contributed to the decline in numbers training in the early 1960s. By the mid-1960s the average GP's list of patients was nearly at the maximum permitted, 3,500, and in designated areas had risen over it. The numbers of designated areas had also increased. Rudolf Klein notes that it was in this period that the number of complaints by patients against their GPs reached its peak, and suggests that the bitterness resulting from their demoralisation and discontent spread over to the patients.[88]

More positive measures were taken to improve distribution of GPs in 1966 when the Review Body of Doctors' and Dentists' Remuneration[89] recommended additional allowances for practice in designated areas.[90] At this point the distribution of medical manpower took an upward turn. The DHSS reported in 1972, in its Annual Report, that the number of principals had continued to increase, and although some of the increase could be accounted for by overseas doctors practising here, the British-born doctors had also increased in number. The average number of patients per doctor continued to decline and was 2,421 in October 1971.

Payment of the general practitioners continued to present difficulties. The negotiations before 1948 rejected payment by salary and agreed to capitation fees from a central pool into which the Treasury paid enough money to cover an estimated appropriate income for all the doctors and an allowance for practice expenses. The pool money was distributed through the Executive Councils.[91] The GPs were on the whole offered better pay than they had been able to command before,[92] but the method of payment tended to reward good and bad alike. In 1966 a new system of remuneration was recommended by the Review body which 'reflected more closely the individual doctor's services for his patients and his practice expenses'[93] based on negotiations on the *Charter for the Family Doctor Service* published by the British Medical Association in 1965. The new system included an annual basic practice allowance, not called a salary, but not related to the size of the doctor's list,[94] special allowances for seniority, group practice and postgraduate training, inducement payments and initial practice allowances to doctors going to designated areas, and assistance towards the cost of ancillary workers and provision and improvement of premises. The average net remuneration in 1972 was £5,575 with an average £2,230 for expenses.

Private practice continued in the family practitioner setting, but, unlike the hospital service, it does not seem to the patient to be an attractive alternative. The British Medical Association in the period of grave dissatisfaction with the National Health Service in 1965 planned a private insurance scheme, which included an annual payment, plus item of service payments. The scheme lasted only three years, getting limited support from practitioners and little from patients. Other private schemes have made little impact on the main body of users.

Squabbles about pay have perhaps reflected some of the less easily identified troubles in general practice. The 1946 Act foresaw general practitioners working in health centres. These were not acceptable to many, and economic difficulties prevented building except in a few instances, but general practitioners did move towards working in groups of their own making. This grouping provided stimulation and interest, and was increasingly necessary as the progress of medicine tended to leave the general practitioners behind. The early lack of interest in training for general practice has reflected the profession's attitude to it, in spite of the declaration by the Cohen Committee that 'the general practitioner must hold the key position in the Health Service'.[95] The Annis Gillie Report, *The Field of Work of the Family Doctor*,[96] suggested that his work had three aspects. He is the patient's first line of defence in times of illness – from birth to death. He acts as intermediary between hospital and patient, referring where necessary and arranging after-care. He can best mobilise and co-ordinate the health and welfare services in the interests of the individual in the community and of the community in relation to the individual. The committee recommended changes in the medical curriculum to give doctors awareness of the community as well as the individual, specific training for work in general practice, and opportunities for the general practitioner to maintain professional competence by part-time work in hospitals and continuing educational activities.[97]

The Todd Report on medical education forecast great changes in the structure of general practice but said that there was 'a continuing need for a first-line preventive, diagnostic and therapeutic service which can deal in general terms with the total medical needs of the patient and when necessary guide him towards specialist services'.[98]

The Annis Gillie Committee estimated that 90 per cent of all medical episodes were handled from start to finish by the GP, which, as the Todd Committee commented, is a very substantial proportion. However, the use the GP makes of up-to-date methods and services may not be entirely satisfactory. Gordon Forsyth and R. F. L. Logan in 1962 estimated that only a very small proportion of general practitioners were using techniques of modern pathology,[99] while Bransby, in his review of psychiatric services,[100] found that the results of surveys of general practice implied a lack of identification of mental illness and limited use of specialist and social services.[101]

General practitioners have also continued to certify incapacity for work, which started under the National Health Insurance legislation in 1911, and which may affect the way in which the doctor is regarded by some of his patients – more as a necessary contact in the procurement of payment than as the 'first line of defence in illness'.

In emergency situations such as the 'flu epidemic or the withdrawal by the GPs of this service as a protest at the Secretary of State's reception of the recommendation of the Review Body on Pay in 1970, certificates can be issued by local social security offices. The Annis Gillie Committee suggested that general practitioners themselves could make a more positive use of these doctor–patient contacts, by using them as an opportunity for screening tests.

The element of choice for the patient is now somewhat curtailed by grouping of doctors and the use of deputising services, which can result in a patient rarely seeing the doctor of his choice. In 1972 a joint working party was set up representing the DHSS, the Royal College of General Practitioners and the BMA General Medical Services Committee under the chairmanship of the Chief Medical Officer of the DHSS to look at the way the organisation of general practice had developed and to make recommendations for the future. The first report in 1973[102] looked mainly at appointment systems, deputising arrangements and diagnostic support.

With changing patterns of disease the need for a family practitioner based in the community grows rather than diminishes. 'If the general practitioner did not exist he (or someone like him) would have to be invented.'[103]

The general dental services

These services began with the severe handicap of too few dentists, which has persisted, so that it is still not possible to provide a complete service on demand. The geographical distribution of dentists has been very unsatisfactory. Cook and Walker in their study of the distribution of dentists[104] found that there was a clear association between social class and the proportion of dentists in a population and a study of adult dental health in 1968[105] showed that the dental health of a population correlated with the ratio of dentists to that population.

Dentists have not been subject to the same restrictions as doctors in regard to the setting up of practice, but Cook and Walker suggested that such restrictions would not be reasonable when even in the best-served areas the proportion of dentists remained below that enjoyed in other European countries.

The method of remuneration did not encourage the best in dental practice. The Tattersall Committee's Report[106] criticised the system, in which the Review Body on Doctors' and Dentists' Remuneration recommends an 'average' income for dentists; and the Dental Rates Study Group devised a scale of fees which would give the average dentist, working a prescribed number of hours, this 'average' income. If more than half the dentists worked faster than the 'average' last calculated they momentarily put up their individual salaries, but in due course a readjustment had to be made by lowering the scale of fees. The Tattersall Committee complained that this system put a premium on speed and took no account of quality. The questions here might be how much 'quality' can the nation afford, and yet how much 'quality' can it safely do without.[107]

In 1969 the principle of seniority payments to dentists was accepted, and those aged between 55–70 were allocated an extra £200 p.a. By 1972 the target average net income was £4,308 p.a. The supply of dentists rose slowly, and an end to the chronic shortage seemed to be in view.

At the inception of the National Health Service the whole range of dental care including dentures was free, but from 1952 charges have been made except for certain categories, such as pregnant and nursing mothers, and young people. The payments since 1968 have been for half the cost of treatment, including dentures, up to a maximum of £10.

Although the local authorities provided a dental service under their maternity and child welfare service the private practitioner dealt with most of the pre-school children, and pregnant and nursing mothers, but the school health service has done rather more of the work with school children. The opportunity for preventive work and screening in the school health service has probably been important and should continue to be so in a situation of general apathy.

The pharmaceutical services

The pharmaceutical services provide drugs under the National Health Service, and in 1948 everyone using the general practitioner service was entitled to free medicines. As the demand for drugs seemed excessive, and extra finance was required, a basic charge for each prescription was imposed in 1952. Pensioners and people on assistance could claim this back, but the system was cumbersome and many either did not claim the refund or did not have prescriptions made up. The prescriptions for that year dropped by 5 per cent. Since 1952 charges have been imposed and removed, and finally imposed again in 1968 on the basis of a payment for each item prescribed. A number of categories were exempted from the charges in an attempt to simplify procedures for needy patients. Retirement pensioners and children simply completed declarations on the back of prescription forms. Ante- and post-natal women got the necessary form with welfare milk token books. The unemployed and their families obtained a refund from the employment exchanges. Recipients of supplementary benefits got an exemption certificate with their order books. People suffering from certain chronic illnesses obtained exemption certificates on application to the Executive Council. Those not exempt in the above categories who expected to require more than twelve prescriptions in six months could get a prepayment certificate for six or twelve months at a cheap rate, throughout the whole period.

The average cost of prescriptions has gone up from 15p. in 1949 to 75p. in 1971 and the number of prescriptions dispensed has risen from 200 million in 1949 to 250 million in 1971.

The cost and the safety of drugs are matters of concern to the government. The Sainsbury Committee of Enquiry into the Pharmaceutical Industry reported in 1967[108] and suggested that the bill to the National Health Service for drugs had been inflated by excessive prices, but contrary to some expectations did not suggest that the industry should be nationalised. The prices are fixed by an agreement between the DHSS and the pharmaceutical industry. On the safety of drugs the Medicines Act of 1968 controls the marketing and trial of new drugs.

The general ophthalmic service

This supplemented the ophthalmic treatment available through the hospital and specialist service, the Executive Councils organising the work of the ophthalmic medical practitioners, ophthalmic opticians and dispensing opticians. In the first two years of the service the demand for spectacles reached its peak.[109]

The status of the non-medical opticians has improved since the Opticians Act, 1958, set up a General Optical Council and required both ophthalmic and dispensing opticians to be registered. The council has the duty of supervising training and executing disciplinary functions.

Adults are charged for lenses and frames, except those unable to pay, who make application to the Ministry of Social Security.

The local authority health committees

Under the 1946 National Health Service Act local authority health committees provided the other half of the community services. They also had duties and powers under the Public Health legislation and in some authorities were made responsible for welfare provisions under the National Assistance Act of 1948, for the elderly, physically handicapped, blind and homeless.

Local authorities had duties under the National Health Service Act to provide health centres, midwifery, home nursing, ambulance and vaccination and immunisation services. They continued to cater for the health needs of mothers and pre-school children, although the GPs and hospitals duplicated some of this work. They had powers and duties in after-care and prevention of illness. Under the 1959 Mental Health Act their powers under Section 28 of the National Health Service Act relating to the community care of the mentally disordered became duties.

Health centres were planned as the focal point for the community services, to end the isolation of GPs and integrate their work with that of domiciliary nurses and the social services. They were also to be used by the hospital service for out-patient clinics, thus improving contact between the personnel in community care and those in hospital. Financial and administrative problems hindered their development. GPs feared a loss of independence and found in the few centres that were operative that the comparatively high rents reduced their own income when this was based solely on *per capita* payments. Ten years after the appointed day only ten had been opened. Other avenues of co-operation were explored, such as attachment of health visitors to general practices and, as the General Practitioners were responding to encouragement from the Ministry to group themselves, the health centres did not seem so essential.

In the annual report of 1961 the Minister said that health centres had not always been successful in furthering co-operation, but it should be noted that little thought had been given to the dynamics of co-operation and co-ordination.

From 1966 when the GPs' method of remuneration was altered to give allowances for premises, and more money was available for capital projects in local authorities, there was a renewal of interest in health centres: 2 were opened in 1965, 8 in 1966 with 40 more in the pipeline; in 1972 there were 365 in operation and 265 more in the building or planning stage.

The maternity and child welfare services are mainly the achievement of local authorities, and under the 1946 Act they were required to provide a full maternity and infant-care service. They had to ensure that there were sufficient domiciliary midwives to deal with the home confinements, then about 30 per cent of the total, give ante- or post-natal care including dental treatment and health advice. The Guillebaud Committee reported that the division of the health services into three branches had its most serious impact on these services,[110] since all the users had the services of a GP, and the hospitals which dealt with three-quarters of confinements also gave ante- and post-natal and infant care. The Cranbrook Committee,[111] set up on the recommendation of the Guillebaud Committee, thought that any reorganisation would create more problems than it would solve. However, over the years the pattern of midwifery has become much more flexible with no rigid demarcation between home and hospital.

By 1972 only about 10 per cent of actual deliveries took place at home but much of the ante- and post-natal care was undertaken in the community. More than half the total number of women confined in hospital were sent home after a short stay – from two to seven days – to the care of the local midwife. One-fifth of the maternity beds available were staffed by GPs.

Other nurses working in the community are the health visitors, school nurses and district nurses; sometimes all functions, including midwifery, have been undertaken by one person.

Health visitors have been involved in community health for a century, but with a gradually changing function. The health education role has remained constant but the areas of ignorance that they deal with have changed. In 1909 they were concerned with infectious illness as well as maternal guidance, which centred to a large extent on teaching mothers how to prevent infectious disease in their babies and homes and they supervised patients discharged from public hospitals. With improvements in public hygiene they became more closely identified with the maternity and child welfare services, giving advice on child-rearing, not only through infant clinics, but in schools.

Increasing affluence and the universality of the National Health Service brought need for a new community role for the 6,000 trained women in the field. Examination of this role by the Jameson Committee,[112] reporting in 1956, presented difficulties of definition. The health visitor's role was described as health educator and social adviser[113] but it was not easy to limit these functions. The report suggested that 'she must take account of the unit – the family – of which the individual forms a part, and not only of physical but psychological and social factors' – an immense task. While mothers still need advice on the physical care of their children, there is no longer a clear distinction between physical and mental hygiene and advice on developmental problems is increasingly needed.[114]

Work with old people has increased. Visits to the elderly doubled between 1964 and 1972, while in the same period visits to pre-school children showed a decline.

Confusion between the work of health visitors and local authority social workers has led to some antagonism, even though the two statutory bodies concerned with their training were closely related.[115] The more social and psychological factors affect a patient's health the more difficult it becomes to define roles. For similar reasons and because of structural and administrative difficulties GPs have also had problems in co-ordinating their work with that of health visitors. The situation began to be eased in the 1960s by some attachments of community nurses – both health visitors and district or domiciliary nurses – to general practices. The Health Service and Public Health Act of 1968 furthered this development by enabling local health authorities to provide for their nurses to attend patients at places other than the patient's home. By 1972, 70 per cent of health visitors and 68 per cent of home nurses were working in association with general practitioners, and the 'Health Team' began to take shape.

The ambulance service which largely takes people between home and hospital was run by local health authorities. Ambulance crews resisted the proposal that the service should be administered by the Regional Hospital Boards, although there was evidence to suggest that a more efficient service could be provided on a larger scale.

Vaccination and immunisation services were also part of the local authorities' work. The National Health Service Act repealed the Vaccination Acts of 1867 and 1907, by which vaccination of infants was compulsory,[116] and in 1970 the routine vaccination of infants was discontinued as the risk of fatality from it was slightly greater than the risk from smallpox. It was considered that an outbreak could be quickly controlled. In 1973 this country had the unenviable distinction of being one of the six countries in the world in which human transmission of smallpox occurred. It was an embarrassing moment in the World Health Organisation smallpox eradication programme when the cradle of Public Health was found to be nurturing the disease.

Prevention of illness, care and after-care was a broadly based power given to the local authorities under the 1946 Act. There were duties relating to the control of tuberculosis in the community. The incidence of this deadly scourge of the nineteenth century has fallen very dramatically due partly to rising standards of living and partly to the development of BCG vaccine. Deaths from TB occur mainly in the older age group who were exposed to infection many years ago. However, it remains a minor threat and one that must be tackled in the community, by early diagnosis and the quick tracing of contacts.

The other major concern of the local authorities under this section of the National Health Service Act was work in the community with the mentally ill and subnormal. Part of the duties of the local health authority was the operation of the law relating to compulsory admission to hospital. Several changes have taken place. In 1948 the officers appointed by the local health authorities to administer the 1890 Lunacy Act were often the people who, as Relieving Officers under the Poor Law, had previously had this responsibility. Called originally Duly Authorised Officers the general movement towards positive preventive community work was signalled by changing their name to Mental Welfare Officers. In the health service reorganisation these officers were incorporated into the Social Services Department, and with the emphasis on generic work their specialism was merged with that of other workers. Their work today is dealt with in the chapter on the personal social services.

Local authority health committees also had responsibility until 1971 for mentally handicapped children who were not able to attend school. The Department of Education and Science then took responsibility for the education of these children, but their health needs were met by hospital and local health authority services.

A service of great importance in keeping the elderly and handicapped as mobile as possible is the chiropody service. From 1959 local authorities were empowered and encouraged to make such provision, and by 1972 all the local authorities had done so, either directly or by delegation to a voluntary organisation.

The importance of preventive work was stressed in the plans for the development of the health and welfare services published in 1963 and revised in 1966.[117] Local authorities were asked to submit their plans for four main categories of clients: the elderly, mothers and young children, the mentally disordered and the physically handicapped. These groups include those clients who may have a multiplicity of needs that can only be met satisfactorily by careful co-ordination of provisions and by co-operation in the field. They were also asked to review their provisions for patients at home and for the homeless.

Liaison

Liaison between the local health authorities, central government and other branches of the National Health Service was undertaken by the

Regional Officers of the DHSS, an office started in the last war. The principal regional officer was required to take an overall view of health matters in his area, with regard not only to the activities of the local health authorities, the RHBs and Executive Councils but also the many interested voluntary agencies, and to collaborate with the Regional Officers of the Social Work Advisory Service of the Ministry of Health.[118]

Some of the difficulties can be imagined when the number of authorities is considered.[119] The RHBs numbered 15 with 330 hospital management committees and 36 boards of governors. The Executive Councils, 134 altogether, geographically were fairly well matched with the 175 local authorities but the GPs being independent contractors may have had patients from more than one Executive Council and local authority area. Where the patients' health problems were compounded by housing difficulties an even more confused situation arose in the counties, where the housing authority was at the urban and rural district level, while the welfare and health services were top-tier functions.[120] For some patients such as the groups mentioned in the previous section their health needs could only be met by care from all three sections of the health service, and the welfare services. No one had authority to draw on all the resources, although the GP was regarded as the co-ordinator.

The 1968 Green Paper referred to these problems when considering the possibility of a new type of local authority responsible for all services. But whether the new health service should be run by area health authorities or by local government there was no doubt that the co-ordination of medical and welfare services needed to be more effective.

Reorganisation

For the consumer the services described in the last section have not changed. Patients see the same family doctors and attend the same hospitals to see the same specialists. Their needs at home are met by the same community nurses. For many of the staff there has been little apparent change. The Staff Advisory Committee[121] in its bulletin of December 1972 said 'we confidently expect that the great majority of staff will be doing the same job after the appointed day in the same place they are doing it today'. The National Health Service Reorganisation Act, 1973, is an amending act, and the major provisions of the 1946 and subsequent Acts remain.[122] The reorganisation is concerned with the administration of the service.

Planning for change

In a foreword to the White Paper, 1972, the Secretary of State pointed

193

out that there had never been any single authority empowered to provide a comprehensive service, planned rationally, in a given area. The basic principles of the service, outlined in the second Green Paper, which have 'stood the test of time',[123] remain fundamental. These are that health care should be paid for out of taxes, with the financial burden of sickness borne by the whole community, that there should be a service of uniformly high quality in all areas and for all people – as yet not achieved – that the doctor's clinical freedom must be protected, and that the family doctor team (the idea of the 'team' is a recent innovation) should be central to the service. But while the principles are constant the desirability of making structural and administrative changes has been appreciated since the Guillebaud Committee in 1956 stressed the urgent need for co-ordination of the service at all levels. They thought it would be premature to propose any fundamental change in structure at that time particularly as any such changes would have to be paralleled by changes in local government. They said, with some foresight, that 'longer experience of the working of the Service and the gradual emergence of a new generation may make comparatively simple many things which now appear difficult or impracticable'.[124] Since the 1960s serious discussions about reorganisation have taken place. The Porritt Report of 1962[125] concluded that all medical services in any area should be in the hands of one authority, which they called an Area Health Board. The lack of overall planning, by which the service could be kept in line with social and medical changes, was deplored, but the concept of a National Health Service, they concluded, was sound.

The magnitude of the changes envisaged required careful consultation and discussion with all interested parties and could only be considered in relation to proposals for the reorganisation of local government and the personal social services.[126] Several documents developed the proposals for change and the major matters for consideration. The first Green Paper presented for discussion purposes in 1968[127] stressed the need to co-ordinate the service in more than name, and said that its proposed area health boards should be 'more than a roof beneath which separate parts of the service . . . could lead distinct and largely unco-ordinated lives'. Finding an administrative unit that would be large enough to be efficient and economical in use of resources yet small enough to be in touch with local needs and interests proved difficult. The first Green Paper was criticised on both counts, as its proposed area health boards, numbering about fifty, depending on the changes in local government boundaries, and designed to be directly responsible to the Minister, were too small to carry out planning of some health service activities; while at local level they seemed to be too big for the participation by staff and public in the everyday running of the service. The Green Paper

194

did not rule out the possibility of the new local authorities being responsible for an integrated health service, but the second Green Paper in February 1970[128] firmly stated that this would not be the case.

The criticisms regarding the size of the area health boards, now referred to as Area Health Authorities, were met by proposing that bodies called Regional Health Councils would carry out some health functions, mainly those of planning for larger populations and including medical training, planning hospital and specialist services, deployment of senior staff and administration of the blood transfusion service. The Councils would not supervise the area health authorities which would still have a direct relationship to the central department, and would cover the same geographical areas as the new local authorities, being about 90 in number. The central department, it was proposed, should increase its activities by taking over from the RHBs their function with regard to major building schemes, and in order to keep in touch with local affairs the regional offices of the central department would be strengthened. The central department would also aim to have more effective control over spending.

At the other end of the scale local participation was to be encouraged by the establishment of district committees which would supervise the services at local level, and channel public and professional opinion up to the area authorities.

The third paper called a Consultative Document came out in May 1971 and introduced yet another element in reorganisation. This was an emphasis on management. The requirements of management efficiency called for a strengthening of the regional level, as the direct relationship of 80–90 area health authorities with the central department would be cumbersome. The proposed regional health authorities would have 'real management responsibility within the chain of command', and there would be 'maximum delegation downwards matched by accountability upwards'. Members of the new authorities, deliberately kept small, would have to be people skilled and experienced in management. Members with these qualities could best be secured by selection rather than election. The document therefore firmly separated the management structure and function from local participation and representation of local interests, the latter need to be met by community health councils.

The consultative document announced the setting up of an expert study to consider the management arrangements for the new structure,[129] while the central department's organisation was also to be scrutinised 'to ensure that it will be fully equipped for its new task'.[130]

The final broad structure was presented in the White Paper of August 1972 and mainly embodied in the Act of July 1973.

195

The proposals were criticised by the Opposition as not being sufficiently democratic, but the Labour Government, returned to power before the day appointed for reorganisation, did not impose any changes. A brief document[131] outlining the government's criticisms of the separation between the management of the service and participation by the people it is serving was published shortly after. Proposals for making the health authorities more democratic were included.

The objectives of reorganisation

These are to unite the health services, establish close links with local authority services, involve the professions and the public in the running of the service and ensure central control over finance through well-defined management structures.[132]

As one of the objectives of reorganisation is government control over spending, and one of the cardinal principles of the National Health Service is clinical autonomy for medical practitioners (which involves decisions about allocation of health resources to patients), there has to be an administrative arrangement whereby the conflict inherent in this situation can be resolved. Professional autonomy is respected by having all professional workers managed by members of their own profession, which also deals with the bogey of lay administration, and there is at all levels advisory machinery whereby the professions involved can be consulted and make their views known.

At the operational – or district – level (see Chart 9) where the resources are allocated to the patients by the professionals there is representative machinery to make joint planning possible. For this purpose differences in staff structure have to be accommodated; for instance the nurses can be represented at district level by the District Nursing Officer as there is a clear hierarchical structure already operating[133] but there is no such hierarchy for the doctors, GPs being under contract of service to the Family Practitioner Committees and the consultants under contract of employment to the regional health authorities. Some hospital consultants are already grouped as previously described under the Cogwheel system of joint planning, but the planning and co-ordination must now extend to all the medical services. This is done by setting up District Medical Committees to act as advisory and planning bodies. GPs and consultants both serve on these committees, and one GP and one consultant are sent as representatives to the Medical Advisory Committee for the Area. In this way it is hoped that both the objective of participation by the profession and that of accountability for spending can be reached.

Participation by the public has been divorced from the manage-

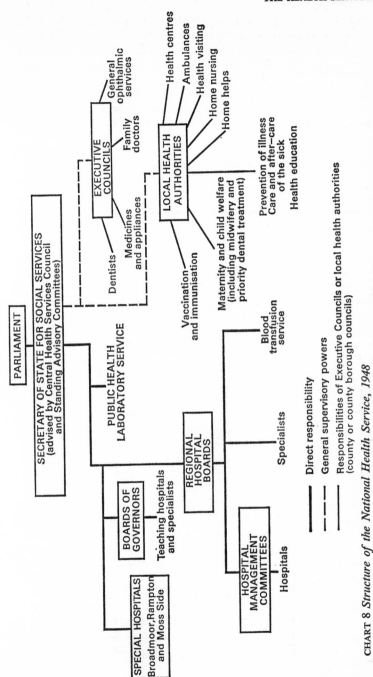

CHART 8 Structure of the National Health Service, 1948

This diagram gives a broad view of the organisation of the National Health Service and omits or simplifies some of the details.

ment structure. The lay members of the regional and area authorities, who are few in number, are not directly representative of the public although there are places for nominations from local authorities. New bodies, the Community Health Council,[134] have been set up for this purpose one for each district, and in a brief life have already had many vicissitudes. The original proposals in the White Paper were criticised in Parliament as giving so little power to the community health councils that they were likely to be toothless watch-

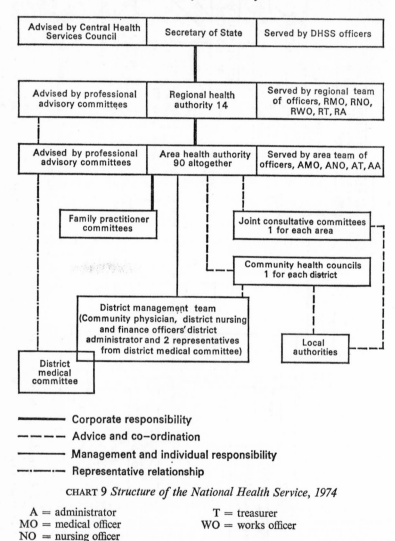

CHART 9 *Structure of the National Health Service, 1974*

A = administrator   T = treasurer
MO = medical officer   WO = works officer
NO = nursing officer

dogs. This situation has improved by making the regional health authorities responsible for appointments to the councils, not the area health authorities as at first proposed, and by reducing the regional health authorities' share of nominations to the council to one-sixth. The local authorities nominate half and the voluntary agencies concerned with health matters in the district the remaining one-third.[135] In order to keep criticism as objective as possible members of a community health council may not also be members of the regional and area authorities, nor may they be members of newly set-up Teams of Officers. The original proposals also excluded staff working in the district covered by the community health council, but the Labour Government decided that they should be able to serve if they were invited to do so. The Labour Government increased the strength of the community health councils in two ways. First, by making it mandatory for a spokesman from the new district management team to attend meetings at the request of the community health council to answer questions; these meetings are open to the public and so present an opportunity for greater involvement and understanding by the consumers. Second, by asking the regional health authorities to consult the community health councils regarding appointments to their area health authority. A National Council is suggested to advise and assist the work of these very new bodies, which have the potential for a very effective contribution to the health service. Although not intended to be part of the complaints machinery of the National Health Service it is possible that the community health councils may be viewed as such by the public. They will be able to act as 'patient's friend' and advise on the lodging of individual complaints, and will also be able to deal with broad areas of complaint, but not individual matters. The public may, however, find this an added confusion in an already confusing area.

The objective of closely linking health and local authority services could probably be best attained by uniting them under one authority. This has been discussed and rejected. Instead a duty to collaborate has been laid on both authorities as recommended by the Working Party set up to discuss collaboration in 1971.[136] In its first report published in 1973, environmental health, personal social services and school health matters were discussed.[137] The Joint Consultative Committees proposed in this report have been set up under the National Health Service Reorganisation Act.[138] As these are considered to be very important to the effective delivery of care by both health and local authorities it is suggested by the DHSS that the chairmen of area health authorities and local authority committees should be appointed to the joint consultative committees and should be supported by their senior officers to consider specific areas of common concern, such as social work support for hospitals, child health, mental health and services for the elderly. Local authorities also have representation on Area Health Authorities.

Duties that were formerly carried out by local authorities other than under the National Health Service Acts have had to be transferred to the new authorities. For instance the notification of births under the Public Health Act, 1936, must now be made to the area medical officer, and arrangements have to be made for housing the domiciliary staff, the midwives and district nurses, who were formerly housed by their employing local authority when necessary.

The objectives of unification and effective management will it is hoped be achieved by the new structure for the National Health Service.

Complaints machinery

Complaints machinery has been discussed in each document concerning reorganisation. The Porritt Committee saw no reason to change the systems already in practice and assumed that the small number of complaints against doctors indicated the public's satisfaction with the service. The alternative explanation is that the machinery, heavily weighted in favour of the doctor, is difficult to work and requires great persistence on the part of the complainant.[139] Doctors must be protected from irrational or malicious attacks and health problems can arouse strong emotions of guilt and hostility. Complaints against GPs were only allowed by the Executive Councils where they concerned breach of contract. In the hospital service complaints were dealt with 'almost entirely internally'[140] but with no further or more impartial appeal except to courts of law where appropriate. Statutory Enquiries occasionally look into serious complaints. The Davies Committee[141] was set up in 1971 to advise on hospital complaints procedures and suggest a code of practice. The pressing need for some other body led to the appointment of a Health Service Commissioner (who was also the Parliamentary Commissioner for Administration) in 1973. Section II of the Reorganisation Act deals at some length with his office and duties.[142]

The new structure

At the time of writing the new structure had been in operation for three months. Brown, Griffin and Haywood in the third report of the Humberside Reorganisation Project[143] say that an 'appraisal of the reorganisation will probably not be practicable until well into 1975'. The description of the new structure is therefore largely based on the White Paper, the Act of 1973, the 'Grey Books', the Health Reorganisation Circulars of the DHSS, and other documents relating to the changes being made. The Grey Book *Management Arrangements for the Reorganised NHS* gives very detailed proposals for the structure which have largely been accepted and should be consulted along with the White Paper (Cmnd 5055).

Although tempting to study, the process of change is beyond the scope of this chapter. However, mention should be made briefly of the way it has been managed. For many months the new authorities worked alongside the old, new staff appointments being programmed to take place during the transitional period. The DHSS instituted a series of Circulars (HRC) in 1972 which were sent out to all bodies concerned with the old and new structures, to advise on developments, explain and inaugurate changes in functions and new procedures. Information bulletins were issued to staff to keep them in touch with developments and regions had their own newsletters, giving information on local happenings. Joint liaison committees of senior staff from the different sections of the health services were set up to guide the various bodies concerned with planning the changes.

At central government level the Secretary of State is, as before, responsible for the National Health Service and is ultimately accountable for its performance and cost. He is advised by the Central Health Services Council as laid down in the 1946 Act, and served by the officers of the Department. In the Department, and its regional offices, the needs of certain categories, such as children, are considered as an entity, cutting across the 'genericism' of reorganisation in health and the local authority social services.[144]

Accountable to the Secretary of State are the fourteen regional health authorities, responsible for regional planning and policies, allocation of resources between the area health authorities and monitoring their performance, the appointment of senior medical staff in all but the area health authorities concerned with the university medical schools, and a variety of services which require regional organisation. The members of the regional health authorities are appointed by the Secretary of State, who has a duty to consult various bodies first, listed in Schedule I of the Act. An innovation is the payment of chairmen, which recognises the heavy demands made on their time. The regional health authorities are advised by regional advisory committees, representing the health services staff. These committees, provided that they are seen to be truly representative of their staff group or profession, are given statutory recognition and must then be consulted by the regional health authority.

The five salaried officers of each regional health authority form a Regional Team of Officers and include medical, nursing and works officers, an administrator and a treasurer. Their task is to work with the area teams of officers in planning and co-ordinating services, and to advise their authority on performance in the areas under its supervision. They are not the managers of the area officers.

The area health authorities, ninety in number, are the third tier of authority. They must provide a comprehensive health service for their area and have taken over all the functions of the hospital management committees and Executive Councils, and most of those of the local health authorities. They serve populations ranging from 1 million to less than one-quarter of a million, and are co-terminous with the new local government boundaries. In London some boroughs are grouped together and thus match the area health authority. They are accountable to the regional health authorities. The chairman of each authority is appointed by the Secretary of State, and the rest of the members by local authorities, the universities, and by the regional health authorities, and should include at least one doctor and nurse. These professional members are in addition to the area advisory committees, and the area team of officers, which includes the area medical officer, nursing officer, treasurer and administrator.

The area team of officers prepares plans for presentation to the region and, with local authority staff, for presentation to the joint consultative committee. Working through that committee they must ensure that medical services are provided for school health, public health and for the social services. They delegate executive responsibility to the district management teams, monitor their performance and co-ordinate their activities. Although the area team of officers are not managers of the district team, and both are responsible directly to the area health authority, the status of the area officers is to be higher than that of the district officers.[145] How this will emerge in practice has yet to be seen. The Central Health Services Council in their Report for 1972 recommended that the district community physician should be of equal status to the area and regional community physicians, and of consultant rank. They felt that the quality of work, at the 'level closest to the patient', should be protected.

Each area health authority covering the university medical and dental schools is responsible for providing clinical facilities and is designated as a Teaching authority, referred to briefly as AHA(T).

The area health authorities also carry out the functions of the former Executive Councils through Family Practitioner Committees[146] and for this are responsible directly to the Secretary of State, not the regional health authorities. They have no managerial control over the GPs who remain independent contractors as before. In the new National Health Service, however, the health centres, in which increasing numbers work, will be under control of the area health authorities and the whole structure will be health orientated with emphasis on the primary care team of which the GP is the leading figure.

The area health authorities will also be 'managers of hospitals' for the purposes of the Mental Health Act, 1959, relating to discharge of patients. Three or more members of a committee or sub-committee of the area health authority, not necessarily themselves members of the authority, will have powers to discharge. Although the committee appointed for these purposes must have one or more area health authority members on it, power to discharge can be exercised by three people who are not area health authority members.[147]

The area health authorities are not representative either of professional or public interests. The professional advisory committees are there to present the interests of the staff and the public is represented by community health councils.

Most Areas are divided into up to five Districts for the practical provision of services, nearly one-third of the smaller area health authorities are not further divided, and the structure and staffing of these is slightly different from the rest.[148]

For the consumer and the staff providing health care the district 'will form the natural community for the planning and delivery of health care',[149] serving populations of about 250,000. It has a District General Hospital, or group of hospitals, although, because the siting of hospitals was in response to needs and government boundaries of years gone by, the District General Hospital may not actually be in the district, or possibly not even within the area health authority boundary. The natural patient 'flow' of the community is the basis on which districts have been identified, but no new boundaries will preclude people using services they have grown accustomed to. Various management arrangements deal with problems of 'overlap'[150] which may also be concerned with the social work service available to the hospital, coming either from the local authority in which the hospital is sited, or from the local authority whose population is largely served by the hospital.

There is no district authority, no group of selected lay people jointly responsible for the service. At district level the health service is fully integrated, and the local professional staff are involved in planning and delivering all health care. There is a district management team composed of the district community physician, district nursing, finance and administrative officers, and two elected representatives from the district medical committee involving all the doctors working in the district, one a hospital consultant, the other a GP. Collectively and individually the team of six is responsible to the area health authority. All members of the team have equal status and none may override the others. In order to ensure that there is no domination of any individual or group the team must come to a consensus of opinion on any matters of decision. Any disagreements that cannot be resolved must be referred to the area health authority.

The role of the community physician is important in that he is concerned with countering at consumer level those developments in the social services as a whole which fragment the consumer's interests. In the Green Paper, 1970, it was stated that the 'services should be organised according to the main skills required to provide them rather than by any categorisation of primary user'. (This is referred to also in the section on environmental health.) The district management team will be responsible for setting up Health Care Planning teams to deal with categories of consumers who have a multiplicity of interdependent needs and who need 'a high level of interaction between hospital and community care'.[151] The community physician will be responsible for the management of these teams which will be multi-disciplinary, and will include workers from outside the health service such as local authority social workers. The groups most likely to benefit from this kind of interaction and planning are the elderly, mentally disordered, children and maternity cases. Promoting and supporting other planning activities thought to be necessary, such as reviewing local provisions, and identifying unmet needs will also be part of the community physician's role.

District organisation will, it is hoped, put an end to the domination of the hospital sector – the acute general hospitals rather than those for chronic conditions. The needs of the acutely ill are more readily met as they require limited care, from a few specialist staff, and show economic and social returns in that patients regain their previous state of functioning. The needs of the chronically ill require much more 'management' in the sense that the resources required are often interdependent and substitutable; they need the help of many and different workers and the pay-off may be only a postponement of greater incapacity.

The allocation of resources in the unified service should lead to economies and better provision, but this leaves untouched the major problem of health finance, one that is not unique to this country. Professor Chester, discussing world problems of financing health care, thinks it possible that 'no country can afford the health care system that it really needs'.[152] Economic setbacks in this country led to cuts in spending in all sectors in 1973, holding up capital projects, and wage increases. The taxpayer is reluctant to shoulder heavier burdens, particularly as the psychological mechanisms of denial lead him to hope and expect that he will have little use for health or social services. Although on the whole satisfied with the National Health Service,[153] individual difficulties, long waiting lists for hospital treatment and public scandals about very impoverished services leave few people in doubt that more money is needed, and there is, for instance, great public sympathy for the nurses' demand for higher pay. But where the extra money is to be found beyond the economics of reorganisation remains a mystery, and where the limits are to be set is a subject that, like death, is carefully avoided.

Issues of life and death

This chapter has so far been concerned with the control of death; in considering family planning, abortion and euthanasia we come to more controversial issues.

Population policy – family planning and abortion

It has always been difficult for the state to influence patterns of fertility. While a woman may feel that the decision about her family size is a matter for herself and her spouse, the total community is obviously concerned about the size and 'shape' of the population. Since the late eighteenth century we have swung in anxiety between over-population and under-population. The equation today is no longer regarded as a simple one of people–food, but includes the quality of life. Damaging inequalities can result from the maldistribution of cultural resources, and larger families can be disadvantaged.[154]

Family limitation by contraception, abortion and infanticide must be as old as man.[155] It was not until the nineteenth century that circumstances were favourable for open discussion of birth control.

When family planning was discussed by the Committee on Abortion[156] in 1939 the population appeared to be still in danger of decline. Consequently the majority believed that birth control advice should be given only on medical grounds. In a minority report Mrs Thurtle said that the wealthy could buy contraceptives, and that the decision by the majority discriminated against and penalised the poor, who had 'visited upon them the shortcomings of their upper- and middle-class sisters'.

Before 1939 local authorities were empowered to give advice to married women who were medically at risk, but not many did.[157] The major work was undertaken by the Family Planning Association (a voluntary organisation that aimed to be a pressure group but found that it had to do the work as well).

Since the 1960s anxiety has again swung to fears of over-population. The 1967 National Health Service (Family Planning) Act enabled local authorities to give advice to all women regardless of medical need or marital status. Development of the services was very uneven and by 1972 there was still one local authority not providing a service either directly or through the agency of a voluntary body. Some were giving a full, free service including a domiciliary service. Until the National Health Service (Family Planning) Amendment Act, 1972, all provision was directed at women. This Act allowed local authorities to provide vasectomy without charge as part of their family planning service. The Select Committee on Science and Technology in 1971 in discussing population came to the conclusion that 'the Government must act to prevent the consequences of population growth becoming intolerable for the everyday conditions of life'. The action that the government took was rather less than hoped for, in that it set up a Population Panel to assess the situation and the available evidence, rather than a Special Office as suggested by the Select Committee. The first report of the Population Panel published in March 1973 recommended the development of comprehensive family planning services as an integral part of the National Health Service.[158] Apart from any stabilisation of the population it should benefit the quality of family life. The report of the Chief Medical Officer of the Department of Health in 1968 acknowledged 'the positive contribution of family planning to family wellbeing'. About 200,000 unwanted pregnancies are thought to occur each year and he pointed out that of the 54,000 children received into care in 1965 about 20,000 could be regarded as unwanted or lacking adequate parental control. This report sees family planning as essential for preventing family suffering and deprivation, regardless of population trends. One of the major tasks seems to be to get families to use the services available.[159]

The question of payment for family planning was debated throughout the passage of the National Health Service Reorganisation Bill. Early proposals had not escaped from the thinking of the 1930s, in that medical need was considered to be the main criterion for free advice and supplies, whereas much evidence pointed to the importance of meeting social needs. This was emphasised when the Lords, led in 'revolt' by Baroness Llewellyn Davies, demanded free family planning for all. The Conservative Government eventually arranged for a family planning service available for all under the National Health Service with supplies on prescription. This meant that families who would normally not pay prescription charges (those on supplementary benefit for instance) would get supplies free. The Labour Government from February 1974 worked towards an entirely free service. One difficulty to be dealt with was the problem of payment to GPs. Family planning advice other than on medical grounds does not fall within the terms of the GP's contract, and new arrangements have to be negotiated.

Although the Registrar-General's returns in the 1970s have reported record low natural increases in population and reductions in the annual numbers born there is still some way to go before stability or zero population growth is reached.

The great availability of contraceptives, and in particular the pill, which is extremely reliable, may have led to the great increase in the incidence of gonorrhoea. The incidence of this disease rose throughout the 1960s but in 1972 showed a slight decline in the number of new cases. It is particularly a disease of young adulthood, occurring mainly in the 18–24 age range.[160]

Abortion describes the termination of a pregnancy up to twenty-eight weeks (sometimes it is used for termination in the first sixteen weeks, later termination being called miscarriage). It is a very significant factor in all industrial societies. Comparative figures are misleading as societies where abortion is legal will produce fairly accurate information, while in other countries this will be concealed. In this country in 1972 there were 156,714 notified abortions.[161] Guesswork suggests that another 50,000 to 100,000 illegal abortions occur each year,[162] apart from spontaneous, or natural, abortions which happen once in every five to ten pregnancies.

From 1803 in this country abortion was a secular crime, but the Infant Life Protection Act, 1929, carried a therapeutic clause in that an abortion carried out in 'good faith' to save the life of the mother was not illegal. This led to confusion of interpretation and there was no case law until 1938 when a gynaecologist, Mr Bourne, notified the police of his intention to terminate the pregnancy of a fourteen-year-old victim of rape.

The committee set up in 1937 to enquire into the prevalence of abortion found that the law relating to abortion was being flouted by all classes of women.[163] They did not recommend any extension of grounds for legal abortion and only a hesitant and limited extension of family planning. Mrs Thurtle in her minority report said that 'it is not possible to enforce a law affecting a large class of persons – in this case the women of the country – unless the law has the sanction of that class'.

After the Bourne case in 1938 the legal grounds for abortion were extended from threat of the life of the mother to threat to her physical and mental health. No provisions were made regarding the physical or mental state of the unborn child, nor the social situation of the family. At its conference on abortion in 1966 the Family Planning Association made a strong plea for the law to be clarified, which was done in the National Health Service (Abortion) Act, 1967. Abortion is legal if it is to protect the life, or physical or mental health of the woman. On 'social' grounds a pregnancy can be terminated if it presents a risk to the physical or mental health of her existing children. It is also legal if the unborn child is considered to be at risk. Two doctors have to agree to the abortion and by an amending Act in 1970 one of them is required to be the doctor who performs or supervises the abortion.

Abortions can be performed only in National Health Service

hospitals or places approved by the Department of Health. Approval was given for one year initially to 59 registered nursing homes, reduced to 55 by 1972. Fees are payable to the homes and the doctors operating there, but not to the National Health Service hospital.

There are great regional differences in numbers of abortions and in the marital status of the patients.[164] Doctors may decide for themselves whether they will perform abortions or not, but the situation of the nurses who have to attend is not so easy. There has been distress reported amongst nurses. They are not involved in the preliminary discussions with the patient that would enable them to sympathise with her need and perhaps thus override their feelings for the unborn child. There appears to be no satisfactory enlargement of the criteria on which decisions can be made without influence by the personal prejudice of the doctor. Punitive attitudes have been revealed which may prevent a decision being made in the best interests of the community, even if it also appears to condone undesirable behaviour in the patient.

Anxiety about the way the Abortion Act was being implemented led to the setting up of a committee in 1971, under the chairmanship of Mrs Justice Lane, to review the working of the Act, but not the principle underlying it. In their balanced and sensible report of 1974,[165] the Committee were 'unanimous in supporting the act, and its provisions' and thought that the gains outweighed any disadvantages.

Euthanasia and decisions about death

Euthanasia, like abortion, is a topic that generates heat. The thought of continuing into extremely ripe old age holds terror for some. Fears of being maintained in life, to be a burden on others and incapacitated oneself, has led to demands for some policy on euthanasia. The Private Member's Bill presented in 1970 by Dr Gray was defeated. It proposed that people should be able to file a declaration for or against euthanasia with their medical records. Reorganisation of the National Health Service should ensure better care for the dying and their families. Discussion during a Lords debate on the National Health Service Reorganisation Bill revealed some of the public disquiet about this aspect of the service, and the desire for death with dignity. More than half the deaths take place in hospital now, and over two-thirds are elderly. Those who die at home often have a need for support and services through a terminal illness. Cartwright's study[166] reveals some of the deficiencies, in particular the lack of collaboration between hospital and community services.

Developments in medicine open prospects of care undreamed of a few years ago, such as kidney machines and 'spare-part' surgery.

The cost of these treatments is infinitely greater than anything previously undertaken, and decisions will have to be made about priorities and expenditure, and whether some people are more worth saving than others. As consumers come to perceive their needs so the demand for treatment increases. People will be less willing to accept discomforts and distress that were once considered an unavoidable and natural part of life. Decisions about life and death are being presented to doctors and patients in a way that was unknown a generation ago.

Conclusion

Towards the end of 1973 Sir George Godber, the Chief Medical Officer of the DHSS, retired after many years in the health service. In his last Annual Report, 1972, he wrote of the advances and achievements of the National Health Service over twenty-five years, and stated, 'in time of need for myself or my family I would now rather take my chance at random in the British National Health Service than in any other service I know'. He pointed out how much of a part of our way of life it is: 'A majority of health professionals have done most if not all their professional work within the Health Service.' About one-third of the population were born into the National Health Service, and many more will remember little if anything of the pre-1948 health services. This may perhaps account for the fears that one of the negative achievements of the National Health Service has been to promote a view of health as something that is obtained by curing sickness rather than by preventing it. The responsibility of the individual for his own habits of life may be lessened rather than supported and guided unless health education is encouraged, and preventive measures that lie outside the National Health Service promoted. Wadsworth and Butterfield[167] note that this disadvantage was foreseen by Sydney and Beatrice Webb in *The State and the Doctor*, 1910, and reflect that the two attitudes to a free health service of fear of abuse and lessening of personal responsibility on one hand, and of the belief that health will be improved on the other, have existed side by side for years. They are not, however, irreconcilable and evidence to support both views can readily be found. Perhaps many would find the Lane Committee's comment on the Abortion Act an apt description of the National Health Service: 'Its advantages outweigh its disadvantages.'

Further reading

The National Health Service has been much studied and written about. It is a vast topic with many facets. Life and health have value in economic and ethical terms, and the management of health care and the quality of the health professionals are of interest to most people at some time. A short reading list will inevitably miss out excellent papers and books.

DHSS publications include:
> *The Annual Report of the DHSS.*
> The annual report of the Chief Medical Officer, *On the state of the public health.* (This has a useful reference section at the end of each chapter.)
> *The Annual Report of the Hospital Advisory Service.*
> *The Annual Report of the Central Health Services Council.*

There are government publications on many special topics, e.g.:
> *The Committee of Enquiry into the Cost of the NHS* (Guillebaud Report), Cmd 9663, HMSO, 1956.
> *Royal Commission on Medical Education* (Todd Report), Cmnd 3569, HMSO, 1968.
> *Committee on the Working of the Abortion Act* (Lane Report), Cmnd 5579, HMSO, 1974.

The Office of Health Economics – founded in 1962 by the Association of the British Pharmaceutical Industry – publishes pamphlets on a variety of topics.

On the development of the health services useful books are:
> BMA, *Health Service Financing*, 1970. This has a long historical introduction.
> BRIAN ABEL-SMITH, *The Hospitals 1800–1948*, Heinemann, 1964.
> W. M. FRAZER, *A History of English Public Health 1934–1939*, Baillière, Tindall & Cox, 1950.
> RUTH HODGKINSON, *Origins of the National Health Service*, Wellcome Medical History Library, 1967. A history of the Poor Law Medical Services between 1834 and 1871.
> KATHLEEN JONES, *A History of the Mental Health Services*, Routledge & Kegan Paul, 1972.

Early studies of the National Health Service include:
> H. ECKSTEIN, *The English Health Services*, Harvard University Press, 1958. (An analytical study of origins and achievements.)
> ALMONT LINDSAY, *Socialized Medicine in England and Wales*, Oxford University Press, 1962.
> ROSEMARY STEVENS, *Medical Practice in Modern England: The Impact of Specialisation and State Medicine*, Yale University Press, 1966. (An account of the development of both medical practice and the National Health Service.)

ARTHUR WILLCOCKS, *The Creation of the National Health Service*, Routledge & Kegan Paul, 1967.

Preparations for change include:

A Review of the Medical Services in Great Britain (Porritt Report), Social Assay, 1962.

The two Green Papers, *The Administrative Structure of the Medical and Related Services in England and Wales*, 1968, and *The Future Structure of the NHS*, 1970.

The Consultative Document, 1971.

The White Paper, *NHS Reorganisation – England*, Cmnd 5055, HMSO, 1972.

The Grey Books, *Management Arrangements for the Reorganised NHS*, and *Collaboration Between the NHS and Local Government*, 1972.

R. G. S. BROWN, *The Changing National Health Service*, Routledge & Kegan Paul, 1973.

Other studies include the Nuffield Provincial Hospitals Trust series edited by G. McLachlan, *Problems and Progress in Medical Care*, Oxford University Press.

Notes

1 The 1973 National Health Service Reorganisation Act became operational in April 1974.

2 1946 National Health Service Act, Section I, (1).

3 1388, 12th Richard II. See Karl de Schweinitz, *England's Road to Social Security*, Barnes, New York, 1943, chapter I.

4 M. W. Susser and W. Watson, *Sociology in Medicine*, Oxford University Press, 1971; A. Cartwright, *Patients and their Doctors*, Routledge & Kegan Paul, 1967, chapter XI; M. E. J. Wadsworth, J. W. H. Butterfield and R. Blaney, *Health and Sickness – The Choice of Treatment*, Tavistock, 1971.

5 See studies such as Thomas Ferguson and A. N. MacPhail, *Hospital and Community*, Oxford University Press, 1954, and Robert Kemp, 'The golden bed', *Lancet*, 14 November 1964.

6 Norman Longmate, *King Cholera – the Biography of a Disease*, Hamish Hamilton, 1966.

7 *General Report on the Sanitary Conditions of the Labouring Population of GB*, HMSO, 1842, p. 144: 'In the great mass of cases . . . the attack of fever precedes the destitution, not the destitution the disease.'

8 See note 5.

9 *Minority Report of the Poor Law Commission*, HMSO, 1909, discusses at length the problems of Poor Law medical services and lack of preventive work.

10 W. M. Frazer, *A History of English Public Health 1834–1939*, Baillière, Tindall & Cox, 1950, p. 451.

11 One of the three working parties set up in 1971 by the DHSS to consider aspects of reorganisation of the National Health Service.

12 DHSS, *The Future Structure of the NHS*, HMSO, 1970. (The second Green Paper.)

13 1973 National Health Service Reorganisation Act, Clause 10.

14 1972 Local Government Act, Section 112.

15 See the *First Report of the Working Party on Collaboration between the NHS and Local Government*, HMSO, 1973, for further discussion of the plans for environmental health services.

16 *First Report of the Royal Commission on Environmental Pollution*, Cmnd 4585, HMSO, 1971.

17 The 1972 *Annual Report of the Chief Medical Officer of the DHSS* discusses some of the problems in the introduction.

18 See Brian Abel-Smith, *The Hospitals 1800–1948*, Heinemann, 1964, and Ruth Hodgkinson, *Origins of the National Health Service*, Wellcome Medical History Library, 1967.

19 *Minority Report of the Poor Law Commission*, part I, chapter 5, HMSO, 1909: 'The Poor Law Infirmaries are growing in popularity ... skilled artisans and the smaller shopkeepers are coming to regard [them] as a municipal institution paid for by their rates and maintained for their convenience and welfare [they] are fast becoming rate-aided hospitals.'

20 The White Paper, *A National Health Service*, Cmd 6502, HMSO, 1944, Appendix A, 'Existing services'.

21 See Kathleen Jones, *A History of the Mental Health Services*, Routledge & Kegan Paul, 1972, for a full and lively account of developments in the mental health field.

22 It is interesting to note that while a great deal has been written on the development of services for the poor there appears to be little collected information on the care of the well-to-do. This is of particular importance in the health service as many of the services made available for all were based on the kind of care that the middle classes usually paid for.

23 See the *Minority Report of the Poor Law Commission*, HMSO, 1909, for a description of the medical policy and practice of the Boards of Guardians; also Ruth Hodgkinson, *op. cit.*

24 See *Minority Report*, chapter 2: 'Phthisis cases are maintained in crowded, unventilated homes where there are unrestrained facilities to convey the disease to their offspring. Diabetes cases live on the rates and eat what they please.'

25 *Op. cit.*, chapter 5, 'The treatment of the sick by the public health authorities', (VI) 'Health visiting'.

26 Herman Levy, *National Health Insurance*, Oxford University Press, 1944.

27 For a very full and clear account of the complaints machinery see Rudolf Klein, *Complaints Against Doctors*, Charles Knight, 1973.

28 In the first three years of the National Health Service nearly 5 million full dentures were supplied, about 1 person in 10 of the total population (figures from the Ministry of Health Information Service).

29 See Mary Stocks, *A Hundred Years of District Nursing*. Allen & Unwin, 1960.

30 See W. M. Frazer, *op. cit.*, and Madeline Rooff, *Voluntary Societies and Social Policy*, Routledge & Kegan Paul, 1957, Part 2, 'The maternity and child welfare movement'.

31 In a speech given in 1909 Dr F. Truby King said: 'The decadence of nations is threatening many lands. France, with its declining birth rate has already become a second-class power. . . . We hear much nowadays about national defence. The safety of nations is not a question of the gun alone, but also of the man behind the gun, and he is mainly the resultant of the grit and self-sacrifice of his mother. If we lack noble mothers we lack the first element of racial success and greatness.' Dr Truby King was a pioneer in the field of infant welfare. Originally employed as Medical Superintendent of a mental hospital in New Zealand, he applied the principles of successful stock breeding that he developed on the hospital farm, to the care of human infants. In a paper to the Farmers' Union he stated that if the same care and attention were given by the government to instructing mothers in how to rear their babies as was then being devoted to the rearing of stock, they would soon save infant lives.

32 The 1918 Education Act gave local education authorities the duty to make arrangements for treatment, and extended the service to secondary schools.

33 See the Report of the Chief Medical Officer of the Ministry of Education for 1956 and 1957, *The Health of the School Child*, in which the first fifty years of the school health service is described.

34 Report of the Feversham Committee, *The Voluntary Mental Health Services*, HMSO, 1939.

35 See Ministry of Education, *Report of the Committee on Maladjusted Children* (Underwood Report), HMSO, 1955, for a description of the growth of child guidance.

36 *Report of the Sheldon Committee on Child Welfare Centres*, HMSO, 1967.

37 *Interdepartmental Report on the Future Provision of Medical and Allied Services*, HMSO, 1920. Other reports of the inter-war years include the *Royal Commission on National Insurance* (1926), which suggested that medical services should be separated from the insurance system and maintained from public funds. The PEP reports on *Public Social Services* (1937) and on the *Health Services* (1937) suggested that there should be a clear separation between the essential health services, which are housing, nutrition, education and insurance, and the sickness service. The sickness service should be centred on the GP, suitably trained, who would act as educator, co-ordinator and counsellor. The BMA reports of 1930 and 1938, *A General Medical Service for the Nation*, suggested the regional organisation of hospital services.

38 Margery Spring Rice in *Working Class Wives*, Penguin, 1939, reported on the survey conducted by the Women's Health Enquiry Committee into the health of women, mothers in particular. The standard of

health was low, the result both of inadequate nourishment, and inability to pay for medical treatment.

39 There was no information available on the numbers and types of hospital beds available in the country. The Ministry of Health had to make surveys of hospital resources in 1938 and 1939.

Further surveys on existing hospital facilities for the whole of Great Britain were started in 1941, some by the Ministry of Health and some by the Nuffield Provincial Hospitals Trust. English and Welsh services were summarised in *The Hospital Surveys – The Domesday Book of the Hospital Service*, produced by the Nuffield Provincial Hospital Trust in 1946.

40 R. M. Titmuss, *Problems of Social Policy*, HMSO, 1950, chapter V.

41 *Ibid.*, chapter XXIV, Part 4.

42 *Social Insurance and Allied Services*, Cmd 6404, HMSO, 1942, Part 6, para. 427.

43 Set up by the BMA and Royal Colleges in 1940.

44 See Sydney and Beatrice Webb, *The State and the Doctors*, Longmans, 1910. They note that one-sixth of all doctors worked as district medical officers for the Poor Law boards. There were perhaps as many or more working for public health authorities.

45 For interesting accounts of the negotiations that took place see Gordon Forsyth, *Doctors and State Medicine*, Pitman, 1973; Arthur Willcocks, *The Creation of the National Health Service*, Routledge & Kegan Paul, 1967; and *Health Service Financing*, BMA, 1970.

46 This antagonism may not have been as widespread as the BMA suggested; nevertheless, an Amendment Act was passed in 1949 which prevented the introduction of full-time salaried service for GPs and dentists except by Act of Parliament. The NHS Act of 1966 was just such an act.

47 See Pauline Gregg, *The Welfare State*, Harrap, 1967, Appendix A.

48 *Report of the Poor Law Commissioners*, HMSO, 1842, p. 41. Dr Duncan, the medical officer of health of Liverpool, reported to the Commissioners: 'It is found that the faculty of perceiving the advantage of a change is so obliterated as to render them incapable of using, or indifferent to the use of, the means of improvement which may happen to come within their reach.' The same problem of apathy remains, and contrasts sadly with Beveridge's idea that the 'individual should recognise a duty to be well and to co-operate with all steps which may lead to diagnosis of disease in early stages'. Robert Kemp, 'The golden bed', *Lancet*, 14 November 1964, noted that among certain groups of patients 'apathy is all too common'.

49 The annual report of the Chief Medical Officer is published by HMSO under the title *On the State of the Public Health*.

50 The Constitution of the Central Health Services Council is contained in Schedule I of the National Health Services Act, 1946. There are 21 medical and 20 lay members. The *Annual Report* is published by HMSO, and gives information on the work of the standing advisory committees.

51 *Report on Ely Hospital*, Cmnd 3975, HMSO, 1969. See also the

Annual Report of the DHSS, Cmnd 4462, HMSO, 1969, p. 43, which describes the new service.

52 *Ibid.*, p. 43. The *Annual Reports of the Hospital Advisory Service* are also published by HMSO. In the 3rd report (for 1972, published 1973) progress was reported as follows: 'During the year it became apparent that the increasing physical resources allocated to hospital development generally and to the long-stay services in particular are beginning to show their effects.'

53 The National Health Service contribution in 1972 was 8¾ per cent of the total source of finance. 70 per cent of the money for the Service came from taxes, and a further 16 per cent from taxes was made available to local authorities for their health and personal social services.

54 *Royal Commission on Medical Education 1965–68*, Cmnd 3569, HMSO, 1968.

55 From the first Ministry circular to the new regional hospital board, in 1947.

56 *Report on the Cost of the NHS*, Cmd 9663, HMSO, 1956. See also the analysis of expenditure on the National Health Service prepared for the Committee by R. M. Titmuss and B. Abel-Smith, *The Cost of the NHS in England and Wales*, 1956.

57 Figures from the Annual Reports show that in England and Wales in 1948–9 hospital and specialist services accounted for 51 per cent of total expenditure (£128 million). In England alone in 1972–3 it was about 57 per cent of total expenditure (about £1,700 million). Comparisons are not straightforward as early reports present joint figures for England and Wales.

58 Ministry of Health, *Hospital Plan for England and Wales*, Cmnd 1604, HMSO, 1962, presenting schemes to be started in the period up to 1971. See also the Central Health Service Council, *The Functions of the District General Hospital* (Bonham Carter Report), October 1969. The DHSS Information Office reported that by 1969 8 district general hospitals had been completed, 83 more were partly complete and 45 more were in progress.

59 See the *Annual Reports of the DHSS* for 1969 and 1970. Also, *Better Services for the Mentally Handicapped*, Cmnd 4683, HMSO, 1971.

60 'The Regional Hospital Boards are responsible for exercising a general oversight ... of the hospital service in their region. It is a corollary of this recommendation that the Ministry should leave the task of supervising the HMCs to the Boards' (Guillebaud Report, Cmd 9663, HMSO).

61 The first Green Paper, 1968, for example noted that the respective roles of the regional hospital board, and hospital management committees were not clear. Of the boards it said: 'Their primary task as originally conceived was planning and co-ordinating development; their intervention in matters of management has grown out of their responsibility for allocating financial resources.'

62 Ministry of Health, *Report of the Committee on Senior Nursing Staff Structures*, HMSO, 1966.

63 Ministry of Health, *Management Functions of Hospital Doctors*, HMSO, 1966. A paper prepared by a sub-committee of the Advisory Committee for Management Efficiency in the National Health Service.

64 Ministry of Health, *First Report of the Joint Working Party on the Organisation of Medical Work in Hospitals*, HMSO, 1967; *Second Report*, HMSO, 1972; *Third Report* (by a different working party), HMSO, 1974.

65 See R. G. S. Brown, *The Changing National Health Service*, Routledge & Kegan Paul, 1973, and Rudolf Klein, *op. cit.*, for useful discussion on the professional role and responsibility.

66 1946 National Health Service Act, Part II, Section 5. Also the 1968 Health Services and Public Health Act, Part I.

67 Figures from T. E. Chester, 'Health Service Reorganised', *National Westminster Bank Review*, November 1973, quoting a study undertaken by Lee Donaldson Associates on behalf of the DHSS. See also Michael Lee, *Opting Out of the NHS*, PEP broadsheet, 527, 1971 – a short and useful discussion on the private sector, which is by no means a simple issue.

68 *Private Practice in the NHS Hospitals*, Cmnd 5270, HMSO, 1973.

69 See the pamphlets of the Institute of Economic Affairs such as Arthur Seldon, *Universal or Selective Social Benefits*, 1967; *After the NHS*, 1968; and Fabian pamphlets such as *Socialism and Affluence*, 1967. The IEA pamphlet by M. H. Cooper and A. J. Culyer, *The Price of Blood*, 1968, and R. M. Titmuss, *The Gift Relationship – from Human Blood and Social Policy*, Allen & Unwin, 1971, present the two sides of the argument.

70 Para. 730. The report suggests that there may be a time when the prophecy will be fulfilled.

71 DHSS, *Facilities and Services of Psychiatric Hospitals in England and Wales in 1966*, HMSO, 1969.

72 Brian Abel-Smith and R. M. Titmuss, in *The Cost of the NHS in England and Wales*, Cambridge University Press, 1957, noted that after the age of forty-five, single people make a greater demand for hospital care than married people. J. R. Butler and M. Pearson, *Who Goes Home*, Bell, 1970, found that long-stay patients often had social difficulties.

73 Ministry of Health, *A Hospital Plan for England and Wales*, HMSO, 1962, para. 17.

74 DHSS, HM (71) 97, *Hospital Services for the Mentally Ill*.

75 DHSS, HM (72) 71, *Services for Mental Illness related to Old Age*.

76 The annual reports of the Chief Medical Officer, *On the State of the Public Health*, give an account of the plans and discussions in the section on mental health. See the report of the conference of the Royal College of Psychiatrists and the DHSS on services for the mentally ill and handicapped, *Approaches to Action*, ed. G. McLachlan, HMSO, 1971. Criticism of the Hospital Plan in the PEP report *Psychiatric Services in 1975* by G. F. Rehin and F. M. Martin, 1963, drew attention to the dependence of hospital usage on community provision, and their second broadsheet, *Towards Community Care*,

1969, commented on the inadequacy of information on which services are based.

77 E. R. Bransby 'Mental illness and the psychiatric services', *Social Trends*, HMSO, 1973.

78 *Ibid.*

79 The Act followed the publication in 1957 of the *Report of the Royal Commission on the Law Relating to Mental Illness and Mental Deficiency*, Cmnd 169, HMSO.

80 Section 44.

81 Part V of the Act deals with the admission of patients concerned in criminal proceedings.

82 Henry R. Rollin, *The Mentally Abnormal Offender*, Pergamon Press, 1969.

83 See bibliography and notes in Henry R. Rollin, *op. cit.*

84 See for instance the *Report of the Committee of Inquiry into Whittingham Hospital*, Cmnd 4861, HMSO, 1972. Also the *Annual Reports of the Hospital Advisory Services*.

85 *Better Services for the Mentally Handicapped*, Cmnd 4683, HMSO, 1971, outlines the existing services and the possible ways of improving them. The lack of information on numbers and needs was being remedied by DHSS financed surveys. The report of the 1970 census of mentally handicapped patients was published in 1972. The DHSS also publishes reports on the facilities and services of psychiatric hospitals, unfortunately with rather a long time-lag, but trends can be seen and regional differences in facilities are made apparent. Pauline Morris's study, *Put Away: A Sociological Study of Institutions for the Mentally Retarded*, Routledge & Kegan Paul, 1969, drew attention to the inadequacies of institutional care, and Barbara Robb's *Says Everything*, Nelson, 1967, made a dramatic impact in its exposure of conditions in geriatric hospitals.

86 The Constitution of the Executive Councils is found in Schedule 5 of the Act, 1946.

87 In 1973 there were over 20,000 GPs, 12,000 dentists, nearly 14,000 chemists and 7,000 opticians.

88 Rudolf Klein, *op. cit.*

89 Set up in 1962 on the recommendation of the *Royal Commission on Doctors' and Dentists' Remuneration* (Pilkington Committee), 939, HMSO.

90 See John Butler, *Family Doctors and Public Policy, A Study of Manpower Distribution*, Routledge & Kegan Paul, 1973.

91 See Pauline Gregg, *The Welfare State*, Harrap, 1967, Appendix A, V, for a short clear account of the system of pay; also Gordon Forsyth, *Doctors and State Medicine*, Pitman, 1966, and *Health Service Financing*, BMA, 1970.

92 R. Klein, *op. cit.*, found that the least affluent quarter of GPs were only marginally better paid than teachers in 1913–14, with an average annual income of £195. The period between the wars was no better for them.

93 See the Minister's *Annual Report* for 1966.

94 In 1972 this allowance was £1,594. From the National Health Service notes (DHSS Information Office) *How the Family Doctor is paid*, August 1972.

95 Central Health Services Council, *Report of the Committee on General Practice within the National Health Service*, HMSO, 1954, pp. 2–3 and para. 12.

96 Central Health Services Council, Standing Medical Advisory Committee, *The Field of Work of the Family Doctor*, HMSO, 1963. (Chairman: Dr Annis Gillie.)

97 Courses for GPs are provided under Section 63 of the Health Services and Public Health Act, 1968.

98 *Royal Commission on Medical Education*, Cmnd 3569, HMSO, 1968.

99 G. Forsyth and R. F. Logan, *Towards a Measure of Medical Care*, Oxford University Press, 1962, and R. F. L. Logan, 'Studies in the spectrum of medical care', in *Problems and Progress in Medical Care*, Nuffield Provincial Hospitals Trust, 1964.

100 R. F. L. Logan, *op. cit.*

101 General Medical Services, *Report of the Joint Working Party on Diagnostic Support for GPs*, HMSO, 1973.

102 See note 101 and *Present State and Future Needs*, Royal College of General Practitioners, 1970.

103 Rosemary Stevens, *Medical Practice in Modern England*, Yale University Press, 1966.

104 Paula Cook and R. O. Walker, 'The geographical distribution of dental care in the UK', *British Dental Journal*, vol. 122, nos 10, 11 and 12, 1967.

105 Government Social Survey, *Survey of Adult Dental Health in England and Wales*, HMSO, 1970. Over one-third of the population had no teeth of their own.

106 'Methods of remuneration', Report of the *Ad-hoc* Sub-committee of the General Dental Services, *British Dental Journal*, vol. 117, 20 October 1964, p. 331.

107 See also John R. Butler, 'Studies in the use of dental care', *Studies in Social and Economic Administration*, vol. 1, no. 3, July 1967.

108 Cmnd 3410, HMSO.

109 The number of pairs of glasses supplied in the six months of 1948 were 1,800,000. In 1949 the number was 6,800,000 and in 1950, 8,300,000. In 1951 charges for lenses and frames were introduced and there was an immediate fall to 4,689,000 in 1951. This may have been in part due to satisfaction of the outstanding pre-service demand. The number has remained at 4–5 million since then.

110 Cmd 9663, HMSO, 1956, paras 631–9, on the maternity and child welfare service.

111 Ministry of Health, *Report of the Committee on the Maternity Services*, HMSO, 1959.

112 Ministry of Health, *An Inquiry into Health Visiting* (Jameson Committee), HMSO, 1956.

113 *Ibid.*, chapter X, 'The fieldwork and functions of the health visitor'.

114 T. Ferguson and A. N. MacPhail, *Hospital and Community*, Oxford University Press, 1954.

115 Set up under the 1962 Health Visitors and Social Work Training Act were the Council for Training in Social Work and the Council for Training of Health Visitors; they shared a chairman until, under the 1970 Local Authority Social Services Act, a new Central Council was set up for all social work training.

116 The first Vaccination Act, making vaccination compulsory for infants, was passed as early as 1853. It was difficult to implement as there were no means for enforcing it.

117 *Health and Welfare, The Development of Community Care*, Cmnd 1973, HMSO, 1963; ditto, Cmnd 3022, HMSO, 1966.

118 In 1968 the name changed to the Social Work Division, and in 1971 it was amalgamated with the Home Office Child Care Regional Service.

119 See the first Green Paper, 1968.

120 A patient admitted from a burnt-out caravan to the regional burns unit in the next regional hospital board was kept in the unit for many weeks beyond his medical need while the local authorities concerned disclaimed responsibility for him. Three were involved – the one in which the burns unit was situated, the one in which his own hospital was situated and from which he was transferred to the burns unit, and the one in which his now non-existent caravan had stood.

121 Set up in April 1972 to safeguard the interests of staff during reorganisation, advise on the transfer of staff, and keep them informed of progress.

122 See Schedule 5 of the National Health Service Reorganisation Act and the Health Service Reorganisation Circular, HRC (73) 26, which gives the provisions of the Health Service Acts from 1948–68 remaining in force.

123 DHSS, *National Health Service: The Future Structure of the National Health Service*, HMSO, 1970.

124 Cmd 9663, HMSO, 1956, para. 730.

125 *A Review of the Medical Services in Great Britain*. The Committee, appointed in 1958, was sponsored by the Royal Colleges and the BMA.

126 The Seebohm Committee's Report, *Local Authority and Allied Personal Social Services*, appeared in July 1968 and the Redcliffe-Maud Committee on *Local Government in England* reported in June 1969. The latter report suggested that local government could be responsible for all health services, but this idea was rejected for reasons discussed in the Green Papers.

127 Ministry of Health, *National Health Service: The Administrative Structure of the Medical and Related Services in England and Wales*, HMSO, 1968.

128 DHSS, *National Health Service: The Future Structure of the National Health Service*, HMSO, 1970.

129 The Management Study Group were assisted by a firm of management consultants (McKinsey & Co.) and by the Health Services Organisation Research Unit of Brunel University. The steering committee

supervising the study group had members from the DHSS and wide representation from the health services. For its terms of reference see the White Paper on National Health Service reorganisation, Cmnd 5055, HMSO, 1972.

130 See the DHSS *Annual Report* for 1972, chapter 2.

131 *Democracy in the National Health Service: Membership of Health Authorities*, HMSO, May 1974.

132 DHSS, *National Health Service – The Future Structure of the National Health Service*, HMSO, 1970.

133 *Report of the Committee on Senior Nursing Staff Structure* (Salmon Committee), HMSO, 1966.

134 See the White Paper, Cmnd 5055, HMSO, 1972, HRC, (74) 4, and the Labour Government paper *Democracy in the NHS*, HMSO, 1974.

135 The Voluntary Agencies are selected by the regional health authorities.

136 The Consultative Document, 1971, announced the establishment of this working party, at the same time as the expert study on management. The reports of these two groups, and the *Report of the Working Party on Medical Administrators* (Hunter Report), are referred to as the Grey Books.

137 DHSS, *A Report from the Working Party on Collaboration between the NHS and Local Government*, HMSO, 1973, on its activities to the end of 1972. Ditto, HMSO, 1973, on its activities from January to July 1973.

138 HRC, (73) 19.

139 See Rudolf Klein, *op. cit.* This is a very readable and lively account of what would appear to be a dull subject.

140 *Report of the Committee on Hospital Complaints Procedure* (Davies Committee), HMSO, 1973.

141 See note 137.

142 He has power to investigate complaints 'that an individual has suffered injustice or hardship through maladministration or failure to provide treatment and care'. DHSS, *Annual Report*, HMSO, 1972.

143 A study of the processes of reorganisation on Humberside has been undertaken by the Department of Social Administration at the University of Hull. Three progress reports have been issued so far, by R. G. S. Brown, S. Griffin and S. C. Haywood, in April and December 1973 and in July 1974.

144 The Health Service Development Group, one of eight groups under the Secretary of State, has a section concerned with social handicap, including the homeless, alcoholics and drug addicts, the elderly and the physically handicapped.

145 The Grey Book, *Management Arrangements for the Reorganised NHS*, chapter 2, p. 21.

146 See Schedule I, Part II, 1973 Act, for membership.

147 HRC, (74) 7.

148 *Management Arrangements for the Reorganised NHS*, Exhibits VI and VII, gives diagrams of the two different structures. The area team of officers and the district management team will combine functions

in the areas without districts and will be called Area Management Teams.

149 The White Paper, Cmnd 5055, para. 45. See HRC, (74) 23 for lists of districts.

150 See the HRC Circulars (73) 4 and 74 (32).

151 *Management Arrangements for the Reorganised NHS*, para. 2, p. 47.

152 Professor T. E. Chester, 'Health Service reorganised', *National Westminster Bank Quarterly Review*, November 1973.

153 The Porritt Committee canvassed public opinion and found a high level of satisfaction with the Service, although this may have been expressed by people who were not using the Service much, if at all, but were glad to know it was there.

154 *Royal Commission on Population*, Cmd 7695, HMSO, 1949, chapters 5 and 14.

155 Ralph Thomlinson, *Demographic Problems*, Dickinson, California, 1967.

156 *Report of The Interdepartmental Committee on Abortion*, HMSO, 1939, reprinted 1966.

157 Ministry of Health Circular, 1937.

158 Cmnd 5258, para. 43.

159 The report of the Chief Medical Officer for 1972 gives information on research into the use of family planning services.

160 See the reports of the Chief Medical Officer, DHSS, for information and figures.

161 *Ibid*.

162 Philip Rhodes, *Paper in the Report of the Proceedings of a Conference on Abortion in Britain held by the Family Planning Association*, Pitman, 1966.

163 See note 156.

164 See the Registrar-General's supplement on abortion, in *Statistical Review of England and Wales*.

165 *Report of the Committee on the Working of the Abortion Act*, Cmnd 5579, HMSO, 1974. Section B of this report gives a very good survey of the many areas of disquiet.

166 *Care of the Dying*, HMSO, 1973. (Proceedings of a National Symposium, 1972.) Ann Cartwright *et al.*, *Life before Death*, Routledge & Kegan Paul, 1973.

167 M. E. J. Wadsworth, W. J. H. Butterfield and R. Blaney, *Health and Sickness: the choice of treatment*, Tavistock, 1971.

7 The personal social services
Eileen Holgate and Olive Keidan

The development of services for people unable to meet all or some of their needs within the confines of their own family and intimate social setting has been haphazard, veering between anxiety about the consequences to society as a whole of aiding its dependent members, and thereby encouraging dependency in others, and the compassion aroused by contact with people who led wretched and impoverished lives. Protection of the weak from exploitation of many kinds, such as child labour, confinement of unwanted relatives in mad-houses, baby farming, has had to reconcile fears about the consequences of interfering with individual liberty, with the need to help the helpless. The growth of personal social services has centred on certain groups which have been identified at different times as having special needs – such as orphans, juvenile delinquents (a different category altogether rather than a facet of the whole group of children in need), the frail elderly, the mentally disordered, the physically handicapped, addicts, immigrants, the homeless – and on the gradual emergence of social work as a profession.

Both statutory and voluntary agencies have made contributions to the development of social work services. These services have been characterised by personal interaction between clients and workers, through which needs are assessed.

In the statutory services emphasis initially and inevitably lay in administering the law and fulfilling the duties and obligations laid on the local bodies. Nineteenth-century developments tended to be dominated on one hand by thoughts of poverty, destitution and the Poor Law, and on the other hand by the growing individualisation of services and the positive approach found in public health. The Education Act of 1870 signalled a comparable involvement by the local boards of education with many families, while the century-long pursuit of protection and care for the mentally disordered, whether rich or poor, had a similar impact on central government and local authority provision.

The services for those who were the concern of the Poor Law authorities covered all their needs albeit at a low level of provision. Health care, education, shelter were all provided by one statutory authority, with Relieving Officers acting as 'fieldworkers' and co-ordinators. The development of separate and specialist provision for some groups of clients enlarged the scope of local authority services, and involved some specialisation by the staff involved. Preparation for work in local authorities was primarily concerned with the orientation of the staff towards their role as paid servants of the corporation or board, and acquiring a knowledge of the law to be administered.[1]

It was in the voluntary agencies that the processes of casework and group work were identified and training for social work as we know it today began. Courses giving a theoretical background to the field-work training of the volunteers who comprised the bulk of the work force were started by agencies such as settlements and the Charity Organisation Society. From these early beginnings grew the first university departments concerned with social work training in Liverpool and London.[2]

A wide range of voluntary agencies grew up alongside the statutory services.[3] Many of their activities prompted a fundamental review of statutory responsibility followed by changes in provision. There was for example a slow development in the safeguarding of children in their own families from the founding of the National Society for the Prevention of Cruelty to Children (NSPCC) in 1889 to the Department of Health and Social Security (DHSS) Memorandum on the management of non-accidental injury to children in 1974. A very recent similar development can be seen in the growing recognition by a few voluntary agencies of 'battered wives' as a group for which special provision should be made rather than as individuals suffering in personal misfortune. The process of interaction and reciprocal involvement seems to have speeded up. The first shelter for battered wives was opened in 1971[4] – and already local authorities are moving towards an acceptance of responsibility in this area of need.

The relationship between voluntary and statutory services and their respective roles was debated throughout the latter part of the nineteenth century. The Charity Organisation Society attempted to make a rational allocation of functions between voluntary and statutory agencies, the former to work with the remediable cases, while the Poor Law dealt with residual problems. There was considerable resistance among voluntary societies to any extension of statutory provision beyond a bare minimum, but pressure was growing for the state to play a more positive role in welfare. The debate culminated in the division of opinion found among the members of the Poor Law Commission of 1905.[5] The First World War and following Depression damped down some of the passion that had characterised discussion, while the gradual extension of positive statutory provisions in income, health, education and employment services removed some of the basis for argument, and pointed the way to the Welfare State.

The statutory services

In 1948 the local authorities shed their duties as destitution authorities and looked forward to what the Ministry of Health in the Annual Report for 1949 referred to as the 'promotion of welfare for all regardless of means'. It has not proved easy to shake off the association of statutory care with poverty, and there is still a tendency to think of poverty as the core problem and to assume that people without financial worries are people without problems.

In the 1948 reorganisation local authorities had duties and powers under the National Assistance Act to provide domiciliary and residential care for the physically handicapped, the elderly and the homeless. Apart from those staff concerned with the blind there were few trained workers available, and very little interest in training.[6] Much of this work was already being undertaken by voluntary agencies who continued to operate alongside the statutory services.[7]

Under the National Health Service Act the local health authorities became responsible among other things for the community care of the mentally disordered. Relieving Officers and welfare workers from the voluntary agency concerned with mental deficiency, the Central Association for Mental Welfare, constituted the bulk of the fieldwork staff. Some preparation for the new work, albeit small, was given through the National Association for Mental Health.

The local authority education departments continued this care of children at risk educationally and emotionally through school health services and child-guidance clinics. The School Welfare Officers evolved from the School Attendance Officers, who were employed by the School Boards to try to ensure that the law regarding compulsory education was being observed.[8] The new Children's Departments of the local authorities set up under the Children Act of 1948 were made responsible for children at risk in their family life. The Home Office, the central government department having responsibility for this new service, started training courses in conjunction with social work departments at several universities before the service was actually launched.

Medical and psychiatric social workers were employed by the new Regional Hospital Boards (RHBs). Although there were well-established professional social work courses there were far too few trained workers in 1948 to meet demand.

The probation service, like the children's departments of the local authorities, was, and today still is, the concern of the Home Office. The officers who worked as servants of the local probation committees were trained under the auspices of the Probation Training Board set up by the Home Office before the war. The Home Office has been more vigorous than the Ministry of Health in promoting social work training. It was not until the Younghusband Working Party reported in 1959[9] that social work training for the health and welfare services was fully considered. Even then the training for residential workers remained sketchy.

In 1948 the central government departments concerned with social work and ancillary services were the Ministry of Health, which had oversight of the local authority health and welfare services, and of the hospital and specialist services, the Home Office which had similar responsibility for the local authority children's departments and the probation service, and the Department of Education, which was responsible for the education services, including school health and welfare.

The problems that such divided responsibility can bring were recognised after 1948. Joint circulars from central government departments to the local authorities in the 1950s urged co-operation in order to deal more effectively with families whose needs lay across organisational boundaries. The movement towards consolidation of the personal social services grew from the realisation that the fragmentation that was inherent in the services could be avoided by focusing on the family rather than on 'needy' categories.

The first move towards a comprehensive family service came in 1960 when the Ingleby Committee,[10] concerned with child neglect and delinquency, concluded that the long-term solution would lie in reorganisation of the various services concerned with the family, and their combination into a unified family service. In 1965, in the White Paper *The Child, the Family and the Young Offender*, it was announced that the government intended to form a small committee to review the organisation of the local authority personal social services in England and Wales. This committee, under the chairmanship of Mr Seebohm, was asked to consider what changes were desirable in order to secure an effective family service. On discussing its brief the committee decided to extend the definition of the family: 'We could only make sense of our task by considering also childless couples and individuals without any close relatives: in other words, everybody.'[11] The report was published in 1968 and came through as an authoritative, sobering document. A case for an organisational change was built on a close analysis of the state of affairs both inside and outside the local authorities. Lack of resources, including trained social workers, inadequate knowledge about the nature of the problems a service was intended to combat, and divided responsibility resulting from organisational fragmentation, led to inadequacies and could lead to muddled situations.[12] A strong case for a radical reorganisation had certainly been made.

The committee proposed each local authority should have a statutory duty to set up a unified Social Services Department providing social work and ancillary services, with its own principal officer, preferably a social worker, serving a separate Social Services Committee. At central government level there should similarly be one Department responsible both for the relationship between central government and the new departments and for the overall national planning of the personal social services together with the intelligence and research services, which were badly needed. On the question of training for social work the Committee recommended that the divisions and specialisms that had characterised training should end and that the three existing bodies concerned with training should be amalgamated.[13] Although the brief had specifically excluded consideration of the probation services and the voluntary sector the Committee found considerable agreement on the need to integrate all social work training including that for probation officers.

Because the very size of the new department might mean a monolithic structure, cumbersome and slow to respond to needs, and because it was vital that social work should communicate itself swiftly and smoothly to people, it was suggested in the report that most of the fieldwork should be undertaken by teams of about twelve professional staff responsible for areas of 50–100,000 population. In order to counter the accusation that people had experienced difficulty in understanding the personal social services and that the services had failed to reach them, the Committee laid emphasis on the need for the services to be community-based. Participation in the planning, organisation and provision of the services was the essence of a community-based social service and there was a new opportunity for voluntary organisations to make their contribution and for local authorities to mobilise these organisations, encouraging them with professional help and financial grants.[14]

The Seebohm Report was well received in social work circles although in local authority circles generally there was some opposition to the proposal of the Committee to impose one set pattern of departmental organisation. In Parliament the report was given a good reception, both Lords and Commons showing near unanimity in accepting the reasoning of the Committee for reorganisational change and the pattern for the future. The Committee had urged swift implementation of the proposals, but the government was awaiting the results of other committees of enquiry whose findings and recommendations would affect plans for reorganising the personal social services. In the end, however, with a General Election pending, the Local Authority Social Services Bill implementing the report was hurried through its final stages and became law on 29 May 1970, the reorganised service being scheduled to start operating from 1 April 1971.

The Act itself was quite a brief one since not all the Seebohm proposals needed legislation for their implementation.[15] It required local authorities to set up a Social Services Committee and to appoint a Director of Social Services together with adequate staff. The functions of the committee were to consist of those which up to that time had been performed by the Welfare and Children's Committees plus some from the Health Committee. Support for the latter had come, since Seebohm had reported, from the second Green Paper on the reorganisation of the National Health Service, in which it had been recommended that all social work should be undertaken by the new local authority Social Services Department.[16]

Initially it was not made clear which central department would have 'overlord' responsibility. This doubt was later resolved when it emerged that child care responsibilities, hitherto belonging to the Home Secretary, would in future lie with the Secretary of State for Social Services who was already responsible for health and welfare matters, but that the Secretary of State for Wales would have responsibility at central level for personal social services in Wales. The Home Secretary would, however, retain, for both England and Wales, his existing responsibilities relating to juvenile courts[17] because of his overriding responsibility for protecting the public and ensuring the rights and liberties of the individual.

Within the DHSS, a new division, the Local Authority Social Services Division, headed by a Deputy Secretary, was set up to undertake the new functions of the Secretary of State for Social Services. A Social Work Division of that Department with regional offices was established. Interestingly, in a service becoming generic, specialist interests were retained at regional level with concern for particular consumer groups.

A Personal Social Services Council as recommended by Seebohm[18] was set up in 1973 as an independent, non-statutory body, to advise the Secretary of State on policy issues and to promote development of the personal social services both statutory and voluntary. Members of the Personal Social Services Council are drawn from public bodies, local authorities, the professions and other institutions. Consumer representation, which Seebohm suggested, is missing.[19] Perhaps further consideration should be given to this omission, particularly as there is little likelihood of any of the members having been, or likely to be, on the receiving end of the service despite its apparent universality. Finance for the council is provided jointly by central government and local authorities.

With regard to training, the Seebohm recommendation that there should be one central body was implemented by the formation in 1971 of the Central Council for Education and Training in Social Work, an independent body with statutory authority to promote education and training in all fields of social work and to award qualifications. It succeeded the two previous training councils in the fields of health and welfare and the care of children and the training committee of the Advisory Council for Probation and After-care.[20]

At local level Social Services Departments, under Directors of Social Services, were established on 1 April 1971, to be responsible for the previously separate services for children, the physically disabled, the elderly, and the mentally ill. A range of other services were included,[21] all adding up to the basis of a comprehensive service to the family in the community. Although in Scotland the probation service became an integral part of the Social Work Departments following the Social Work (Scotland) Act, 1969, it was not included in the reorganisation in England and Wales. The dilemma facing education welfare officers as to whether to remain within the education service or to transfer to social services remained, and still remains, unresolved. Hospital social workers remained in the Health Service and were only transferred with much reluctance in April 1974.

Change inevitably poses a threat and brings anxiety. It was, therefore, with very mixed feelings that social workers from separate departments merged with each other and set about establishing a generic service. Whereas, particularly in children's departments, the social workers had constituted a high proportion of the personnel, they were joined by home helps, occupational therapists and an increasing number of other groups, which effectively highlighted the minority status of the social worker in the new departments (see Chart 10).[22]

Before any real consolidation could take place there was a further upheaval occasioned by the reorganisation of local authority boundaries on 1 April 1974. In the two-tier system of county and district levels, Social Services Departments in metropolitan county areas were placed at district level but otherwise remained at county level. Some local authorities were untouched by the change, others not only became part of larger areas but changed counties as well. April 1 1974 also heralded the restructuring of the National Health Service. This latter change affected Social Services Departments by adding the statutory responsibility for providing social work support for the health service and a statutory responsibility to co-operate.

This partnership by statute should, in the long term, help towards a reduction in use of hospital beds by those people whose needs would be met within the community, with local authorities providing a range of residential and domiciliary support services, recognising that many people now in hospital do not require skilled medical and nursing care and would benefit considerably from living in the community. Legislation lays down what personal social services the local authority should provide and, in recent years, this has been on an increasing scale as there is a widening appreciation of need. The long-term objective of a Social Services Department is, according to the Seebohm Report, to provide a 'community-based and family-oriented service available to all, reaching beyond the discovery and rescue of social casualties and enabling the greatest possible number of individuals to act reciprocally, giving and receiving service for the well-being of the whole community'.[23] A worthy objective indeed.

Work of the Social Services Department

A comprehensive service is the sum of the parts which make up the whole and in order to see the range of responsibilities and to begin to appreciate the scale of work undertaken by the Social Services Departments it is necessary to select some aspects for detailed study. A starting point for a family-oriented service seems to lead naturally to a focus on children, for whom the family remains today, despite doubts expressed from time to time about its functional usefulness, an important social institution.

Children and families

There is value in looking back in the past, in order better to comprehend the present child care services. Only a brief survey can be given here, but it is hoped that some of the more important landmarks may emerge in the process.

Like many other social services, those for children have developed in piecemeal fashion, often erratic in execution and limited in the attainment of objectives. If a single word can describe the process it is 'pragmatism', the treatment of each problem as it arises and in the context of the needs of the moment. It is only of late that a picture has emerged of services working on common principles. In the past if a child was said to be destitute he became the responsibility of one agency; if endangered or delinquent, that of another; if in need of temporary care because of, say, his parent's illness, then of yet another. Yet despite this compartmentalisation the saving feature was that progressively over the course of time his needs were being recognised and the last century, in particular, was a period of massive

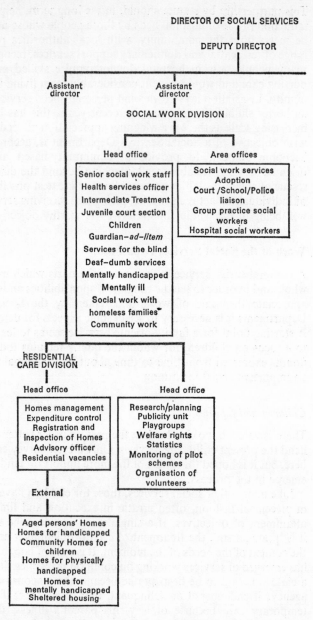

CHART 10 *A model of a local authority Social Services Department*

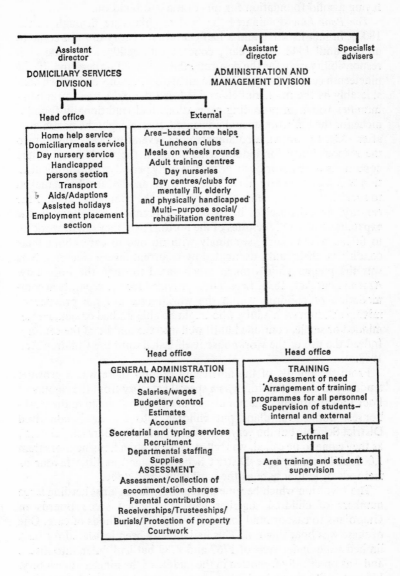

generation of legislation for children. In the reign of Queen Victoria more than 100 Acts for the welfare of children were passed, thereby laying a solid foundation for this century to build on.

The Poor Law dominated the field of child care throughout the 1800s; in fact its three and a half centuries' history did not come to an end until 1948. In its early concern with children the state took responsibility only for the destitute, the orphaned or deserted. In the nineteenth century the numbers in all these situations had grown considerably as the industrial cities displaced the old agricultural communities which in preceding generations had traditionally found a niche for the unfortunate and unwanted. Increasingly the parish and, after 1834, the union, a combination of several parishes, discharged the responsibility for indoor relief through the workhouse, where conditions were notoriously grim. The early period of institutionalisation was a particularly harsh one for children. Those who managed to survive their early years of life might, at the commencement of the century, find themselves hived off as apprentices to labour in the expanding mills and factories of the north. There they might work up to fifteen hours a day, seemingly with no one to care about their conditions, their ranks decimated by recurrent fever epidemics. Nor was the pauper child's plight much eased through the Poor Law Amendment Act, 1834. Legislation provided for the separate accommodation of children within the workhouse, but the practice of mixing children with adults who might be able-bodied or sick, feeble-minded or senile, continued until well into the middle of the century. Indeed the use of the workhouse itself lasted until the Children Act, 1948.

From the middle of the nineteenth century there was a growing tendency to extract children as a special category from the rigours of Poor Law treatment. The popularity of education spread to the workhouses. Some Guardians put children into the newly-conceived District Schools but the very size of some of these 'Barrack Schools', as they came to be called, was self-defeating, often housing more than 1,000 children. In time District Schools gained as little favour as methods of indoor care as the workhouse had done.

The revulsion which became increasingly felt against herding large numbers of children together had already led some Boards of Guardians to cast around for more acceptable methods of care. One of these was boarding out. This had already been legislated for on a limited scale under Acts of 1767 and 1782 but had fallen into disuse and was practically forgotten in the middle of the nineteenth century. Interest in it was revived when some Boards considered that, since outdoor relief could be granted in occasional cases when orphan children were placed with relatives or friends, it might usefully be extended to cover other children. It was, as one writer on the period has pointed out,[24] simply an extension of the use of outdoor relief administered in a more enlightened manner and involving closer supervision. To begin with, rural unions engaged in the practice but later industrial areas joined in. Support came from such public figures as Matthew Davenport Hill, Charles Dickens and Mary Carpenter, and the Poor Law Board after a very cautious appraisal of the system gave official approval in 1870. Even so it is well to remember that boarded-out children formed only a minority of pauper children in the care of the Guardians and as late as 1908 comprised only 8,659 compared with a total of 69,080 on indoor relief. Some local Boards experimented with other methods of care as well, such as cottage homes, on the model of those used on the Continent and already adopted by some voluntary child care organisations in this country. Towards the end of the century they became popular with other Boards, who saw this method of care as a distinct improvement over both the District School and the workhouse, which had such a stultifying effect on children's development.

The Poor Law care of children came under the scrutiny of the Royal Commission on Poor Law Relief, but the majority report of 1909 put forward no specific recommendation beyond urging that Poor Law children were to be brought up in the best possible way and that their care was to be administered by a single authority which should also be the authority to look after the needs of adults. Their report emphasised the curative and restorative nature of Poor Law treatment and it was left to the minority report, largely the work of Beatrice Webb, to stress the need for preventive work to reduce the incidence of destitution and other causes that led to children having to come into care at all. It was the minority report, too, which, in advocating the break-up of the Poor Law, recommended that the existing child care service should be incorporated in the education service which had recently become the administrative responsibility of the larger local authority units.

In spite of this the provision for care was dominated by the Poor Law until 1948, even though the Boards of Guardians had been abolished and their functions transferred to county councils and county borough councils, and the Children and Young Persons Act, 1933, whilst largely a consolidating measure, extended the provisions for children in need of care or protection.

DEVELOPMENT OF SERVICES FOR CHILDREN Protection of children not in the care of the Poor Law developed as different problems were revealed.

Baby farming, by which infants were placed for reward with strangers, was mainly concerned with illegitimate children. London in particular had a large number of private lying-in establishments

233

from which the infants might go, ostensibly for 'adoption' at a premium of anything up to £100. In reality the infants would be farmed out with private foster-mothers for a round sum or a small weekly payment. Since there were no laws for the compulsory registration of births and deaths before 1836, there was no disincentive to the neglect of infants, and every place freed by the death of one became available to another live infant, giving rise to yet one more lucrative transaction. After a particularly scandalous case involving the murder of a number of young children through neglect, Parliament set up a Committee on the Protection of Infant Life in 1871 and, after the shocking revelations made to that committee about the state of baby farming, passed the Infant Life Protection Act in 1872. Further scandals indicated the weakness of these provisions and it required stronger legislation in 1896 and then 1908 before the worst excess could be curbed. By then rising living standards coupled with improved employment opportunities had served to reduce the problem of baby farming.

Neglect of children and cruelty by their own parents could go unchecked in the last century because a man's children, like his wife, were regarded as his property to do with virtually as he pleased. Some early legislation existed, such as an Act of 1824, which prohibited a man from procuring his child to beg, and equally he would be guilty of an offence if he killed or injured his child, but there was little by way of law which discouraged a parent from neglecting his children. In any case it was virtually impossible to remove a child from his parent however badly he treated him. The family was inviolable and children's wrongs were none the less parents' rights. So strongly held was this principle, which even so benign a champion of children as Lord Shaftesbury was loath to see breached, that it was not until nearly the end of the century that the campaign calling for authorised intervention on behalf of neglected children gained headway.

In 1868 Boards of Guardians had been given power to prosecute parents who wilfully neglected their children but this applied only where these children had become the direct concern of the authorities, and left untouched the mass of families outside their ambit. Action for these came through the formation of a number of voluntary societies pledged to secure the prevention of cruelty to children. They were modelled on similar ventures in North America and their initial aim was to publicise the seriousness and extent of child neglect and cruelty. In 1889 these societies, most of which had by this time amalgamated into a national organisation, under the able direction of their secretary Benjamin Waugh, successfully initiated the first of the great pieces of protective legislation – the Prevention of Cruelty and Protection of Children Act. This strengthened not only the law relating to the punishment of adults for acts of wilful cruelty or neglect, but also provided for the removal of children from cruel and neglectful parents to a safer environment.

The child offender, unlike the orphaned or destitute or cruelly treated child who excited public compassion, remained the object of profound social disapproval for most of the nineteenth century. The principles of individual responsibility and retributive justice were strongly bound up in attitudes toward him and reflected in the policies relating to his treatment. For a long time too he was regarded as meriting equal treatment with adults before the law. Reduced to its simplest terms it meant that if he was caught committing any one of numerous offences, however trivial, he merited punishment. As late as 1880, Sir William Harcourt told the House of Commons of children of ten or eleven years of age who were constantly being committed to prison for several weeks of hard labour for such crimes as playing pitch and toss, obstruction in the streets, trampling down of grass and throwing stones and breaking windows.

Early efforts in the 1830s were directed at segregating young offenders from adults in prisons, even to the extent of providing a separate prison at Parkhurst for this purpose with the object of avoiding contamination with the hardened adult criminal and for providing training with the object of reforming rather than merely punishing child offenders. But it was not until well into the middle of the century that the Reformatory Schools movement inspired by Mary Carpenter made it possible for young offenders to be sent to these or the similarly conceived industrial schools for training and education. Side by side with this development, differentiation was gradually being applied in methods of trial, certain offences committed by juveniles being reduced from indictable to summary status, thereby avoiding trial by jury in an increasing number of cases. But the provision of a separate and modified juvenile court system did not become a reality until the Children Act, 1908, which was an important landmark in the history of the treatment of children who came before a court for any reason. During the Second World War Margery Fry and Max Grunhut suggested that the interests of both young offenders and society would be better served by abandoning legal and procedural considerations and concentrating on the welfare of the offender.[25] This line of thought was later examined by the Ingleby Committee but rejected by them in favour of further modifications of the juvenile court procedures. But the Kilbrandon Committee,[26] Scotland's equivalent to Ingleby, and the Labour Party Committee under the chairmanship of Lord Longford, took up the same theme and opted, in slightly different forms, for abandoning the concept of criminal responsibility for young people under sixteen and concentrating instead on treating their criminality on welfare lines. In 1965, the Labour Government published a White Paper on the subject under the title of *The Child, the Family, and the Young Offender* based on the Longford Report. The radical proposal to abolish juvenile courts in favour of family councils run by the local authority children's departments produced considerable opposition. It was later modified in a further White Paper, *Children in Trouble*. The Children and Young Persons Act, 1969, was based on this White Paper.

Child-care services in the 1940s were included in the general reappraisal of social services. At that time the care and supervision of children was allocated to different departments according to the legal definition of their functions. These departments included public assistance committees, education and health committees at local level and the Home Office and Ministries of Health and Education at central level. Not surprisingly there was a good deal of confusion over which department did what and for whom. The war years had produced a great number of children who required public care because of the disruption of family life and the increase in juvenile delinquency. The evacuation schemes, too, had shown up a great many child problems which might otherwise have remained hidden within the anonymity of the large industrial cities. A severe strain was placed on the local authorities' limited amount of accommodation for children, which in any case was already outdated.

In 1944 correspondence in *The Times*, initiated by Lady Allen of Hurtwood, drew attention to the generally poor situation of children in care, stressing that many orphaned, destitute or neglected children still lived under the chilly stigma of 'charity'. Too often they formed groups isolated from the main stream of life and education, few of them knowing the comfort and security of individual affection. As a result the Care of Children Committee was set up under the chairmanship of Miss (later Dame) Myra Curtis. Even before the Curtis Committee reported, the tragic case of the O'Neill children forced its attention on the nation, a case in which these children had been boarded out by a local authority with foster parents who neglected them to the point where one of them died.[27] The incident showed as nothing else could have done so vividly to what tragedy administrative muddle could lead. The report of the Committee in 1946 provided the blueprint for the Children Act, 1948, which placed a duty on local authorities to set up specialised Children's Committees under the central guidance of the Home Office.

The family today pays considerable regard to its child-rearing functions. Improved standards of living and the development of educational, health, social security and other social services have brought considerable refinement to family life. When we consider this aspect we find that parents not only provide for their child's nurture but, for the first few years of his life, act as the chief socialising agents, thereby greatly influencing the pattern of his life. Parents do, in fact, provide the basic model of family life for their offspring which will affect them not only through childhood, but also much later in adulthood. Partly through the diminution of the importance of the extended family in child rearing, partly through social changes, husband and wife form much more of a partnership in marriage than was previously the case. This makes for a far greater equality between the sexes in which boundaries of the role of each are no longer so rigidly defined. However, not all families function equally well in performing their child-rearing tasks. This may be because of personal factors or simply as a result of having to cope with inadequate housing or too little money.

ONE-PARENT FAMILIES One-parent families are a particularly vulnerable section of the community. Until recently the fatherless family was singled out as having the greatest difficulties, particularly the unsupported single mother.[28] Now the needs of motherless families are increasingly being recognised.[29] There are more than 1 million motherless or fatherless children living in about 620,000 one-parent families in Great Britain, i.e. one in ten of all families. It is estimated that about 520,000 are fatherless, of which 310,000 are divorced or separated, 120,000 widowed and 90,000 single.[30] Although our society is geared both economically and socially to two-parent families, they do not have the prerogative for happiness, as mounting divorce statistics testify,[31] and some families benefit from the withdrawal of an unsatisfactory parent. There is, however, sufficient research to indicate that for numbers of one-parent families the position is very difficult indeed. They constitute one of the fastest growing groups at poverty level in the country with nearly a quarter of a million living on supplementary benefit. Housing problems are often acute and many families have to find new accommodation[32] when they become fatherless and are quite unable to afford a mortgage. They have, therefore, to compete for the declining supply of rented accommodation. As poverty and poor housing are problems associated with two-parent families also, perhaps the distinctive features of single parenthood are loneliness and isolation. A parent may wish to work for social reasons but may be prevented because of having young children for whom no suitable day-care facilities are available. The problems may become so overwhelming that the parent sees no option but to place the children in care. In the year ending March 1973, 7,125 children were received into the care of local authorities in England because of the lack of a parent. *The Report of the Committee on One Parent Families* (Finer Report), 1974, proposed amongst its many recommendations a non-contributory Guaranteed Maintenance Allowance, which would be large enough to offer a choice to a parent of whether or not to work.

CHILDREN IN NEED OF CARE While every effort is made to prevent the breakdown of the family unit it is important to remember that not all parents are able to sustain a child-nurturing role. The child is now no longer seen as the 'chattel' of the parents; he is viewed as a person in his own right needing, in some circumstances, to be removed from his natural parents to permanent substitutes.

The 1948 Act underlined the requirement that each child in public care should be treated according to his own needs and abilities. While making it obligatory to rehabilitate a child with his relatives or friends if consistent with his welfare,[33] no legislation for preventive work was included and this shortcoming became increasingly evident as difficulties were experienced in providing acceptable substitutes to the child for his own family and social workers became frustrated by not being able to offer assistance to a growing number of families with problems which affected all areas of their life. The Ingleby Committee had recommended that children's departments be given extended powers to promote the welfare of children and to work with families to prevent their breakdown under stress and consequent separation. There was widespread approval for Section I of the subsequent Children and Young Persons Act, 1963, giving the mandate for preventive work, which became the special responsibility of local authority children's departments, who developed ways of assisting families at risk. Some operated rent-guarantee schemes to prevent eviction, set up family advice centres, helped pay relatives' fares to look after children and helped in a number of miscellaneous ways that would have been impossible before the Act.[34] The Social Services Departments continue to use their powers under the 1963 Act for preventive action, often in a variety of imaginative ways. Nevertheless, family breakdowns continue to occur and children have to leave their own homes, temporarily or permanently.

The 1972–3 DHSS statistics reveal that there were about 90,000 children in care in England, many of them received as a result of temporary deprivation.[35] Considering the upset experienced by most children in being removed from familiar surroundings, the question must be asked whether it was necessary for 15,000 to be in care because of the short-term illness of a parent and another 3,600 because of confinement. Full investigation of all requests for care is essential to discover what alternatives are available and also to identify families which may be at risk.[36]

Foster care This was strongly urged by the Curtis Committee as the best form of substitute care – short of adoption, which is the legal integration of a child into another family, and the Children Act, 1948, specified that where possible a child must be boarded out.[37] In the five years immediately after 1948 the proportion boarded out rose from 35 per cent to 52 per cent. As a consequence of fostering being widely favoured, residential care was seen as a last resort and therefore undervalued. Even the disbanding of the large barrack-like children's homes and the creation of smaller ones, many on ordinary housing estates, did little to alter the view of them held by social workers. There has, however, been a reappraisal of foster care, as it was realised through experience that it was not necessarily the best course for every child. Physical or mental handicap may rule it out in some cases, whilst in others the child may remain so attached emotionally to his own family that it is undesirable to attempt to place him in a substitute family. The failure rate is estimated to be high, probably half of the children placed on anything but a very short-term basis are returned from fostering to be placed elsewhere by the local authority.[38]

Foster parents are recruited from all sections of the community and a fair proportion are relatives of the child. A difficulty that social workers have to cope with in the fostering situation is the fear felt by foster parents that a foster child who has been treated for a long time as a member of the family may have to be returned to his parents if they demand it. The local authority has some power to reduce this possibility. If a care order has been made by a court a parent cannot demand the child's return without the court's consent. In other cases the local authority may assume parental rights over the child.[39] But instances do occur where a child is returned to his natural parents against his own and the foster parents' wishes, and they raise the issue of who is morally, if not legally, entitled to rear the child, the natural parent who was prevented from doing this or the foster parent who stepped in to fill the gap. To such questions there can be no generalised answers.

Fostering is a much cheaper method of public care than placement in a children's home. While the work is constantly being praised as an example of important community service and suggestions are made that foster parents should be accepted as equal colleagues of social workers,[40] recognition of their service is not reflected in the form of remuneration. There are exceptions, but on the whole local authorities pay allowances to cover maintenance only perhaps fearing that higher payments would attract undesirable applicants. In May 1974, foster parents organised themselves into a National Foster Care Association aiming, amongst other things, to improve the quality of the service given to children in care throughout the UK, to work for foster parents to have an effective share in policy-making on child care and to demonstrate to the community and to professional agencies the value of the service provided by foster parents and see this acknowledged by enhanced payments for all foster parents.

Adoption   Until the first Adoption Act, 1926, it was not possible for a parent to divest himself of his rights, liabilities and duties in relation to a child. Although what were known as *de facto* adoptions existed in practice these were not recognised in law and a parent could reclaim his child from the *de facto* adopters, who had very few safeguards for contesting this. The *de facto* adoption process came into focus particularly during the First World War in connection with the widespread campaign to help Belgian orphans and it was largely as a result of this that England and Wales, lagging behind most other developed countries in this respect, passed the first adoption legislation which was designed to 'confer the privilege of parents upon the parentless'.[41] Today adoption is covered in the main by the Adoption Act, 1958, which lays down in considerable detail substantive law and procedure designed to protect not only the child to be adopted but also the natural and adoptive parents. Adoption statistics used to reflect the social difficulties for women who gave birth to children outside marriage, the majority of adoptions being childless couples adopting illegitimate babies. Now greater efforts are being made to enable the single mother to keep her baby, society is more accepting of unmarried parenthood, the pill offers protection from unwanted pregnancies and abortion is more freely available. In an annually decreasing number of adoption orders being made,[42] the percentage of parents adopting their own children is rising, probably reflecting higher rates of divorce and remarriage as well as the increase in the number of unmarried mothers keeping their children and adopting them on marriage.[43]

With the shortage of babies for placement, statutory and voluntary adoption agencies are either closing their lists or widening their horizons. Children hitherto considered to be unadoptable because of being physically or mentally handicapped, of mixed race or past infancy are now being successfully placed for adoption and today adoptive parents may be older and already have children of their own. The integration of an adopted child into a family does bring about problems which one would not expect to see in families in which the members are bound to each other by blood ties, but there is evidence that in many families this artificial grafting process has resulted in happiness for adopted children and adoptive parents alike. A longitudinal study of adopted children published in 1972[44] showed that at the age of seven they were doing as well and often better than children living with both natural parents and considerably better than illegitimate children brought up by their own mothers. It will be interesting to know whether this position is maintained at adolescence when the search for personal identity, particularly of an adopted child, may become acute.[45]

A considerable number of couples have by-passed adoption

agencies and negotiated privately for adoptive children, as the law allows. Many of the private adoptions are arranged through 'third parties', persons who act as intermediaries putting parents and prospective adopters in touch with each other, a practice which causes concern although there is no proof that it is any less successful than agency-arranged adoption.[46]

[Aspects of adoption law have been criticised and there has been pressure for changes to be made. In 1972, the *Report of the Departmental Committee on the Adoption of Children* (Houghton Report) recommended that it should be possible for a mother to relinquish her child to an adoption agency before it was placed with adoptive parents and for her to take a final decision about adoption at an early stage so that adoptive parents could be assured that there was no possibility of a later change of mind necessitating the removal of the child.[47] The Committee also recommended that foster parents who have had the care of a child for five years or more should be able to apply for an adoption order without the risk of removal of the child by parents before the court hearing.] This recommendation has been criticised by social workers partly because they do not accept that any specific length of time is proof of the quality of a placement and partly because they fear that parents genuinely unable to care for their children might be deterred from placing them in public care. The Committee's recommendations were incorporated in a Private Member's Bill presented to Parliament in 1973.[48] Supported by all parties and most social workers, it seemed guaranteed to be accepted but, on the day of the second reading on 9 February 1974, Parliament was dissolved and the Bill was, therefore, lost. It is expected that the new government will sponsor a Bill in the near future which will strengthen further legislation relating to children.[49]

Recent research[50] has suggested that there are several thousand children with special needs currently in residential care who would benefit from fostering or adoption. The distinction between these two resources is becoming blurred as older children with knowledge of, and ties with, their family of origin, traditionally fostered, are now being placed in adoptive homes. It is argued that adoption gives a child greater security because there is a legal commitment. But, as with marriage, the legal bond does not determine the quality of the relationships, and there is no equivalent of divorce in adoption in the UK.

Child Protection Local authorities have protective and supervisory functions for children who are privately placed in foster homes by their parents for a continuous period. The current law on child protection is contained in the Children Act, 1958, as amended by the Children and Young Persons Act, 1969. This, broadly speaking, places an obligation on people to notify the local authority of their intention to act as foster parents for periods of more than six days to children not related to them. The authority then has a duty to investigate the matter and in certain cases may prohibit the placement or allow it to go forward provided specified conditions are observed. Private homes must be visited regularly unless exempted by the local authority. In recent years there has been a substantial increase in the number of children privately placed. In 1960, 6,837 had been notified to local authorities in England and Wales and in 1970 this number had risen to an estimated 10,811.[51] This reflects to some extent the number of people from abroad who, unacquainted with conditions here, often have considerable difficulty in finding placements or assessing their suitability. Even though recent amending legislation has made a genuine effort to clarify some of the difficulties which local authorities have experienced in administering the law, problems relating to such matters as the legal status of private foster parents and children will remain. This is inevitable in an area where, as indeed in all areas of child care, there are conflicting interests to be borne in mind. First, it is now commonly accepted that the welfare of children, in this case those below the upper limit of the compulsory school age, should be protected. Second, the law should take account of the rights of a parent to place his child with a family through a private arrangement. Third, the law should not be so stringent as to make it impossible for a good neighbour or friend to act as voluntary host to a child as and when need arises. Compromise in the legislation has resulted in a set of complex, detailed duties, powers and prohibitions. Even with the legislation some private fostering arrangements are most unsatisfactory. Holman[52] advocates a much greater control of all children placed under the Child Protection legislation and a more positive approach to supervision by statutory social work agencies.

Day care   Nearly 5 million married women go out to work, of whom about 1 million have children under five years old. Surprisingly little has been done to help these working mothers. Where help is not forthcoming from amongst their own family circle they are forced to make unsatisfactory arrangements with private individuals.[53] Very few mothers can afford to have paid help in the home to look after a small child.

Officially sponsored or approved day care is provided by local authority day nurseries and nursery schools[54] and registered private nurseries and child-minders. Local authority day nurseries existed before the Second World War but it was during the war years that they were greatly developed as part of government policy to free mothers for essential war work. After the war their number was allowed to fall on the grounds that, in the interest of the health and development of the child no less than for the benefit of the mother, the proper place for a child under two was with her at home. At the same time the intention was voiced of encouraging the growth of nursery schools for the three – fives.[55] A few years later the Ministry of Health actively discouraged local authorities from providing day nursery places because of the public expense involved, particularly where the need arose solely from the mother's desire to supplement the family income by going out to work.]

In the report compiled on behalf of the National Society of Children's Nurseries by a working party under the chairmanship of the late Dr Yudkin, it was pointed out that it was irrelevant to think of places in relation to the total pre-school population.[56] Some areas have far greater needs than others. But even in the highly industrial areas of the country where need might be expected at a high level, the provision of day nursery accommodation showed great variation. The acute shortage of places, even in areas where the population per 1,000 of the child population under five was relatively high, has meant that priority is given to special categories of families: unsupported mothers, those with poor health or those with exceptionally deprived living conditions – leaving, indeed, little if any room for others who may want day care for other good reasons. Existing nurseries usually have waiting lists despite the fact that graded charges are made to parents. The Yudkin Report suggested that private nurseries, which are usually run on a commercial basis, are more likely to be used by middle-class families who see their value in terms of the educational advantages for their young children, than by working mothers.

Yudkin's report, which followed closely on the Plowden Report, was very likely instrumental in rekindling interest in an area which had received little publicity since the war years. The provision of additional nursery places in selected areas was approved in the projects included in the Urban Programme which was announced by the government in July 1968. Initially thirty-four local authorities with areas of special social need were included in the programme, largely financed by the government; its provisions were subsequently enshrined in the Local Government Grants (Social Needs) Act, 1969.

In the absence of local authority nurseries, working mothers and others who must place their children during the daytime can make use of other recognised facilities, either with registered child-minders or in registered private day nurseries. Both methods are governed by the Nurseries and Child Minders Regulations Act, 1948, amended by Section 60 of the Health Services and Public Health Act, 1968. This was initiated in response to the disquiet which had arisen over inadequacies and loopholes in the earlier legislation which led to many children being cared for by unregistered daily minders who escaped the scope of the regulations. The child-minding laws, like private fostering, attempt to steer a course midway between trying not to discourage relatives, friends or neighbours from offering day-care for a child and at the same time ensuring that, as far as is possible, his health, welfare and safety are protected. Only people who take a child under five, not related to them, for daily minding for reward are affected by the extensive powers to impose requirements or make prohibitions relating to the suitability of minders and premises.

There has recently been an upsurge of interest in child-minding. A government-aided Child-minding Research Unit established in Cambridge has not only highlighted some of the enormities of illegal minding but it has also sparked off a great deal of response in local authorities, some of which are now prepared to subsidise day foster homes, providing equipment and arranging training for child-minders. There is also a Childminders Action Movement,[57] which aims to improve standards generally and to have child-minding fully integrated into the whole child care pattern as providing a valuable social service and offering an essential form of community care.

The recent development of play groups for children of all ages has tended to confuse discussion of the need for adequate day-minding facilities. Play groups are intended mainly to provide a social, educational experience for children and by no means only for those considered deprived in some way. They do not normally cater for any one child on a daily basis. Day-minding, on the other hand, must be available on a continuous basis for each child and is primarily intended to give relief to a hard-pressed parent or to enable her to follow employment.

Court work Where the state assumes an obligation to intervene between parents and their children the final arbiter is usually the court. The most common case is where the child has committed some act which, if committed by an adult, would have been liable to criminal prosecution. But the state also has a right or duty to intervene where there is neglect or ill-treatment of a child, where he is in moral danger or lacks control. The rules and procedures in these cases are governed by the Children and Young Persons Acts, 1933–69. Under these Acts, certain agents are authorised in emergency to remove children temporarily from their homes and bring them before the court. These are the police, local authority social services departments and the NSPCC. It is unusual to find a voluntary organisation like the latter with such powers as it gained in 1889 and doubts are sometimes voiced about the appropriateness of such an arrangement in view of the expansion of local authority responsibilities in this direction.

A child under the age of fourteen years or a young person under seventeen[58] may be brought before a juvenile court under care proceedings. The grounds on which such action can be taken have been frequently modified over the years, but the law is quite specific about what the case must rest on. Court action can result in a parent losing custodial rights over the child and the child too may find his liberty restricted. So a balance must be preserved between the welfare of the child as the court sees it, and the rights of parents and of the child himself. Currently, the grounds for action are established by Section 1 of the Children and Young Persons Act, 1969. They consist of a series of six alternative conditions plus a requirement that the court must be satisfied that the juvenile is in need of care or control which he is unlikely to receive unless a specified order is made. The six conditions cover:

(a) prevention of proper development or neglect of the child;
(b) being involved in situations in a household in which another child has been found to be neglected;
(c) exposure to moral danger;
(d) being beyond parental control;
(e) not receiving efficient full-time education;
(f) having committed an offence other than homicide.

If any of the grounds can be substantiated, it is still necessary to satisfy the court that it is not possible to bring about any improvement in the situation except through one of the orders it has the power to make. In effect, this means that the initiating agency must have taken steps to find out whether any action has been or could be taken to prevent the case from coming to court at all. Avoidance of compulsory action through the courts is an important theme in the recent legislation and has become an objective of social work support given to families.[59]

Parents and others in charge of children are sometimes prosecuted in connection with offences against them. One of the advances in recent legislation has been that it is now not necessary to prove that parents have committed specified offences, or, if they have, that these have been wilfully committed before it becomes possible to bring a child before the juvenile court as being in need of care. In other words, much more attention can now be paid to the welfare needs of children.

The inclusion of the sixth condition for care proceedings, that the child has committed an offence, was inserted as a means of enabling young offenders to be dealt with in the same way as other children in need of care.

Proceedings in a juvenile court are normally far less formal than in an adult court. Nevertheless, they are legal proceedings and this sometimes seems to conflict with the fact that, in deciding on the kind of treatment for the youngster before them, the magistrates must have regard for his welfare.[60] If the 1969 Children and Young Persons Act is ever fully implemented all children under fourteen who commit offences will be the subject of care proceedings in the juvenile court. New procedures will also ensure that prosecution is avoided for as many young persons under seventeen as possible. The government elected in 1970 decided not to implement these procedures for young persons and to postpone full implementation of those for children. This means that children of ten and over still remain liable to prosecution for offences, although informal procedures ensure the avoidance of this for many children.

Because the new procedures require evidence that the parents are unlikely to provide adequate care or control unless an order is made, investigation by the local authority social services departments is a prerequisite of court action. This involves consultation and co-operation between the departments and the police, who are increasingly willing to consider the social needs of a child before deciding on prosecution.

In theory there should be far fewer juveniles appearing before juvenile courts now, and of those who do more should be dealt with by way of care proceedings. When the juvenile court is satisfied that the case for care has been made out, it can make a limited number of orders. These fall into two categories. In the first type of order, the court decides that the child or young person may remain at home. The parent may be required to take proper care or exercise effective control, or a supervision order may be made with or without certain conditions, placing the child under the supervision of an officer of a local authority or a probation officer. The second type of order is a care order where the court in effect removes the child from home by assigning his care to the local authority. Special provision may also be made in cases where mental treatment is required.

Orders which allow children and young persons to remain at home are made for relatively short periods, for example the maximum period for a supervision order is three years. A requirement for *Intermediate Treatment* may be attached to a supervision order by a court. The term, not found in the Children and Young Persons Act, 1969, was used in the White Paper *Children in Trouble* to describe a new form of treatment intended to enable a juvenile under supervision to come into contact with different environments, interests, and experiences in association with others of his own age[61] 'intermediate' between measures which either leave him at home with his parents or remove him to the care of the local authority.[62] The range of available facilities, both residential and non-residential, is set out in schemes proposed by Children's Regional Planning Committees. It is too soon to comment on the effectiveness of intermediate treatment as the scheme became operative only in 1973.[63] The concept of inter-mediate treatment is imaginative and creative. The danger is that it may become rigid and standardised in practice.

The new procedures for dealing with young offenders, together with the system of supervision orders, transfers to the local authority much of the work previously undertaken in this field by the probation service. The Social Services Departments are finding themselves fully stretched by both these additional onerous responsibilities.

With the increased concern felt about children whose future may be prejudiced by the break-up of their parents' marriage, care orders or supervision orders can be made under the Matrimonial Proceed-ings (Magistrates' Courts) Act, 1960, or the Matrimonial Causes Act, 1965. Under these Acts, courts which deal with matrimonial disputes involving separation and divorce must ensure that adequate provision is made for the children of the marriage. The number of care orders, although increasing, is well below 500 a year but many more supervision orders are made.[64] Wards of court can be dealt with similarly under the Family Reform Act, 1969.

A care order, under which the local authority is given parental rights, can last up to the time a young person reaches eighteen, or, in certain cases, nineteen.[65] But the order can be revoked by the court before that time on the application of either the local authority, the child or young person himself, or his parent.

The local authority to whose care the juvenile is committed has considerable power in deciding where and with whom the child may live, but the keynote of the care order is that it allows the local authority to treat the child in the same way as other children in its care. Like them he may be placed with foster parents or in residential accommodation. The care order also gives the local authority power to allow the child to return to his own home, the order itself remaining in force.

As a result of the 1969 Children and Young Persons Act, the approved school system was restructured and incorporated into a generic system of community homes which included all the residen-tial establishments of the local authority together with some volun-tary homes providing a range of specialised care according to the needs of children.[66] The type and size of children's homes has under-gone change. The large children's homes housing hundreds of child-ren and institutional in character have now all disappeared and given way to an increasing number of smaller establishments, more often than not situated unobtrusively amongst other houses in residential areas. Everything is done to encourage a relaxed atmosphere, as opposed to the regimented and impersonal regimes which were in vogue not so many decades before. Even where, by present-day stan-dards, large children's homes are in use, accommodating say fifty children, it is possible to divide them into smaller and more personal groups.

Developments in residential care continue all the time. Thus, for example, concern about the needs of especially disturbed children has given rise in many areas to the establishment of special homes serviced by psychologists, psychiatrists and other medical advisers. In order to help a small minority of children so damaged by their early experiences as to be beyond effective care in any local authority home, Youth Treatment Centres have been set up administered directly by the Secretary of State, DHSS.[67]

Parental contributions Originally considered as a means of discouraging 'feckless' parents from handing over the care of their children to the state, these are still obligatory. Nowadays the obligation is explained as desirable on the grounds that it helps to reduce the burden of public expenditure and also brings home to parents their continuing responsibility and duty to take over the care of the children as soon as possible. The average contribution for each child works out at about 5 per cent of the average cost of maintaining a child in care, but it must be remembered that many parents have insufficient means, relying for their income on social security benefits and therefore making no contributions.

Adults with special needs

Adults with special needs were grouped together for Poor Law purposes as the Aged and Infirm. These have generally been exempt from the constraints imposed on the able-bodied, who resorted to begging or Poor Relief, but most of the effort to do more than maintain them at a minimal level either by out relief or in an institution came from charitable activity.

THE ELDERLY The elderly have long been objects of charity and today we still assume that they will be willing recipients of the attention of young volunteers and will not suffer any stigmatisation thereby. Alms, almshouses, sheltered housing, parish and friendly visiting have a long and continuing history. The impact of old age in an industrial society, particularly on earning capacity, was realised largely through the work of Charles Booth, and the idea of a pension as of right grew from his promotion of this cause.[68] The 1908 Old Age Pension Act established for the first time a specific age at which one could be officially elderly and not expected to earn a living. The inflexibility of this, endorsed by the 1926 Contributory Pension Scheme, may have done some disservice to those employed in heavy industry or rapidly changing industries who may not be able to continue in work until retirement age. They are neither pensioners nor disabled, but with the disadvantages of both.

A development that had some significance concerning responsibility for the elderly was the abolition of the household means test in 1941, which relieved children of the duty to support parents with whom they lived and 'shifted the obligation to look after those who are old . . . from the family and from the household to the community as a whole'.[69] Geographical mobility, increasing affluence leading to young couples setting up separate households, working women and changes in the size and shape of families from few generations with large sibling groups, to four- and even five-generation families with much smaller sibling groups, have meant that some elderly people cannot be cared for by their families at all and others not without outside help. A new factor in this situation has been developments in medicine which can keep alive, and possibly heavily dependent, old people who would previously have died after a short illness, and this can put a great strain on the family. It seems from various studies[70] that the elderly have not on the whole been rejected by their families, but more flexible welfare provisions have had to grow from the rather rigid divisions of 1948 when the National Assistance Act ended the Poor Law. The tasks of the latter were reallocated between the National Assistance Board – dealing with financial assistance – and the local authorities who through welfare committees, or joint health and welfare committees,[71] had a duty to provide residential accommodation for all needing 'care and attention',[72] while the new National Health Service provided hospital and medical care. Unfortunately the divisions met administrative rather than clients' needs. Difficulties arose when the clients did not conform to categories which put the sick into hospital and the fit into Homes.[73] Clients not fit enough for admission to a Home, needing more medical care and supervision than was provided and yet not really in need of hospital care, were shuffled uneasily between the two. 'Body swapping' between Homes and hospital solved some of the problems but at the cost of the dignity of the client who, having become physically and financially dependent, lost all power to have any say in decisions about his future. Even with a good income the frail elderly were and still are at the mercy of those who care for them, although safeguards are provided through the duty placed on local authorities to register private Homes.[74]

A demarcation line between health and welfare was provided by the Ministry in 1965 on the basis of the quantity and quality of nursing care needed.

The original hope that residences for the elderly should house no more than 35 people and should quickly replace the Poor Law buildings was dashed by increasing demand and restrictions on building. The review of the first ten years of the service in the Ministry's Annual Report for 1958 revealed that although small Homes had increased from 63 to 990 the numbers of people in residential accommodation, mainly elderly and infirm, had almost doubled. Waiting lists and the development of domiciliary care led to a population in the Homes that was more infirm and older. This increase in infirm residents required a higher staff-ratio and some local authorities built larger units to make more efficient use of trained staff such as nurses and night staff, which added to the movement away from the idea of a 'home-like' Home. Mental infirmity in old age, as with physical infirmity, required services across the administrative boundaries of health and welfare, and within the health service across the boundaries of psychiatry and geriatrics. Problems of disposal between hospital and Homes arose when local authority residential staff, often untrained, were faced with the care of disturbed old people, while in psychogeriatric units overcrowding and staff shortage reduced the possibilities of amelioration of conditions and led to scandals of poor care and ill-treatment.

The main activity of local welfare authorities was concerned with the duty imposed on them under Part III of the National Assistance Act to provide residential accommodation. Under this Act they were also allowed to make agency arrangements with voluntary agencies providing accommodation or domiciliary welfare service. It was not until 1962 that the National Assistance (Amendment) Act gave local authorities powers to provide domiciliary services that would enable old people to continue to live in their own homes; but, while the legislation for children allowed local authority money to be spent on individual families to prevent children having to be received into care, no similar provision was made for adults; further, the Health Service and Public Health Act, 1968, specifically prohibits any payment to old people by local authorities. In 1963 the local authority plans for health and welfare provision in the future were published.[75] The elderly were described as needing first and foremost a home of their own, support of various kinds to enable them to stay there and residential accommodation when necessary. Only slowly have the needs of the elderly and their supporting families been recognised. Laundry services, home helps, chiropody, meals on wheels, holiday relief and day care, clubs and recreational facilities have all been developed as ways of maintaining the elderly in their own homes, and have slowly broken down the rigidity imposed by the legislative restrictions of 1948. Subsequent legislation (the Amendment Act of 1962 and the Health Services and Public Health Act of 1968) has extended the duties and powers of local authorities in health and welfare services and the story is one of slow expansion to meet need in more flexible and imaginative ways.

The Seebohm Committee criticised the piecemeal provisions and lack of overall planning. They recognised that planning depends to a great extent on the identification of need, which is far from easy with a heterogeneous group like the elderly, and on the assessment of existing provisions, which again is not easy since the family, the community and other social services all make varying and inter-dependent contributions to the care of the elderly.

Since 1971 the local authorities have continued to exercise their functions for the elderly. Under the National Health Service Re-organisation Act they have a duty to collaborate with the health services, which is an important aspect of work with the elderly; and in drawing up the ten-year plans to 1983, they are urged by the DHSS to consult with and involve voluntary organisations and not to forget the role of the volunteer.

The elderly today represent about 16 per cent of the population; their numbers will increase over the next two decades, as will their average age, thus putting heavier pressures on the social services. Unlike childhood, old age does not begin and end within a specific period, so that families and public services cannot clearly foresee where their duties will begin and end.

The proportion of elderly living alone has more than doubled in the past two decades. The 1971 Census[76] revealed that of the 8 million elderly people in private households a quarter lived alone and a quarter with only their spouse, while the survey by Amelia Harris[77] in 1971 showed that about half a million women over sixty-five were handicapped in some way and one-third of these lived alone.

The domiciliary services of the local authorities have increased. They have a duty to provide a home-help service, which was increased by 11 per cent between 1971 and 1972, with nearly half a million households being helped, most of the recipients being elderly. Meals services, both local authority and voluntary, also increased in this period.[78] Some are served at clubs, but rather more than half at home. Many clients get only one or two meals per week. For those at home alone the social contact may be as valuable as the dinner. The health service also helps to keep the elderly as independent as possible in their own homes by mitigating infirmity and improving mobility, through chiropody and physiotherapy services. The inter-disciplinary health care planning teams concerned with the elderly should be able to organise more efficient services for them.

Recreation and social contacts have largely been the domain of voluntary agencies and it is hard to see how the Social Service Departments could undertake all that is necessary in this work, although it has been argued that trained social workers should under-take the visiting.[79] As more than 95 per cent of the elderly live in private households the task could be immense.

Residential provision continues to be the major activity of local authorities for the elderly. The Seebohm Committee found that three-quarters of the residents were over 75 and one-third over 85. The higher rate of admissions since has increased the proportions in the higher age groups. Between 1967 and 1972 the 65–74 age group in residential accommodation increased by 1,000, the 75–84 by 4,000 and the 85+ by 8,000.

A consequence of this increase in very old people is the growing concern about mental disorder in old age. The incidence of senile dementia increases sharply with very old age. In his report for 1972 the Chief Medical Officer refers to the major policy document HM(72)71 which was issued concerning services for mental illness related to old age. The report distinguished between the needs of those whose illness (usually depressive) can respond to treatment and those who suffer from senile dementia, with deterioration of person-ality, impairment of memory and sometimes behaviour disorders. The latter need service based on co-operation between psychiatrists, geriatricians and the social services. The need to plan provision beyond medical care alone is recognised by the transfer at central government level of oversight of psychogeriatrics services from the Mental Health Division to the Division for the Socially Handicapped, which is also responsible for the aged in general.

The Hospital Advisory Service in its report for 1972 wrote of the hostility it had found in the hospital service towards geriatrics and geriatric staff, and although they did not say so presumably the rejection extends to the patients as well. In their earlier report they noted that psychogeriatric patients can frequently be found in large wards in mental hospitals under poor conditions, and that their presence in increasing proportion tends to lead to a deteriorating service. All these factors make it difficult to create a forward-looking multi-disciplinary service that can work across administrative boundaries.

The local authorities' concern with the elderly must, therefore, be flexible and must reach out to workers in other services, to voluntary agencies and to volunteers. Not all old people need help at all times and some not at any time. The problem is to put people in touch with services when the time comes. Often the deciding factor is an illness that reveals the slowly mounting difficulties the old person has had to face. Many ideas for crisis warning arrangements have been tried out, and many ideas for avoiding illness and accidents have been proposed, but none are foolproof. In the care of the elderly, as with children, the local authorities are very vulnerable to criticism. In avoiding criticism there is the possibility that they will harass with the best intentions people who have begun to close in their lives and wish for no more than the bare minimum. Local authorities may have to have the courage to protect their clients from service as well as give it.

In cases where old people, or any others who are the concern of the Welfare Authority, are found to be living in insanitary conditions, neither receiving proper care and attention from others nor able to care for themselves, they can be compulsorily removed under Section 47 of the National Assistance Act. The local authority must apply to the court, with medical evidence, for authority to remove the person to a hospital or Home for up to three months. Only after careful enquiry, bearing in mind the interests of the old person, and of others who might be suffering from the nuisance, will the medical, social and legal authorities take this step.

The local authority must also under Section 48 take responsibility in lieu of relatives and friends for care of the movable property of people in hospital or removed to Homes and take steps to see that their own home is locked and all people who may be concerned notified – in fact to act as a responsible friend or relative.

Finally, under Section 50, if there are no relatives or friends to do so, local authorities can arrange for burial or cremation, and must respect the wishes of the deceased.

As with children, the local authority tries to fulfil where necessary the functions of the family for the elderly members of society.

THE PHYSICALLY HANDICAPPED The physically handicapped fared better under the 1948 legislation than the elderly. A difficulty that occurs in discussing adults with special needs by categories, such as the elderly and the physically handicapped, is that the categories are by no means mutually exclusive. Blindness is now largely a handicap of old age, so are arthritis and rheumatism. However, provision for the physically handicapped was initially concerned with adults who would have been working and joining in community life if they had not suffered through some disabling accident, illness or congenital malfunctioning. As well as meeting the residential needs of this group local authorities had powers to make available domiciliary employment and recreational facilities, and had duties for the welfare of the blind deriving from the Blind Persons Acts of 1920 and 1938.

Definitions of physical handicap were approached warily. Blindness was perhaps the easiest category to establish, as educational needs can sift out children who cannot see well enough to read, while for adults the inability to perform work for which eyesight is essential was the definition used by the National Assistance Act. Hearing defects were divided into three categories – deafness with speech impairment, deafness without speech impairment (usually arising after language has been acquired) and 'hard of hearing'.

Deafness in children can be mistaken for mental subnormality, and requires careful diagnostic techniques. Both education and employment services are required to make special provision for these disabilities. Although grouped together the social response to the blind and the deaf is markedly different. It is much easier to communicate through the spoken word than the written word, and deaf people in consequence suffer greater loneliness and isolation.

Other disabilities described in the 1948 legislation as the concern of local welfare authorities were 'substantial' and 'permanent' incapacity through illness, injury and congenital deficiency. In the DHSS tables these are grouped as General Classes. They contain a higher proportion of people of working age than of elderly. The major disabilities of these two age groups are different. Of the elderly nearly half are suffering from arthritis and rheumatism, while among those of working age nearly half are suffering from organic nervous diseases (such as epilepsy, multiple sclerosis). Diagnosis and assessment of a handicap is not easy. Amelia Harris[80] in considering definitions of impairment disablement and handicap, refers to the confusion between 'disability' and 'handicap' and the fact that in common usage they appear to be interchangeable; but not all disabilities leave people handicapped. She uses disablement to describe 'loss or reduction of functional ability' and handicap to describe 'the disadvantage or restriction of activity caused by disability'. Peter Townsend[81] considers another dimension, the individual's perception of his disability *vis-à-vis* his life situation may profoundly affect the extent to which he plays the disabled 'role'.

The DHSS figures do not tell the full story as there is no compulsion to register, nor is registration a prerequisite to obtaining welfare help. The Blind Register is probably the most complete. At the time that the personal social service departments were set up in 1971 there were about 96,000 registered blind people (68,000 of them over 65), 34,000 registered partially sighted (21,000 of them over 65), 40,000 in the three deaf categories and 234,000 in the general classes.

The needs of these people as described in *Health and Welfare*, 1963, are for diagnostic help and guidance on adjustment to handicap, care at home with domiciliary services and home adjustments or hostel and Home care, employment opportunities, recreation and holiday provisions with help where necessary with transport. Local authorities have powers under 1948 and 1962 legislation to alter homes and fittings so that the handicapped can be as independent as possible but where a client is in need of permanent hospital care the provisions tend to be medically rather than socially orientated. There have been too few severely handicapped young people in many areas to justify expenditure on separate accommodation and many have either 'grown up geriatric' or been rescued by voluntary agencies like the Cheshire Homes.[82] The numbers are not large; Amelia Harris found that only 20 per cent of the appreciably or severely handicapped were under thirty years old. Nevertheless, concern about the special needs of the young disabled was expressed in the Chronically Sick and Disabled Persons Act, 1970, which required the Secretary of State to make an annual report to Parliament of the numbers of younger people in homes provided by local authorities under the National Assistance Act, which also housed people over sixty-five. In the report for 1972 there were 8,000 so placed but more than half of these were sixty and over.

Amelia Harris's study gave information on the situation of the disabled in the community. Out of 3 million identified as disabled, although not necessarily handicapped, more than half were over sixty-five. Of the severely handicapped and very severely handicapped a surprising number were estimated to be living alone. These were mainly elderly people. Very few of the very severely and severely handicapped were registered with the local authority, but many not registered had had help.

Increasing demand for help for the disabled found expression in the Chronically Sick and Disabled Persons Act of 1970. In Section I of the Act the local authorities have a duty to enquire into the numbers and needs of the disabled, and the onus on the client to make the first move appeared to have been transferred to the local authority. In a subsequent circular[83] the local authorities were advised that they need not seek out *all* the disabled and that a sample survey would suffice. The intention is thus interpreted not in terms of identifying all individuals in need, but of planning for future services on the basis of more accurately estimated demand.[84]

This Section of the Act came into operation in October 1971 after the new personal social services had been in operation for six months, and in some areas proved to be a great added strain to a service struggling to establish itself. It has, however, aired the problem of the disabled and drawn attention to unmet needs.

A more important provision for the general well-being of the disabled was contained in Section 4, which made it mandatory for public buildings to allow for the access of the disabled. If it becomes a matter of course for buildings to be designed so that the disabled can use them freely it will more readily promote their integration into the normal life of the community. Public transport can still pose problems.

Local authorities were also given powers under the Act to install telephones and television sets but in practice provision has sometimes been held up by lack of resources. A publicity booklet about the services available for the handicapped was published and circulated by the DHSS in 1972; about 2 million copies were distributed.[85]

255

More publicity came from the appointment by the Labour Government early in 1974 of Mr Alf Morris as Minister with Special Responsibility for the Disabled. Mr Morris had been instrumental in promoting the 1970 Act.

Mobility of disabled people was the subject of a survey undertaken by Lady Sharp on behalf of the government. In her report, in 1974,[86] she suggested that the diffusion of responsibility between different bodies presented difficulties in making best use of resources including those of the disabled person himself. The DHSS is responsible for vehicle service, but some confusion exists about the criteria on which allocation of help rests. Originally a powered vehicle was to replace a lost limb, but there has been increasing pressure for non-driving disabled people to be helped, and the social as well as mobility needs of the disabled be considered. The Sharp Report concluded that while severe physical disability should not of itself be an entitlement to a car, 'all the circumstances of the household should be taken into account'.

The local authority has the responsibility for providing aids and chairs for temporary use.

THE MENTALLY DISORDERED   Like the elderly and physically handicapped, the mentally disordered have need for a range of co-ordinated services, and like them have suffered from a lack of public interest and shortage of resources in all sectors. In hospitals and in medical research mental illness and mental deficiency have been the poor relations,[87] while community resources have never met demand. The role of local authorities has changed from provision before 1948 of hospital and institutional care closely associated with the Poor Law, to an increasing involvement in community care.[88] With the National Health Service Act of 1946 the local authority hospitals passed into the care of the Regional Hospital Boards. The institutions providing accommodation under the National Assistance Act were the province of the local welfare authorities, but the large quasi-medical institutions housing mental defectives went to the RHBs. Local authority health departments had powers under the 1946 National Health Service Act to provide 'prevention, care and after-care services' for illnesses which include mental disorders, and later, under the 1959 Act, the power to provide this service for the mentally disordered became a duty.

The pioneer work in community care was done by voluntary agencies[89] closely supported by the Board of Control.[90] After-care for the mentally ill discharged from institutions was started in 1877 by the forerunner of the Mental After Care Association[91] which demonstrated the value of support on discharge, the need for hostels and the importance of contact with the families.

256

Separate community and domiciliary care for mentally defectives was slow developing, because until the latter part of the nineteenth century the range, causes and effects of mental deficiency were not sufficiently well established to allow for adequate provisions to be made.[92] At the turn of the century, when there was already great concern about the possibility of national physical deterioration, the social problems that clustered around feeblemindedness coupled with the apparent high fertility-rate of these people aroused fears of national mental deterioration. Efforts to help mental defectives fell into two main categories: for the severe subnormals – the idiots and imbeciles – there was need for institutional care, other than in work-houses, lunatic asylums and prisons, and for the 'improvable' ones need for training and special educational facilities. The social in-adequacy of the defectives meant that they all needed protection and supervision to a greater or lesser degree. Many voluntary agencies were founded in the nineteenth and twentieth centuries to offer in-patient care, training, after-care, and supervision. The most widely known and vigorous was the Central Association for Mental Welfare which grew out of the National Association for the Care of the Feebleminded, founded in 1895.

The legislation providing services for mental defectives grew up gradually, dealing with one aspect after another, and splitting the duties and provisions between different agencies. Under the Poor Law, Boards of Guardians dealt with pauper defectives, usually in the workhouse. Defectives could also be certified under the Lunacy Act, 1890, and sent to lunatic asylums. The Mental Deficiency Act, 1913, set up Mental Deficiency Committees of the local authorities to provide institutional care, supervision and guardianship, training and occupation. In 1929 these committees took over from the Boards of Guardians the responsibility for pauper defectives. The local education authorities also had duties under the Education Acts to ascertain defectives in the area and to provide special classes and schools, but this did not extend to supervision of the special school leavers.[93] The quality of care provided varied greatly between one authority and another. Many delegated the work of community care to voluntary agencies such as the Central Association for Mental Welfare, which not only carried out the statutory supervision, but ran occupation centres and employed home teachers.

From 1948[94] the local health authorities had transferred to them the duties relating to certification and admission to hospital under the Lunacy Act of 1890 and under the Mental Treatment Act of 1930, and although the latter Act made voluntary admission to hospital possible there were still forms to complete and supervision to ensure that the voluntary patient was truly volitional. These duties were formerly carried out by Relieving Officers, who were able to choose in 1948 which of their two main activities they would pursue: they could either work for the National Assistance Board, dealing with relief of financial distress, or they could work for the local health authority as Duly Authorised Officers dealing with the mentally ill and subnormal. Other duties of the local authority concerned care of the mentally subnormal, under the 1913 Mental Deficiency Act, which required local authorities to ascertain the defectives in their area and supervise them in their own homes, admit them to residential institutions, supervise them should they be discharged on licence, provide occupation centres. Voluntary agencies such as the Central Association for Mental Welfare were very active and often carried out the local authority functions. The local health authorities in 1948 took over most of the work and many of the workers. The third kind of mental health worker, the Psychiatric Social Worker, who was expected to extend the activities of local health authorities from the crisis-orientated and legalistically based work to a casework service, did not materialise in sufficient numbers to make any impact at all. The Mackintosh Committee,[95] reporting in 1951, found that of over 300 professionally qualified practising psychiatric social workers only 8 were employed by local health authorities, and the Younghusband Committee[96] reporting eight years later found that the numbers had risen only to 26 full-time and 5 part-time workers.

The 1954 Royal Commission on the Law Relating to Mental Illness and Mental Deficiency was concerned basically with the outmoded forms by which mentally disordered patients were received for treatment and the isolation of their care from the rest of health and welfare services. They suggested that 'most people are coming to regard mental illness and disability in much the same way as physical illness and disability'. The legislation that followed the Royal Commission in 1959 brings together again for administrative purposes the mentally ill and those of subnormal intelligence, calling these conditions collectively 'mental disorder'. The term also includes psychopathic disorders. Section 4 of the Act defines and classifies mental disorder.

Severe subnormality This describes the condition of people who suffer from arrested or incomplete development of mind and are unable or unlikely to be able to lead an independent life, or guard against exploitation.

In the 1970 Census of mentally handicapped patients in hospital about two-thirds were found to be suffering from severe mental handicap. Physical and behavioural incapacities requiring medical and nursing care are often associated with this condition, but about a quarter of the severely subnormal hospital residents were not so incapacitated and could presumably have been accommodated in hostels within the community had facilities been available. The 1959 Act places a duty on local authorities to provide residential accommodation for those not needing hospital care, but it was not until the end of the 1960s that pressure for a change from hospital to community, as advocated by the Royal Commission of 1954, began to gather force. The Secretary of State for Health and Social Services allocated more money to local authorities for these needy groups (see also the chapter on the health services) and in the plans for the reorganisation of the National Health Service the hospitals for severely mentally handicapped patients were in the future to be smaller, and to serve one health area, thus promoting collaboration with local authority services and other health services. The hope that the isolation of the severely handicapped will end rests on this collaboration. Regional Hospital Boards and local authorities were asked in 1971 to undertake joint planning exercises and by the time the 1972 Annual Report was published some success was noted.[97] In some areas social admissions to hospitals could be ended, as the local authority provisions could meet need.

These local authority services should include a range of residential, occupational and domiciliary care. The paper *Better Services for the Mentally Handicapped*,[98] published in 1971, reported that the local authorities had concentrated their limited efforts in the previous decade on residential homes and junior training centres, but comparatively little had been done in face of need. Out of the 174 local authorities in England and Wales in 1969, 28 had no residential places at all for children or adults, 69 had no places for children and 31 no places for adults – in all, 128 authorities with major deficiencies. In the 1972 DHSS Annual Report progress in work on training centres and residential homes is noted. A 55 per cent increase in residential places (or work in progress) over 1971 is reported, representing nearly 1,000 places. Altogether 8,000 places for adults, including foster homes and lodgings, were available, but as the calculated need in 1969[99] was for 37,000 places the target will take thirty years to reach at this pace.

Apart from occupation, training and residential care, local authority social service departments must help families care for their handicapped members at home, which includes casework, counselling and welfare aids. 'Social workers should work with the family and with the staff of the residential home, the foster parent or landlady. They should also be in contact with other people as need arises.'[100] With shortage of all resources the pressures on the families and services are very great.

Guardianship, under Section 6 of the 1959 Act, continues a provision that began with the 1913 legislation. It allows for a mentally ill or severely subnormal patient of any age who could live in the community provided there was adequate protection and control, to be placed under the supervision of a guardian. Similarly people under twenty-one suffering from subnormality or a psychopathic disorder can be placed under the guardianship order. The local authority can act as guardian, and so can the parents of the patients. The advantage of a guardianship order before 1948 was that parents maintaining a severely subnormal child at home could receive a guardianship allowance from the local authority. Today it allows parents to exercise authority with support of the local authority that would normally not be appropriate for an adult child, and gives supervision to the handicapped person in the community. It is possible for instance to exercise control over the patient's place of residence, and attendance at a training centre. The procedures applying to guardianship applications are as stringent as those for compulsory admission under Section 26 of the 1959 Act and require both medical and social services approval for presentation to court.

Subnormality This is the second category described in the 1959 Act and refers to people whose condition includes subnormality of intelligence, and 'requires or is susceptible to medical treatment or other special care or training'. There is no clear demarcation line between these two categories, but an intelligence quotient of 50 'is commonly taken as a broad dividing line'[101] although it is accepted that it is not a precise measure and decisions about need for treatment and care must be based also on emotional stability, physical endowments and the quality of support available in the family and community. At the upper end of the subnormal range there is again no clear dividing line and many will lead ordinary lives even though they suffer from a mild degree of subnormality. The hospital census (see note 13) found that about one-third of the inmates had IQs above 50 and of these more than half had no disabilities that required hospital care. Their needs were social rather than medical and represented a shortfall in community provision.

Psychopathic disorder Psychopathic disorder refers to people who may or may not suffer from subnormality of intellect, but whose behaviour is abnormally aggressive or seriously irresponsible, and who require or would be susceptible to medical treatment. This category represents a tidying up of the mental deficiency legislation concerned with 'moral defectives'. The 1959 Act specifically excludes promiscuity or immoral conduct as being in themselves evidence of mental disorder. Defining these in anything other than personal and value-laden terms would be difficult. However, the Royal Commission discusses at length the problem of the psychopath: 'The difficulty is that what distinguishes psychopathic patients from ordinary citizens is their general behaviour, not loss of reason, or serious lack of intelligence.'[102] Many psychopaths have therefore not been liable to treatment under the mental deficiency or the lunacy legislation and yet have been in need of protection themselves, or in need of a control broader than the criminal law would allow. The Royal Commission concluded that compulsory powers should be available to ensure training and supervision during adolescence and early adult life. Any guardianship order relating to a psychopath must be made before the age of 21 and be terminated at 25, by which time the patient should have shown either some adjustment to the demands of life, or that further training and supervision would have no effect.

Mental illness[103]   This is not defined in the Act, but is taken to refer to a disorder of mind in patients who have previously functioned normally. Mentally subnormal people may also develop mental illness. The range of mental illness is vast, extending from severe and very disabling schizophrenic breakdowns to a mild anxiety state in response to unusual stress. Equally extensive therefore must be the social service provisions, from residential care and sheltered occupation centres for the permanently mentally disabled to social work services in out-patient clinics and day hospitals and support of people at periods of particular stress, such as bereavement. The 1963 *Health and Welfare* plans found that referrals of mentally ill people to local authorities varied greatly in different areas and assumed that needs were not being met. Studies of the distribution of social malaise[104] showed a concentration of mentally ill patients in rundown areas of cities, but this uneven distribution of potential need could not explain all the wide variation in demand. The *Health and Welfare* plans assumed that the purpose of the community services for the mentally ill was to provide help in all main aspects of ordinary life, in the home and at work. Since 1963 the pressure has grown to transfer as much as possible of treatment and care of the mentally ill to the local community, through in- patient care in District General Hospitals, the use of day hospitals and residential accommodation between hospital and home. The Seebohm Committee found evidence of great need of social work and community care but few resources to meet it.

Rehin and Martin in their 1969 PEP broadsheet reported that mental welfare officers were psychiatric- rather than social-work orientated and that much of their work concerned the processes of admission to hospital, with little time given to prolonged support and after-care. The inheritance of 1971 was a continuation of the statutory activities of Mental Welfare Officers under the 1959 Act.

Apart from the need for a representative of society to oversee any interference with liberty, or act in lieu of relatives where necessary,

261

the role of the social worker and the dissipation of skills and time in admission of patients to hospital should be re-examined. GPs have complained since 1971 that the service they had formerly received from mental welfare officers had deteriorated. It should, however, be remembered that the involvement of the mental welfare officer derived from his predecessor, the Relieving Officer, whose duties were as an officer of the Parish and Board of Guardians. In company with constables, overseers and justices he had duties relating to pauper lunatics and those, pauper or not, who were not under proper control. Admission to asylums for anyone other than a pauper was on the application of the spouse or any other relative, who also undertook to visit the lunatic. Where the application for admission did not come from a relative the connection between the alleged lunatic and the petitioner had to be disclosed. The involvement of the Relieving Officer in the role of petitioner grew with his involvement in the administration of the Lunacy Act, and its very complicated procedures. The continuation of this role in 1948 was perhaps a natural consequence of the great upheavals of that time and the almost complete absence of psychiatric social workers in local authority mental health services. That social workers have any greater ability in removing patients to hospital than community nurses, doctors or ambulance men has not really been demonstrated.

Prevention and after-care   The duties of local authority personal social services in the prevention, care and after-care of mental disorder were examined by the Seebohm Committee. In the chapter on prevention they discussed ways in which people likely to be subjected to social stress could be identified and helped. To a large extent the preventive work relies on referrals from workers in other services who must, therefore, be knowledgeable about social work and the contribution that it can make.

Other work of Social Services Departments

PUBLIC RELATIONS   This is an important method of increasing knowledge about social work and the social services. Despite the ever-increasing demand for these services, the general public and some who might be effective in referral still know little of the work of the Social Services Departments and tend only to associate them with breakdown and failure. The Seebohm Committee was concerned that those people who needed help should be encouraged to seek it and stressed that the setting up of one statutory department concerned with most aspects of welfare was an essential first step in making the services more easily accessible.[105] But to have a service on the doorstep is not necessarily to have it used, although availability is obviously important. A survey undertaken in 1969 in South Wales[106] highlights some of the difficulties of a pre-Seebohm situation and there is little evidence that currently the social services are any more used by the general public. Timidity, fear that workers in a bureaucratic organisation will be remote, that they might treat people curtly, keep away those who need the reassurance of a friendly, supporting service. Others are afraid there might be repercussions in asking for help, some unfortunate result for them because they seem not able to cope. Pride and independence also prevent some people from asking for what is still considered by many as 'charity'. The view that only problem people use the social services is one that dies hard. Self-referral requires a perception of the problem as being appropriate to the agency. People whose knowledge of social work is vague or relates to ideas of charity workers are likely to turn to 'agencies' that they know of and feel able to use, such as the family doctor service, and will present those symptoms that gain them a hearing. For the anxious or bereaved, physical symptoms are plentiful enough to justify a medical consultation.

For departments as large as the reorganised local authority Social Services Department, offering potentially an unlimited social service to everyone, it is important that they are identifiable and what they have to offer and to whom is extensively known. It may not be sufficient to have an information officer housed in the Town Executive's department. An effective public relations officer within the structure of the Social Services Department itself would be of immense value, giving information about the service to the general public, dispelling the myths and fantasies about social work and social service and relating to the media, which are extending their interests into all aspects of social problems. Newsletters and guidebooks are being produced in some areas but developing a dialogue with the community demands a full-time commitment and a high degree of expertise. The Social Services Department might find the publicity primer produced for voluntary organisations (who have long since accepted the importance of publicity, albeit primarily for financial purposes) of value.[107]

Ultimately there may be sufficient resources of manpower for an individual social worker to become personally known in his area and to have sufficient understanding of its needs to take the appropriate service to the consumer. Stimulating demand for a public service is not necessarily a difficult task. The danger currently is that needs identified could overwhelm the resources and lead to frustration and anger. But that does not appear to be a good enough reason to keep the public in ignorance of what is available. Good communication between the public and the service is essential. So important has this aspect become that a group of information officers, calling themselves the York Group, have inaugurated a National Association of Information Communications in the Social Services.

WELFARE RIGHTS The entitlement of the individual or family to financial benefits, services or exemptions from charges built into the complex system of the Welfare State is an aspect of work increasingly being undertaken by Social Services Departments. There has been a growing awareness in the last few years of the low rate of take-up of benefits. In 1971 the government spent more than £700,000 on publicising new benefits, including some £400,000 on television and press advertising. Such efforts, in the short term, are beneficial but claims drop radically when publicity is reduced and cost precludes prolonged national campaigns.[108] Whilst ignorance of the right to claim is partly the reason for the low take-up rate, many people are deterred because of a dislike of 'charity', the stigma of the means test, confusion about where to apply and anxiety about completing official forms.

Various voluntary organisations have been active in the welfare rights field but local authorities are now beginning to accept this as their responsibility. This move confounds those who have criticised local authorities for not making people more aware of their rights and who have claimed that some departments responsible for providing benefits might not wish to have these entitlements more widely known. In 1972, Manchester's Social Services Department was the first to appoint a Welfare Rights Officer[109] to investigate and develop ways of informing people at 'grass-roots' level about welfare benefits. There seems, in fact, to be a strong case for a specialist officer although some social workers would argue that welfare rights are as 'generic' as any other aspect of the work of the department, and that consideration of entitlements is an aspect of casework. Strong feelings are roused by the welfare rights casework controversy. It is worth reflecting that it may be easier to deal with family problems as manifestations of societal, structural inadequacies rather than attempt to deal with the more difficult and perhaps more frightening ones of personal interaction. Much more constructive is the view that every effort should be made to ensure that all entitled to benefits receive them,[110] and that there should be continued action at all levels to make benefits more widely known. There would seem to be an excellent opportunity for statutory and voluntary organisations to workout a strategy together to provide as comprehensive a welfare rights service as possible. As it is so difficult, even for experts, to find their way through the administrative jungle of benefits and means-tested benefits, there may be an argument for establishing a separate specialist service with the client able to have direct access to the legal profession.[111]

COMMUNITY WORK Community work is now considered an important aspect of social services work, and is a rapidly developing area of social work practice. While the theory of community work evolved mainly in underdeveloped countries and the USA,[112] there has been experimental work in this country from the 1950s.[113] The Home Office in 1969 promoted research projects in seven inner urban areas, which were predominantly experiments in community organisation.[114]

The principal objective of community work has been described as being to help organisations and groups within the community (geographical community or community of interest) to identify their own needs and their own interests and to act in consort to influence policy and to get resources to meet those needs and to develop the confidence and skill to achieve their own interests in a way that will lead to the improvement and greater fulfilment in life for themselves and for other members of the community.[115]

The local authority community workers should enable voluntary organisations and individuals to participate in seeking to understand needs in the community and in trying to meet those needs. They must also try to modify the tranquillising effect that the universal provision of a variety of social services may have on the individual's view of his role and responsibilities in society.

RESEARCH The importance of research for social planning and for evaluating the adequacy and appropriateness of services was emphasised by the Seebohm Committee.[116] Consequently a number of Social Services Departments have established research sections but not all Directors of Social Services have accepted the value of this aspect of their work. Agency-based research exists to increase the operational efficiency of the organisation and to assist in decisions on the allocation of resources and priorities. Hampered, however, by the small number of people employed in research sections, the length of time needed for some projects and the special knowledge required of research techniques, co-operation with universities and polytechnics is being sought.[117] A clearing house for local authority Social Services Departments research is run by the Institute of Local Government Studies at the University of Birmingham which issues a regular bulletin, providing information about research projects at all stages in local authorities throughout the country.

The effectiveness of Social Services Departments

After two major upheavals[118] and no time for consolidation, it is impossible to measure the effectiveness of local authority Social Services Departments. Establishing a service that is potentially so

265

all-embracing that its parameters are undefinable and with no experience to fall back on has made demands which at times have seemed overwhelming. Greater public awareness of services available, additional legislation placing extra responsibilities on Social Services Departments has meant that an excessively demanding situation has been created. Increased pressure, unfamiliarity with some of the problems, high turnover of staff and a loss of expert skills has meant a disruption, and undoubtedly a dilution, of services. It is argued that the strength of the Social Services Departments now lies in their size. They are able to make more economic use of resources, they command a substantial share of local authority finance and they have a much more powerful position in the local authority organisations than the separate smaller departments which were amalgamated in 1971.

Probation and After-care

To describe the Probation and After-Care Service as a benevolent, family service might seem almost contradictory when it is so closely aligned with the courts, yet a closer look at its tasks seem to support such a description. Its history goes back to the appearance of the Police Court Mission in 1876,[119] which provided voluntary workers to assist offenders appearing before the London courts. At the same time in the USA a system of probation was being developed.

In Great Britain, the Probation of Offenders Act, 1907, authorised the appointment of probation officers, describing their function thus: 'to advise, assist, befriend'. This somehow encapsulated the caring elements of a professional social work relationship and it was retained not only in the Criminal Justice Act, 1948, but also reappeared in the Children and Young Persons Act, 1969, which placed on local authority social workers the main responsibility for supervising juveniles.[120]

The general requirements of a probation order are that the probationer lead an honest and industrious life, be of good behaviour and keep the peace and inform the probation officer of any change of employment and address. A strict time-limit of between one and three years is imposed by the duration of the order into which special requirements may be written. Offenders over the age of fourteen years must agree to the order and it is argued that, in fact, there is no choice because the alternative may have seemed worse and the apparent lack of real choice is sometimes seen as a barrier in the relationship between the probationer and the probation officer. There is no denying that the legal authority of the court is an aspect of a probation order and has become embedded in the probation officer's social work. The value of probation is that it offers help to the offender within the community. Whilst the probation officer has a great deal of autonomy in relation to an individual probationer for whom he is responsible by order of the court, he is also responsible to the community.

Work with the offender remains central to the probation service, but the service has gradually become involved in the after-care of people discharged from detention centres, borstals and prisons. Voluntary organisations had previously undertaken much of this work and continue to do a great deal. In October 1964 a Probation and After-care Department was formed in the Home Office, the central government department responsible for the service. As the main object of after-care is the reintegration of the offender into the community, participation of ordinary members of the community was accepted as a necessary part of the process and the probation officers began to recruit groups of volunteers to assist them in their task of rehabilitation. By 1966 probation officers were seconded for limited periods for welfare work in the prisons as part of an effective system of 'through care', a process which begins immediately an offender receives a prison sentence and extends to his return to the community. To work successfully this system requires close liaison between probation officers concerned with prisoners inside the prison and those concerned with his family outside prison.

The Criminal Justice Act, 1967, confirmed the transformation of the Probation Service into the Probation and After-care Service. It also added new duties connected with parole, a form of conditional release from prison offering the offender responsible supervision in the open as soon as it is commensurate with public interest. The final decision to grant parole licence lies with the Parole Board which works in close co-operation with the probation service.[121] But, with the prison population increasing and with no reduction in crime, the effectiveness of prison sentences was increasingly being questioned. Following the 1970 Wootton report,[122] the Criminal Justice Act, 1972, legislated to reduce the number of prison sentences by providing alternative methods of sentence to the courts, supervision orders with suspended prison sentences, community service orders, probation day training centres and deferred sentences.

As a result of the Act, day training centres were set up in Liverpool, Sheffield, South Wales and London, each one being run in an experimental, individual way, offering therapeutic, practical and educational activities. Day training centres are not a cheap resource as compared with the Community Service orders where the offender follows his own employment, but carries out an unpaid community task for not less than 40 or more than 240 hours in a year. The pilot scheme, tried out in five areas, has been judged so successful that this provision will extend to all areas from 1975.

Currently the prison population has been reduced[123] and efforts are being made to reduce it even further and to help more offenders to remain in the community. In 1974 the Home Secretary's Advisory Council on the Penal System proposed major efforts to deal with young adult offenders – particularly as it is the 17- to 20-year-olds who so often feature in criminal statistics – by offering further facilities for treatment in the community. The Council's main recommendations are that detention centres, borstals and prison sentences should be abolished and two new court orders introduced, a Custody and Control order and a Supervision and Control order, the latter to be exercised by probation officers, who have criticised the proposal because it seems to represent a move away from the caring and befriending role to one of controlling and punishing.

Whatever his future duties, the probation officer already has a wide range of responsibilities including other mandatory ones in relation to social enquiry reports for courts, divorce court welfare duties, guardian *ad litem* duties in respect of adoption placements made by local authorities, and voluntary activities such as matrimonial conciliation and consent to marry.

The Probation and After-care service retained its independent, specialist status despite the Seebohm Committee's concern about this in relation to a unified Social Services Department[124] and despite the example set by the Scottish reorganisation when it became absorbed into the generic Social Work Departments. One argument for remaining separate was that a service primarily for offenders must remain immune from the possible vagaries of local politics.

The probation officer, as a mediator between the offender and society, considers his client best served by an agency that, although managed locally, is funded and guided by the Home Office. Probation is an established but rapidly developing service, one which saw the value of volunteers, which experimented in group work before it became a fashionable method of social work, and which is now determinedly moving in to the community. Whilst reflecting changes in society and questioning its role, probation emerges as a confident, progressive profession.

Non-statutory services

Voluntary agencies

In 1948 Lady Williams in her introduction to *Voluntary Social Services since 1918*[125] asked, 'have the voluntary services outlived their usefulness?' This question posed at the end of the Second World War expressed something of the great changes that had been taking place in society. Statutory provisions had largely eliminated the need for charity which had been the *raison d'être* of many voluntary agencies. With the expected reduction in the manifestation of poverty those agencies most concerned with the particular evils that seemed to be a consequence or a cause of poverty – disease, ignorance, crime, mental deficiency – were faced with a need to review or relinquish their activities.

The Central Association for Mental Welfare, for example, handed over its functions to the new local authority mental health departments with a sense of satisfaction in this culmination of its pioneering work. The National Association for Mental Health, however, handed over its fieldwork activities in mental after-care, but continued its important work in teaching, propaganda and in the co-ordination of promotion of services for the mentally disordered.

The National Council of Social Service continued and extended its threefold function. Today it promotes co-operation between different agencies at local level through local councils of social service; and at national level between agencies pursuing similar objectives in different localities. It also offers advice and specialist help in setting up and running voluntary organisations, through personal contact and a wide range of publications.

The wide variety of voluntary agencies, some very well supported by public money, makes anything more than a broad description difficult. They include national organisations with very specific functions, local organisations with general welfare aims, self-help groups, community activities and many more variations on similar themes. Their workers may be paid, professionally qualified staff, or untrained volunteers. It is, however, possible to examine the work of a number of these agencies, which exemplify some of the current trends in the voluntary sector and in social work in voluntary agencies. The specialist nature of some of these agencies has remained unchanged in the changing world of the statutory social services. Their very specialism, implying as it does an expertise, is an attractive consideration for social workers amidst the anxieties of practice in a generic service and, with salaries coming into line with local authority social work, voluntary organisations have little difficulty in obtaining professionally trained people.

The professionalisation of some voluntary organisations has made it increasingly difficult to draw clear lines of demarcation between the statutory and voluntary field. The Family Service Unit is an example of this, developing from a small agency, which during the Second World War started experimental preventive work with families in a way that was much criticised because it was so personal and intense,[126] to a fully professional service staffed by trained social workers and offering regular and frequent contact over a long period of time to a limited number of chosen families who face overwhelming

269

social, economic and personal handicaps. Also, as a voluntary organisation it receives substantial grants from the local authorities in which it works, and since 1971 there has been an increase in the number of referrals from local authorities of clients requiring long-term support.

Dr Barnardo's, another fully professional voluntary social work service, differs from the Family Service Unit by virtue of the fact that it receives no financial help from national or local government and is dependent on voluntary contributions, but on the other hand from the range of activities undertaken it might appear that its work is indistinguishable from that of local authority Social Services Departments.

Established by Dr Barnardo, who was foremost among the late nineteenth century pioneers for social reform, it is a Christian organisation which originally provided homes for destitute children in the East End of London. Now moving rapidly away from its traditional residential care image into a pioneering and socially orientated one, it has developed into a widespread organisation, particularly in the densely populated areas, providing a full family service with the focus on children deprived of a caring, stable family environment. It offers a comprehensive family care service working on the principle that a child should be helped, if possible, in the context of its own family using whatever method of social work intervention is appropriate. Play schemes, babysitters, day-centres, holidays, are examples of services provided. For children who require placement away from their own homes there are still the Dr Barnardo's residential establishments, including residential schools for physically handicapped, emotionally disturbed and educationally subnormal children. As with the Family Service Units, the relationship with the local authority is regarded as mutually advantageous.

The National Marriage Guidance Council is an agency which differs from Barnardo's and Family Service Unit in that although engaged in social work it did not until recently employ professionally qualified social workers. Established as a voluntary organisation with volunteer counsellors in the late 1930s in response to the growing concern about the rising divorce rate, it first received a government grant in 1948. Currently it receives about two-thirds of its income from the government. The work the counsellors undertake is seen by the Marriage Guidance Council as overlapping the sphere of medicine, social work, education and pastoral care. Its own image is of a 'grass roots' organisation dependent on tapping good-will locally to provide voluntary counsellors for the well-being of the community. Already, however, this voluntary agency is changing direction. Some workers trained as counsellors by the Marriage Guidance Council are now employed by local authority Social

Service Departments, while the Council has started to employ paid, professionally qualified social workers.

While voluntary agencies are free to innovate and experiment, or work with clients who may be unacceptable to the city fathers as worthy of public aid (an example might be vagrants), those agencies that rely heavily on such aid may find that they have to accept the constraints of oversight and accountability.

Volunteers

Reference has already been made to the contribution of volunteers in both statutory and voluntary agencies and it is interesting to note that with the increase in the number of needs which the community recognises as having to be met by welfare services the wheel has gone full circle in relation to who gives the help. The volunteer of the nineteenth and early twentieth centuries, whilst not wholly disappearing, gave way to the qualified professional social worker, who in his turn has begun to accept the volunteer back again.

In June 1966, the National Council of Social Service and the National Institute for Social Work Training, recognising the urgent need to examine the contribution made by volunteers to the work of voluntary and statutory agencies, set up a committee under the chairmanship of Miss Geraldine Aves to enquire into the role of voluntary workers in the social services in England and in Wales.[127] The Committee reported positively on volunteers, seeing them as resources and the voluntary nature of their engagement as an expression of participation and practical democracy. They seemed to have special gifts to offer – gifts of time, permanence, independence of outlook. It is an interesting commentary on the present state of social work that volunteers, rather than professional social workers, are seen as having time and offering continuity. The latter used to pride themselves on these aspects of their work.

Demands on social services are such that professional workers are constantly under pressure. The contribution of volunteers is valuable as long as they are not regarded as a substitute for professional staff in order to maintain a service more cheaply. Keen amateurs offer an extension and enrichment of the services, as demonstrated, for example, in hospitals and in the probation service which have recruited, organised and supported voluntary workers for several years. The need to have an organiser responsible for the co-ordination of volunteer effort within the agency has been demonstrated in various projects.[128]

The Aves Report recommendation that a focal point for all aspects of the work of volunteers should be established resulted in the setting up of the Volunteer Centre in London in 1973, funded by central government and the voluntary sector. An Association of Volunteers in Social Work has also been established to bring together all kinds of volunteers in order to pool experience and to offer a collective voice on social issues.

A new arrival in the voluntary section is the 'conscripted volunteer', for example, the probationer undertaking community work as part of his 'treatment'. The therapy is for giver as well as receiver and clearly underlines one of the most important aspects of voluntary effort.

Self-help groups

The most striking development in voluntary effort in recent years has been the emergence of self-help groups. Self-help was, of course, a great virtue in nineteenth-century England and was possibly most evident in Friendly Societies and Mutual Benefit Societies. Whilst the older voluntary organisations, such as Barnardo's, are regrouping and finding new roles, there are today lively new groups attempting to meet their own needs.

One such group is Gingerbread, the eye-catching name for an association of one-parent families with its national headquarters in London, where it offers a twenty-four-hour telephone service for lone parents needing help and advice, and an increasing number of local branches. Members are divorced, separated, widowed, unmarried, prison spouses or parents whose partners are seriously disabled, and a substantial number of men is included. The local groups aim to provide a warm, friendly atmosphere, to help combat the loneliness and isolation which confront so many one-parent families and also to act as a pressure group for provision of better services for one-parent families and their children. The organisation has proved to be a welcome addition particularly at the local level to the National Council for One-Parent Families, with whom it works very closely. That it met a need was dramatically demonstrated by the rise in membership from 5 to 5,000 in four years.

Pressure-group activity combined with the satisfactions of social contact and sharing has been demonstrated by the Disablement Income Group, while the National Society for Mentally Handicapped Children (largely the work of parents of such children) has moved from a self-help situation to be an employer of paid professional staff, moving into the vacuum unexpectedly created when the Central Association for Mental Welfare handed over its functions to the local authorities in 1948.

The value of self-help is recognised and forms an important part of community work in local authority and in voluntary agency activity.

272

The churches as providers of social services

In the latter part of the nineteenth century and the early years of the twentieth, the churches and individual Christian philanthropists played a large part in the development and provision of personal social services. Today the basic unit of the Anglican and Roman Catholic Church remains the parish, and the parochial system gives the parishioner 'the inalienable right to be cared for by the parson of the parish'[129] but the vast increase in population and the steady decline in the number of clergymen makes this care impossible, while the decline in church affiliation might also make it unacceptable to many members of the community. It would be difficult to decide who constitutes the flock today and what the difference is between pastoral care and social work. Pastoral care, the caring activity of the church, is caring for the 'whole person', but social work, the caring activity of the state, also offers care to the 'whole person'. Is the priest, therefore, faced with a loss of congregation, redefining his role today by undertaking social work in the community? Is the social worker taking over some of the traditional role of the clergy, e.g. helping people who have been bereaved? A note in the Aves Report, 'we are aware that religious bodies of all denominations are increasingly finding themselves challenged to define what might be their special contribution to meeting human needs of all kinds whether at national or local level',[130] might sound like a comment on an institution which had lost its way. Instead a vigorous ecumenical movement is gaining ground. At local level group ministries are being established in some areas with a single church serving all denominations and the clergy actively involving themselves together in the community.

The British Council of Churches is the central co-ordinating body and as such can act on behalf of all churches on issues of importance. An example is the Community and Race Relations Unit, acting for the improvement of relationships between the majority of the population and racial minorities. Another is the British Church Housing Trust which involves the churches in the voluntary housing movement, providing houses to supplement the local authority provision.

The Roman Catholic Church in seventeen of its dioceses in England and Wales has for many years run children's agencies which are now all registered adoption agencies. Following the establishment in 1968 of the Social Welfare Commission, a consultative and advisory body for matters relating to social welfare, a Child Care Committee was set up in 1971 giving the church, for the first time, a central point of reference for discussions and negotiations with central government on child care matters. The Roman Catholic Church has also a long history of effort for the single homeless, and offers a housing advice service as well.

273

An outstanding figure in the work of the Church of England was Josephine Butler, whose concern for the situation of women led to the development of moral welfare work[131] which eventually became the direct responsibility of the church. Josephine Butler College was established in 1920 to train moral welfare workers who worked with unmarried parents and their children.[132] While the development of statutory social services covered much of the work pioneered by the church, there was no specific provision for unmarried parents and their children, so moral welfare work continued, staffed and financed by the Church of England in all the dioceses of the country. The demand for this service reached its peak in 1966-8 when there were about 100 homes and 350 social workers dealing with an average of 24,000 families a year.[133] Many social services departments have now taken over responsibility for unmarried parents although, in some cases, by mutual agreement, the church continues to do this work grant aided by the local authority.

The basic dilemma, however, remains regarding the special contribution the churches should make in personal social services. It was exemplified when the Roman Catholic Church set up a committee recently to consider the needs of the elderly and to decide where it could help, not wishing to supplant or duplicate existing work but having special concern 'where the church seems to have something special to offer'.[134] The Church of England in a discussion paper, 'The church and its social work', 1973, seems to be suggesting the further development of casework, group work and community work to be undertaken by trained social workers under the aegis of the church but it does not clarify the role of the clergy in the parish apart from their pastoral role.

If the church's aim is the promotion of man's spiritual and material well-being it should be proclaiming the relevance of its particular message to people in the modern world without needing to translate its parochial service into casework, group work and community work terms.

Industry as a provider of personal social services

Industry is not usually acknowledged as a purveyor of personal social services; nevertheless it is responsible in a fragmented and as yet largely undocumented way for some highly organised services.

The various Factory Acts safeguard the work force generally, and trade unions, described in the Aves Report as 'the prime example of self-help organisations',[135] assist particular sections mainly in relation to conditions and wages. A number of companies are now beginning to recognise that personal problems at home or at work can affect performance and that boredom and frustration on the shop floor or strain and anxiety at management level may result in sickness and absenteeism. There would seem to be a need for a counselling service available to all employees aimed at reducing tension and improving performance. Because the personnel officer may seem to be too closely aligned with management, it has been suggested that a Personal Welfare Officer be appointed who would be able to remain independent.[136] Another possibility, tried by the Liverpool Personal Service Society in the 1960s, is the secondment of a social worker from a separate agency.

As the demand for female workers continues, more companies are offering subsidised nursery facilities in order to attract women with young children into the labour market or to re-employ those who have left to have children. Provision is made occasionally for school children before and after school during term time as well as in school holidays.[137] The Child Minding Research Unit would like it to be compulsory for large companies to provide grant-aided day nurseries. Such a resource would be valuable for lone fathers who wish to continue in employment and to care for their children, as well as for women with children. Perhaps industry could also introduce meaningful Flexitime so as to make it unnecessary for many very young children to be taken to child-minders before parents and children are fully awake or to have to be collected late in the day following an evening shift.[138]

An increasing concern in the community for the elderly is reflected in industry, where attention has been turned to older and retired employees, pre-retirement courses being offered to the former and social clubs, day centres and pension schemes as well as home and hospital visiting by paid workers and volunteers being provided for the latter.

Since the 1944 Disabled Persons (Employment) Act, industry has had to offer employment to the handicapped. A useful partnership should be possible between local companies and social services organisations in order to promote further the well-being of the disadvantaged and to extend schemes for the employment not only of the handicapped but also of ex-prisoners and others with social problems. Industry does, of course, give routine tasks to hospital patients and others to be undertaken in sheltered workshops.[139]

Conclusion

We cannot be entirely satisfied with the social services, nor should we be. Every step taken to improve the quality of life and relieve burdens has a consequence in altered perceptions of one's own duties, responsibilities and rights. Thus the base from which social services spring is a changing one. New methods of care replace old ones and are abandoned in turn. The old ways are re-examined in the light of new insights and assessments of need. There is an uneven progression which brings not only the anxieties always associated with change, but also its challenges and hopes.

Further reading

Because the literature on the personal social services is so extensive, it is only possible to give a brief supplement to the books already mentioned in the text.

On *social services* generally see chapter 1 and the *Report of the Committee on Local Authority and Allied Personal Social Services*, Cmnd 3703, HMSO, 1968. *The Report of the Poor Laws Commission*, 1909, gives very full information on services at the turn of the century.

On *social work* Routledge & Kegan Paul publish the Library of Social Work series, edited by Noël Timms. Allen & Unwin publish the Readings in Social Work series for the National Institute for Social Work, compiled by Eileen Younghusband.

On *children and families* the National Children's Bureau offers a wide range of publications. The NSPCC also has a number of publications, including research reports on non-accidental injury to children. Other useful reading is:

J. BOWLBY, *Maternal Care and Mental Health*, World Health Organisation, 1951.

R. FLETCHER, *The Family and Marriage in Britain*, 3rd ed., Penguin, 1973.

R. HOLMAN, ed., *Socially Deprived Families in Britain*, Bedford Square Press, 1970.

M. KELLMER PRINGLE, *The Needs of Children*, Hutchinson, 1974.

A. F. PHILP, *Family Failure*, Faber, 1963.

M. RUTTER, *Maternal Deprivation Re-assessed*, Penguin, 1972.

J. STROUD, *Services for Children and their Families*, Pergamon, 1973.

H. WILSON, *Delinquency and Child Neglect*, Allen & Unwin, 1962.

On *probation*, see the following:

Advisory Council on the Penal System, *Young Adult Offender*, HMSO, 1974.

F. V. JARVIS, *Probation Officers Manual*, Butterworth, 1969.

On *adults with special needs*, see:

Association of Psychiatric Social Workers, *Ventures in Professional Co-operation – Mental Health Clinic, Hospital and Community*, 1960.

D. COLE and J. UTTING, *The Economic Circumstances of Old People*, Occasional Papers in Social Administration, no. 4, Codicote Press, 1962.

DHSS, *Mobility of Physically Disabled People* (Sharp Report), HMSO, 1972.

HUGH FREEMAN, ed., *Progress in Mental Health*, Churchill, 1969. Proceedings of the seventh International Conference on Mental Health.

W. JAEHNIG, 'Seeking out the disabled', *The Year Book of Social Policy* (ed. Kathleen Jones), 1972.

D. LEES and S. SHAW, eds, *Impairment, Disability and Handicap*, Heinemann, 1974.

THOMAS MAGOON *et al.*, *Mental Health Counsellors at Work*, Pergamon, 1969.

F. M. MARTIN and G. F. REHIN, *Towards Community Care – Problems and Policies in the Mental Health Services*, PEP, 1973.

Ministry of Pensions and National Insurance, *Financial and Other Circumstances of Retirement Pensioners*, HMSO, 1966.

A. MORRIS and ARTHUR BUTLER, *No Feet to Drag*, Sidgwick & Jackson, 1972.

National Association for Mental Health, *New Ways with Old Problems*, Conference Report, 1969.

National Council of Social Service, *Over Seventy*, 1954. A report of an investigation into the social and economic circumstances of 100 people over seventy years of age.

Office of Health Economics, *Mental Handicap*, HMSO, 1973.

JULIA PARKER, *Local Health and Welfare Services*, Allen & Unwin, 1965.

Psychiatric Rehabilitation Association, *The Mental Health of East London*, Psychiatric Research Unit Report, 1969.

NESTA ROBERTS, *Our Future Selves*, Allen & Unwin, 1970. A history of the National Old People's Welfare Council.

J. H. SHELDON, *The Social Medicine of Old Age*, Oxford University Press, 1947. One of the earliest attempts in this country to look at the health problems of the elderly and to show the close link between health and other social factors.

K. SODDY and R. AHRENFELDT, eds, *Mental Health in the Service of the Community*, Third Report of the international study group of the World Federation for Mental Health, 1967.

GRETA SUMNER and RANDALL SMITH, *Planning Local Authority Services for the Elderly*, Allen & Unwin, 1969.

P. TOWNSEND and D. WEDDERBURN, *The Aged in the Welfare State*, Occasional Papers in Social Administration, no. 14, Bell, 1965.

See also chapter 6 for further reading.

Notes

1 Relieving Officers could take the certificate of the Poor Law Examinations Board set up in 1910.

2 See the accounts of training in Eileen Younghusband, *Report on the Employment and Training of Social Workers*, Carnegie UK Trust, 1947, and Marjorie Smith, *Professional Education for Social Work in Britain*, Allen & Unwin, 1953.

3 See Kathleen Woodroofe, *From Charity to Social Work*, Routledge & Kegan Paul, 1962, and Madeline Rooff, *Voluntary Societies and Social Policy*, Routledge & Kegan Paul, 1957.

4 Chiswick Women's Aid Centre was set up in 1971 to provide a temporary home for battered wives and their children. With increasing recognition of the problem, centres in other parts of the country are being established. See Erin Pizzey, *Scream Quietly or the Neighbours will Hear*, Penguin, 1974.

5 *Report of the Royal Commission on the Poor Laws*, HMSO, 1909. Also Una Cormack, *The Welfare State*, Loch Memorial Lecture, Family Welfare Association, 1953, reprinted in A. V. S. Lochhead, *A Reader in Social Administration*, Constable, 1968.

6 Julia Parker, *Local Health and Welfare Services*, Allen & Unwin, 1965.

7 Madeline Rooff, *op. cit.*

8 The Annual Report of the Ministry of Education for 1950, Cmnd 8244, looked back on fifty years of work in the field of education, but did not mention the education welfare officer.

9 *Report of the Working Party on Social Workers in the Local Authority Health and Welfare Services*, HMSO, 1959.

10 *Report of the Committee on Children and Young Persons*, Cmnd 1191, HMSO, 1960.

11 *Report of the Committee on Local Authority and Allied Personal Social Services* (Seebohm Report), Cmnd 3703, HMSO, 1968, para. 32.

12 'The home help service, a day nursery, nursery school or a residential nursery might all provide means whereby a motherless child could be cared for providing in the first three instances the father was able to take charge at night. But these services are the responsibilities of three different committees and departments, which look at the problems from somewhat different points of view, have rather different methods of trying to solve it, and different orders of priority in deciding how much of their total resources should be devoted to the particular service required' (*op. cit.*, para. 98).

13 Central Training Council in Child Care, Council for Training in Social Work and the Advisory Council for Probation and After-care.

14 Seebohm Report, para. 482.

15 Local Authority Social Services Act, 1970.

16 See chapter 6, note 128.

17 See Home Office Circular no. 294/1970.

18 Seebohm Report, paras 640–3.

19 *Ibid.*, para. 641.

20 The Council was set up by the Health Visiting and Social Work (Training) Act, 1962, as amended by Statutory Instruments 1221 and 1241 of 1971.

21 See Local Authority Social Services Act, 1970, Schedule I.

22 This model of a Social Services Department has been compiled by the authors from several different local authority structures. Individual Social Services Departments will vary in matters of detail.

23 Seebohm Committee, para. 2.

24 V. George, 'The origins of the boarding out system', *Child Care News*, no. 46, 1966.

25 M. Fry *et al.*, *Lawless Youth*, Allen & Unwin, 1947.

26 *Report on Children and Young Persons (Scotland)*, Cmnd 2603, HMSO, 1964.

27 *Report of the Boarding Out of Denis and Terence O'Neill 1945–6*, Cmnd 6636, HMSO, 1946.

28 M. Wynn, *Fatherless Families*, Michael Joseph, 1964. See also D. Marsden, *Mothers Alone*, revised ed., Penguin, 1973.

29 V. George and P. Wilding, *Motherless Families*, Routledge & Kegan Paul, 1972.

30 *Report of the Committee on One-Parent Families* (Finer Report), Cmnd 5629, HMSO, 1974.

31 Figures for divorces in Great Britain totalled 27,000 in 1961, 62,000 in 1970 and 77,000 in 1971. The sharp increase in 1971 reflects the Divorce Reform Act which came into effect in England and Wales at the beginning of that year. See *Social Trends*, no. 3, HMSO, 1972.

32 Statement by National Council for One-Parent Families, 2234/MW, 31 October 1973.

33 Children Act, 1948, Section 1 (3), (a) and (b).

34 J. S. Heywood and B. K. Allen, *Financial Help in Social Work*, Manchester University Press, 1971.

35 See DHSS, *Health and Personal Social Services Statistics*, HMSO, 1973.

36 'Short-term care matters because it provides the means of entry to a family that has hoisted a signal of distress', H. R. and E. B. Schaffer, *Child Care and the Family*, Occasional Papers in Social Administration no. 25, Bell, 1968.

37 Children Act, 1948, Section 13(1), (a). See also Children and Young Persons Act, 1969, Section 49, which provides greater flexibility of provision.

38 See R. A Parker, *Decisions in Child Care*, Allen & Unwin, 1966.

39 Children Act, 1948, Section 2 and Children and Young Persons Act, 1963, Section 48.

40 For further discussion see V. George, *Foster Care*, Routledge & Kegan Paul, 1970, pp. 79–80 and 224–6.

41 W. Clarke Hall and A. C. L. Morrison, Law Relating to Children and Persons, Butterworth, 7th ed., 1967, p. 640.

42 Peak figure of 24,831 adoption orders in 1968; in 1971, 21,495 adoption orders (*Statistical Review of England and Wales*, HMSO, annually).

43 See Table 3, *Adoptions by Natural Parents*, Report of the Departmental Committee on the Adoption of Children, Cmnd 5107, HMSO, 1972.

44 J. Seglow, M. Kellmer Pringle and Peter Wedge, *Growing up Adopted*,

National Foundation for Educational Research in England and Wales, 1972.

45 F. H. Stone, 'Adoption and identity', *Child Adoption*, no. 58, 1969.

46 J. Seglow, M. Kellmer Pringle and Peter Wedge, *op. cit.*, p. 157.

47 Under the present Adoption Law it is possible for the natural mother to withdraw her consent up to the time of the court hearing.

48 Presented by Dr David Owen, Labour MP for Plymouth Sutton.

49 This is as a result of the continued pressure to make alterations in the law and procedure relating to adoption, fostering and guardianship.

50 Jane Rowe and Lydia Lambert, *Children Who Wait*, Association of British Adoption Agencies, 1973.

51 The number notified to local authorities in England in 1973 was 10,900 (*Annual Report of the DHSS*, Cmnd 5700, HMSO, 1973).

52 Robert Holman, *Trading in Children*, Routledge & Kegan Paul, 1973.

53 Brian Jackson, 'The childminders', *New Society*, 29 November 1973.

54 For nursery schools see chapter 2.

55 Ministry of Health Circular, 221/45, 1945.

56 S. Yudkin, *0–5, A Report on the Care of Pre-School Children*, National Society of Children's Nurseries, 1967, p. 10.

57 M. Manning, 'The community needs a childminders' charter', *Community Care*, 1 May 1974.

58 The Children Act, 1908, defined a child as a person under 14 and a young person as one who is 14 but under 16. The upper age limit was raised to 17 years by the Children and Young Persons Act, 1933.

59 Effective preventive work will depend increasingly on consultation and co-operation amongst services. See *Children in Trouble*, Cmnd 3601, HMSO, 1968, para. 18.

60 Children and Young Persons Act, 1933, Section 44 (1), states: 'Every court in dealing with a child or young person who is brought before it, either as being in need of care or protection or as an offender or otherwise, shall have regard to the welfare of the child or young person.'

61 *Children in Trouble*, Appendix C. For further information on this subject see *Intermediate Treatment*, HMSO, 1972.

62 Regional Planning Committees, first mentioned in the White Paper *Children in Trouble*, were established under the Children and Young Persons Act, 1969, Section 35, to prepare plans for a system of community homes in their areas and to prepare schemes for intermediate treatment.

63 For further information see *Intermediate Treatment Project*, HMSO, 1973.

64 See DHSS, *Children in Care of Local Authorities in England at March 31st 1973*, HMSO, 1974.

65 Children and Young Persons Act, 1969, Section 20 (3), (a) and (b).

66 *Ibid.*, Sections 35–48.

67 *Youth Treatment Centres*, HMSO, 1971.

68 Charles Booth wrote several books and pamphlets on the problems of old age and poverty.

69 From a speech by Pethick-Lawrence when the bill was debated in the

House, quoted Karl de Schweinitz, *England's Road to Social Security*, Barnes, New York, 1943.

70 Peter Townsend, *The Family Life of Old People*, Penguin, 1963; D. Cole and J. Utting, *The Economic Circumstances of Old People*, Occasional Papers in Social Administration, no. 4, Codicote Press, 1962.

71 About two-thirds of local authorities had separate welfare committees.

72 National Assistance Act, 1948, Section 21. Residents have to pay at least a minimum charge for accommodation, which removes one of the taints of the Poor Law. If unable to pay the minimum charge the Supplementary Benefits Commission pay it, and provide weekly pocket money. All residents retain enough money for personal needs.

73 In 1957 an attempt was made to assign responsibility but shortage of places in hospitals and homes still sometimes prevented care being given in the appropriate place. See the Annual Report of the DHSS, *Ten Year Review*, HMSO, 1958.

74 The DHSS *Annual Report*, HMSO, 1972, gives information on voluntary and private homes for elderly and disabled people. There were 23,887 elderly residents in voluntary homes and 18,820 in private homes.

75 Ministry of Health, *Health and Welfare: the Development of Community Care*, Cmnd 1973, HMSO, 1963.

76 See the article by D. C. L. Wroe, 'The elderly', *Social Trends*, 1973.

77 Amelia Harris, *Handicapped and Impaired in Great Britain*, Office of Population Censuses and Surveys, HMSO, 1971.

78 The Seebohm Committee found that there had been a five-fold increase in the number of meals served between 1962 and 1968.

79 See Julia Parker, *Local Health and Welfare Services*, Allen & Unwin, 1965, chapter 5.

80 See note 69.

81 Peter Townsend, 'The disabled in society', Lecture given to the Royal College of Surgeons, May 1967.

82 The DHSS figures for 1971 show that out of a total of 222,597 'General Classes' registered in England, 5,656 were under 16, and 13,431 were between 16 and 29. There is no indication how many were very severely handicapped.

83 DHSS, 12/70 August.

84 See the article by Walter Jaehnig, 'Seeking out the disabled', *Year Book of Social Policy* (ed. Kathleen Jones), 1972.

85 *Help for Handicapped People*, HMSO, July 1972.

86 *Mobility of Physically Disabled People*, HMSO, 1974.

87 Kathleen Jones in *A History of the Mental Health Services*, Routledge & Kegan Paul, 1972, points out that only 1 per cent of the Medical Research Council's funds had been spent on mental health in the early years of the National Health Service, while in the hospital service, where mental disorders take up nearly half the available beds, only about 16 per cent of capital expenditure in the first five years went to mental hospitals and institutions.

88 See chapter 6.

89 See Madeline Rooff, *op. cit.*, Part III.
90 The Board of Control was a central government body that before 1948 had large supervisory duties relating to mental health services. After 1948 it retained responsibility for the procedures under mental health legislation relating to individuals and was a body to which appeal regarding certifications could be made.
91 First called the After-care Association for the Female and Friendless Convalescent on leaving Asylums for the Insane.
92 Kathleen Jones, in *A History of the Mental Health Services*, discusses the influence of Dr A. F. Tredgold's *Mental Deficiency*, the first clinical textbook on the subject. He thought that mental deficiency was a clearly distinguishable condition – 'between the lowest normal and the highest ament, a great and impassable gulf is fixed'.
93 1899 and 1914 Elementary Education (Defective and Epileptic Children) Acts, and the 1921 Education Act.
94 The *Report of the Royal Commission on the Law Relating to Mental Illness and Mental Deficiency* has a useful summary of provisions after 1948. See also Kathleen Jones, *A History of the Mental Health Services*.
95 *Report of the Committee of Social Workers in the Mental Health Services* (Mackintosh Report), Cmnd 8260, HMSO, 1951.
96 *Report of the Working Party of Social Workers in the Local Authority Health and Welfare Services* (Younghusband Report), HMSO, 1959.
97 DHSS, *Census of Mentally Handicapped Patients in Hospital in England and Wales, 1970*, HMSO, 1972.
98 Cmnd 4638, HMSO, 1971.
99 *Ibid.*, Table 5.
100 *Ibid.*, para. 166.
101 *Ibid.*, para. 26.
102 Royal Commission on the Law Relating to Mental Illness and Mental Deficiency, 1957.
103 See E. R. Bransley, 'Mental illness and the psychiatric services', *Social Trends*, HMSO, 1973.
104 See for example the study by Margaret Castle and Elizabeth Gittus, 'Distribution of social defects in Liverpool', *Sociological Review*, vol. 5, no. 1, 1957.
105 Seebohm Report, paras 145, 146.
106 B. Glastonbury, M. Burdett and R. Austen, 'Community perceptions and the personal social services', *Policy and Politics*, vol. 1, no. 3, March 1973.
107 C. Sladen, *Getting Across: a Publicity Primer for Voluntary Organisations*, Bedford Square Press, 1973.
108 *Welfare Rights Stalls*, A National Innovations Centre Leaflet, undated.
109 P. Burgess, 'Rights man in welfare', *New Society*, 13 September 1973.
110 The DHSS booklet *Family Benefits and Pensions* gives general guidance and is revised regularly.
111 See the foreword by S. Burkeman to the *SWAG Report*, British Association of Settlements, 1974.

112 In underdeveloped countries scarcity of resources, limited social services, underemployment of the working population and the strong bonds of the extended family make community work obviously relevant. In the USA the emphasis on self-help as an ideal and a tradition of neighbourliness, even if superficial in nature, lend support to community action.

113 See John Spencer *et al.*, *Stress and Release in an Urban Estate*, Tavistock, 1964, and E. U. Goetschius, *Working with Community Groups*, Routledge & Kegan Paul, 1969.

114 An account of this can be found in John Banks, 'The role of central government' in Anne Lapping, ed., *Community Action*, Fabian Society, 1970.

115 *Some Guidelines for the Appointment of a Community Worker*, Association of Community Workers, revised ed. May 1974. Available from the Department of Social Administration, University of York.

116 Seebohm Report, chapter XV.

117 For instance, Portsmouth Social Services Department and Portsmouth Polytechnic established a joint Social Services Research and Intelligence Unit in 1972.

118 (1) Reorganisation of the local authority personal social services in 1971, and (2) the reorganisation of local authority boundaries in 1974.

119 F. V. Jarvis, *Advise, Assist, Befriend, A Brief History of the Probation and After-care Service*, National Association of Probation Officers, 1972.

120 Section 14: 'it shall be the duty of the supervisor to advise, assist and befriend the supervised person.'

121 See the section on parole in J. F. S. King, *The Probation and After-care Service*, Butterworth, 1969.

122 *Non-Custodial and Semi-Custodial Penalties*, HMSO, 1970.

123 The total prison population in 1971 comprised 38,673 males and 1,035 females and in 1972 37,348 males and 950 females. See the structural tables in *Report on the Work of the Prison Department 1971–2*, Cmnd 5489, HMSO, 1972.

124 Seebohm Report. para. 704.

125 Henry Mess, *Voluntary Social Services since 1918*, Routledge & Kegan Paul, 1948.

126 The workers turned their hands to anything, doing scrubbing, cooking and shopping. They were on Christian name terms with their clients when other social workers were addressed more formally.

127 Geraldine Aves, *The Voluntary Worker in the Social Services*, Allen & Unwin, 1970.

128 See I. Sparks, *Voluntary Family Counsellors*, Dr Barnardo's Volunteers' Project, Liverpool University Press, 1974.

129 K. Slack, *The British Churches Today*, SCM Press, 1970.

130 National Council of Social Services, *The Voluntary Worker in the Social Services*, 1969, para. 31. Published by Allen & Unwin, 1970.

131 M. P. Hall and I. V. Howes, *The Church in Social Work*, Routledge & Kegan Paul, 1965.

132 The college is now closed.

133 'Moral welfare to Seebohm', *Journal of the Institute of Social Welfare*, 1972.
134 Newsletter published by the Social Welfare Commission April/May 1974.
135 *The Voluntary Worker in the Social Services*, National Council of Social Services, 1969, para. 29.
136 Dudley Balaam, 'Personnel at its most personal', *Industrial Society*, February 1973.
137 J. West, *Company Day Nurseries*, Institute of Personnel Management, 1970.
138 B. Jackson, 'The childminders', *New Society*, 29 November 1973.
139 See chapter 3.

8 Law as a social service
Clive Davies

Law is often recognised as 'the oldest and richest of the social sciences',[1] but seldom as the oldest, most pervasive and richest of the social *services*. It is not readily viewed in this light, partly because 'it has always been there' and partly because so many people (including such eminent thinkers as Plato and Marx[2]) regard law as inimical to mankind, a social *dis*service – or at best a necessary evil. Yet the provision by the state of a set of legal rules, means for their enforcement and a system of tribunals to determine disputes arising under them meets all the criteria of 'social service' suggested earlier in this book:[3] it results from collective action, is designed to meet social needs and is motivated by 'social' rather than narrowly economic considerations. And among the declared aims of law in contemporary Western societies, quite apart from the maintenance of a 'Welfare State', are the provision of social order, the maximising of individual liberty and the protection of the weak against the strong (including the citizen against the state) – 'services' hardly to be sneezed at, however much taken for granted by those of us accustomed to live under what Dicey called 'the Rule of Law',[4] and even though, like other social services, unevenly and imperfectly provided.

Law, however, is more than merely one social institution among many. It is the fundamental social institution, the basis of all others. To a great extent, law *is* society. The answer to the question whether law shapes society or society shapes law (do most people refrain from murder, for example, because it is forbidden by law, or is murder forbidden by law because most people refrain from it?) is that both statements are true: the relationship is reciprocal. While 'every legal system serves the purposes of its society',[5] and primitive, feudal, capitalist, socialist and Welfare State societies all evolve systems of law to suit their own requirements,[6] it is also true that legal systems, in turn, determine the structure and functioning of societies.

285

The close connection, even identity, of a society and its law might seem too obvious to require emphasis but it is often overlooked. Thus the recent critic of English law who thought that it could not 'by itself remove the major inequalities from society. They derive from differences in wealth, education and power'[7] failed to see that inequalities in wealth, education and power are not immutable differences like those in height, weight, beauty and (more arguably) intelligence that law must accept as inevitable, but socially created and legally supported differences, which law may seek to reduce or remove, as indeed it has been doing, in diverse ways, throughout much of the world in this 'egalitarian' twentieth century.

There is much more to law, then, than the traditional image of bewigged counsel arguing nice points before robed judges, and it would be inadequate to confine a discussion of law as a social service to 'legal aid as a social service'. It is necessary to attempt to look at law and legal institutions in their wider aspect: at substantive law (the basic rules laid down by law) as well as adjective law (the ancillary rules providing for their implementation).

Law and justice, though closely connected in most people's minds,[8] are separate concepts. One difference, that law is found everywhere and justice nowhere, arises not only because justice represents perfection, unattainable in an imperfect world, but also because there is too little agreement among mankind as to where justice lies: it depends on one's ideology and where one happens to stand. Some people, for example, think socialism just: others think it theft. Justice is like the rainbow or the stuff that pipe-dreams are made of – agreeable to contemplate but profitless to pursue. A more practical quest is for the elimination or reduction of the more blatant and avoidable *in*justices, as they seem to us, in society.[9] Such may arise from three sources: the content, quality and adequacy (or lack of them) of the law itself; unequal knowledge and understanding of the law among those who are subject to it; and unequal access to the services of lawyers and the courts. They are discussed successively in the following sections.

1 Law and its reform

A society's law is the formal part of the set of rules by which its people live and are governed. Consensus and conflict theorists disagree whether law represents more closely the tacitly agreed wishes of society in general or the wishes of its ruling class.[10] Current English law,[11] like most systems, is a mixture of both – there is undoubted consensus, for example, for the laws prohibiting murder, rape and theft, but not for the laws abolishing capital punishment, flogging and birching. Those of us who do not like all that we see of the law in operation are free in a Parliamentary democracy to try to change it, and can hardly fail to succeed if the consensus (or even a bare majority) is with us, given sufficient ability, determination, good organisation and time.[12] English law is nothing if not flexible.

For contemporary English law is the product of more than 1,000 years' continuous 'organic' growth. Earlier in this century Sir William Anson likened it to 'a house . . . of rambling structure . . . built by many hands . . . convenient rather than symmetrical'.[13] There may be too strong a hint of affection, not to say complacency, in that description: Sir William probably gave little thought to the discomforts of those confined to the house's bleaker attics and more dismal basements, still less to those obliged to clean its chimneys and drains; his viewpoint was from the drawing-room. But rambling old houses have drawbacks as well as advantages even for those who own and control them, and another dispute is between those who think that the time has come to knock the old place down and replace it with a modern structure, and those who believe that it can be modified yet again to meet the strains of the late twentieth century as it has met, with relative success, those of previous times.

The law is to be found in *Acts of Parliament* (or statutes) and *case law* (or precedents, or judge-made law). Until the mid-nineteenth century, case law was the major part and statute law a mere appendage, but now 'more law is made by Parliament and Ministers of the Crown than by judges',[14] a consequence of the shift towards a more closely controlled society and the Welfare State. Confusingly for most laymen, case law is composed of two separate streams, *common law* and *equity*: common law, the older and still principal part, originally developed in early Norman times from the customary law of the Anglo-Saxons, while equity originated in the thirteenth century as a supplement to remedy the grosser defects of the common law. For centuries they were administered in two separate systems of courts; the Judicature Acts, 1873-5, fused the two systems of courts, but retained the separateness of the two systems of law, so that a right or remedy today may still be either 'legal' or 'equitable', and thus subject to different rules.

Another division is between *private law*, governing the relationships of citizens among themselves (marriage and divorce, wills and intestacy, contract, tort and so on), and *public law*, governing the relationship between citizen and state (criminal law, constitutional law and administrative law). More familiar to most people is the division between *civil law*, which provides remedies for citizens injured or aggrieved by the actions of others, and *criminal law*, which provides punishment or other sanctions for actions treated as wrongs committed (primarily) against the state. The importance of this distinction is emphasised by the provision of, broadly speaking, separate sets of courts,[15] the greater degree of stigma attached to criminal behaviour and the different burdens of proof applying to civil and criminal proceedings – the plaintiff in a civil case need prove his case only 'on a preponderance of probabilities', but a criminal prosecution must be proved 'beyond reasonable doubt'.

The beginning of the nineteenth century, soon after the eminent jurist Sir William Blackstone had described English law as 'the best birthright and noblest inheritance of mankind',[16] was the period of the 'Waltham Black' code, when nearly 150 crimes (many petty) were punishable by death, when small children could be hanged for stealing and when the ordinary Englishman had little contact with law except when he, or someone he knew, found himself in the dock on a criminal charge. Common people had little notion of having any rights at law, still less of pursuing them to court. Nineteenth-century law now seems openly to have served the interests of *laissez-faire* capitalism, particularly those of entrepreneurs. There was scant protection for employees, tenants or consumers, for the doctrine of freedom of contract meant that people must be bound by the terms of agreements 'voluntarily' entered – little allowance being made for the social realities of differences in the parties' knowledge, wealth and bargaining-power. Workpeople were especially disfavoured: the common law doctrines of common employment (that a workman injured as a result of the negligence of a fellow-workman had no redress against his employer), of contributory negligence (that a person injured in an accident for which he was even partly responsible had no claim at all) and that 'a personal action dies with the person' (that a person's dependants had no claim in respect of an accident resulting in his death) all militated against the interests of working people at a time when industrial accidents maimed and killed with horrifying frequency. Few working men had the vote till quite late in the century, and, though the Combination Acts (which outlawed trade unions, while leaving employers free to combine) were largely repealed in 1824, their effects lingered on much later – the Tolpuddle Martyrs were tried in 1834. Those who could or would not work were subject to the 'deterrent' harshness of the Poor Law, described elsewhere in this book.[17] Female inferiority was a doctrine as firmly established as *laissez-faire*: women were without the vote and married women without the right to control their own property.

The past century has brought reforms in all these areas. Common employment, contributory negligence and 'personal actions die with the person' were abolished by statute in, respectively, 1948, 1945 and 1846–1934.[18] The rights of workpeople to form unions and strike were firmly established in 1871 and 1906.[19] Statutory attempts have also been made to secure minimal conditions of employment for certain classes of worker[20] – though such provisions can have only limited effect in a society where supply and demand and relative bargaining-power continue to dominate such issues. Attempts to protect tenants have been made by a long line of Landlord and Tenant and Housing Acts, discussed elsewhere,[21] and to protect consumers by a succession of Food and Drugs legislation, the Sale of Goods Act, 1893, and, most recently, the Fair Trading Act, 1973. The rigours of the Poor Law have been replaced by the relative generosity of Social Security.[22] And women achieved the right to vote on the same terms as men in 1929 and the right to control their property after marriage in 1935.

The most important socio-legal changes of the twentieth century, however, have been made by the great public law statutes creating our mixed-economy Welfare State society – the various nationalising Acts and the statutes providing for education, the health service and the other social services. Major statutory reforms in private law (realms more generally thought of as 'lawyers' law') include the simplification of land law by the property legislation of 1922–5, the introduction of legitimation and adoption in 1926,[23] the improvement of divorce law by the Act of 1937[24] and subsequent statutes, and of the law of inheritance in 1925–38[25] and the introduction of the citizen's right to sue the Crown in 1945:[26] judicial legislation, too, has continued, by such relatively little-publicised steps as the introduction of legal abortions as early as 1939,[27] and the extension of tortious liability in negligence in 1932[28] and intimidation in 1964.[29] In criminal law the major development has been the adoption of a more humane attitude to young offenders in the Children and Young Persons Acts of 1933 and 1969, though another landmark of law reform was the Criminal Justice Act, 1948, which abolished flogging and birching and sought to lay the foundations for a more constructive post-war penal policy.

The past decade has been an unusually active period in law reform: an unprecedented spate of books and pamphlets critical of the law (see Further Reading) in the mid-1960s, was followed by the passage of statutes, many of which brought in reforms suggested in the books. (It is gratifying, in particular, to look at Lord Gardiner's book, *Law Reform Now*, published in 1964, today, ten years later, to find that nearly half of the reforms suggested there have been effected. Among the statutes were the Criminal Law Act, 1967, abolishing the ancient and anomalous distinction between felonies and misdemeanours, the Parliamentary Commissioner Act, 1967, establishing the British Ombudsman, the Sexual Offences Act, 1967, legalising most forms of homosexual activity, the Abortion Act, 1967, putting on a statutory footing the law given in the judgement of 1939, the Theft Act, 1968, rationalising and modernising the law relating to offences against property, the Children and Young Persons Act, 1969, transferring to social workers a greater share of the responsibility for the treatment of young offenders, and the Divorce Reform Act, 1969, providing a completely new basis for the law of divorce, apart from important Acts introducing changes in the machinery and administration of the law, some of which are mentioned in Section 3, below.

Criticism of the law remains, quite rightly, strong, but it is hard to judge which reforms will secure priority. Arguably the most urgent need for reform is in the mundane sphere of taxation law, for greater social equality and improved social services (if they are what society really wants) can be achieved only by taxation: yet (legal) 'tax avoidance' and (illegal) 'tax evasion'[30] are widespread, revenue law being viewed as a kind of game, in which taxpayers try to find loopholes in the law while Parliament tries to stop them. In a complex economy the task of devising a fair and effective system of taxation must be difficult, and it is not made easier by the employment of able and highly paid experts to thwart the intentions of Parliament, nor by the fluctuating tax policies of successive governments. Improvements, however, could be made, with will and application; a start might be made, possibly with more than symbolic value, by abolishing the judge-made rule that taxing statutes must be interpreted 'restrictively', that is in favour of the taxpayer[31] – and so against the interests of the beneficiaries of taxes (the old, the sick and people who cannot work).

Wider assent would doubtless be given to the need for clarification of the law. As Mr Justice Scarman has said,[32] law must be complex (because human behaviour is complex and there must be rules of law to cover its every aspect), but it need not be obscure. Law which can be found only in assorted statutes (enacted at the rate of nearly 100 a year) and cases (reported at the rate of over 1,000 a year), some of them centuries old, is highly obscure. In Sir Leslie's view, consolidating and codifying statutes should have high priority, and few would disagree, but Parliamentary time is not easily found.

The law relating to compensation for tort is a 'forensic lottery', in one writer's words,[33] in which a person is likely to receive compensation if he is injured by a car but not if injured by a bicycle (because motorists must be insured while cyclists need not), compensation depending, in any case, on the chance of reliable witnesses happening to be available. For years debate has continued about replacing the 'fault' or 'liability' basis of tort (that compensation should be payable only by someone who is negligent or in some other way at fault) by the 'insurance' idea (that every injured person should be entitled to compensation – from a central, presumably state-organised, pool of funds – irrespective of the tortfeasor's financial standing and degree of fault).[34] An obstacle to this reform is that 'fault' theory accords with most people's idea of what is morally right.

The issue of civil liberty leads to continuous controversy between libertarians, jealous to preserve and extend civil rights (the rights of the individual against the state and its agents the police), and the 'law and order' faction, who would curtail such rights in the interests of greater social order. The former school of thought is ably represented by the National Council for Civil Liberties (NCCL);[35] the latter has no such continuous sounding-board but is equally ably represented from time to time by eminent policemen[36] and men of law[37] and may well constitute a 'silent majority'. The question arises most often in the sphere of criminal procedure and evidence, where the law is regularly castigated from opposite flanks as acquitting too many who are guilty[38] and convicting too many who are innocent.[39] Do such converse criticisms cancel each other out, suggesting that the present system is working reasonably well, or do they support each other in urging the need for radical reappraisal?

Criminal law in general, indeed, still marred by such anachronisms as the caging of a (presumptively innocent) defendant in a 'dock' in court, the power of magistrates to imprison without trial by refusal of bail[40] and of Crown Court judges to do so for contempt of court,[41] seems a ripe field for reform to its many critics. Both more subtly and more fundamentally, the substantive rules of criminal law are criticised for systematically discriminating against the poor, weak and uneducated by treating their typical forms of wrong-doing (assault, simple theft, burglary) as crimes, while leaving unpunishable the more sophisticated but, arguably, equally anti-social misconduct (mental cruelty, excessive profiteering, environmental pollution) typical of the educated, rich and powerful;[42] reform in this area, going to the roots of society as well as of criminal law, would present great difficulties both in drafting and subsequent enforcement, even if it commanded popular support (which is doubtful). All these issues arise in the sphere of juvenile crime: there is widespread tolerance for the errors of youth, but most crime is committed by juveniles, and all crime is at best an irritating nuisance, at worst a frightening menace; society's consequent ambivalence between the concept of juvenile offenders as 'children in trouble'[43] requiring help, and as 'little criminals' requiring punishment, is perennial.

The law is capable, in theory, of adding almost infinitely to the 'enlargement of rights' thought by Professor Titmuss[44] to be the hallmark of the Welfare State. The right to a dwelling, to a job and to privacy, for example, sound desirable, but all present problems. The first would require dispossession of the 'overhoused' to make room for the homeless, a course of action acceptable to few. The second could be realised in practice only by creating large numbers of state-provided jobs, which could be construed as a return to the workhouse or chain-gang solution, worse than the present system of enforced idleness on 'the dole'. So too, one man's rights to privacy is a restriction on everyone else's right to knowledge. On all of these issues there is too much disagreement for the path ahead to be at all clear.

What can the law do, within the existing social framework, to help the deprived and underprivileged in a general way? Much of the above is relevant, of course – especially the redistribution of wealth by more effective taxation and the right to a (reasonably paid) job and to shelter; but the law relating to the provision of education and health services is highly relevant too. Is law the best instrument for attacking discrimination against women, coloured people, ex-prisoners, ex-mental patients, gypsies and other travellers, the unintelligent and other disadvantaged groups? These, too, are questions about which society in general (like the 'experts') is uncomfortably divided and undecided.

Parliament, the prime agency of law reform, cannot easily act when the wishes of society are so far from clear: MPs, in any case, lack expertise, and Parliament is too preoccupied with other matters. Government departments attempt to keep under review the law affecting their own work, but they also are too preoccupied with day-to-day management to have much time for wider horizons and the more distant future. Accordingly *ad hoc* government committees and working parties are set up from time to time to examine and report on specific issues. In recent times, too, permanent committees have been established to keep the law under constant review: the (part-time) Law Revision Committee and Criminal Law Revision Committee, and the (permanent) Law Commission; the last-named body, whose establishment in 1965 was possibly the most far-reaching step in twentieth-century law reform,[45] has produced a ceaseless flow of working papers and reports, many of them resulting in legislation.[46] The Commission's primary function, however, is the Augean Stable task of examining the tangled mass of existing law, clarifying it and enabling it to work more effectively, rather than to address itself to the large 'political' legal issues mentioned above.

Effective pressures for more controversial changes in the law, in fact, come principally from permanent and *ad hoc* interest and pressure groups and occasionally from idiosyncratic individuals. Thus industry, the professions and the trade unions strive constantly to preserve and expand their rights and privileges at law: bodies like Justice, the Howard League, the NCCL, the NSPCC and the RSPCA work ceaselessly to advance their various aims; other bodies spring to life from time to time to meet particular situations, such as the construction of a new airport (the Cublington Residents' Association), a flood of pornography (Lord Longford, Mrs White-house and the Festival of Light) or the abuse of legal process by drug manufacturers (the Thalidomide Parents' Association); while strongly-motivated individuals like A. P. Herbert (divorce law reform in the 1930s) and Raymond Blackwood (enforcement of the Gaming Acts in the 1960s) may sometimes achieve changes in the law if they are well placed, persistent, able and fortunate. If, as Eugen Ehrlich said, 'the centre of gravity of law is in the will of the people',[47] their will expresses itself in curiously roundabout ways.

2 Public legal knowledge

The legal maxim 'ignorance of the law excuses no man' has the corollary that everyone knows the law – an absurd proposition, for even lawyers are often ignorant of large areas of law outside their own specialisms. Every Man cannot be his Own Lawyer any more than he can be his own doctor, because he lacks the necessary lengthy training; but just as it is good for a man's physical and medical health to have a working knowledge of his principal bodily functions and the like, so is it good for his legal, social and political health to have a general understanding of the main principles of law.

Such a basic understanding is generally lacking. Englishmen down the ages, learning that solicitors' offices and law-courts are places best avoided, have viewed law with distaste and fear. But ignorance of law is a disadvantage in a complex and impersonal society where it may be encountered suddenly and unbidden. The legally ignorant are too much at the mercy of smart alecs, cheats, the unscrupulous, the powerful, the knowledgeable, users of small print and others who can exploit them. Laws against tenant harassment and unfair trading practice, for example, cannot help people who know nothing of them or the rights and remedies they give.

One of the virtues of the English legal system is often said to be the part played by ordinary people in its administration. Lay justices (JPs) are indeed regularly and fairly deeply involved, but they are only some 20,000 and far from representing all sections of society – though the basis of selection has broadened somewhat in recent decades. Jury service also involves lay people in the work of the courts, but the commitment is neither regular nor deep; the basis of their selection, too, has broadened considerably in recent years, by the removal of property qualifications and the reduction of the qualifying age to eighteen[48] – Lord Devlin's description of the jury as 'male, middle-class, middle-aged and middle-minded' is less accurate than it was. Surprisingly few people avail themselves of the daily free entertainment offered in the courts: those who do usually find the experience both impressive and instructive.

Schools provide little education in legal matters. A-level law, it is true, is offered at some secondary schools, but it is not a popular choice, and in any case academically-inclined sixth formers are a very small proportion of the school population. All that most school children learn about law is a few disconnected anecdotes, having little relevance to the child's own life. Emphasis is laid on the law's aggrandisement and mystique, so that it comes to be seen as distant and remote, to be treated with awe, reverence and fear rather than an ever-present influence in daily life that, in a Parliamentary democracy, is supposed to belong to ordinary people, to control and shape for their own use and benefit.

One of the results of the present heightened interest in legal reform has been the suggestion that legal education be introduced into schools.[49] The Law Society has been preparing film strips on various aspects of law for school children, and the National Committee of the Young Solicitor's Group has suggested that young lawyers should give talks in schools. Increasing numbers of lawyers, particularly the young, are anxious to cultivate greater social awareness than the profession has traditionally been credited with, a spirit which might well find a mutually useful outlet in involvement with schools. Few school teachers feel equipped to teach law, and there is a dearth of non-academic books on law for school children.[50] Legal education for children, like sex education twenty years ago, is virtually unexplored territory. Many would argue that it is neither desirable nor necessary and even its advocates tend to disagree about approach, method and subject-matter. One useful approach might be to begin with the child himself, exploring in the context of his own day-to-day life and relationships such socio-legal concepts as the nature of rules, rule-enforcement, rights and duties and property. Such a method of study might lead to a much-needed de-mystification of law, a better appreciation of what law can and cannot achieve and an understanding that rules of law can be made and unmade at will: law would be brought down to earth, to the level of everyday life, where it rightly belongs.[51]

Public legal education, however, is not a matter of widespread interest today, and may not become one. This is to be regretted, because a wider public knowledge of law might have two important consequences for society. At the individual level, a person can function better if he has a fairly clear idea of his rights and duties: he is less likely to become either a victim of injustice or a menace to others. At the more general social or political level, it seems important at a time when increasing numbers of people are for diverse reasons turning to violent and other extra-legal remedies for various kinds of real or imagined wrongs that there should be a wider understanding of the virtues as well as the limitations of our present system of government and the practicable alternatives available.

3   The services of lawyers and the courts

Lawyers

The 20,000-odd solicitors of England and Wales are the general
practitioners of law in that it is they who deal first with members of
the public. They are generally thought of as office-bound, and many
do specialise in non-litigation work like conveyancing, but they have a
right of audience in the lower courts (where some 98 per cent of
cases are heard) and some do a great deal of advocacy. The 3,000-odd
barristers (or counsel) are akin to consultants in that they may be
approached only through a solicitor, though their training period is
shorter and their examinations somewhat easier than those of the
junior branch of the profession. Barristers have a sole right of audience in the superior courts (where they appear wigged and gowned)
and they are traditionally thought of as advocates, though many
specialise in paperwork and are seldom seen in court; in general it is
from the Bar that judges are drawn. The division between the two
branches, like so much else in English law, is less logical than time-
honoured, and the argument for fusion is raised periodically, but it
receives little support from solicitors and less from the Bar; there is
little general public interest in the question.

Lawyers have traditionally served the interests of the well-to-do
(though, in doing so, they may incidentally have served the interests
of individual liberty for all) and still broadly do today, service of the
large corporations and house-owners having succeeded that of the
great landowners in earlier times. Legal education reflects this bias:
much attention is given to land law, conveyancing, wills and intestacy,
company law, trusts, taxation and the complexities of civil procedure
in the superior courts, very little to branches of law that affect the
poor, such as welfare law, furnished tenancies, industrial accidents,
fair rent legislation or juvenile court and administrative tribunal
procedure.[52] It is reflected, too, in the situation of solicitors' offices,
which are many in the business quarters and middle-class residential
areas but few in working-class districts. (Barristers' chambers are
confined to the centres of the great cities, some three-quarters of them
in London.) Lawyers' fees, of course, are well beyond the means of
ordinary people.

A rudimentary system of legal aid for the poor existed from
mediaeval times in civil cases in the *in forma pauperis* procedure, and
from the nineteenth century in the better-known dock brief.[53] The
Poor Prisoners Defence Acts of 1903 and 1930 put criminal legal aid
on a statutory footing, but very few defendants were represented
down to 1945. The Rushcliffe Committee Report[54] of that year led
to the passing of the Legal Aid and Advice Act, 1949,[55] still the

principal Act. Applications for legal aid in civil cases are dealt with by local Legal Aid Committees of the Law Society, those in criminal cases by the court. People with very low incomes and capital receive free legal aid; the modestly well-to-do are ineligible; those between the two extremes may be granted legal aid but be required to make a contribution according to a sliding scale. The lawyer receives his normal fee for the work, less 10 per cent.[56]

Spending on legal aid has grown from less than £1 million in 1945 to some £25 million in 1972, a large increase, even allowing for inflation, and a measure of expansion of the service. Some critics, indeed, consider it deplorable – especially the expenditure on criminal defences.[57] On the other hand there is well-documented evidence of a large unmet need.[58] The 1974 annual official *Report on Legal Aid and Advice*[59] succinctly summarised some of the deficiencies:

> We have little doubt that (a) there are many people whose legal rights are . . . at present going wholly by default; (b) some of these are unaware even that they possess such rights; others realize it but either do not know how to obtain help in enforcing them or lack the money or the ability, or both, to do so; (c) there is a severe overall shortage of solicitors in the country and . . . their geographical distribution is very ill-suited to serve the poorer and more disadvantaged sections of the community; (d) there are considerable areas of the law, notably those relating to housing, landlord and tenant matters and welfare benefits where expert advice and assistance is urgently needed but is often hard to come by.

Other recurring criticisms are that the financial limits have always been too low, so that going to law is a luxury available to the very rich (who can afford it) and the very poor (who receive legal aid), but not to those between; that too high a proportion of expenditure is on divorce (85 per cent of expenditure in civil cases in 1972);[60] that legal aid has never been made available for tribunals;[61] that too little money is available for criminal appeals – of the thousands of such appeals reaching the Court of Appeal each year, the majority are 'home-made', often semi-literate scrawls on prison notepaper. The Legal Advice and Assistance Act, 1972, which introduced 'new legal aid' (making it easier to get up to £25 worth of free legal advice) did nothing to meet these particular criticisms.

The deficiencies of officially-provided legal aid are mitigated by a number of supplements, some well established and some more recent: a systematic survey carried out in three London boroughs in 1968–70[62] found that, in addition to the (few) solicitors offering their services under the official scheme, legal aid and advice were being given by nine 'legal advice centres' (mainly nineteenth-century charitable foundations in the 'poor man's lawyer' tradition), local authority legal departments and rent officers, Citizens' Advice Bureaux, Members of Parliament and political parties, local authority services, the probation service, the courts, the police, hospitals, social security officers, trade unions, newspapers and miscellaneous other individuals and organisations. In recent years 'duty solicitor' schemes and 'neighbourhood law centres' have begun in London and other cities. Under duty solicitor schemes a rota of solicitors is arranged to provide free legal advice at court to people recently arrested and charged with crimes.[63] Law centres, a very different concept, are staffed by full-time salaried lawyers who offer a continuous service of advice in all legal matters to the people of particular underprivileged districts.[64] The scene is thus rapidly-developing and somewhat confusing: one observer has described it as 'like the police before Peel'[65] – fragmentary, unsystematic and incomplete.

Among various proposals for further reform are the establishment of a 'public defender' responsible for advising everyone charged with crime, the extension of lay advocacy (and even 'self-advocacy'), the introduction of the 'contingent fee' system found in some states of the USA (whereby the lawyer acts for an indigent client on the basis that he receives no fee if the action is lost but a share of the proceeds if it is won) and, more wholesalely, the introduction of a 'National Legal Service' providing a universal and all-embracing service on the model of the National Health Service.[66] Perennial obstacles in the path of reform are the shortage of funds (reflecting the problem of priorities within all the social services, and in national expenditure generally) and the insufficiency of lawyers to supply legal advice to all who need it. Another is the conflict between those who wish to see an expansion of legal aid and advice within the existing framework (retaining, in particular, the autonomy of the legal profession) and those who contend that a solution can be found only by creating a new salaried legal service responsible either to the state (the National Legal Service model) or to community action projects (the neighbourhood law centre model). Thus, although the will for change has never been stronger, the way forward is far from clear.

Courts and tribunals

The English court system,[67] like English law, is a bewildering mixture of old and new. The House of Lords, the Court of Appeal (Civil Division) and the High Court all have mediaeval origins, but the Court of Appeal (Criminal Division) was first established (as the Court of Criminal Appeal) in 1908. The new Crown Court, set up by the Courts Act, 1971, replaces the former courts of assize and quarter sessions, both dating from mediaeval times. County Courts were not established till 1846. Magistrates' courts (which deal with the great majority of criminal cases and have important civil jurisdiction too) have existed continuously since the fourteenth century. The experimental Westminster Small Claims Court (intended, like the earlier Manchester Arbitration Scheme, to settle minor disputes cheaply, informally and quickly) first sat in January 1974.[68]

Administrative tribunals[69] are largely twentieth-century innovations, concomitants of the Welfare State. There are now more than sixty different kinds of tribunal and they have evolved unsystematically, in response to different needs, so that they vary greatly not only in size, jurisdiction and composition but also in nature and function. Some (like social security tribunals) were established because the ordinary courts were too expensive, formal and slow; others (like planning tribunals) because the courts lacked expertise, policy consciousness or doctrinal flexibility. In some cases (like the Transport Tribunal) there is only one tribunal, based in London; in others (like general commissioners or income tax and social security tribunals) there are hundreds, distributed throughout the country. In terms of numbers of cases dealt with and the aggregate cash value of those cases, the most important tribunals are those dealing with such matters as income tax liabilities, social security benefits and rent control; but tribunals which adjudicate less frequently (like planning tribunals and the professional disciplinary committees) make decisions which profoundly affect the lives of the individuals concerned and are also highly relevant to a crucial social problem – the balance between social control and individual liberty. Some tribunals have 'judicial' powers, that is powers to determine the facts of disputes and to decide them according to law: others have 'quasi-judicial' powers, powers to decide cases according to the requirements of 'policy' rather than fixed rules of law. From some tribunals there is a full right of appeal to the courts, from some a right of appeal only on points of law, and from others no right of appeal, but a right of access to the courts by seeking a 'prerogative order' of certiorari, mandamus or prohibition; not surprisingly, the provisions for judicial review of tribunals has been described by one authority as 'cluttered . . . up with an incoherent, complex, inefficient and jumbled mass of rules'.[70] In 1957 the Franks Committee made detailed recommendations on the constitution and working of tribunals:[71] some led to reforms while others (such as the provision of legal aid for tribunals and their power to subpoena witnesses) have remained unimplemented.

The most common complaints about courts have changed little over the centuries: that they are dilatory and expensive, and often do injustice. A more recently emphasised criticism is that they are, for social and economic reasons, beyond the reach of ordinary people, so that legal rights are without remedies. More specifically, criticisms are made from time to time of the archaic dress and speech, the jury system, the conduct of prosecutions by the police, the use of unpaid and untrained lay magistrates, the social isolation of professional judges and the characteristically Anglo-Saxon adversary mode of trial – that is, the 'gladiatorial combat' model as opposed to the inquisitorial or 'truth-seeking-tribunal' model favoured in European countries; all of these, of course, have their defenders.

A simple remedy for many of the deficiencies would be a great increase in the number of courts, a solution that would take time (for judges cannot be produced overnight) as well as money (where once again the problem of priorities within the social services arises). The rationalisation of the Crown Court by the Courts Act, 1971,[72] is too recent for proper evaluation, but most commentary so far (from consumers as well as lawyers) has been favourable. A similar restructuring and rationalisation of magistrates' courts and administrative tribunals is widely regarded as due.

A more radical change would be the re-arrangement of the courts' existing work-load to conform more closely to the demands of social benefit and justice. At present, for example, the division of work between the High Court and the County Courts is determined solely by the cash value of claims, and in practice the use made of the appellate courts is determined by the same test – and so, in many cases, by the wealth of the parties. So too, on the criminal side, although the broad rule is that cases go to the Crown Court or a magistrates' court according to the gravity of the offence charged, in a wide range of offences (including many motoring offences, also theft and kindred offences) the accused has a choice; the option for a Crown Court trial (with its greater thoroughness and better chance of acquittal) depends more on the ingenuity, advisedness, experience and wealth of the accused than on the objective importance of the case. The jurisdiction of administrative tribunals has been determined by historical accident; disputes arising in such areas as rents, industrial injuries and welfare rights often fall automatically to be decided by a tribunal – more cheaply, informally and expeditiously than in an ordinary court.

As these examples show, the English legal system often appears to offer two separate classes of adjudication – 'Rolls-Royce' justice for the rich, powerful and well-connected, and 'mini' justice for lesser folk. Thus a business firm's multi-thousand-pound suit or a rich man's trial for drunken driving, though hardly of greater *social* consequence than an unemployed workman's claim for £5 a week or an uneducated youth's trial for burglary, will normally receive a much more careful and expert hearing. So blatant an operation of market-place principles ('you gets what you pays for') is arguably as

299

inappropriate in the sphere of law as it is increasingly coming to be seen in the spheres of education and medicine.

There is little general interest in such questions at present, however, and it may be that a system in which, as Lord Birkenhead cynically observed, 'the courts, like the Ritz Hotel, are open to all', is indeed generally acceptable to society at its present stage of development.

The path ahead

This brief and necessarily elliptical account of English law and its institutions has dwelt more on its weaknesses than on its virtues. That is not because its virtues are not recognised. It is not enough to say that it is the best system we have, and that, miraculously (if sometimes creakingly), it works – and works quite well compared with many of our other social institutions. It must also be said that its better aspects (particularly the incorruptibility of our judges, including 'the great unpaid', the lay magistrates) are admired and envied by the world. It may even be, as its many admirers claim, 'the best in the world'. But it is certainly not, in Sybille Bedford's words, 'the best we can do', and it will never be that without ceaseless informed criticism.

Law offers a better reflection of society than any other social institution because as well as being fundamental and all-pervasive it is also highly exposed. Its present state of muddle and confusion reflects the uncertainties, ambivalences, conflicts and, perhaps most of all, apathy in late twentieth-century Britain about the kind of society its people want.

Further reading

Of the many excellent general introductory books about English law for the student and general reader, P. S. James, *Introduction to English Law*, 6th ed., Butterworth, 1966, and William Geldart, *Elements of English Law*, 7th ed., Oxford University Press, 1966 (a shorter book), are among the most widely read.

Books about the English legal system (dealing principally with the machinery of the law, the court system and the development of the various branches of law) are likewise abundant and include A. Kiralfy, *The English Legal System*, 4th ed., Sweet & Maxwell, 1967, and G. R. Y. Radcliffe and A. G. N. Cross, *The English Legal System*, 4th ed., Butterworth, 1964. Two recent 'readers' or 'source-books', Geoffrey Wilson, *Cases and Materials on the English Legal System*, Sweet & Maxwell, 1973, and Michael Zander, *Cases and Materials on the English Legal System*, Weidenfeld & Nicolson, 1973, are both collections of the raw materials of law-making.

Of special interest to social workers is Michael Zander, *Social Workers, Their Clients and the Law*, Sweet & Maxwell, 1974, a clear and comprehensive *vade mecum*; J. D. McClean, *The Legal Context of Social Work*, Butterworth, 1975, a somewhat longer work, has been announced but not published at the time of writing.

Two brilliantly perceptive accounts by a laywoman are Sybille Bedford's *The Faces of Justice*, Collins, 1961 (comparing English and foreign legal proceedings), and her *The Best We Can Do*, Collins, 1958 (about the trial of John Bodkin Adams). Ronald Rubinstein (another layman), *John Citizen and the Law*, 3rd ed., Penguin, 1952, is now unfortunately out of print.

The separate branches of English law (e.g. family law, divorce, criminal law, equity, tort, etc.) are admirably covered by a wide range of books too many to be catalogued here. In most branches the reader has a choice between introductory students' texts (often supplemented by books containing extracts of cases and statutes) and the larger, more comprehensive, practitioners' works: thus in criminal law, for example, he may choose between Rupert Cross and P. Asterley Jones, *Introduction to Criminal Law*, 7th ed., Butterworth, 1972, a simple introduction (supported by R. C. Cross and P. A. Jones, *Cases on Criminal Law*, 5th ed., Butterworth, 1973), J. C. Smith and B. Hogan, *Criminal Law*, 3rd ed., Butterworth, 1973, a longer and more penetrating students' textbook and J. F. Archbold, *Criminal Pleading, Evidence and Practice*, 38th ed., Sweet & Maxwell, 1973, 'the criminal practitioners' bible'.

More critical accounts of English law are given in Brian Abel-Smith and Robert Stevens, *Lawyers and the Courts*, Heinemann, 1967; the same authors' *In Search of Justice*, Allen Lane, 1968; Michael Zander, *Lawyers and the Public Interest*, Weidenfeld and Nicolson, 1968; and Michael Zander, ed., *What's Wrong with the Law?*, BBC, 1970. John Parris, *Under my Wig*, Barker, 1961, offers a more personal, amusing and irreverent critique. Martin Mayer, *The Lawyers*, Dell, 1967, a popular critical paperback about law in the USA, is worth the British reader's attention if only because so many American legal issues and problems become those of Britain a decade or so later.

The more amorphous areas of jurisprudence, law in relation to society and the sociology of law, are dealt with in Dennis Lloyd, *The Idea of Law*, Penguin, 1964 (a very lucid layman's introduction to jurisprudence); W. Friedman, *Law in a Changing Society*, Penguin, 1964; Morris Ginsberg, *On Justice in Society*, Penguin, 1965; Alan Harding, *A Social History of English Law*, Penguin, 1966; Harry Street, *Freedom, the Individual and the Law*, Penguin, 1963, N. S. Timasheff, *An Introduction to the Sociology of Law*, Harvard University Press, 1939; and G. Gurvitch, *Sociology of Law*, Kegan Paul, 1947.

Some of the theoretical issues raised in this chapter are taken further in Pauline Morris, Richard White and Philip Lewis, *Social Needs and Legal Action*, Martin Robertson, 1973.

Latest editions of books should always be consulted when possible; in a period of rapidly changing law a book that is even a few years out of date can be very misleading.

Notes

1 Lon L. Fuller, *Anatomy of the Law*, Penguin, 1971, p. 9.
2 See Dennis Lloyd, *The Idea of Law*, Penguin, 1964, chapter 1, 'Is law necessary?'
3 See chapter 1, p. 1 in this volume.
4 A. V. Dicey, *Law of the Constitution*, Macmillan, 1885.
5 Martin Mayer, *The Lawyers*, Dell, 1967, p. 261.
6 See H. H. Gerth and C. Wright Mills, eds, *From Max Weber*, Routledge & Kegan Paul, 1948, p. 185.
7 Anthony Lester in Michael Zander, ed., *What's Wrong with the Law?*, BBC, 1970, p. 22.
8 Thus most European languages make one word serve for both 'law' and 'justice' – *jus, droit, recht, diritto*. Anglo-Saxon usage seems to emphasise their distinctiveness.
9 Thus JUSTICE (the name adopted by the British section of the International Commission of Jurists) has contented itself with particular causes, often with considerable effect.
10 A useful short discussion of the argument appears in Peter Worsley, ed., *Introducing Sociology*, Penguin, 1970, chapter 8, by W. W. Sharrock.
11 'English' law has been that of England and Wales since the conquest of 1535: Scotland and Northern Ireland have separate systems.
12 Time is of the essence: thus abortion, homosexuality and divorce law reform took decades, land law reform centuries.
13 Sir William Anson, *The Law and Custom of the Constitution*, Clarendon Press, 1922, p. 1.
14 Sir Alfred Denning, *The Changing Law*, Stevens, 1963, p. 6.
15 But there is overlapping: thus magistrates' courts have civil as well as criminal jurisdiction.
16 Sir William Blackstone, *Commentaries on the Law of England*, Cadell, 1793, vol. 4, p. 443.
17 See chapter 1 in this volume.
18 Law Reform (Personal Injuries) Act, 1948; Law Reform (Contributory Negligence) Act, 1945; Fatal Accidents Acts, 1846 and 1864, and Law Reform (Miscellaneous Provisions) Act, 1934.
19 Trade Union Act, 1871; Trade Disputes Act, 1906.
20 E.g. Contracts of Employment Act, 1963, Redundancy Payments Act, 1965, Industrial Relations Act, 1971; and see chapter 4, in this volume.
21 See chapter 5 in this volume.

22 Ministry of Social Security Act, 1966; and see chapter 4 in this volume. See also Harry Calvert, *Social Security Law*, Sweet & Maxwell, 1974.

23 Legitimacy Act, 1926, Adoption of Children Act, 1926: see Margaret Puxon, *The Family and the Law*, Penguin, 1963, chapter 9.

24 Matrimonial Causes Act, 1937: see Puxon, *op. cit.*, chapter 3.

25 Administration of Estates Act, 1925; Inheritance (Family Provisions) Act, 1938; see Puxon, *op. cit.*, chapter 12.

26 Crown Proceedings Act, 1947.

27 *R.* v. *Bourne* [1939] 1 KB 687.

28 *Donogue* v. *Stevenson* [1932] AC 562.

29 *Rookes* v. *Barnard and Others* [1964] AC 1129.

30 The distinction is well settled at law, though not everyone accepts its morality.

31 *Russell* v. *Scott* [1948] AC 422.

32 Sir Leslie Scarman, 'Need the Law be obscure', in Michael Zander, ed., *op. cit.*

33 Terence Ison, *The Forensic Lottery*, Staples Press, 1967.

34 See, e.g., JUSTICE, *No Fault on the Roads*, Stevens, 1974.

35 Monthly publication *Civil Liberty* and occasional other publications.

36 Sir Robert Mark, Annual Dimbleby Lecture, November 1973.

37 See, e.g., Lord Hailsham, *The Times*, 18 June 1974.

38 Sir Robert Mark, *loc. cit.*

39 See, e.g., Clive Davies, 'The innocent who plead guilty', *Law Guardian*, March 1970; Susanne Dell, *Silent in Court*, Bell, 1971.

40 See, e.g., Clive Davies, 'Imprisonment without sentence', *New Society*, 27 March 1969; Keith Bottomley, *Prison Before Trial*, Bell, 1970.

41 See, e.g., *Balogh* v. *St Albans Crown Court*, reported in *The Times*, 4 July 1974.

42 See, e.g., Dennis Chapman, *Sociology and the Stereotype of the Criminal*, Tavistock, 1968.

43 Home Office, *Children in Trouble*, Cmnd 3601, HMSO, 1968.

44 Richard M. Titmuss, *Essays on 'The Welfare State'*, Allen & Unwin, 1958, chapter 2.

45 See Sir Leslie Scarman, *Law Reform: The New Pattern*, Routledge & Kegan Paul, 1968.

46 See Law Commission, *Eighth Annual Report, 1972–3*, Cmnd 58, HMSO, 1973.

47 E. Ehrlich, *Fundamental Principles of the Sociology of Law*, Harvard University Press, 1936, p. 199.

48 Criminal Justice Act, 1972.

49 See, e.g., E. F. M. Stary, 'Legal education in schools', *Law Notes*, April 1974.

50 But Methuen's New General Studies series (for young people) includes a forthcoming title, Steve Burkeman, *Crime and Punishment*.

51 The suggested programme, it is appreciated, is a product of the positivist view of law; natural law thinkers would desire a different approach: see Dennis Lloyd, *op. cit.*, chapters 4 and 5.

52 See Michael Zander, 'Clinical legal education', *New Law Journal*, 22 February 1973.

53 Whereby a prisoner in the dock, if he has £2.22½p., may choose any barrister present in court to represent him; dock briefs have become less common (though by no means obsolete) since the growth of legal aid.

54 Home Office, *Report of the Committee on Legal Aid and Advice in England and Wales* (*Chairman: Lord Rushcliffe*), Cmnd 6641, HMSO, 1945.

55 'Legal aid' officially means assistance in litigation, 'legal advice' being on matters apart from litigation; but in general usage (and in this chapter) the term 'legal aid' is used to cover both.

56 See E. J. T. Mathews and A. D. M. Oulton, *Legal Aid and Advice*, Butterworth, 1971.

57 See Alan Paterson, *Legal Aid as a Social Service*, Cobden Trust (NCCL), 1970, pp. 11 and 13.

58 *Ibid.*; also the twenty-third annual official report on legal aid (see the following note).

59 Lord Chancellor's Office, *Legal Aid and Advice: Report of the Law Society and Comments and Recommendations of the Lord Chancellor's Advisory Committee, 1972–3* (*Twenty-third Report*), HMSO, 1974.

60 Institute of Judicial Administration, *Priorities in Legal Services*, University of Birmingham, 1974.

61 *Ibid.*

62 Brian Abel-Smith, Michael Zander and Rosalind Brooke, *Legal Problems and the Citizen*, Heinemann, 1973.

63 See Marjory Jackson, 'Duty solicitor schemes', *Legal Action Group Bulletin*, September 1974.

64 See 'Neighbourhood law centres: some background information', *Legal Action Group Information Sheet 2*, 1974.

65 Richard White in *Priorities in Legal Service*, note 60 *supra*.

66 See Jeremy Smith, 'A national legal service', *New Law Journal*, 29 November 1973.

67 See H. G. Hanbury, *English Courts of Law*, Oxford University Press, 1967, or R. M. Jackson, *The Machinery of Justice in England*, 6th ed., Cambridge University Press, 1972.

68 See *The Times*, 29 January 1974, or *Law Notes*, March 1974.

69 Harry Street, *Justice in the Welfare State*, Stevens, 1968, and Kathleen Bell, *Tribunals in the Social Services*, Routledge & Kegan Paul, 1969, offer the fullest accounts of administrative tribunals to date, though both are incomplete: see too R. M. Jackson, *op. cit.*, chapter 6. Surprisingly, in view of the importance of tribunals, the literature on the subject is meagre and there is as yet no single comprehensive work.

70 Harry Street, *op. cit.*, chapter 3.

71 Home Office, *Report of the Committee on Administrative Tribunals and Enquiries*, Cmnd 218, HMSO, 1957. The chairman was Lord Franks.

72 See Home Office, *Report of the Royal Commission on Assizes and Quarter Sessions*, Cmnd 4153, HMSO, 1969. The chairman was Lord Beeching.

9 Towards a social policy
Anthony Forder

Marshall has pointed out that at the beginning of the twentieth century the future of the country was seen in terms of a choice between a modified *laissez-faire* capitalism and socialism.[1] But by the middle of the century a third way had been found, a combination of capitalism with economic planning and universal social services, that became known as the 'Welfare State'. With varying emphases, other Western countries have developed a similar approach to economic and social problems. Thoënes,[2] in defining the major character-istics of the 'Welfare State', added democracy to government-sponsored welfare and a capitalist system of production. He saw the Welfare State as a new form of society which could be compared with feudal, liberal and socialist societies.

If one considers the policies that led to the creation of the post-war welfare capitalist state, some of the new elements were as much con-cerned with supporting the capitalist system as with social welfare. Measures concerned with the maintenance of full-employment and the planning of the economy – at least planning in the 1960s if not in the immediate post-war period – can be seen as a modification of *laissez-faire* to make capitalism more effective within its own terms by reducing uncertainty and maintaining stability. Similarly govern-ment intervention in industrial training has been designed to counter-act a situation in which the costs of training had become an externality for individual firms to the detriment of industry as a whole.

Other measures were aimed much more at giving greater priority to social objectives. They were designed to cope with the externalities of the economic system, particularly those that created costs for families; to protect aspects of our culture that were undervalued by the economic system, such as the protection of the countryside and the maintenance of historical monuments; and to distribute resources with regard to 'need' instead of 'demand'. Here real conflicts emerge between the values of the welfare and capitalist systems.[3] Capitalism emphasises individual self-determination within a system in which self-interest is harnessed to the common good by using resources as an incentive to action. Resources are therefore distributed as rewards for contributions to the common good. The competitive attitudes and the inequalities that result are accepted as a reasonable price to pay for individual autonomy. In contrast the welfare system places primary importance on the distribution of resources according to need which in turn implies an emphasis on equality. The main incentive to action is an appeal to altruism and the common good, rather than self-interest as such. Co-operation is stressed rather than competition. The paternalistic role of the expert as the arbiter of need has been accepted as a necessary corollary of the system, though this is increasingly being disputed. Certain aspects of this conflict have already been discussed in the conclusion to chapter 4. The implicit conflict of values is explored further in the argument between the economists of the Institute of Economic Affairs and Professor Titmuss at the end of this chapter.

But the distribution of power may be as important or more important than the distribution of resources and here the political system takes its place. Democracy and *laissez-faire* capitalism both spring from the same ideals of individual freedom and responsibility so both stress the right and the ability of the individual to make rational choices in contrast to the paternalism of welfare. But individual power is weighted differently in the two systems. In democracy each vote is of equal weight, and votes are distributed equally. In the economic system units of money are also of equal weight, but their unequal distribution gives individuals unequal power. The gradual extension of the franchise throughout the nineteenth and twentieth centuries has provided a political power to counterbalance economic power, and this has been an important factor in enabling the welfare system to rise beside and within the economic system. *Laissez-faire* capitalism could hardly have been converted into welfare capitalism without the state first having become democratic. Yet the democratic system and the welfare system also have their conflicts. Mention has already been made of the fact that welfare is paternalistic in tendency. At the same time democracy by biasing decisions in favour of majority opinion may lead to the neglect of minority interests, which are important concerns of welfare.

Control in the welfare system

Within the welfare system there are three main groups with responsibility and power: professional workers, administrators and committee members who are representatives of the community or, in the case of voluntary organisations, of subscribers, and may be elected or appointed in some other way. Between these three there is a natural rivalry based on authority derived from different sources.

The authority of professional workers like doctors, lawyers or architects rests on their expertise. On the basis of this expertise they claim the right to make certain decisions which others without that expertise are not in a position to criticise. They expect a wide measure of freedom and discretion in the exercise of their responsibilities both in serving their clients and in developing new techniques. They do not expect to have to carry lay people or even the body of their colleagues with them in every significant decision.[4] However, the expertise of the professional is usually, perhaps always, in a relatively narrow field. If the needs of his clients are to be met effectively the co-operation of other members of his own profession and of members of other professions is often necessary. This requires co-ordination. Moreover it is difficult or even impossible for the individual professional worker to evaluate the priority that should be given to the needs of his clients, as against the needs of others, because of his own involvement. Such co-ordination requires administration.

The authority of the administrator derives from his overall view of the resources of an agency and the needs they must meet, together with his understanding of co-ordinating procedures. Co-ordination of the work of a number of individuals inevitably involves some loss of freedom for them. This may be accepted willingly if the objectives of the co-ordinated policy are understood and approved and the administrative procedures are seen to promote those objectives. But such an ideal is not easy to achieve especially in a large organisation. The result is that there is often conflict between professional and administrative workers. The issues involved in this conflict as revealed in various studies are discussed in P. M. Blau and W. R. Scott's *Formal Organisations*.[5]

The loss of freedom for any one professional group through co-ordination and administration may be minimised by ensuring that control is kept in the hands of members of its own profession, as doctors have tended to dominate medical care, and social workers have sought to control their own departments. But skill in administration is not normally included in professional training. Since promotion within a professional service is often dependent on the exhibition of professional skill rather than administrative ability, it may be a matter of chance whether the administration of a service gets into competent hands. For example, in universities administrative ability is not highly regarded as a justification for promotion, and more weight is often given to scholarship than to administrative ability in appointing a professor who may be required to administer a department.

Committee members derive their authority from their accountability to those who provide the money for the service. They do not generally possess the knowledge and expertise of the administrative and professional workers in the service, on whom they are dependent for much of the information on which their decisions must be based as well as for carrying out those decisions in practice. This makes it difficult for them to feel confident that they are in fact exercising their responsibilities appropriately. There is a division of responsibility, but the lines of the division are not clear and may be drawn differently by committee members and their officers, so that the former want to be involved in decisions which the latter regard as their prerogative. A working relationship requires mutual confidence which takes time to develop, and can be upset by a change in the committee or in the chief officers of the services. But even if a working relationship is established which is satisfactory to both parties, this does not mean that the division of responsibility is appropriate. A complaisant committee or a passive chief officer may fail to fulfil their appropriate responsibilities to the detriment of the service or of other services.

A dramatic example of the struggle for control between professional, administrative and political élites is provided in Arthur Willocks's account of *The Creation of the National Health Service*.[6] Once the need for a national health service was accepted, the civil servants of the Ministry of Health produced a plan with a simple, unified structure leaving the primary responsibility for the service with the local authorities. This plan was so unacceptable to the medical profession that it was quickly dropped and a new plan produced, giving far more freedom to professional interests. Gradually this plan was modified in response to different pressures until the tripartite structure of the National Health Service Act, 1946, was created. This gave almost total independence to general practitioners, and separated the administration of the hospitals under predominantly medical influence from other related services that were left under the control of local authorities more directly accountable to the electorate. The new reorganisation in 1974 has seen a continuation of that struggle that appears to have strengthened professional interests, and to some extent administration, at the expense of democratic control.

The role of the public

The need to maintain an appropriate balance between the administrative, the professional and the political élites is clear, and their obvious interdependence helps to ensure this. In some cases the balance will shift too far in one direction or the other but such a balance is likely to be unstable. Further protection to the balance of power is provided by the use of other élite groups, such as justices of the peace, trade union leaders and the hierarchy of the churches, in positions of influence and power. But the most serious weakness in the present structure is the limited influence of the general public, particularly in its role as consumer of the social services.

The government, using the term in its broadest sense to include the staff of government services as well as the country's political rulers, is dependent on the public for its resources. It is also, less obviously, dependent on the public as consumers of the social services. The state needs a healthy, literate and responsible adult population to ensure current stability, security and prosperity; it needs well-educated, well-adjusted and well-nourished children as a guarantee for the future; it needs to feel that there is adequate provision for its old people both for its own peace of mind and for an assurance of personal security for the future. These conditions will only obtain if the public does make use of the social services in an appropriate way. But this is a long-term view, and most decisions, professional, administrative and political, are concerned with more immediate issues in which those who provide the services find themselves bound within a structure which allows them little latitude for flexible action. In consequence when they are faced with demands for a different kind of service from the public or other critics, they tend to react defensively. Their desire to be allowed to get on with the job in the best way they know is not purely selfish, although self-interest plays its part. There is indeed a real difficulty for professional and other workers in social services in distinguishing between what is best for themselves and what is best for their clients.

Both as payers for and consumers of the social services, the public has considerable difficulty in influencing the provision that is made. In both capacities, they are dependent on the knowledge, skill and integrity of those responsible for the services and, in general, can only respond to the initiative of others. Many of the issues are complex and technical so that only the well-informed can even ask the right questions, let alone evaluate the answers. Moreover, it is in the interests of those who are responsible for the services to make political or personal issues appear to be technical issues.[7] This simplifies their task and enables them to act decisively and therefore, from some points of view, more effectively. The siting of the third London airport at Stansted was justified on technical grounds until public pressure raised the political issues. At a different level, a surgeon will often make an authoritative recommendation for an operation on health grounds without considering the relevance of social issues. The training of professional workers indeed often encourages this approach by focusing attention on certain technical issues and thereby encouraging a blindness to wider questions. Further support may be given by the process of segmentation discussed in chapter 1.

The problem is complex, and no single approach can provide an answer to it. In the past, considerable reliance has been placed on the role of elected representatives. It is the weakness of this system that has been one of the driving forces in the promotion of local government reform described earlier.[8] Periodic elections provide only a modicum of control over political representatives, and none at all over the details of policy. This would be true even without the dependence of the representatives on their appointed officers. The public has almost no influence on the choice of candidates by political parties, and policy is offered in packages which have to be accepted or rejected as a whole. Moreover, the amount of communication that can take place between an elected representative and his constituents is necessarily limited and usually takes place in such a way that it is impossible for him to judge the general significance of any complaints or proposals that are made. This problem is even more intense in services which are run directly by central government.

Apart from ignorance and lack of skills, consumers of the social services also suffer because they are divided and have low status in the services and often outside them.

While almost all citizens contribute to the cost of services, and therefore have a common interest in economy, over other issues their interests are likely to conflict. The consumers of most services are minorities in society as a whole. For example even parents with dependent children are a minority in the adult population of this country, as Margaret Wynn has pointed out.[9] Parents of children with specific handicaps will be an even smaller minority. Many of those in greatest need are the scapegoats of society against whom even others in similar need may unite. So the particularity of individual need and the nature of its incidence tends to isolate consumers from one another.

In recent years there has been a considerable growth of consumer groups with specific needs, such as associations of people with specific handicaps. These groups meet several needs, giving social support and practical advice, raising money for specific objectives as well as exerting political pressure. Frequently in their membership they include some professionals from the services with an interest in the specific condition. Many groups have also risen whose common interests are based on geographical contiguity – tenants' associations and community councils. A few associations have also been created to represent wider interests, such as the Hospital Patients' Association, but these often have a smaller membership than associations that bring together those whose more limited concerns but deep anxieties make possible a more wholehearted and focused commitment. The value of such consumer groups has increasingly been recognised by professionals within the services and by government, and active stimulation has been widely advocated. A new occupational group, community workers, has now grown up specifically to meet this need.

Consumers of the social services also generally have a low status within them. Where the services are provided through hierarchical organisations, as they generally are, consumers are the lowest level in the hierarchy. They are often also in a very dependent position because of the compelling nature of their needs or because of the social support for the discipline to which they are subjected. The fear of gaining a reputation as a trouble-maker is very real. This low status in the services is often reinforced by low social status in other spheres. As Pinker[10] has suggested, many of the clients of the social services may be conditioned to the acceptance of a poor service by their experience of the economic market. Perhaps the provision of social services through the economic market was only satisfactory at all because most of those who could pay for services were of an equal or superior social status to the professionals, and so had the authority of status as well as the power of money to back their position. So one of the most important arguments in favour of universal services is that they cover those with high social status as well as those with low, so that the influence of all consumers over the services is likely to be more effective.

Both low status and ignorance can be counteracted by the support and assistance of advisers and advocates. Much advice and some advocacy is provided by workers in the social services employed mainly for other purposes. Social workers particularly have begun to see advocacy as an important part of their role.[11] Councils have been set up to represent consumers like the consumer councils of the nationalised industries. Councillors and MPs see advocacy as part of their role. It is a function of consumer associations and of other pressure groups.

Additional protection for consumers is provided by procedures for dealing with complaints and appeals. These are sometimes informal, through often reluctant referral up the hierarchy. Sometimes they are formal, involving a system of tribunals which may be more or less dominated by professional interests.[12] Final appeals may reach the courts or the appropriate Minister. Most people, for a variety of reasons, are reluctant to complain openly, and if any system for dealing with grievances is to be effective, it is essential that complaints are treated sympathetically and even encouraged, instead of being met with the defensiveness which is a common natural response. It is also important that there should be more openness in the system. The principles on which decisions are based should be publicly

311

available.[13] People also need to know the reasons for particular decisions, preferably in writing, where the decision constitutes a denial of service, as otherwise they are not in a position to query them.

Because it is so difficult for private citizens to pursue complaints through the intricate machinery of bureaucracy, and to penetrate the curtain of defensiveness, particularly in services operated by central government, the Parliamentary Commissioner was appointed to investigate complaints involving maladministration in Central Government Departments, referred to him by Members of Parliament.[14] Nicknamed the 'Ombudsman' after the officer with similar functions first introduced in Norway, the role of the Parliamentary Commissioner has been criticised both because of the legal limitations of his powers – for example, he cannot call for the amendment of a bad decision if there has been no maladministration – and for the narrow interpretation placed on his functions by the first incumbent. The position of Parliamentary Commissioner for the Health Services has now been added to his duties.

One significant dilemma concerns the level at which decisions are taken. The greater the discretion at lower levels of administration, the more possibility there is of flexible decisions to meet the needs of the particular situation, whether at the level of the individual, the family or some wider community unit. This can help the consumer, both directly and through the greater possibility of more flexible co-ordination between services at the appropriate level. Yet the greater the discretion, the more possibility there is of arbitrary decisions and variations of standards of provision. This dilemma can be seen in the arguments about the relationships between central government and local authorities;[15] in the attacks on the discretion given to officers of the Supplementary Benefits Commission,[16] and in the doubts expressed about the role of child care officers in the administration of financial grants under the Children and Young Persons Act, 1964.[17] Somehow selection, training, supervision and control need to be related more closely to the level of responsibility and the discretion which is to be exercised.

A study of consumer consultative machinery in the nationalised industries identified three features of particular significance for effective intervention on the consumer's behalf.[18] The first was the extent to which such bodies were representative of cross-sections of relevant and informed consumer opinion. The second was the extent to which the bodies were organised at levels which correspond to those of the decision-making bodies with which they were most directly concerned. The third was the right of the bodies to pursue the consumer's case to higher levels of authority, when response had failed at their own level. This may take place within the existing administrative machinery, or a parallel system of adjudication may be set up through the courts or through administrative tribunals.

These three features are of general importance in the development of consumer influence. The first perhaps presents the greatest problems, not so much where individual complaints are being pursued, but where issues are at stake that affect a number of consumers whose needs and interests may vary. It is a matter of first establishing contact, which is difficult, and then maintaining communication in both directions as the situation develops, which is even more difficult. A central problem is that of continuing to negotiate with the relevant decision-making bodies, which involves seeing their point of view, without being subtly converted to neglect of the views of those whose interests are being represented. Fulfilment of the second criterion, the creation of different levels of representation, intensifies the problems by creating additional barriers to communication between negotiators at the top and consumers at the bottom.

The welfare system and relative deprivation

In Britain the concentration of major changes in social policy in the few years from 1944 to 1948 tended to obscure the extent to which these measures were, in Beveridge's words about his own proposals, 'a natural development from the past'. In one sense it is inevitable that unless a state suffers some dramatic destructive experience new services will tend to develop from the old and make use of institutions, methods and skills developed in the past. In Britain, however, this process of adaption is particularly evident, being combined with a tendency to meet problems one by one as they arise rather than by the development of a consistent policy.

This approach has certain advantages. Gradual change is more easily acceptable to the majority of people. At the same time *ad hoc* measures do not require a prior agreement about long-term aims and general principles, so that temporary alliances can be made to deal with each specific problem. Sometimes this can lead to more rapid progress than might otherwise be possible, but it also creates problems. Gaps and inconsistencies and difficulties in co-ordination are almost inevitable. Logic and efficiency are sacrificed to the demands of existing interests, while the greatest improvements will often accrue to those in the best bargaining position. Individual examples of such anomalies can be found in all the social services described in this book.

But the gradualness of change may have had more fundamental results. The question now raised by some sociologists is how far the whole edifice of social services should be seen not as an instrument of social justice, but as a support for the basic inequalities established

313

in earlier forms of society.[19] Certainly the apparatus of the post-war welfare state seems to have done surprisingly little to change these basic inequalities.

In the field of education, despite the vast increase in the numbers of students at universities, the proportions from working-class families has scarcely changed from pre-war levels.[20] The highest positions in the Armed Forces, the Civil Service, the judiciary and politics are still largely monopolised by those who have been educated in the fee-paying public schools and at Oxford and Cambridge Universities.[21] Only in the Anglican Church has there been some decline in this respect, which may reflect its declining influence. At the other extreme evidence suggests that the extent of illiteracy is no lower and may be higher than before the war.[22]

At work, Routh's study of relative earnings between different occupational classes showed remarkable consistency between 1906 and 1960.[23] What changes there were, were concentrated in relatively short periods of time and were often partially reversed in the next period of change. The last major change before 1960 took place in 1941–3. This work has not been brought up to date beyond 1960, but the spread of incomes before tax has remained remarkably consistent between 1950 and 1970.[24]

In the field of social security comment has already been made on the extent to which redistribution is horizontal rather than vertical. Taking the whole field of taxation and benefits the redistributive effects are still relatively small if a comparison is made with the pre-war period. Webb and Sieve, after reviewing all the evaluative studies on this topic, concluded:[25]

> We are now in a position to answer the questions we asked earlier about the role of social policy in producing greater inequality (*sic*). To judge from Nicholson's findings the answer must be largely a negative one, for neither pre- nor post-redistribution incomes have become substantially more equal since before the war. At any one time welfare policies seem to be effective in reducing inequality; but the major post-war changes which have been so widely assumed to be beneficial and equalitarian, have made no difference to estimates of inequality.

In housing, thirty years of post-war housing policy and town planning has still failed to eradicate homelessness (which in its strictest definition appears to be on the increase), to bring all homes up to a minimum standard or to provide a reasonable environment in the old slum areas or in most of the new estates into which the people from the inner city areas have been decanted.

Only in the field of health can one retain some optimism,[26] and

314

even here because of the effect of the failure of other services on health social class differences may remain very high, for example in infant mortality rates.[27]

Social justice

Webb and Sieve in their quoted conclusion seem to assume that 'equalitarian' changes are necessarily also beneficient. This is an assumption behind much critical writing on the social services. It is a value judgement that will not necessarily be universally acceptable. The issue depends partly on a definition of social justice, and partly on the extent to which social justice is seen as being compatible with or taking precedence over other goals, such as economic growth.

Runciman has put forward three commonly accepted definitions of social justice in the distribution of resources:[28]

There are, broadly speaking, three different and mutually incompatible theories of social justice: the conservative, the liberal and the socialist. In the conservative theory, social justice consists in a social hierarchy, but a hierarchy governed by a stable system of interconnected rights and duties. Those at the top are the holders not merely of privilege but of responsibility for the welfare of those below: and through the recognition that different strata in society have different functions to fulfil, the hierarchy is accepted without dissension or envy as long as the responsibilities imposed on each class are in fact properly exercised.

In the liberal theory, by contrast, there is also a hierarchy; but this hierarchy is only legitimate if it has been arrived at from a position of initial equality. The liberal is not against inequality, but against privilege. He demands equality not of condition but of opportunity. He places a value not on an elite of caste, or inherited culture, but of individual attainment.

The socialist theory, finally, is the strictly egalitarian theory. It may, or may not require as a corollary that the state should play a predominant part in economic affairs. This is really only a means to an end – the maximum of social equality in any and all its aspects.

In this Runciman is not perhaps strictly fair to the socialist ideal, which is perhaps better expressed as 'From each according to his ability, to each according to his need'. He goes on to consider whether it is possible to conceive some criteria of social justice on which inequalities of class and status might be rationally determined. He suggests that it is essential that those who are deciding what would be socially just would have to imagine that they themselves could not

315

know the position they would occupy with regard to the various criteria that might be considered, such as relative ability, and differing family responsibilities. Runciman suggests that it is unlikely that arbiters in such a position would come down in favour of complete equality. For example, special merit, and the contribution of the individual to the well-being of the community, might be regarded as deserving of reward, while great weight would probably be given to each person's social needs and responsibilities. Although it is impossible to forecast the actual weight that would be given to different criteria, it seems certain that the distribution of income would be different from the present distribution, and there would be little room under such a system for inherited wealth.

Runciman adds a caveat that because social justice demands change, this is not necessarily sufficient justification for trying to effect it, for the process of effecting the change may be too damaging to all those involved to be worthwhile. Yet pressures are mounting for change. There is increasing awareness of the waste of human resources due to deprivation of various kinds.[29] At the same time racial, industrial and other conflicts appear to be mounting as people begin to make wider comparisons for themselves. Certainly any attempt to develop a consistent policy for the social services must take into account a number of vital issues concerned with differential incomes. How should resources be divided between the employed and the non-employed? To what extent should resources be used to reward special ability, hard work, and industrial enterprise and savings, rather than to meet social needs? Does the cultivation of a privileged élite still have the same importance for us as it appears to have done for earlier generations, or does the interdependence of a technological society require for its stability and progress more equality of income, status and power? How far should preference be given to the future rather than the present, by devoting resources to investment in capital goods; in houses and other buildings that will meet the standards of the future; in technological change; and in the education and development of the next generation of workers, parents and citizens? And finally, perhaps, how far can we tolerate or afford to tolerate the increasing inequalities between nations in face of their growing interdependence?

The concept of poverty

The question of social justice is closely related to the question of poverty. Comment has already been made in chapter 4 on the concept of the poverty line and the move to a comparative definition of poverty, related to average earnings. But real income is more important than monetary income as a determinant of poverty. In the words of a study prepared for the Social Science Research Council,[30] people are

> poor because they are deprived of the opportunities, comforts and self-respect regarded as normal in the community to which they belong. It is therefore the continually moved *average* standards of that community that are the starting points for an assessment of its poverty and the poor are those who fall sufficiently far below these average standards.

Once one sees poverty in these terms, the way in which different forms of deprivation reinforce each other and are closely correlated becomes obvious. Families without a father generally have a low income, are more likely to live in sub-standard accommodation as well as lacking the emotional support that a father can give to the family. At the same time, with the possible exception of widows, the mother's position produces stigma. Chronic sickness and disability reduce income as well as increasing medical and dependency needs.[31]

Baratz and Grigsby,[32] in a very radical approach to the concept of poverty, see it as lying in this correlation of 'severe deprivations and adverse occurrences' with inadequate economic resources. So they consider that poverty should be measured by indices showing how deprivation and adverse occurrences are distributed among different income groups. For instance, if disability, poor working conditions, sub-standard houses, and effective participation in the political process were likely to be found equally among the rich and the poor, one could say that there had been a reduction in the extent of poverty.

The Social Science Research Council in its study went on to analyse different theories of the causation of poverty, which implied different methods of attack. Poverty can be seen as being due to personal inadequacies, leading to attempts to supplement income in various ways, or to improve earning power. It may be attributed to the failure of various institutions such as the educational system or the social services, leading to attempts to reform these. Or it may be seen as the product of a social system which requires that some people should be very highly rewarded and others poorly rewarded. In this case no attempt to improve people or institutions will reduce the differentials, whether the concept of social justice is 'conservative' or 'liberal'. The weakest members of society will inevitably be poor in a comparative sense.

Two approaches to the future of the social services

One of the problems of developing rational discussion of priorities is that few people declare honestly to themselves the biases created

317

by their own interests, with the result that they are prepared to maintain basically inconsistent positions. Students, for instance, can simultaneously support greater selectivity in provision of social services benefits, but campaign for the abolition of a parental means test for their own grants without considering whether or not there is a common principle involved. In these circumstances, it may be of particular value to consider the views of two groups that have each tried to develop a consistent line of argument, although from opposing points of view. Both groups consider it desirable that a higher proportion of the gross national product should be spent on social services, and that more resources should be devoted to the needs of the most handicapped; both groups accept a democratic political system and are concerned that consumers should have more influence on the services provided; to these ends, they would both welcome a reduction in the power of professional groups. With so much agreement about ends, it might seem that disagreement could only be over technicalities. Yet behind each view lies a different ideal of human relationships.

The first view is put forward by a group of writers whose names are associated with the Institute of Economic Affairs, including several economists.[33] In essence, their view is the nineteenth-century liberal-economic approach adapted to new circumstances, an approach that is rejected by many economists today. They start from an appreciation of money as a most useful tool in an industrial society particularly when it is used in a market in which buyers and sellers are in direct contact. It provides a measure of the value that is placed on goods and services, and, therefore, a means of deciding priorities. It is a convenient method of rewarding work, effort and enterprise, and of ensuring, for those who cannot work, that their needs are met. It does this in a way that leaves the maximum responsibility for choice with the individual. By his choice, if monopoly can be prevented, the individual is also able to influence the quality and quantity of the goods and services provided, and ultimately create a balance between supply and demand. This is contrasted with the lack of incentive where needs are met regardless of individual effort, the lack of choice where goods and services are provided in kind rather than in cash, and the excess demand that is created where the individual does not have to consider his own priorities.

Behind this view of the significance of money as a tool, lies an acceptance of an individualistic approach to life, and of the importance of competition and reward in stimulating individual effort. There is no doubt that competition and reward can be effective in this way, at least for those who have expectations of success. Competition played an important part in Britain's Industrial Revolution and still does in many aspects of our lives. Moreover, as a motivating force, it has become institutionalised in the socialising process within our educational system, not only in individual academic study, but even in team sports. Thus, it has become an important part of our psychological processes, and it is difficult for most of us, especially for those who have had to struggle for success in this system, to conceive a progressive society based on other forms of motivation.

A competitive system is also a very useful method of selecting the members of an élite in a meritocracy. This group of writers stresses the importance of entrepreneurial and other skills associated with an élite in a technological society, although they accept the need to restrict the monopoly powers of professional groups.

A measure of inequality in the distribution of wealth and income is an inevitable concomitant of a competitive system based on financial rewards. This they accept. However, there is a minimum level of poverty, below which people should not be allowed to fall, and the state should ensure this by providing for the needs of the poor on a test of means as well as need. In order to ensure that adequate resources are available to reward exceptional effort, skill or initiative, the minimum level of poverty is conceived in absolute rather than relative terms. This is not easily reconcilable with the view that is also expressed – without any evidence being given for it – that inequalities of income can be expected to grow less with the increase of national productivity. The emphasis on individual choice requires that benefits to the poor should be given in cash or some equivalent form which enables them to make their own decisions about priorities in expenditure, for example, vouchers exchangeable for a variety of different services according to need.

The same emphasis on choice makes them support a wider extension of private provision of social services in such fields as health and education. Their own research in this country and American experience shows, in their view, that a larger private sector would result in those in the middle and higher income ranges putting a larger proportion of their income into social services than they are prepared to pay in tax. This could mean that a higher proportion of the gross national product was devoted to social services with a general improvement in quality. These writers also assume that in a private market the direct monetary link between the giver and receiver of the service would give the latter more control over the quality of the service.

The second approach to the development of the social services can be found in the writings of R. M. Titmuss, Brian Abel-Smith, Peter Townsend and others, whose names have been associated with the Department of Social Administration at the London School of Economics. Starting from a sociological rather than an economic point of view, and also a more radical approach,[34] these writers have less faith in the effectiveness of money as a tool for measuring value, for providing a rational basis for deciding social or individual priorities, or for relating supply with need. Perhaps even more fundamental is their doubt of the relevance of an individualistic, competitive ethic to the problems of a modern industrial society in which specialisation has reached so high a level that co-operation is essential for efficiency.

Competition is seen as being destructive as well as constructive in its effects. It can be destructive because it inhibits co-operation, because it often destroys the self-respect of those who lose out in the struggle, and because it produces anxiety, which at a low level stimulates effort, but at a higher level can paralyse action. The role of competition in our present society is recognised but other motives for action are also seen as significant. Even within a competitive system, cultural attitudes in defiance of competition have persisted; effort that receives no financial reward is still put into employment, and there is a continued willingness to engage in voluntary activities, to help others. These writers believe that if the changes that are taking place in our society can be directed aright, co-operation can be given a more predominant place.

Inequalities of wealth and income are seen as undesirable, and in the long run unnecessary. They are undesirable partly because they are inequitable and partly because they are dysfunctional. Relative poverty restricts the opportunities for valuable experiences of many kinds for individuals and families, and results in a waste of their abilities and resources. These inequalities, moreover, tend to perpetuate a hereditary élite and to concentrate command over resources, and hence power, in the hands of a few. This may not be appropriate in a society whose future depends on the responsibility and understanding of the manual worker, the trade unionist and the ordinary citizen, as well as on the honesty and ability of the manager, the executive officer, the civil servant, and the political leader.

It might be expected that these writers, in the interest of equality, would agree in recommending that benefits and services should be given selectively to those in need rather than on a universal basis. However, they believe that experience in this country and in the USA shows that benefits subject to a test of means lead to a sense of stigma and discrimination, which often results in the rejection of the services. Moreover, the existence of a substantial private sector alongside public social services tends to attract a higher proportion of available resources into the former. Those who use the public services would receive a poorer service than under a universal system, and would lack the knowledge, skill and influence necessary to protect their own interests. The provision of universal services is thus seen as a method of ensuring that priority is given to need regardless of income, and that the quality of the public services is supported by a strong and influential body of consumers.

In the view of these writers, it is dangerous to put too much reliance on a single mechanism for managing services as complex as health, education or income maintenance. The economic market provides a method of assessing demand for a service but not for assessing need; it provides a method of rationing scarce resources, but not a fair one: it provides only a limited control over the quality of complex services. Political action through government or pressure groups is one way by which the individual strengthens his position; social research provides a variety of alternative methods of assessing need as well as demand; social work has developed ways of ensuring a more adequate dialogue between the consumer and the service, and an alternative method – not necessarily fairer – of rationing resources. Further techniques may be found in time. Indeed it might be argued that we have reached a stage at which greater progress could be achieved if fewer resources were devoted to technological invention, and more to research into ways of making better use of the technological and other knowledge that we have already at our disposal.

To some extent, these two approaches epitomise the dilemma of man's situation. On the other hand, each man is an individual, conscious of his individuality, his personal achievements, and his personal freedom. Yet the full development of individual personality depends on the quality of social relationships; and personal achievement and freedom are enhanced by co-operative action in the control of the environment. Co-operative action requires the surrender of some aspects of personal freedom and some opportunity for individual initiative, yet if too much freedom is lost, adaptation to change, even change itself, becomes more difficult.

A market economy is one way of achieving joint action with a maximum of personal freedom, but this freedom has in the past been very unevenly distributed. It may be possible to modify the economic market so that it extends freedom further. But the price of personal freedom may be higher than we want to pay, and there may be different and perhaps greater satisfactions to be found in co-operative achievement.

Further reading

This chapter can be regarded as a continuation of chapter 1, so that some of the books referred to in that chapter and at its end are relevant to this one. Two subjects have, however, been explored somewhat more fully: first, the role of social services in our society, and second, the problem of poverty, to which some of the books mentioned in chapter 4 refer.

The role of the social services

In the list below, Pinker provides a broad historical account of the theoretical bases or the lack of them in the study of social administration, and concludes with an account of current sociological contributions. Becker is an American contribution at a time when sociology was first acknowledging its need to be relevant. Davies, Boaden and Donnison examines issues of decision-making, the first two at a broad level, the latter through case-studies. Thoënes is concerned with the shift of power to a new decision-making élite as a result of the development of the Welfare State, underestimating the continued importance of political factors. Titmuss and the Institute of Economic Affairs are discussed in the text:

HOWARD S. BECKER, ed., *Social Problems: A Modern Approach*, John Wiley, 1966.

P. M. BLAU and W. R. SCOTT, *Formal Organisations: A Comparative Study*, Routledge & Kegan Paul, 1963.

NOËL BOADEN, *Urban Policy-making: Influences on County Boroughs in England and Wales*, Cambridge University Press, 1971.

BLEDDYN DAVIES, *Social Needs and Resources in Local Services*, Michael Joseph, 1968.

D. V. DONNISON, VALERIE CHAPMAN *et al.*, *Social Policy and Administration: Studies in the Development of Social Services at the Local Level*, National Institute for Social Work Training, Allen & Unwin, 1965.

Institute of Economic Affairs, *Towards a Welfare Society*, 1967.

ROBERT PINKER, *Social Theory and Social Policy*, Heinemann, 1971.

PIET THOËNES, *The Elite in the Welfare State*, ed. J. Banks, Faber & Faber, 1966.

R. M. TITMUSS, *Commitment to Welfare*, Allen & Unwin, 1968.

Poverty and income distribution

The books in the list that follows represent a range of different approaches to the problem of poverty reflecting the great increase of interest in this subject in recent years. Townsend is an important examination of theoretical issues; Holman examines the extent of different kinds of deprivation in Britain and their interrelationship; Coates and Silburn is a case study of an area (others are referred to in note 29). The other books are mainly concerned with the distribution of income, and in the case of Atkinson, wealth. Titmuss was a seminal work breaking the complacency created by the accepted figures from the inland revenue. Routh, Webb and Sieve, Runciman and Wootton are all discussed in the text. Jackson and Stack are further analyses:

A. B. ATKINSON, *Unequal Shares: Wealth in Britain*, Allen Lane, 1972.

KEN COATES and RICHARD SILBURN, *St Anne's: Poverty and Morale*, Nottingham University Press, 1967.

R. HOLMAN, ed., *Socially Deprived Families in Britain*, NCSS, 1970.

DUDLEY JACKSON, *Poverty*, Macmillan, 1972.

GUY ROUTH, *Occupation and Pay in Great Britain, 1906–60*, Cambridge University Press, 1965.

W. G. RUNCIMAN, *Relative Deprivation and Social Justice*, Routledge & Kegan Paul, 1966.

THOMAS STARK, *The Distribution of Personal Income in the United Kingdom, 1949–63*, Cambridge University Press, 1972.

R. M. TITMUSS, *Income Distribution and Social Change*, Allen & Unwin, 1964.

PETER TOWNSEND, *The Concept of Poverty: Working Papers on Methods of Investigation and Life Styles of the Poor in Different Countries*, Heinemann, 1970.

ADRIAN L. WEBB and JACK E. B. SIEVE, *Income Redistribution and the Welfare State*, Occasional Papers in Social Administration no. 41, G. Bell, 1971.

BARBARA WOOTTON, *The Social Foundations of Wages Policy*, Allen & Unwin, 2nd ed., 1962.

Of the periodicals listed below, the following are particularly useful: *Social Trends*, an annual government publication which includes two or three articles in each issue as well as statistical tables and charts giving information and a range of important issues; *The Year Book of Social Policy*, which provides commissioned articles on important issues that have arisen during the year. Some focus on a particular theme, others on disparate subjects. The themes in past issues have been, Social Services Departments (1971), Education (1972), Local Government and Health Service Reforms (1973):

British Journal of Social Policy
Problems and Policies
Social and Economic Administration
Social Trends (HMSO, annually)
The Year Book of Social Policy, ed. Kathleen Jones (annually, hardback).

Notes

1 T. H. Marshall, *Social Policy*, Hutchinson, 1965, pp. 28–30, 96.
2 Piet Thoënes, *The Elite in the Welfare State*, ed. J. A. Banks, Faber and

Faber, 1966, p. 125: 'The Welfare State is a form of society character-ised by a system of democratic, government-sponsored welfare placed on a new footing and offering a guarantee of collective social care to its citizens, concurrently with the maintenance of a capitalist system of production.'

3 See T. H. Marshall, 'Value problems of welfare-capitalism', *Journal of Social Policy*, vol. 1, 1, January 1972.

4 See D. S. Lees, *Economic Consequences of the Professions*, Research Monograph no. 2, Institute of Economic Affairs, 1966, for a discussion of the effects of some of these claims.

5 Routledge & Kegan Paul, 1963. See also Mark Abrahamson, *The Professional in the Organisation*, Rand-McNally, 1967.

6 Routledge & Kegan Paul, 1967. See also Anthony Forder, 'Lay committees and professional workers in the English probation service', *Social and Economic Administration*, October 1969.

7 Piet Thoënes, *op. cit.*, Part II.

8 Pp. 11–15.

9 Margaret Wynn, *Family Policy*, Michael Joseph, 1970, pp. 23–5.

10 R. Pinker, *Social Theory and Social Policy*, Heinemann, 1971, pp. 142–3.

11 See chapter 7, p. 264.

12 Kathleen Bell, *Tribunals in the Social Services*, Routledge & Kegan Paul, 1969.

13 Harry Street, *Justice in the Welfare State*, Stevens, 1968, p. 108 *et seq.*

14 See the Annual Reports of the Parliamentary Commissioner for details of his work, and Harry Street, *op. cit.*, chapter 5, for critical comments. Also Sir Alan Marre, 'Some reflections of an Ombudsman', *Social and Economic Administration*, vol. 9, no. 1, Spring 1975.

15 J. A. G. Griffith, *Central Departments and Local Authorities*, Allen & Unwin, 1966, chapter 8. See also the discussion in the various reports on local government reform quoted in chapter 1.

16 E.g. Tony Lynes, 'The secret rules', *Poverty*, no. 4, Autumn 1967.

17 Jean S. Heywood and Barbara K. Allen, *Financial Help in Social Work: A Study of Preventive Work with Families under the Children and Young Persons Act, 1963*, Manchester University Press, 1971.

18 Consumer Council, *Consumer Consultative Machinery in the National-ised Industries*, HMSO, 1968, chapter 6.

19 See the discussion of these issues in Victor George and Paul Wilding, 'Social values, social class and social policy', *Social and Economic Administration*, vol. 6, no. 3, September 1972.

20 See Trevor Noble, 'Intragenerational mobility in Britain', *Sociology*, vol. 8, no. 3, September 1974. In his notes at the end of the article the author refers to other articles on this topic.

21 David P. Boyd, 'The educational background of a selected group of England's leaders', *Sociology*, vol. 8, no. 2. May 1974.

22 See K. B. Start and B. K. Wells, *The Trends of Reading Standard*, for the National Foundation for Education Research, 1972. Commissioned by the Department of Education and Science.

23 Guy Routh, *Occupation and Pay in Great Britain, 1906–60*, Cambridge University Press, 1965, p. 147. See also Barbara Wootton, *The Social Foundations of Wages Policy*, Allen & Unwin, 1955 and 1966.

24 *Social Trends*, no. 2, 1971, table 29. In 1949–50 average income in the lower quartile was 61 per cent of the median, and in the upper quartile 141 per cent. In 1969–70 the proportions were 64 per cent and 139 per cent respectively.

25 Adrian L. Webb and Jack E. B. Sieve, *Income Redistribution and the Welfare State*, Occasional Papers in Social Administration no. 41, G. Bell, 1971, chapter 7.

26 Martin Rein, 'Social class and the health services', *New Society*, 20 November 1969.

27 The child health section of the Annual Reports of the Chief Medical Officer of the Department of Health and Social Security refer to this problem. See particularly the report for 1972.

28 W. G. Runciman, 'Social justice', *The Listener*, 29 July 1965, reprinted in Eric Butterworth and David Weir, *The Sociology of Modern Man*, Fontana/Collins, 1970, p. 308. See also W. G. Runciman, *Relative Deprivation and Social Justice*, Routledge & Kegan Paul, 1966, which includes a historical study of inequalities of class, defined in terms of income, of status and of power, and a contemporary survey of attitudes.

29 For examples of studies demonstrating the interdependence of need in different fields, see: Charles Vereker and J. B. Mays, *Urban Redevelopment and Social Change*, Liverpool University Press, 1961; Ken Coates and Richard Silburn, *St Anne's*, Nottingham University Press, 1967; J. W. B. Douglas, *The Home and the School*, Macgibbon & Kee, 1964; J. B. Mays, *Education and the Urban Child*, Liverpool University Press, 1962. A fuller discussion of the issues is contained in R. Holman, ed., *Socially Deprived Families in Britain*, National Council of Social Services, 1970.

30 Social Science Research Council, *Research on Poverty*, Heinemann, 1968, p. 5.

31 For a full discussion and evidence see R. Holman, ed., *op. cit.*

32 Morton S. Baratz and William E. Grigsby, 'Thoughts on poverty and its elimination', *Journal of Social Policy*, vol. 1, 2, April 1972.

33 See *Towards a Welfare Society*, Occasional Paper no. 13, 1967, Institute of Economic Affairs, for an account of these views and a list of publications relating to them.

34 The Institute writers, however, regard themselves as 'radical reactionaries'.

Index

Abel-Smith, Brian, xxii, 319
Abortion, 205–8 *passim*; Act, 207, 208, 209, 289; legal grounds for, 207; notified (statistics), 207
Acton Society Trust, 75
Addicts, 222
Administrative Tribunals and Enquiries, Committee on, see Franks Committee
Administrators, 306; authority, 307
Adoption, 238, 240–2; Acts, 238; agencies, 240, 241
Adult education, *see* Education (adult)
Age Concern England, 19
Ageing, *see* Elderly persons
Albemarle Report, 43
Allen, Lady Marjory of Hurtwood, 236
Almoners, *see* Social work (medical and psychiatric workers)
Ambulance service, 191
Annis Gillie Committee/Report, 185, 186
Anson, Sir William, 287
Approved schools, *see* Schools (approved)
'Approved Societies', 170
Arbitration, *see* Wages
Asylums, lunatic, *see* Mental hospitals
Atkinson, A. B., 117
Aves Report, 271–2, 273

Baby: farming, *see* Children (baby-farming); minding, *see* Day care
Bains Report, 15, 18, 19
Balance of payments, xxiv, 8
Baratz, Morton S. and Grigsby, William E., 317
Barlow Report, 131
Barnardo, Dr Thomas J., 270, 272
Barristers, 295
'Battered wives', 223
Bedford, Sybille, 300
Benefits, *see* Occupational benefits, *and see under* Social security
Bentham, Jeremy, 3
Bevan, Aneurin, 175
Beveridge Report, 7, 9, 16, 91–2, 96–8, 113, 169, 175, 313
Birmingham, 173, 265
Birth control, *see* Family planning
Births and deaths, registration, 234
Bismarck, Otto E. L., Prince, 5
Blackstone, Sir William, 288
Blackwood, Raymond, 293
Blau, P. M. and Scott, W. R., 307
Blind persons, 109, 224, 253; Acts, 253; statistics, 254
Board of Education, *see* Department of Education and Science
Boarding out, *see* Children (fostering)
Boards of Health, 127, 164
Booth, Charles, 5, 248
Borstals, 5

Routledge Social Science Series

Routledge & Kegan Paul   London and Boston

68–74 Carter Lane   London EC4V 5EL
9 Park Street   Boston   Mass 02108

Contents

*Authors wishing to submit manuscripts for any series in
this catalogue should send them to the Social Science Editor,
Routledge & Kegan Paul Ltd, 68–74 Carter Lane,
London EC4V 5EL*

●*Books so marked are available in paperback
All books are in Metric Demy 8vo format (216 × 138mm approx.)*

International Library of Sociology

General Editor   John Rex

GENERAL SOCIOLOGY

Barnsley, J. H. The Social Reality of Ethics. *464 pp.*
Belshaw, Cyril. The Conditions of Social Performance. *An Exploratory Theory. 144 pp.*
Brown, Robert. Explanation in Social Science. *208 pp.*
● Rules and Laws in Sociology. *192 pp.*
Bruford, W. H. Chekhov and His Russia. *A Sociological Study. 244 pp.*
Cain, Maureen E. Society and the Policeman's Role. *326 pp.*
Gibson, Quentin. The Logic of Social Enquiry. *240 pp.*
Glucksmann, M. Structuralist Analysis in Contemporary Social Thought. *212 pp.*
Gurvitch, Georges. Sociology of Law. *Preface by Roscoe Pound. 264 pp.*
Hodge, H. A. Wilhelm Dilthey. *An Introduction. 184 pp.*
Homans, George C. Sentiments and Activities. *336 pp.*
Johnson, Harry M. Sociology: *a Systematic Introduction. Foreword by Robert K. Merton. 710 pp.*
Mannheim, Karl. Essays on Sociology and Social Psychology. *Edited by Paul Keckskemeti. With Editorial Note by Adolph Lowe. 344 pp.*
Systematic Sociology: *An Introduction to the Study of Society. Edited by J. S. Erös and Professor W. A. C. Stewart. 220 pp.*
Martindale, Don. The Nature and Types of Sociological Theory. *292 pp.*
●**Maus, Heinz.** A Short History of Sociology. *234 pp.*
Mey, Harald. Field-Theory. *A Study of its Application in the Social Sciences. 352 pp.*
Myrdal, Gunnar. Value in Social Theory: *A Collection of Essays on Methodology. Edited by Paul Streeten. 332 pp.*
Ogburn, William F., and **Nimkoff, Meyer F.** A Handbook of Sociology. *Preface by Karl Mannheim. 656 pp. 46 figures. 35 tables.*
Parsons, Talcott, and **Smelser, Neil J.** Economy and Society: *A Study in the Integration of Economic and Social Theory. 362 pp.*
●**Rex, John.** Key Problems of Sociological Theory. *220 pp.*
Discovering Sociology. *278 pp.*
Sociology and the Demystification of the Modern World. *282 pp.*
●**Rex, John** (Ed.) Approaches to Sociology. *Contributions by Peter Abell, Frank Bechhofer, Basil Bernstein, Ronald Fletcher, David Frisby, Miriam Glucksmann, Peter Lassman, Herminio Martins, John Rex, Roland Robertson, John Westergaard and Jock Young. 302 pp.*
Rigby, A. Alternative Realities. *352 pp.*
Roche, M. Phenomenology, Language and the Social Sciences. *374 pp.*
Sahay, A. Sociological Analysis. *220 pp.*
Urry, John. Reference Groups and the Theory of Revolution. *244 pp.*
Weinberg, E. Development of Sociology in the Soviet Union. *173 pp.*

FOREIGN CLASSICS OF SOCIOLOGY

●**Durkheim, Emile.** Suicide. *A Study in Sociology. Edited and with an Introduction by George Simpson. 404 pp.*
Professional Ethics and Civic Morals. *Translated by Cornelia Brookfield. 288 pp.*
●**Gerth, H. H.,** and **Mills, C. Wright.** From Max Weber: *Essays in Sociology. 502 pp.*
●**Tönnies, Ferdinand.** Community and Association. (*Gemeinschaft und Gesellschaft.) Translated and Supplemented by Charles P. Loomis. Foreword by Pitirim A. Sorokin. 334 pp.*

SOCIAL STRUCTURE

Andreski, Stanislav. Military Organization and Society. *Foreword by Professor A. R. Radcliffe-Brown. 226 pp. 1 folder.*
Coontz, Sydney H. Population Theories and the Economic Interpretation. *202 pp.*
Coser, Lewis. The Functions of Social Conflict. *204 pp.*
Dickie-Clark, H. F. Marginal Situation: *A Sociological Study of a Coloured Group. 240 pp. 11 tables.*
Glaser, Barney, and **Strauss, Anselm L.** Status Passage. *A Formal Theory. 208 pp.*
Glass, D. V. (Ed.) Social Mobility in Britain. *Contributions by J. Berent, T. Bottomore, R. C. Chambers, J. Floud, D. V. Glass, J. R. Hall, H. T. Himmelweit, R. K. Kelsall, F. M. Martin, C. A. Moser, R. Mukherjee, and W. Ziegel. 420 pp.*
Jones, Garth N. Planned Organizational Change: *An Exploratory Study Using an Empirical Approach. 268 pp.*
Kelsall, R. K. Higher Civil Servants in Britain: *From 1870 to the Present Day. 268 pp. 31 tables.*
König, René. The Community. *232 pp. Illustrated.*
●**Lawton, Denis.** Social Class, Language and Education. *192 pp.*
McLeish, John. The Theory of Social Change: *Four Views Considered. 128 pp.*
Marsh, David C. The Changing Social Structure of England and Wales, 1871-1961. *288 pp.*
Mouzelis, Nicos. Organization and Bureaucracy. *An Analysis of Modern Theories. 240 pp.*
Mulkay, M. J. Functionalism, Exchange and Theoretical Strategy. *272 pp.*
Ossowski, Stanislaw. Class Structure in the Social Consciousness. *210 pp.*
Podgórecki, Adam. Law and Society. *About 300 pp.*

SOCIOLOGY AND POLITICS

Acton, T. A. Gypsy Politics and Social Change. *316 pp.*
Hechter, Michael. Internal Colonialism. *The Celtic Fringe in British National Development, 1536–1966. About 350 pp.*
Hertz, Frederick. Nationality in History and Politics: *A Psychology and Sociology of National Sentiment and Nationalism. 432 pp.*

Kornhauser, William. The Politics of Mass Society. *272 pp. 20 tables.*

Laidler, Harry W. History of Socialism. *Social-Economic Movements: An Historical and Comparative Survey of Socialism, Communism, Co-operation, Utopianism; and other Systems of Reform and Reconstruction. 992 pp.*

Lasswell, H. D. Analysis of Political Behaviour. *324 pp.*

Mannheim, Karl. Freedom, Power and Democratic Planning. *Edited by Hans Gerth and Ernest K. Bramstedt. 424 pp.*

Mansur, Fatma. Process of Independence. *Foreword by A. H. Hanson. 208 pp.*

Martin, David A. Pacifism: *an Historical and Sociological Study. 262 pp.*

Myrdal, Gunnar. The Political Element in the Development of Economic Theory. *Translated from the German by Paul Streeten. 282 pp.*

Wootton, Graham. Workers, Unions and the State. *188 pp.*

FOREIGN AFFAIRS: THEIR SOCIAL, POLITICAL AND ECONOMIC FOUNDATIONS

Mayer, J. P. Political Thought in France from the Revolution to the Fifth Republic. *164 pp.*

CRIMINOLOGY

Ancel, Marc. Social Defence: *A Modern Approach to Criminal Problems. Foreword by Leon Radzinowicz. 240 pp.*

Cain, Maureen E. Society and the Policeman's Role. *326 pp.*

Cloward, Richard A., and **Ohlin, Lloyd E.** Delinquency and Opportunity: *A Theory of Delinquent Gangs. 248 pp.*

Downes, David M. The Delinquent Solution. *A Study in Subcultural Theory. 296 pp.*

Dunlop, A. B., and **McCabe, S.** Young Men in Detention Centres. *192 pp.*

Friedlander, Kate. The Psycho-Analytical Approach to Juvenile Delinquency: *Theory, Case Studies, Treatment. 320 pp.*

Glueck, Sheldon, and **Eleanor.** Family Environment and Delinquency. *With the statistical assistance of Rose W. Kneznek. 340 pp.*

Lopez-Rey, Manuel. Crime. *An Analytical Appraisal. 288 pp.*

Mannheim, Hermann. Comparative Criminology: *a Text Book. Two volumes. 442 pp. and 380 pp.*

Morris, Terence. The Criminal Area: *A Study in Social Ecology. Foreword by Hermann Mannheim. 232 pp. 25 tables. 4 maps.*

Rock, Paul. Making People Pay. *338 pp.*

● **Taylor, Ian, Walton, Paul,** and **Young, Jock.** The New Criminology. *For a Social Theory of Deviance. 325 pp.*

SOCIAL PSYCHOLOGY

Bagley, Christopher. The Social Psychology of the Epileptic Child. *320 pp.*

Barbu, Zevedei. Problems of Historical Psychology. *248 pp.*

Blackburn, Julian. Psychology and the Social Pattern. *184 pp.*

●**Brittan, Arthur.** Meanings and Situations. *224 pp.*

Carroll, J. Break-Out from the Crystal Palace. *200 pp.*

●**Fleming, C. M.** Adolescence: Its Social Psychology. *With an Introduction to recent findings from the fields of Anthropology, Physiology, Medicine, Psychometrics and Sociometry. 288 pp.*

● The Social Psychology of Education: *An Introduction and Guide to Its Study. 136 pp.*

Homans, George C. The Human Group. *Foreword by Bernard DeVoto. Introduction by Robert K. Merton. 526 pp.*

● Social Behaviour: *its Elementary Forms. 416 pp.*

●**Klein, Josephine.** The Study of Groups. *226 pp. 31 figures. 5 tables.*

Linton, Ralph. The Cultural Background of Personality. *132 pp.*

●**Mayo, Elton.** The Social Problems of an Industrial Civilization. *With an appendix on the Political Problem. 180 pp.*

Ottaway, A. K. C. Learning Through Group Experience. *176 pp.*

Ridder, J. C. de. The Personality of the Urban African in South Africa. *A Thematic Apperception Test Study. 196 pp. 12 plates.*

●**Rose, Arnold M.** (Ed.) Human Behaviour and Social Processes: *an Interactionist Approach. Contributions by Arnold M. Rose, Ralph H. Turner, Anselm Strauss, Everett C. Hughes, E. Franklin Frazier, Howard S. Becker, et al. 696 pp.*

Smelser, Neil J. Theory of Collective Behaviour. *448 pp.*

Stephenson, Geoffrey M. The Development of Conscience. *128 pp.*

Young, Kimball. Handbook of Social Psychology. *658 pp. 16 figures. 10 tables.*

SOCIOLOGY OF THE FAMILY

Banks, J. A. Prosperity and Parenthood: *A Study of Family Planning among The Victorian Middle Classes. 262 pp.*

Bell, Colin R. Middle Class Families: *Social and Geographical Mobility. 224 pp.*

Burton, Lindy. Vulnerable Children. *272 pp.*

Gavron, Hannah. The Captive Wife: *Conflicts of Household Mothers. 190 pp.*

George, Victor, and **Wilding, Paul.** Motherless Families. *220 pp.*

Klein, Josephine. Samples from English Cultures.
1. Three Preliminary Studies and Aspects of Adult Life in England. *447 pp.*
2. Child-Rearing Practices and Index. *247 pp.*

Klein, Viola. Britain's Married Women Workers. *180 pp.*

The Feminine Character. *History of an Ideology. 244 pp.*

McWhinnie, Alexina M. Adopted Children. *How They Grow Up. 304 pp.*

● **Myrdal, Alva,** and **Klein, Viola.** Women's Two Roles: *Home and Work. 238 pp. 27 tables.*

Parsons, Talcott, and **Bales, Robert F.** Family: Socialization and Interaction Process. *In collaboration with James Olds, Morris Zelditch and Philip E. Slater. 456 pp. 50 figures and tables.*

SOCIAL SERVICES

Bastide, Roger. The Sociology of Mental Disorder. *Translated from the French by Jean McNeil. 260 pp.*

Carlebach, Julius. Caring For Children in Trouble. *266 pp.*

Forder, R. A. (Ed.) Penelope Hall's Social Services of England and Wales. *352 pp.*

George, Victor. Foster Care. *Theory and Practice. 234 pp.*
Social Security: *Beveridge and After. 258 pp.*

George, V., and **Wilding, P.** Motherless Families. *248 pp.*

●**Goetschius, George W.** Working with Community Groups. *256 pp.*

Goetschius, George W., and **Tash, Joan.** Working with Unattached Youth. *416 pp.*

Hall, M. P., and **Howes, I. V.** The Church in Social Work. *A Study of Moral Welfare Work undertaken by the Church of England. 320 pp.*

Heywood, Jean S. Children in Care: *the Development of the Service for the Deprived Child. 264 pp.*

Hoenig, J., and **Hamilton, Marian W.** The De-Segregation of the Mentally Ill. *284 pp.*

Jones, Kathleen. Mental Health and Social Policy, 1845-1959. *264 pp.*

King, Roy D., Raynes, Norma V., and **Tizard, Jack.** Patterns of Residential Care. *356 pp.*

Leigh, John. Young People and Leisure. *256 pp.*

Morris, Mary. Voluntary Work and the Welfare State. *300 pp.*

Morris, Pauline. Put Away: *A Sociological Study of Institutions for the Mentally Retarded. 364 pp.*

Nokes, P. L. The Professional Task in Welfare Practice. *152 pp.*

Timms, Noel. Psychiatric Social Work in Great Britain (1939-1962). *280 pp.*

●   Social Casework: *Principles and Practice. 256 pp.*

Young, A. F. Social Services in British Industry. *272 pp.*

Young, A. F., and **Ashton, E. T.** British Social Work in the Nineteenth Century. *288 pp.*

SOCIOLOGY OF EDUCATION

Banks, Olive. Parity and Prestige in English Secondary Education: a Study in Educational Sociology. *272 pp.*

Bentwich, Joseph. Education in Israel. *224 pp. 8 pp. plates.*

●**Blyth, W. A. L.** English Primary Education. *A Sociological Description.*
1. Schools. *232 pp.*
2. Background. *168 pp.*

Collier, K. G. The Social Purposes of Education: *Personal and Social Values in Education. 268 pp.*

Dale, R. R., and **Griffith, S.** Down Stream: *Failure in the Grammar School.*
108 pp.

Dore, R. P. Education in Tokugawa Japan. *356 pp. 9 pp. plates.*

Evans, K. M. Sociometry and Education. *158 pp.*

●**Ford, Julienne.** Social Class and the Comprehensive School. *192 pp.*

Foster, P. J. Education and Social Change in Ghana. *336 pp. 3 maps.*

Fraser, W. R. Education and Society in Modern France. *150 pp.*

Grace, Gerald R. Role Conflict and the Teacher. *About 200 pp.*

Hans, Nicholas. New Trends in Education in the Eighteenth Century.
278 pp. 19 tables.

● Comparative Education: *A Study of Educational Factors and Traditions.*
360 pp.

Hargreaves, David. Interpersonal Relations and Education. *432 pp.*

● Social Relations in a Secondary School. *240 pp.*

Holmes, Brian. Problems in Education. *A Comparative Approach. 336 pp.*

King, Ronald. Values and Involvement in a Grammar School. *164 pp.*

School Organization and Pupil Involvement. *A Study of Secondary
Schools.*

●**Mannheim, Karl,** and **Stewart, W. A. C.** An Introduction to the Sociology
of Education. *206 pp.*

Morris, Raymond N. The Sixth Form and College Entrance. *231 pp.*

●**Musgrove, F.** Youth and the Social Order. *176 pp.*

●**Ottaway, A. K. C.** Education and Society: An Introduction to the Sociology
of Education. *With an Introduction by W. O. Lester Smith. 212 pp.*

Peers, Robert. Adult Education: *A Comparative Study. 398 pp.*

Pritchard, D. G. Education and the Handicapped: *1760 to 1960. 258 pp.*

Richardson, Helen. Adolescent Girls in Approved Schools. *308 pp.*

Stratta, Erica. The Education of Borstal Boys. *A Study of their Educational
Experiences prior to, and during, Borstal Training. 256 pp.*

Taylor, P. H., Reid, W. A., and **Holley, B. J.** The English Sixth Form.
A Case Study in Curriculum Research. 200 pp.

SOCIOLOGY OF CULTURE

Eppel, E. M., and **M.** Adolescents and Morality: *A Study of some Moral
Values and Dilemmas of Working Adolescents in the Context of a
changing Climate of Opinion. Foreword by W. J. H. Sprott. 268 pp.
39 tables.*

●**Fromm, Erich.** The Fear of Freedom. *286 pp.*

● The Sane Society. *400 pp.*

Mannheim, Karl. Essays on the Sociology of Culture. *Edited by Ernst
Mannheim in co-operation with Paul Kecskemeti. Editorial Note by
Adolph Lowe. 280 pp.*

Weber, Alfred. Farewell to European History: *or The Conquest of Nihilism.
Translated from the German by R. F. C. Hull. 224 pp.*

SOCIOLOGY OF RELIGION

Argyle, Michael and **Beit-Hallahmi, Benjamin.** The Social Psychology of Religion. *About 256 pp.*

Nelson, G. K. Spiritualism and Society. *313 pp.*

Stark, Werner. The Sociology of Religion. *A Study of Christendom.*
  Volume I. *Established Religion. 248 pp.*
  Volume II. *Sectarian Religion. 368 pp.*
  Volume III. *The Universal Church. 464 pp.*
  Volume IV. *Types of Religious Man. 352 pp.*
  Volume V. *Types of Religious Culture. 464 pp.*

Turner, B. S. Weber and Islam. *216 pp.*

Watt, W. Montgomery. Islam and the Integration of Society. *320 pp.*

SOCIOLOGY OF ART AND LITERATURE

Jarvie, Ian C. Towards a Sociology of the Cinema. *A Comparative Essay on the Structure and Functioning of a Major Entertainment Industry. 405 pp.*

Rust, Frances S. Dance in Society. *An Analysis of the Relationships between the Social Dance and Society in England from the Middle Ages to the Present Day. 256 pp. 8 pp. of plates.*

Schücking, L. L. The Sociology of Literary Taste. *112 pp.*

Wolff, Janet. Hermeneutic Philosophy and the Sociology of Art. *About 200 pp.*

SOCIOLOGY OF KNOWLEDGE

Diesing, P. Patterns of Discovery in the Social Sciences. *262 pp.*

● **Douglas, J. D.** (Ed.) Understanding Everyday Life. *370 pp.*

● **Hamilton, P.** Knowledge and Social Structure. *174 pp.*

Jarvie, I. C. Concepts and Society. *232 pp.*

Mannheim, Karl. Essays on the Sociology of Knowledge. *Edited by Paul Kecskemeti. Editorial Note by Adolph Lowe. 353 pp.*

Remmling, Gunter W. (Ed.) Towards the Sociology of Knowledge. *Origin and Development of a Sociological Thought Style. 463 pp.*

Stark, Werner. The Sociology of Knowledge: *An Essay in Aid of a Deeper Understanding of the History of Ideas. 384 pp.*

URBAN SOCIOLOGY

Ashworth, William. The Genesis of Modern British Town Planning: *A Study in Economic and Social History of the Nineteenth and Twentieth Centuries. 288 pp.*

Cullingworth, J. B. Housing Needs and Planning Policy: *A Restatement of the Problems of Housing Need and 'Overspill' in England and Wales. 232 pp. 44 tables. 8 maps.*

Dickinson, Robert E. City and Region: *A Geographical Interpretation* *608 pp. 125 figures.*

The West European City: *A Geographical Interpretation. 600 pp. 129 maps. 29 plates.*

● The City Region in Western Europe. *320 pp. Maps.*

Humphreys, Alexander J. New Dubliners: *Urbanization and the Irish Family. Foreword by George C. Homans. 304 pp.*

Jackson, Brian. Working Class Community: *Some General Notions raised by a Series of Studies in Northern England. 192 pp.*

Jennings, Hilda. Societies in the Making: *a Study of Development and Redevelopment within a County Borough. Foreword by D. A. Clark. 286 pp.*

●**Mann, P. H.** An Approach to Urban Sociology. *240 pp.*

Morris, R. N., and **Mogey, J.** The Sociology of Housing. *Studies at Berinsfield. 232 pp. 4 pp. plates.*

Rosser, C., and **Harris, C.** The Family and Social Change. *A Study of Family and Kinship in a South Wales Town. 352 pp. 8 maps.*

RURAL SOCIOLOGY

Chambers, R. J. H. Settlement Schemes in Tropical Africa: *A Selective Study. 268 pp.*

Haswell, M. R. The Economics of Development in Village India. *120 pp.*

Littlejohn, James. Westrigg: *the Sociology of a Cheviot Parish. 172 pp. 5 figures.*

Mayer, Adrian C. Peasants in the Pacific. *A Study of Fiji Indian Rural Society. 248 pp. 20 plates.*

Williams, W. M. The Sociology of an English Village: *Gosforth. 272 pp. 12 figures. 13 tables.*

SOCIOLOGY OF INDUSTRY AND DISTRIBUTION

Anderson, Nels. Work and Leisure. *280 pp.*

●**Blau, Peter M.,** and **Scott, W. Richard.** Formal Organizations: *a Comparative approach. Introduction and Additional Bibliography by J. H. Smith. 326 pp.*

Eldridge, J. E. T. Industrial Disputes. *Essays in the Sociology of Industrial Relations. 288 pp.*

Hetzler, Stanley. Applied Measures for Promoting Technological Growth. *352 pp.*

Technological Growth and Social Change. *Achieving Modernization. 269 pp.*

Hollowell, Peter G. The Lorry Driver. *272 pp.*

Jefferys, Margot, *with the assistance of Winifred Moss.* Mobility in the Labour Market: *Employment Changes in Battersea and Dagenham. Preface by Barbara Wootton. 186 pp. 51 tables.*

Millerson, Geoffrey. The Qualifying Associations: *a Study in Professionalization. 320 pp.*

Smelser, Neil J. Social Change in the Industrial Revolution: *An Application of Theory to the Lancashire Cotton Industry, 1770-1840. 468 pp. 12 figures. 14 tables.*

Williams, Gertrude. Recruitment to Skilled Trades. *240 pp.*

Young, A. F. Industrial Injuries Insurance: *an Examination of British Policy. 192 pp.*

DOCUMENTARY

Schlesinger, Rudolf (Ed.) Changing Attitudes in Soviet Russia.
2. The Nationalities Problem and Soviet Administration. *Selected Readings on the Development of Soviet Nationalities Policies. Introduced by the editor. Translated by W. W. Gottlieb. 324 pp.*

ANTHROPOLOGY

Ammar, Hamed. Growing up in an Egyptian Village: *Silwa, Province of Aswan. 336 pp.*

Brandel-Syrier, Mia. Reeftown Elite. *A Study of Social Mobility in a Modern African Community on the Reef. 376 pp.*

Crook, David, and **Isabel.** Revolution in a Chinese Village: *Ten Mile Inn. 230 pp. 8 plates. 1 map.*

Dickie-Clark, H. F. The Marginal Situation. *A Sociological Study of a Coloured Group. 236 pp.*

Dube, S. C. Indian Village. *Foreword by Morris Edward Opler. 276 pp. 4 plates.*

India's Changing Villages: *Human Factors in Community Development. 260 pp. 8 plates. 1 map.*

Firth, Raymond. Malay Fishermen. *Their Peasant Economy. 420 pp. 17 pp. plates.*

Firth, R., Hubert, J., and **Forge, A.** Families and their Relatives. *Kinship in a Middle-Class Sector of London: An Anthropological Study. 456 pp.*

Gulliver, P. H. Social Control in an African Society: a Study of the Arusha, Agricultural Masai of Northern Tanganyika. *320 pp. 8 plates. 10 figures.*

Family Herds. *288 pp.*

Ishwaran, K. Shivapur. *A South Indian Village. 216 pp.*

Tradition and Economy in Village India: *An Interactionist Approach. Foreword by Conrad Arensburg. 176 pp.*

Jarvie, Ian C. The Revolution in Anthropology. *268 pp.*

Jarvie, Ian C., and **Agassi, Joseph.** Hong Kong. *A Society in Transition. 396 pp. Illustrated with plates and maps.*

Little, Kenneth L. Mende of Sierra Leone. *308 pp. and folder.*

Negroes in Britain. *With a New Introduction and Contemporary Study by Leonard Bloom. 320 pp.*

Lowie, Robert H. Social Organization. *494 pp.*

Mayer, Adrian, C. Caste and Kinship in Central India: *A Village and its Region. 328 pp. 16 plates. 15 figures. 16 tables.*

Peasants in the Pacific. *A Study of Fiji Indian Rural Society. 248 pp.*

Smith, Raymond T. The Negro Family in British Guiana: *Family Structure and Social Status in the Villages. With a Foreword by Meyer Fortes. 314 pp. 8 plates. 1 figure. 4 maps.*

SOCIOLOGY AND PHILOSOPHY

Barnsley, John H. The Social Reality of Ethics. *A Comparative Analysis of Moral Codes. 448 pp.*

Diesing, Paul. Patterns of Discovery in the Social Sciences. *362 pp.*

● **Douglas, Jack D.** (Ed.) Understanding Everyday Life. *Toward the Reconstruction of Sociological Knowledge. Contributions by Alan F. Blum. Aaron W. Cicourel, Norman K. Denzin, Jack D. Douglas, John Heeren, Peter McHugh, Peter K. Manning, Melvin Power, Matthew Speier, Roy Turner, D. Lawrence Wieder, Thomas P. Wilson and Don H. Zimmerman. 370 pp.*

Jarvie, Ian C. Concepts and Society. *216 pp.*

Pelz, Werner. The Scope of Understanding in Sociology. *Towards a more radical reorientation in the social humanistic sciences. 283 pp.*

Roche, Maurice. Phenomenology, Language and the Social Sciences. *371 pp.*

Sahay, Arun. Sociological Analysis. *212 pp.*

Sklair, Leslie. The Sociology of Progress. *320 pp.*

International Library of Anthropology

General Editor   Adam Kuper

Brown, Paula. The Chimbu. *A Study of Change in the New Guinea Highlands. 151 pp.*

Lloyd, P. C. Power and Independence. *Urban Africans' Perception of Social Inequality. 264 pp.*

Pettigrew, Joyce. Robber Noblemen. *A Study of the Political System of the Sikh Jats. 284 pp.*

Van Den Berghe, Pierre L. Power and Privilege at an African University. *278 pp.*

International Library of Social Policy

General Editor   Kathleen Jones

Bayley, M. Mental Handicap and Community Care. *426 pp.*

Butler, J. R. Family Doctors and Public Policy. *208 pp.*

Holman, Robert. Trading in Children. *A Study of Private Fostering. 355 pp.*

Jones, Kathleen. History of the Mental Health Service. *428 pp.*

Thomas, J. E. The English Prison Officer since 1850: *A Study in Conflict. 258 pp.*

Woodward, J. To Do the Sick No Harm. *A Study of the British Voluntary Hospital System to 1875. About 220 pp.*

International Library of Welfare and Philosophy

General Editors Noel Timms and David Watson

● **Plant, Raymond.** Community and Ideology. *104 pp.*

Primary Socialization, Language and Education

General Editor Basil Bernstein

Bernstein, Basil. Class, Codes and Control. *2 volumes.*
  1. *Theoretical Studies Towards a Sociology of Language. 254 pp.*
  2. *Applied Studies Towards a Sociology of Language. About 400 pp.*

Brandis, W., and **Bernstein, B.** Selection and Control. *176 pp.*

Brandis, Walter, and **Henderson, Dorothy.** Social Class, Language and Communication. *288 pp.*

Cook-Gumperz, Jenny. Social Control and Socialization. *A Study of Class Differences in the Language of Maternal Control. 290 pp.*

● **Gahagan, D. M.,** and **G. A.** Talk Reform. *Exploration in Language for Infant School Children. 160 pp.*

Robinson, W. P., and **Rackstraw, Susan D. A.** A Question of Answers. *2 volumes. 192 pp. and 180 pp.*

Turner, Geoffrey J., and **Mohan, Bernard A.** A Linguistic Description and Computer Programme for Children's Speech. *208 pp.*

Reports of the Institute of Community Studies

Cartwright, Ann. Human Relations and Hospital Care. *272 pp.*

●   Parents and Family Planning Services. *306 pp.*

  Patients and their Doctors. *A Study of General Practice. 304 pp.*

● **Jackson, Brian.** Streaming: *an Education System in Miniature. 168 pp.*

Jackson, Brian, and **Marsden, Dennis.** Education and the Working Class: *Some General Themes raised by a Study of 88 Working-class Children in a Northern Industrial City. 268 pp. 2 folders.*

Marris, Peter. The Experience of Higher Education. *232 pp. 27 tables.*

  Loss and Change. *192 pp.*

Marris, Peter, and **Rein, Martin.** Dilemmas of Social Reform. *Poverty and Community Action in the United States. 256 pp.*

Marris, Peter, and **Somerset, Anthony.** African Businessmen. *A Study of Entrepreneurship and Development in Kenya. 256 pp.*

Mills, Richard. Young Outsiders: *a Study in Alternative Communities. 216 pp.*

Runciman, W. G. Relative Deprivation and Social Justice. *A Study of Attitudes to Social Inequality in Twentieth-Century England. 352 pp.*

Willmott, Peter. Adolescent Boys in East London. *230 pp.*

Willmott, Peter, and **Young, Michael.** Family and Class in a London Suburb. *202 pp. 47 tables.*

Young, Michael. Innovation and Research in Education. *192 pp.*

●**Young, Michael,** and **McGeeney, Patrick.** Learning Begins at Home. *A Study of a Junior School and its Parents. 128 pp.*

Young, Michael, and **Willmott, Peter.** Family and Kinship in East London. *Foreword by Richard M. Titmuss. 252 pp. 39 tables.*
The Symmetrical Family. *410 pp.*

Reports of the Institute for Social Studies in Medical Care

Cartwright, Ann, Hockey, Lisbeth, and **Anderson, John L.** Life Before Death. *310 pp.*

Dunnell, Karen, and **Cartwright, Ann.** Medicine Takers, Prescribers and Hoarders. *190 pp.*

Medicine, Illness and Society

General Editor   W. M. Williams

Robinson, David. The Process of Becoming Ill. *142 pp.*

Stacey, Margaret, *et al.* Hospitals, Children and Their Families. *The Report of a Pilot Study. 202 pp.*

Monographs in Social Theory

General Editor   Arthur Brittan

●**Barnes, B.** Scientific Knowledge and Sociological Theory. *About 200 pp.*

Bauman, Zygmunt. Culture as Praxis. *204 pp.*

● **Dixon, Keith.** Sociological Theory. *Pretence and Possibility. 142 pp.*

●**Smith, Anthony D.** The Concept of Social Change. *A Critique of the Functionalist Theory of Social Change. 208 pp.*

Routledge Social Science Journals

The British Journal of Sociology. *Edited by Terence P. Morris. Vol. 1, No. 1, March 1950 and Quarterly. Roy. 8vo. Back numbers available. An international journal with articles on all aspects of sociology.*

Economy and Society. *Vol. 1, No. 1. February 1972 and Quarterly. Metric Roy. 8vo. A journal for all social scientists covering sociology, philosophy, anthropology, economics and history. Back numbers available.*

Year Book of Social Policy in Britain, The. *Edited by Kathleen Jones. 1971. Published annually.*

Printed in Great Britain by Unwin Brothers Limited
The Gresham Press Old Woking Surrey
A member of the Staples Printing Group